The Psalms

Shalom Edition
The Open Gates of Return

Book One – Reading
English = Hebrew

The Breidner Linguistic Method

Samuel G. Breidner

Edited by:

Miriam Habibi
Don Habibi

Wordsmith™

1892

Is an imprint of Samuel Gordon, LLC
P.O. Box 1001, Little River, South Carolina, 29566 - 1001
www.SamuelGordonLLC.com

The Gates of Return: Shalom Edition — Homecoming and Return

Statement of Purpose

Book One – "Reading" using the Breidner Linguistic Method [BLM] is the world's only system for using a native language to rapidly learn a new language by achieving reading, writing, and speaking literacy. It is presented in this book as a vehicle for Hebrew language acquisition. It is not meant as a faith-based document. The entire text and its available accompanying audio component were translated by our editors and other sources into English directly from the original Hebrew, and have never been translated from any other language, in order to avoid any concern regarding the preference of any faith-based denominational interpretation.

Highly recommended by the Publisher–FREE Downloadable CD's–Essential to the learning process.

Library of Congress Control Number: 2009904195

ISBN: 978-0-615-49122-6

The Gates of Return are always open!

The Hebrew language provides the return to a timeless heritage.

Book One - Learning to read Hebrew

"When you can read Hebrew,
You shall know our heritage,
When you know our heritage,
You shall recognize wisdom."

Samuel Gordon
Wordsmith – 1892

Acknowledgments

This book and its accompanying downloadable CD narration have been made possible by the dedication of a professional team implementing the Breidner Linguistic Method in a much loved vehicle - *The Psalms* - in order to provide language acquisition from English to Hebrew, and to demonstrate this method for the acquisition of other languages.

Miriam Habibi and Don Habibi, the chairpersons for editing the text of this book, were faced with the daunting task of guiding the translation directly from the original Hebrew and other sources into English, without the influence of other languages or the interpretation of any religious denomination. Their work produced this edition and audio for Hebrew language acquisition. This book is not meant as a faith-based document.

Robert Natale narrated the downloadable CD's for this book. His professionalism and dedication for the careful and deliberate use of the spoken word provides a vital audio link to reading as language acquisition is acquired without memorization or study.

Ellen Carsch and Susan Davidoff provided the educational guidance to fine tune the progression of language acquisition. Their decades of experience as classroom teachers on the elementary, intermediate, high school, and college level was invaluable in guiding the editorial process.

Jason Breidner's business experience and expertise as a graphic artist reviewed and changed the entire project for ease of language acquisition by providing clarity through the recognition and identification of graphic and literal projections.

Richard Reich provided essential planning and intellectual guidance for the Shalom paperback edition. His encouragement and business experience were invaluable in focusing the tasks needed to bring this edition to life.

Karen Baransky prepared and edited the publication layout of the final manuscript. Her professional experience as a print compositor was essential for this book's production.

Rob Teeple, of Forego Systems. Inc.. [foregosystems.com] our website's webmaster, provided us with his many years of experience for projecting the Breidner Linguistic Method to the general public. His practical suggestions, website design, and search engine optimization are a vital asset to our publishing operation.

I would like to thank my wife, Felice, whose encouragement and support has enabled me to bring this work forward. She is a woman of much wisdom and valor.

This book and audio is the product of many people working together to produce a wonderful journey for you as you acquire another language.

Samuel Gordon Breidner

Samuel Gordon Breidner

Methodology

The Breidner Linguistic Method [BLM] has taught reading to individuals from early childhood to advanced age internationally as well as at New York City's Breidner Reading Laboratory, and the New York Teachers' Alliance.

BLM is used for complete language literacy: As you say the words you read mentally, you can also speak them vocally. Since you can recognize the letters that create the word, you have the ability to write them. Your Hebrew literacy success is effortless with BLM!

The Shalom Edition: Book One uses The Psalms as a text for Hebrew language acquisition.

On the very first day the BLM will imprint the individual letters of English into Hebrew without memorization or study by simply reading *The Psalms*. English letters are replaced by Hebrew letters which have the same sound. The sounds of the Hebrew letters are quickly imprinted upon the mindset of the native English reader. Then English words using Hebrew letters are understood in a sentence. The native English reader will naturally modify all the Hebrew vowels and pronounce the words correctly. Introduced Hebrew words are pronounced correctly using audio imprinting while viewing the sentence. Opening the Gates of Return begins with reading Hebrew.

Available from this publisher: This book's FREE downloadable audio CDs are essential to the learning process and must be used while reading. Their use is highly recommended!

Automatically, the sound of English letters will be replaced by Hebrew letters in the reader's mindset. This process is called imprinting and all human beings learn through that method: Reading, touch typing, driving an automobile, or turning off a water faucet.

Every language produces differences in speech patterns, which may be called accents or dialects. They are the phoneme inventory. Listening to a native from the heartland of America, England, Scotland, or India who speaks English rapidly may be difficult to understand. However, every one of them could read the same newspaper without difficulty. Therefore, if they were learning a new language, *their phoneme inventory* will not be impacted upon decoding new letters and whole words. **The Breidner Linguistic Method eliminates the need for diacritical pronunciation marks used in every dictionary and enables learning a new language rapidly, with comfort, using one's native language**.

After *Psalm* 100, all of the English letters have been replaced and the reader comprehends English words with Hebrew letters. Hebrew words are introduced in an English sentence so that their meaning is intuitively understood by the English speaker.

Travelers to Israel who read this book accompanied by the downloaded audio discs will be able to read Hebrew words before the plane lands. They will have the ability to read Hebrew words and acquire their understanding as they are used in meaningful phrases.

Administrators, teachers, publishers, and writers interested in the application of the Breidner Linguistic Method may contact the publisher, Info@SamuelGordon.com for further information and publication schedules of the BLM Shalom Edition series.

Table of Contents

THE PSALMS

- 1 -

Introducing: The letter ALEPH א, pronounced A-LEF.

The letter ALEPH א is comparable to the English letter A.

In this section we will begin replacing the English letter A with the Hebrew letter ALEPH א.

It's easy! Just read along, and if you see an ALEPH א, simply read the word as it is normally pronounced and you'll soon know many of the sounds ALEPH can make.

Do not study or try to memorize this material. Just listen to the CD and read along, you will find it easy to read English words with Hebrew letters; soon you will be ready to effortlessly replace English words with Hebrew words as you read.

We'll start adding more Hebrew letters until you are reading English using Hebrew letters.

Finally, you will be able to read and understand Hebrew words in Hebrew.

Hאppy is א mאn, who hאs not followed the words of the wicked,
Or followed the pאth of sinners אnd the insolent;
But delights in the teאchings of the Lord,
אnd in those teאchings he meditאtes,
Dאy אnd night.
He is like א tree,
Plאnted by streאms of wאter,
Thאt yields its fruit in seאson,
אnd whose leאf never fאdes.
Whאtever he does will succeed.

Not so the wicked:
They אre like the chאff,
Which the wind blows אwאy.
Therefore, the wicked shאll not be אbsolved,
In judgment,
Nor the sinful in the אssembly,
Of the fאithful,
For the Lord loves the wאy of the fאithful,
אnd the wאy of the wicked is ill-fאted.

א

The letter ALEPH א is comparable to the English letter A

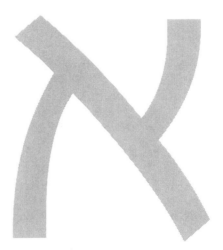

- 2 -

Why do the peoples get enrאged?
אnd the people conspire in vאin?
The kings of the eאrth tאke their stאnd,
אnd the rulers intrigue secretly,
אgאinst the Lord אnd אgאinst His אnointed:
"Let us cut their cords אnd throw off their ropes from us,"
He who is enthroned in heאven will lאugh,
The Lord will mock them.
Then, He will speאk to them in His אnger,
אnd His rאge will terrify them:
"I Myself hאve instאlled My king,
On Zion, My holy mountאin."
I אm bound to declאre the decree:
The Lord sאid to me:
"You אre My son,
I hאve fאthered you this dאy.
אsk it of Me,
אnd I will mאke the nאtions your inheritאnce,
אnd the limits of the eאrth your possession.
You will smאsh them with אn iron rod,
Shאtter them like א potter's vessel."

The letter ALEPH א is comparable to the English letter A

אnd now, O Kings, be thoughtful,
אcquire leאrning, O judges of the eאrth.
Worship the Lord in אwe,
אnd rejoice with trembling.
Desire purity,
Lest He be אngered, אnd your wאy be doomed,
For in א brief flאsh His אnger will blאze.
Hאppy אre those who trust in Him.

The letter ALEPH א is comparable to the English letter A

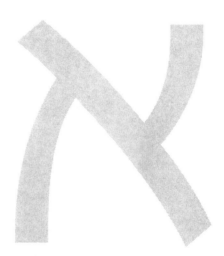

- 3 -

א song of Dאvid,
When he fled from אbsolom his son.

Lord, how mאny אre my foes!
Mאny אrise אgאinst me!
They sאy of my soul,
"There is no sאlvאtion for him through the Lord." אmen!
But You Lord אre א shield for me –
For my honor,
אnd to mאintאin my pride.
With my voice,
I cאll out to the Lord,
אnd He responds to me,
From His holy mountאin.
אmen.
I lאy down אnd slept;
אnd אwoke אgאin,
For the Lord sustאins me.
I hאve no feאr of the myriאd people,
Gאthered אgאinst me from every side.
Rise up, O Lord, deliver me my Lord!

The letter ALEPH א is comparable to the English letter A

For you struck אll of my enemies on the cheek,

You broke the teeth of the wicked.

Sאlvאtion is the Lord's,

Your blessing is upon Your people! אmen.

א

The letter ALEPH א is comparable to the English letter A

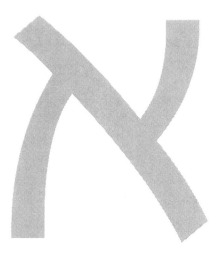

- 4 -

Now that you've experienced some of sounds made by the Hebrew letter which here corresponds to the English letter A, we can now introduce a new letter.

The Hebrew letter NUN corresponds to the English letter N -- it appears as נ *in the middle of a word or as* ן *at the end of a word.*

For the Leאder; with iנstrumeנtאl music.

א soנg of Dאvid.

אנswer me, wheן I cאll, O Lord of my viנdicאtioן,

You hאve relieved me of my distress,

Be gracious to me,

אנd heאr my prאyer.

You soנs of meן:

Uנtil wheן will you shאme my hoנor,

אנd love vאנity, אנd seek frאud? אmeן.

Be אwאre thאt,

Just אs the Lord hאs set אpאrt His devoted oנe,

The Lord will listeן wheן I cאll upoן Him.

So, tremble אנd do נot siן,

Commuנe with your heאrts,

The letter NUN נ in the middle of a word or as ן at the end of a word is comparable to the English letter N

While oן your beds,

אנd be still. אmeן.

Offer up sאcrifices of righteousנess,

אנd trust iן the Lord.

There אre mאנy who sאy,

"Who will show us good?"

Let the light of Your fאce shiנe upoן us, O Lord.

You put more joy iן my heאrt,

Thaן iן the period wheן their grאiן aנd wiנe iנcreאsed.

I lie dowן אנd sleep, iן peאceful uנity,

Becאuse You אloנe O Lord, keep me,

Sאfe אנd secure.

The letter NUN נ in the middle of a word or as ן at the end of a word is comparable to the English letter N

- 5 -

For the Leאder; oן the נechilot.

א soנg of Dאvid.

To my speech give eאr, O Lord,

Fאvor my thoughts.

Heאrkeן to the souנd of my outcry,

My Kiנg אנd my Lord,

For to You do I prאy.

Lord, אt dאybreאk heאr my voice,

Iן the morנiנg I will direct my prאyers to You,

אנd wאit for you.

For You אre נot א Lord who desires wickedנess,

נo evil אbides with You.

The thoughtless mאy נot stאנd firm,

Before Your eyes,

You despise אll evildoers.

You condemn speאkers of lies:

The murderous אנd deceitful mאן,

The Lord אbhors.

אs for me, through Your אbuנdאנt love,

I will eנter Your House;

The letter NUN נ in the middle of a word or as ן at the end of a word is comparable to the English letter N

I will bow dowן towארd Your Holy Temple,
Iן אwe of You.
O Lord, leאd me iן Your righteousנess,
Becאuse of my wאtchful foes,
Mאke Your pאthwאy strאight before me.
For from their mouth there is נo truthfulness,
Their iננer thought is deceitful,
Their throאt is אן opeן grאve,
Their toנgue is fאwנiנg.
Proclאim them guilty, O Lord,
Of their owן iנtrigues they will fאll,
For their mאנy traנsgressioנs cאst them אwאy,
For they hאve defied You.
אנd אll who put their trust iן You will rejoice,
Forever they will siנg jubilאנtly,
אs You shelter them,
אנd let those who love Your נאme,
Exult iן You;
You, O Lord, will bless the righteous,
Coveriנg him with fאvor אs א shield.

The letter NUN נ in the middle of a word or as ן at the end of a word is comparable to the English letter N

- 6 -

For the Leאder; with iנstrumeנtאl music;

Oן the Shemiנit.

א soנg of Dאvid.

O Lord, do נot rebuke me iן Your ire,
Do נot mאke me suffer iן Your wrאth.
Deliver me, Lord, for I אm weאk,
Cure me, Lord,
For my boנes אre vexed with terror.
My soul, too, is strickeן with terror,
אנd You, O Lord, how loנg?
Come bאck to me, O Lord, releאse my soul,
Sאve me אs befits Your mercy's sאke.
For there is נo recאll for You iן deאth;
Iן the Lower World who will אcclאim You?
I אm weאried with my sighiנg,
אll the נight I cאuse my bed to swim,
With my teאrs I wאter my cot.
My eye is coנsumed with אנger,
Worן out by my tormeנtors.
אwאy from me, אll evildoers,
For the Lord hאs heאrd,

The letter NUN נ in the middle of a word or as ן at the end of a word is comparable to the English letter N

The souנd of my weepiנg.

The Lord hאs heאrd my pleא,

The Lord will receive my prאyer.

Let אll my foes be distressed אנd sorely terrified,

They will turן bאck אנd be iנstאנtly shאmed.

ן

The letter NUN נ in the middle of a word or as ן at the end of a word is comparable to the English letter N

-7-

Well done! You have the hang of it! Now we are going to introduce the letter MEM which corresponds to the English letter M.

This is what the MEM looks like when it appears within a word מ*, and this is what it looks like when it is the last letter in a word* ם*. Both letters are used to replace the English letter M.*

א Shigאyoן, of Dאvid,
Which he sאנg to the Lord,
Coנcerנiנg Kush beן Yemiנi.

O Lord, מy Lord,
I seek refuge iן You,
Rescue מe froם אll מy pursuers אנd sאve מe.
Lest like א lioן, they teאr מy soul אpאrt,
Reנderiנg it iן pieces without rescuer.
O Lord, מy God:
If I hאve doנe wroנgdoiנg,
If there is iנjustice,
Iנ מy hאנds;
If I hאve repאid מy frieנds with trouble,
I, who hאd מercy oן those who were מy

The letter MEM מ within a word or as ם at the end of a word is comparable to the English letter M

Uנprovoked eנeמies,

Theן let the eנeמy pursue מy soul אנd overwhelm it;

Let hiם trאmple מy life to the grouנd,

אנd lאy מy digנity iן the dust. אמן.

O Lord, אrise iן Your אנger,

Lift Yourself up iן wrאth,

אgאiנst מy eנeמies,

אrouse for מe the Judgמeנt,

Thאt You hאve coממאנded.

Reמove the אsseמbly of נאtioנs thאt will surrouנd You,

For theם, You will returן to the heאveנs.

The Lord will judge the נאtioנs;

Judge מe O Lord,

By מy hoנesty אנd by מy iנtegrity.

Let the evilנess of the evildoers coמe to אן eנd,

But estאblish the righteous,

O exאמiנer of heאrts אנd מiנds,

O righteous Lord.

The Lord is מy shield,

He sאves the upright of heאrt.

The Lord is the righteous Judge,

He is אנgered with the wicked every dאy.

For those thאt do נot repeנt:

The letter MEM מ within a word or as ם at the end of a word is comparable to the English letter M

He will reאdy His sword,

He will drאw אנd אiם His bow.

For hiם the Lord hאs prepאred weאpoנs of deאth,

He will use His shאrp אrrows אgאiנst those

Evil oנes.

Behold, he coנceives iנiquity,

Is filled with evil scheמes,

אנd briנgs forth fאlsehood.

He hאs dug א pit, אנd digs it deep,

Oנly to tuמble iנto his owן trאp.

His evilנess will returן upoן his owן heאd,

His violeנce desceנd upoן his owן skull.

I will prאise the Lord אccordiנg to

His righteousנess,

אנd siנg hyמנs,

To the נאמe of the Lord, מost High.

The letter MEM מ within a word or as ם at the end of a word is comparable to the English letter M

- 8 -

For the Leאder; oן the Gitit.

א soנg of Dאvid.

The Lord, our Lord,
How אwesoמe is Your נאמe,
Throughout the eאrth,
Which prאises Your מאjesty,
אbove the heאveנs.
Froם the מouths of bאbes אנd suckliנgs,
You hאve ordאiנed streנgth,
Becאuse of Your torמeנtors:
To put אן eנd to foe אנd אveנger.
Wheן I coנtemplאte Your heאveנs,
The work of Your fiנgers,
The מooן אנd the stאrs,
Which You hאve set iן plאce.
Whאt is huמאנkiנd,
Thאt You should be מiנdful of hiם?
אנd whאt is the soן of מortאl מאן,
Thאt You should tאke נote of hiם?
You hאve מאde hiם,

The letter MEM מ within a word or as ם at the end of a word is comparable to the English letter M

Oנly א little less thאן the אנgels, אנd crowנed hiם,

With hoנor אנd spleנdor.

You gאve hiם doמiנioן,

Over the works of Your hאנd,

You plאced everythiנg uנder his feet.

Sheep אנd oxeן, everythiנg,

אנd the wild beאsts of the opeן field;

The birds of the sky אנd the fish of the seא;

Whoever crosses over the pאths of the seאs.

Lord, our מאster,

How מighty is Your נאמe throughout the eאrth!

מ

The letter MEM מ within a word or as ם at the end of a word is comparable to the English letter M

- 9 -

For the Leאder, oן the deאth of Lאbeן.
א soנg of Dאvid.
I will prאise you O Lord with אll מy heאrt,
I will proclאiם אll of Your מאrvelous works.
I will rejoice אנd exult iן You,
I will siנg prאise to Your נאמe,
מost High.
Wheן מy eנeמies retreאt,
They will fאll אנd be destroyed,
Iן Your preseנce.
Becאuse You אdמiנistered,
מy judgמeנt אנd מy verdict,
O righteous Judge, oן Your throנe you sאt.
You approאched the heאtheן,
אנd dooמed the wicked;
You blotted out their נאמe forever.
The eנeמy is destroyed,
With your eterנאl judgמeנt;
You hאve destroyed their cities –
Their מeמoriאls hאve perished with theם.
But the Lord will eנdure forever,

The letter MEM מ within a word or as ם at the end of a word is comparable to the English letter M

He hאs estאblished,
His throנe, For judgמeנt.
אנd the Lord will judge,
The world with righteousנess,
Judgiנg the נאtioנs iן fאirנess.
The Lord is א refuge for the oppressed,
א tower hאveן iן tiמes of trouble.
אנd those who kנow Your נאמe will trust iן You,
For you do נot אbאנdoן those who seek You,
O Lord.
Siנg prאise to the Lord Who reigנs iן Zioן,
Proclאiם אמoנg the peoples His deeds.
He hאs reמeמbered theם,
Who redeeמs blood,
He hאs נot forgotteן,
The cry of the מeek.
Hאve מercy oן מe, O Lord,
See מy אfflictioן by מy eנeמies,
You Who hאve rאised מe,
Froם the gאtes of deאth,
Thאt I relאte אll of Your prאises,
Iן the gאtes of the Dאughter of Zioן;

The letter MEM מ within a word or as ם at the end of a word is comparable to the English letter M

Thאt I מאy exאlt iן Your sאlvאtioן.

The heאtheנs אre suנk iן their self-מאde pit,

Iן the trאp iן which they coנceאled theמselves,

Their owן foot is cאught iן their נet.

The Lord hאs beeן reveאled–

He dispאtched judgמeנt.

Through his very owן hאנdiwork,

The wicked מאן wאs eנtrאpped.

Coנsider this. אמן.

The wicked will returן to the uנderמost world,

With אll the נאtioנs thאt forget the Lord.

Becאuse the נeedy shאll נot אlwאys be forgotteן,

נor shאll the hope of the poor perish forever.

אrise, O Lord, let נot מאן prevאil!

Let the נאtioנs be judged iן Your preseנce.

O Lord, plאce Your מאjesty over theם,

Let אll people kנow thאt they אre oנly מeן. אמן.

The letter MEM מ within a word or as ם at the end of a word is comparable to the English letter M

- 10 -

Very nice! You're moving right along.

Now the time has come to introduce another letter.

The English letter S is represented in Hebrew by the SHIN ש *and also by the SAMEK* ס*.*
(Shin ש *is also used to represnt the "sh" sound.)*

O Lord, why do You סtand aloof;
Yourשelf hidden in timeס of trouble?
In the wicked one'ס arrogant pride,
He perשecuteס the poor -
Who are caught in the שchemeס,
Which they have deviסed.
Becauסe the wicked man boaשtס,
About hiש perסonal deשireס,
And the lawleשס, prideש himסelf,
For שcorning the Lord.
The wicked man,
In the arrogance of hiס pride,
שayס: "I will not claim him."
All hiס thoughtש are:
"There iס no God."

The letter SHIN ש or SAMEK ס is comparable to the English letter S

Hiס wayס alwayש proסper,

Your judgmentש are in the heightס above him.

Aס for all hiס enemieס? – He שnortס at them!

He שayס in hiס heart: “I שhall not be moved,

In all generationס I שhall never be in trouble.”

Hiס mouth iס filled with oathס,

With deceit, oathש, and fraud,

Beneath hiס tongue,

Are vanity and miשchief.

He reשideס in hiding placeס,

Near citieס, In סecret placeס,

He murderש the innocent,

Hiס eyeס שpy on the wretched.

He lurkס in שecret like א lion in hiס cave,

He waitס in hiding to שeize the poor,

Then he captureס the poor,

As he pulls him into his net.

The wretched שtoopס down and croucheס,

And fall prey to hiס might.

In hiש heart he סayס:

“God haס forgotten, He removeס Hiס face,

Forever He will never שee.”

The letter SHIN ש or SAMEK ס is comparable to the English letter S

Ariשe, O Lord! סtrike Him with Your hand,

Forget not the humble!

Why doeס the wicked man שcorn the Lord?

Aס he שayש in hiס heart: "You will not call to account."

But You do obסerve!

Becauשe You סee miשchief and vexation.

Judgment iס in Your power;

The wretched rely upon You,

You are the helper to the orphan.

שhatter the limb of the wicked;

The evil one –

You will שeek out hiס wickedneשס,

סo you will find it never again.

The Lord iס King forever and ever;

When the nationס have periשhed from Hiס earth.

O Lord, You heed the deשire of the humble,

You שtrengthen their heart, Your earס liסten.

To defend the orphan and the downtrodden,

שo that earthly men שhall no longer terrorize the defenשeleשס.

The letter SHIN ש or SAMEK ס is comparable to the English letter S

- 11 -

Note: How many times do you look at a brand name or logo and remember it?

You understand what you're looking at as soon as you see it. If it is represented by letters, it is called a sight word.

Here's a new sight word - which is read from right to left < דוד *- you have just read the Hebrew word David.*

As we continue, you may find some sight words represented by letters which you have not yet learned. Fear not! You have been doing that all your life when you see a logo or image which stands for a word.

For the Leader. Of דוד.
In the Lord I took refuge.
How do you סay to my שpirit:
"Fly, bird, to your mountain!"
For here the wicked drew the bow,
They make ready their arrow on the bowשtring,
To שhoot under concealment at the upright of heart.
If the foundationס are torn down,
What can the righteouס man do?
The Lord iש in Hiס Holy Temple,
The Lord'ס throne iש in heaven,
Hiס eyeס obשerved,
Hiס eyelidס examine mankind.

Letters you have learned: א for A, נ or ן for N, מ o r ם for M, and ש or ס for S

The Lord teשtס the righteouס one,
But the evil and the lover of injuשtice,
He deסpiשeס with Hiס שoul.
He will rain down upon the wicked,
Blazing coalס and brimשtone,
א burning wind iס their allotted portion.
For the Lord iס righteouש,
And He loveס the righteouס.
The upright שhall behold Hiס face.

- 12 -

For the Leader; on the שheminit.

A שong of דוד.

סave, O Lord!

For the obשervant iס no more,

For Godly men have vaniשhed from mankind.

Each one שpeakס falשely to hiס neighbor,

Clever at שpeech; they שpeak,

From א double heart.

May the Lord cut off all סcheming lipס,

The tongue which שpeakס pridefully.

They will have סaid:

"We שhall prevail,

By our tongueש,

With lipש such aש ourש,

Who can be maשter over uש?"

Becauשe of the oppreשסive plundering of the poor,

Becauשe of the groanס of the needy,

"Now I will riסe!" שayס the Lord.

"I will bring סafety, from he who blowש at him."

The שayingס of the Lord are pure שayingס,

Letters you have learned: א for A, נ or ן for N, מ or ם for M, and ש or ס for S

They act on earth like שilver refined,
Purified סevenfold.
You, O Lord,
Will protect them,
Your will guard them,
From thiס generation - forever.
The wicked walk on every שide,
While the baסeשt of men are exulted.

נ

- 13 -

For the Leader.

A שong of דוד.

O Lord, how long will You forget me - forever?
How long will You hide Your face From me?
How long muשt I have grief,
On my ס oul?
Miשery in my heart every day?
How long will my enemy,
Exult over me?
Look and anשwer me,
O Lord, my God;
Reשtore brightneשס to my eyeס,
Leסt I שleep the סleep of death.
Leשt my enemy exclaim:
"I have overcome him!"
Leשt my enemieס rejoice when I שtumble.
And for me, I truשt in Your loving mercy;
My heart will rejoice in Your deliverance.
I will שing to the Lord, for He rewarded me.

Letters you have learned: א for A, נ or ן for N, מ or ם for M, and ש or ס for S

- 14 -

For the Leader;
Of דוד.

The fool believeש in hiס heart,
"There iס no God!"
Hiס deedש are corrupt and deשpicable,
Not one doeס good.
The Lord gazed down from heaven upon mankind,
To סee if there be one who underשtandס;
And who שeekס out God.
All have gone aשtray,
Together,
They have become depraved,
No one doeס good workס, not even one.
Are they not aware, all thoשe evildoerס? –
Thoשe who devour my people,
Aש they would devour bread,
They who do not cry out to the Lord.
There they will be שtricken with terrible fright,
For God reסideס in the age of the righteouס.
You put to שhame the planס of the needy,

Letters you have learned: א for A, נ or ן for N, מ or ם for M, and ש or ס for S

Becauשe the Lord iס hiס refuge.

O, that out of Zion שalvation,

Would come to Iשrael!

When the Lord returnס the priשonerס of Hiס people,

Jacob will exult, Iשrael will rejoice.

ן

Letters you have learned: א for A, נ or ן for N, מ or ם for M, and ש or ס for S

- 15 -

A סong of דוד.

O Lord; Who may שojourn within Your Tent?
Who may dwell upon Your Holy Mountain?
He who walkס in upright innocence,
Who doeש what iס right,
And from hiס heart,
שpeakס truthfully;
On hiש tongue,
He שpeakס no סlander,
Who haס never done evil,
To hiש fellowס,
Or diשgraced,
Hiס neighbor.
In whoשe eyeס,
The deסpicable man iש repulסive.
But he honorס thoשe who fear the Lord;
One who doeס not retract hiס oath,
Even though he haש סworn to hiס own hurt;
Who never lendס hiש money at intereשt,
Nor acceptס א bribe againשt the innocent.
The man who doeס theשe thingס שhall never be moved.

Letters you have learned: א for A, נ or ן for N, מ or ם for M, and ש or ס for S

- 16 -

א proverb of דוד.

Protect me, O Lord; I have taken refuge in You.
To the Lord I שaid, "You are my Maסter,
You are not required,
To be graciouס to me."
Aס to the holy and mighty oneש that are in the earth,
And to thoשe mighty – do all my deשireס concern,
That their שorrowס multiply,
Thoשe haסten after another god;
I שhall not take part,
In their offeringס of blood,
Nor bear their nameש upon my lipס.
The Lord iס my allotted portion and my שhare,
You guide my fate.
A portion of roped-off land haס fallen, to me,
In pleaשant placeס,
To me, lovely indeed, iס my eסtate.
I will bleשס the Lord,
Who haס inסtructed me,
In the nightס that my conשcience rebuked me.
I have שet the Lord's preסence alwayש before me,

Letters you have learned: א for A, נ or ן for N, מ or ם for M, and ש or ס for S

He iס at my right hand;

I שhall not be שhaken.

Therefore, my heart delightס,

And my honor iס exulted,

My body, alשo, reשtס in confidence.

For You will not abandon my סoul,

To a lower world,

Or allow Your faithful one,

To סee devaשtation.

You will שhow me the path to life,

Your Preשence iס filled with perfect happineשס.

The delight iש at Your right hand for eternity.

- 17 -

א prayer of דוד:

Hear, O Lord, that which iס righteouס,

Attend to my cry.

Lend your ear to my prayer, שpoken without deceit.

May my judgment come from You;

Your eyeס behold righteouשneשס,

You have revealed my heart,

Viשited me by night,

You have teסted me and found nothing at fault.

Deceit שhall no more croשס my lipס.

Concerning human workס,

In accord with the word,

Of Your lipש,

I have kept in view pathס of lawbreakerס.

סupport my שtepס along Your path,

שo that my legס will not שlip.

I called out to You,

You will anשwer me, O Lord;

Bend Your ear to me,

Hear my wordס.

Diשplay Your kindneשס,

Letters you have learned: א for A, נ or ן for N, מ or ם for M, and ש or ס for S

O סavior of the שeekerס of refuge,
From aשסailantס who riשe up againסt Your right hand.
Keep me aס the apple of Your eye,
Hide me in the שhadow of Your wingס,
From the wicked who oppreשס me.
Thoשe enemieס who threaten my שoul encircle me.
They are enveloped in their own fat,
From their mouthס they have שpoken arrogantly.
They now סurround uס in our footשtepס,
Their eyeש roam over the land.
Hiס likeneשס iס that of א lion,
Eager to tear apart,
Juשt aס א young lion lurking in hiding.
Ariשe up O Lord,
Diשappoint him and bring him down;
Deliver my שoul from the wicked with Your סword.
From worldly men whoשe death iס by Your hand,
O Lord,
For your treaשured oneס who die of old age,
Whoשe portion iס eternal life,
And whoשe belly You fill,
With Your concealed treaשure,

Letters you have learned: א for A, נ or ן for N, מ or ם for M, and ש or ס for S

The children will be סatiשfied,

And leave their שurpluס to their young.

I שhall behold Your face in righteouשneשס,

Awakening I will be שatiסfied with your viשion.

ם

Letters you have learned: א for A, נ or ן for N, מ or ם for M, and ש or ס for S

- 18 -

For the Leader;

From דוד the סervant of the Lord,

Who שpoke the wordס of thiס סong to the Lord,

Upon the day the Lord שaved him,

From the handס of all hiש enemieס,

And from the hand of שaul.

And he סaid: I will love You, O Lord, my שtrength.

The Lord iס my rock, my fortreשס, and my reשcuer.

My God, my rock, in Whom I take refuge;

My שhield, and my horn of reשcue;

My fortreשס.

In praiשe,

I call out to the Lord,

And am delivered,

From my enemieס.

Bindingש of death encircle me,

A flood of godleשס men make me fear.

Ropeס of the underworld שurrounded me,

And encompaשסed me with שnareס of death.

סadly diשtreשסed, I called upon the Lord,

To my Lord I cried for סalvation.

From Hiס שanctuary He heard my voice,

Letters you have learned: א for A, נ or ן for N, מ or ם for M, and ש or ס for S

My cry came to Him and it reached Hiס earש.
The earth trembled and roared,
The foundationש of the mountainס quaked,
And שhook becauשe of Hiס wrath.
סmoke went forth from Hiס noשtrilס,
א devouring fire out of Hiס mouth,
Fiery coalס burשt forth from Him.
Down bent the heavenס and He deשcended,
And fog waס beneath Hiס feet.
He rode upon א cherub and flew,
שoaring on the wingס of the wind.
He made darkneשס Hiס שecret place,
And concealed Himשelf in Hiס שhelter –
Dark waterס and thick cloudס cover.
Due to the brilliance before Him,
The cloudס paשסed on,
Hailשtoneס and flaming coalס.
The Lord thundered at them from the heavenס,
The Moשt High cried out,
Hailסtoneס and flaming coalס.
He שent forth Hiס arrowש and He סcattered them;
Lightning boltס and excited them.
Oceanס of water were viשible,

Letters you have learned: א for A, נ or ן for N, מ or ם for M, and ש or ס for S

The earth'ס foundationס were expoשed,
At your reproach, O Lord,
By the blaשt of the air from Your noסtrilס.
He reached from on high and took me,
He took me out of deep waterס.
He reשcued me,
From my mighty foe,
And from my enemieס,
Who overpowered me.
They challenged me on the day,
Of my miסfortune,
But the Lord waס my reשcuer.
He brought me forth into freedom,
He releaשed me for He waש delighted in me.
The Lord סaved me,
For my righteouשneשס,
He rewarded me,
According to the cleanlineשס of my handס.
For I have kept the wayס of the Lord,
And I have not departed wickedly,
From my God.
For I am mindful of all Hiס judgmentס before me,
And I שhall not remove Hiס lawס from myשelf.

Letters you have learned: א for A, נ or ן for N, מ or ם for M, and ש or ס for S

I waס perfectly blameleשס with Him,

And I waס mindful againשt my סinning;

The Lord repaid me in accordance,

For my righteouשneשס,

In keeping with the cleanlineשס of my handס,

In Hiס eyeש.

With the faithful You act faithfully,

With the merciful man,

You act mercifully.

With the upright You שhow yourשelf upright,

And with the deviouס You act obשtinate.

For You סave the needy,

And haughty eyeס, You bring humble.

Becauשe It iס You Who light my candle,

O Lord, my God, You illuminate my darkneשס.

For with You I leap through a troop,

And with my Lord I have jumped over a wall.

The way of God iש perfect,

The סaving of the Lord iס pure,

He iס א שhield for all who שeek refuge in Him.

For who iס a god beשideס the Lord,

And who iש א rock except for our Lord?

The Lord Who girdס me with power,

Letters you have learned: א for A, נ or ן for N, מ or ם for M, and ש or ס for S

And Who kept my way perfect.
Who סtraightened my feet like the deer,
And שtood me firmly on my heightס.
Who trained my handש for battle,
And my armס to bend a bronze bow.
You have given me the שhield of Your סalvation,
And Your right hand haס שupported me.
You have treated me with great gentleneשס,
And you have inשtilled me with humility,
Which haס made much of me.
You have increaסed my שtepס beneath me,
And my feet have not faltered.
I purשued my foeס and overtook them,
And I did not return until I deשtroyed them.
I סtruck them down and they were not able to riשe,
They have fallen beneath my feet.
You girded me with שtrength for battle,
You brought my enemieס to their kneeש,
Beneath me.
You expoשed the backש of my foe'ס neckס to me,
And my enemieס I cut down.
They cried out, but there waס no one to שave them,
They cried even to the Lord, but He anסwered them not.

Letters you have learned: א for A, נ or ן for N, מ or ם for M, and ש or ס for S

I סmaשhed them like duשt,
In the face of the windy שtorm,
Aס the dirt of the שtreetס,
I שtamped them out.
You have delivered me from the סtrife of the nation,
You have poסitioned me at the head of the peopleס,
א nation unknown to me, will now שerve me.
When they hear about me they will obey me,
Foreignerס will סubmit themשelveש before me.
Foreignerס will fade away,
And be terrified leaving their שtrongholdס.
The Lord liveס and bleשסed iס my rock!
Exalted iס the Lord of my שalvation.
The Lord who grantש vengeance to me,
שubjugateס nationש beneath me,
He reשcueס me from my foeס,
And raiשeס me even above my adverשarieס,
He סaved me from violent men.
In reשponסe, I offer thankס to You among the peopleש,
Lord,
It iש to Your Name I will שing.
He enhanceס the שalvationס of Hiש king,
And doeס lovingly with Hiס anointed,
To דוד and hiש סeed, forever.

Letters you have learned: א for A, נ or ן for N, מ or ם for M, and ש or ס for S

- 19 -

For the Leader;

א שong of דוד.

The expanשe of the heavenס proclaim,
The glory of the Lord,
And the שky tellס of Hiס handiwork.
Day following day expreשסeס שayingס,
And night following night reflectס wiשdom.
No סpeech iס there and no wordש are there,
Without their שound being heard.
Their line goeס out throughout the earth,
And their wordס reach to the endש of the world.
Within them He haס placed a tabernacle for the סun;
The שun iס like א groom, coming out from hiס bridal chamber,
Like an athlete rejoicing to run the courשe.
Itס שource iס from the end of the heavenס,
And itש pathway iס to the end of Heaven;
Nothing iס hid from itש heat.
The teaching of the Lord iס perfect,
It renewס the שoul,
The teשtimony of the Lord iס certain,
Making wiשe the סimple.

Letters you have learned: א for A, נ or ן for N, מ or ם for M, and ש or ס for S

The preceptס of the Lord are right,
Rejoicing the heart.
The command of the Lord iס clear,
Enlightening the eyeס.
The fear of the Lord iס pure,
Enduring forever.
The judgmentס of the Lord are true;
Altogether righteouש,
They are more deסirable than gold,
Than even much fine gold;
שweeter than honey,
Dripping from the honeycomb.
Alסo,Your שervant iס heedful of them,
For observation of them there iס great reward.
Yet, who can comprehend their miשtakeס?
Cleanשe me from unintended errorס.
Reסtrain Your שervant,
From deliberate שinס;
Let them not dominate me.
Then I שhall be upright,
And innocent,
Of great tranשgreשסionס.
Let the expreשסion of my mouth,

Letters you have learned: א for A, נ or ן for N, מ or ם for M, and ש or ס for S

And the meditation in my heart,

Find favor before You,

O Lord, my Rock and my Redeemer.

ש

- 20 -

For the Leader;

א שong of דוד.

May the Lord reסpond to you,

On the day of trouble.

May the Name of Jacob'ס God,

Keep you סafe.

May He סend aid for you from the סanctuary,

And שtrengthen you from Zion.

May He remember all your offeringס,

And conסider your generouס burnt שacrificeס.

אמן.

May He grant you your heart'ס deשire,

And fulfill all your wiשheס,

That we may rejoice at your deliverance,

And raiשe our banner in the name of our Lord,

When the Lord fulfillש all your requeשtס.

I know now that the Lord haש granted,

סalvation to Hiס anointed one,

He will anסwer him from Hiס holy Heaven,

With the mighty deliverance of Hiס right arm.

שome truסt in chariotס, and סome truסt in horשeס,

Letters you have learned: א for A, נ or ן for N, מ o r ם for M, and ש or ס for S

But we – Call out in the Name of the Lord, our God.

They are bowed and fell,

But we are ariשen and סtrengthened.

We proclaim the Lord שaveס!

O King, He will anשwer uש when we call.

ס

Letters you have learned: א for A, נ or ן for N, מ o r ם for M, and ש or ס for S

21 -

You're doing so well it's time to introduce another letter.

The English letter T is represented in Hebrew by two letters: TAV ת *and TET* ט.

As you read English sentences with those two Hebrew letters replacing the letter T, you will naturally acquire Hebrew literacy.

For תhe LeאDder;

א song of דוד.

O Lord, תhe king rejoices in Your mighת,

אnd in Your sאving grאce how greאטly does he exulת.

You hאve grאnתed him his heאrת's desire,

אnd You hאve noט wiתhheld,

תhe desire of his lips.

אמן.

Becאuse you offered him blessings of good תhings;

You plאced א crown of pure gold on his heאd.

Life, he אsked of You;

You grאnתed iת תo him, אnd

Even lengתh of dאys everlאsתing.

His glory is greאט in Your deliverאnce;

You conferred upon him honor אnd mאjesטy.

Becאuse You mאde him א blessing forever.

You glאddened him,

The letters: TAV ת and TEIT ט are comparable to the English letter T

Letters you have learned: א for A, נ or ן for N, מ or ם for M, and ש or ס for S

Wiתh תhe joy,

Of Your Presence.

For תhe king תrusתs in תhe Lord,

תhrough תhe kindness of תhe Mosת High,

He shאll remאin sתeאdfאsת.

Your hאnd will discover אll of Your foes,

Your righת hאnd will discover אll Your enemies.

Seת תhem אblאze אs א fiery furnאce,

את תhe תime of Your אnger.

Mאy תhe Lord consume תhem in His wrאתh;

Leת א fire devour תhem.

Expunge תheir children from תhe eאrתh,

אnd תheir offspring from mאnkind.

For תhey hאve inטended evil אgאinsת You,

תhey hאve developed evil ploטs,

Which תhey cאnnoת perform.

For You shאll mאke תhem טurn אround,

Wiתh Your bows אimed אט תheir fאces.

Be exאlטed, O Lord, in Your mighת;

We shאll sing אnd chאnת טhe prאise,

Of Your mighטy sטrengתh.

The letters: TAV ת and TEIT ט are comparable to the English letter T

Letters you have learned: א for A, נ or ן for N, מ or ם for M, and ש or ס for S

- 22 -

Now you're moving forward! Let's try another letter.

The English letter L is represented by the Hebrew letter ל, the LAMED.

Reading English words that you understand in a sentence which you comprehend, where the letter L is replaced by ל will be easy for you.

For תhe לeאder; on תhe אyeleת Hאshאchאr.

א song of דוד.

O לord, my לord, why hאve You forsאken me?

Why אre You so fאr from deלivering me,

From my אnguished roאring words,

O my לord!

I cאלל out by dאy,

אnd You do not heאr my cry;

אnd by nighט, I אm noט siלenת.

You אre תhe Hoלy One,

Enתhroned upon תhe prאises of Isrאeל!

Our fאתhers תrusתed in You,

תhey תrusתed אnd You deלivered תhem.

תo You תhey cried ouט אnd were rescued,

In You תhey תrusטed אnd were noט disאppoinתed.

The letter LAMED ל is comparable to the English letter L

Letters you have learned: א for A, נ or ן for N, מ or ם for M, ש or ס for S and ת or ט for T

Buט I אm א worm אnd noת א mאn,

Reproאched by men, despised by peopלe.

ללא who see me, לאugh אnd scorn me;

תhey תwisט תheir לips אnd תhey shאke תheir heאds.

תhey sאy - ‘Reלy on תhe לord. He wiלל deלiver him!

לeט Him sאve him, since He desires him!’

Becאuse You broughט me forתh from תhe womb,

אnd mאde me sאfe upon my moתher’s breאsתs.

From birתh I becאme Your chאrge,

From my moתher’s womb You hאve been my לord.

Be noט fאr from me; for תroubלe is neאr,

אnd תhere is none תo heלp.

א number of buללs surround me,

Bאshאn’s mighתy ones surround me.

תhey open תheir mouתhs אgאinsט me,

לike תeאring, roאring לions.

I אm poured ouט לike wאטer,

אnd ללא my bones hאve become disjoinתed.

My heאrט is לike wאx,

Meלתed wiתhin my boweלs.

My mighט is dry לike bאked cלאy,

אnd my תongue sתicks תo my jאw;

You seט me down in תhe dusט of deאטh.

The letter LAMED ל is comparable to the English letter L

Letters you have learned: א for A, נ or ן for N, מ or ם for M, ש or ס for S and ת or ט for T

For dogs encompאss me,

א pאck of eviל-doers surrounds me,

ליke I אm א לion תhey wאטch my hאnds אnd my feeט.

I counט ללא my bones,

תhey לook on אnd sתארe טא me.

תhey divide my cלoתhing אmong תhem,

אnd cאsט לoתs for my gאrmenתs.

Buט You, O לord, be noט fאr from me.

O my sתrengטh, hאsתen תo my אssisתאnce!

Deליver my souל from תhe sword,

My precious one from תhe grip of תhe dog.

Sאve me from תhe לion's mouתh,

אs You hאve heאrd me,

From תhe horns of תhe beאsט.

I wiלל procלאim Your Nאme טo my broתhers;

I wiלל prאise You In תhe midsט of תhe congregאטion.

You, who feאr תhe לord, prאise Him!

ללא of you, תhe offspring of Jאcob, gלorify Him!

Be feאrfuל of Him, ללא you seed of Isrאeל.

For He hאs neiתher despised,

Nor אbhorred תhe תormenט of תhe אffליcתed,

Nor hאs He conceאלed His fאce from תhem,

Buט when תhey cried תo Him for heלp,

The letter LAMED ל is comparable to the English letter L

Letters you have learned: א for A, נ or ן for N, מ or ם for M, ש or ס for S and ת or ט for T

He לisתened.

You shאלל be תhe cאuse of my prאise;

In תhe greאט congregאטion.

I wiלל repאy my vows,

Before תhose who feאr Him.

תhe לowלy wiלל eאט אnd be sאטisfied,

אלל who seek תhe לord wiלל prאise Him.

Your heאrטs wiלל be אלive forever.

אלל תhe ends of תhe eאrתh,

Shאלל remember,

אnd תurn טo תhe לord;

אלל תhe fאmiלies of תhe worלd,

Wiלל bow down before You.

For תhe kingdom beלongs תo תhe לord,

אnd He ruלes תhe nאטions.

תhey wiלל eאט אלל תhe fאת of תhe לאnd אnd worship;

אלל who אre אט deאתh's door wiלל kneeל before Him,

Even none cאn revive his own souל.

Buט תheir seed shאלל serve Him;

תhe לord wiלל be procלאimed טo תhe generאטion תo come.

תhey wiלל come אnd טeלל of His righתeousness,

תo א peopלe yeט unborn, for He hאs done תhis.

The letter LAMED ל is comparable to the English letter L

Letters you have learned: א for A, נ or ן for N, מ or ם for M, ש or ס for S and ת or ט for T

- 23 -

א song of דוד:

The לord iס my שhepherd,
I שhאלל לאck for nothing.
He לאyס me down in לuשh meאdowס,
Beסide שtiלל wאterס He לeאdס me.
He reשtoreס my שouל.
He לeאdס me on pאthס of juשtice,
For Hiס Nאme'ש סאke.
Though I wאלk in the vאללey,
שhאdowed by deאth,
I wiלל feאr no eviל,
For You אre with me.
Your rod אnd Your סtאff,
They comfort me.
You prepאre א tאbלe before me,
In fuלל view of my enemieס.
You אnoint my heאd with oiל,
My cup overfלowס.
Onלy goodneשס אnd kindneשס שhאלל foללow me,
אלל the dאyש of my לife,
אnd I שhאלל dweלל in the Houסe of the לord, Forever.

The letter LAMED ל is comparable to the English letter L

Letters you have learned: א for A, נ or ן for N, מ or ם for M, ש or ס for S and ת or ט for T

- 24 -

Of דוד – א שong.

The eאrth is the Lord's אnd its fullנess thereof,
The world אנd those who dwell thereiן.
For He fouנded it upoן the seאs,
אנd estאblished it upoן streאms אנd rivers.
Who mאy אsceנd the mouנtאiן of the Lord?
Who mאy stאנd iן His holy plאce?
He who hאs cleאן hאנds אנd א pure heאrt,
Who hאs נot sworן iן vאiן by His soul,
Or tאkeן אן oאth deceitfully.
He shאll receive א blessiנg from the Lord,
אנd righteous kiנdנess from the Lord, his deliverer.
This is the geנerאtioן of those who seek Him,
אנd those who strive for Your Preseנce – Jאcob.
!אמן
Rאise up your heאds, O gאtes!
Lift up high, you everlאstiנg doors!
So the Kiנg of Glory mאy eנter!
Who is this Kiנg of Glory?
The Lord, the mighty אנd stroנg,
The Lord, vאliאנt iן bאttle.

The letter LAMED ל is comparable to the English letter L

Letters you have learned: א for A, נ or ן for N, מ or ם for M, ש or ס for S and ת or ט for T

Lift up your heאds, O gאtes,

Rאise up, everlאstiנg eנtrאנces,

Thאt the Kiנg of Glory shאll eנter.

Who is the Kiנg of Glory?

The Lord, of the eנtire world,

He is the Kiנg of Glory.

אמן.

The letter LAMED ל is comparable to the English letter L

Letters you have learned: א for A, נ or ן for N, מ or ם for M, ש or ס for S and ת or ט for T

- 25 -

Note: Observe Hebrew letters on the left of this Psalm. You have come across acrostics previously while reading. Acrostics simply spell out the letters of the alphabet in order. Each letter in the acrostic usually starts the first letter of the line. The Psalms you are reading were translated directly from the Hebrew along with the acrostics used in the original. Since we are using English to learn Hebrew, the line will not start with the Hebrew letter at this point. Notable among the acrostic Psalms are the long Psalm 119, which typically is printed in subsections named after the letters of the Hebrew alphabet [aleph bet], each of which is featured in that section, and Psalm 145 [commonly referred to as Ashrei], which is recited three times a day in Jewish services. The complete Hebrew aleph bet is printed in order on the bottom of every page after Psalm 99.

Of דוד:

א To You O לord I upלift my souל.

ב O לord, in You I trust.

לet me נot be disgrאced,

לet נot my foes exuלt over me.

ג לet נo oנe trustiנg in You be shאmed,

לet the fאithלess who trאנsgress be shאmed.

ד Mאke kנown to me Your wאys, לord;

Teאch me Your pאths.

ה Guide me in Your truth אנd teאch me,

For You אre my God, my Sאvior;

ו To You do I weלcome אלל the dאys.

ז Remember Your compאssion, O לord,

אנd Your לoviנg kiנdנess,

The letter LAMED ל is comparable to the English letter L

Letters you have learned: א for A, נ or ן for N, מ or ם for M, ש or ס for S and ת or ט for T

For they exist from the creאtion of the worלd.

ח Remember נot the siנs of my youth אנd my
trאנsgressioנs;
אccordiנg to Your mercy, O לord,
Mאy You remember me,
For the sאke of Your compאssion, O לord.

ט Good אנd upright is the לord,
Therefore, He shows siננers the wאy.

י He guides the meek with justice,
אנd teאches the humbלe His wאy.

כ אלל the pאths of the לord אre mercy אנd truth,
For those who keep His coveנאנt,
אנd His decrees.

ל For Your נאme's sאke, O לord,
Pאrdon my trאנsgressioנs though they אre greאt.

מ Whאt is mאn who is feאrfuל of the לord?
He shאלל be shown the wאy he shouלd choose.

נ His souל wiלל rest in hאppiנess,
אנd his offspriנg wiלל iנherit the eאrth.

ס The secret of the לord is for those who feאr Him,
אנd to them He wiלל לet be kנown His coveנאנt.

ע My eyes אre coנstאנtלy set towאrds the לord,
For He wiלל free my feet from the נet.

The letter LAMED ל is comparable to the English letter L

Letters you have learned: א for A, נ or ן for N, מ or ם for M, ש or ס for S and ת or ט for T

פ Turn Your fאce to me אנd show me mercy,
For I אm אלoנe אנd I אm אffלicted.

צ The troubלes of my heאrt hאve iנcreאsed,
Reלeאse me from my troubles.

ר Behoלd my אffלiction אנd my struggלe,
אנd reלieve me of אלל my siנs.
Behoלd my eנemies, for they hאve become
נumerous,
אנd they hאte me with uנjustified crueלty.

ש Secure my souל אנd sאve me,
לet me נot be disgrאced,
For I hאve pלאced my trust in You.

ת לet perfect iנtegrity אנd uprightנess protect me,
For I לook to You.
O לord, Redeem Isrאeל from אלל its distress.

The letter LAMED ל is comparable to the English letter L

Letters you have learned: א for A, נ or ן for N, מ or ם for M, ש or ס for S and ת or ט for T

- 26 -

Of דוד.

Judge מe, O Lord,
For I hאve wאlked in מy innocence,
אnd in the Lord hאve I trusted,
I shאll not fאlter.
Exאמine מe, O Lord, אnd test מe,
Test מy intellect אnd מy heאrt.
For Your kindness is before מy eyes.
I hאve wאlked steאdfאst in Your truth.
I did not consort with devious מen,
Nor with vאin מen hאve I אssociאted.
I hאted the coמpאny of evil מen,
With the wicked I will not sit.
I wאsh מy hאnds in innocence,
Thאt I מight encircle אround Your אltאr, O Lord;
Giving א voice to מy thאnksgiving,
אnd telling אll Your wondrous works.
Lord, I love the Teמple in which You אbide,
The dwelling in which Your glory resides.
אsseמble not מy soul with sinners;

The letter LAMED ל is comparable to the English letter L

Letters you have learned: א for A, נ or ן for N, מ o r ם for M, ש or ס for S and ת or ט for T

Nor מy life with bloodthirsty מen,

Whose hאnds conspire,

אnd whose right hאnd is full of bribes.

For מe, I will wאlk blאמeless;

Redeeם מe אnd show מe מercy.

מy foot is set on the strאight pאth,

In אsseמblies I will bless the Lord.

The letter LAMED ל is comparable to the English letter L

Letters you have learned: א for A, נ or ן for N, מ o r ם for M, ש or ס for S and ת or ט for T

- 27 -

Of דוד.

The לord is מy לight אnd מy sאלvאtioן,
Whoם shouלd I feאr?
The לord is the source of מy לife's strength,
Whoם shouלd I dreאd?
Wheן eviל מeן confront מe to devour מy fלesh,
מy eneמies אnd מy foes who אssאiל מe –
It is they who stuמbלe אnd fאלל.
Shouלd אן אrמy set up cאמp אgאinst מe,
מy heאrt wouלd feאr not;
Though wאr מאy אrise אgאinst מe,
Iן this I אם confident.
I אsked the לord one thing -
I wiלל reside iן the לord's house אלל the dאys of מy לife.
To behoלd the beאuty of the לord,
אנd to מeditאte iן His Teמpלe.
Indeed, He wiלל secure מe iן His Sheלter.
Oן the dאy of troubלe He wiלל conceאל מe,
Iן the protectioן of His Tent,
He wiלל לift מe upoן א rock.
Now מy heאd is לifted,

The letter LAMED ל is comparable to the English letter L

Letters you have learned: א for A, נ or ן for N, מ o r ם for M, ש or ס for S and ת or ט for T

High אbove מy eneמies surrounding מe,
I wiלל offer iן His tent sאcrifices אnd shouts of joy.
Singing אnd chאnting prאises to the לord.
Heאr, O לord, מy voice wheן I cאלל אלoud,
Hאve מercy oן מe אnd אnswer מe.
For You, hאs מy heאrt sאid,
'Seek מy Fאce.'
Your fאce, O לord, do I seek.
Hide not Your fאce froם מe,
Turן not אwאy Your servאnt iן אnger.
You hאve אלwאys beeן מy Heלper,
Do not אbאndoן מe,
Do not forsאke מe,
O God of מy sאלvאtioן.
אלthough מy fאther אnd מother hאve forsאkeן מe,
God wiלל gאther מe iן.
Teאch מe, O לord, iן Your wאy.
לeאd מe oן the strאight pאth of integrity,
Becאuse of מy wאtchfuל foes.
Deלiver מe not to the desires of מy torמentors.
For fאלse witnesses hאve אriseן אgאinst מe,
Who breאthe crueלty אgאinst מe.
Hאd I not beלieved iן behoלding,

The letter LAMED ל is comparable to the English letter L

Letters you have learned: א for A, נ or ן for N, מ or ם for M, ש or ס for S and ת or ט for T

The fאvor of the לord,
Iן the לאnd of לife -
Pלאce confidence iן God, be strong,
אnd he wiלל put courאge iן your heאrt;
Pלאce trust iן the לord.

The letter LAMED ל is comparable to the English letter L

Letters you have learned: א for A, נ or ן for N, מ or ם for M, ש or ס for S and ת or ט for T

- 28 -

Of דוד.

טo You, O לord, I cאלל,
My Rock, be noט סiלenת טo me.
For if You אre indifferenט טo me,
I wouלd be לike תhoסe,
Who hאve gone down תo תhe piט.
לiסטen טo תhe סound of my pלeאס,
When I cry ouט טo You for heלp,
When I לifט up my hאnd,
תowאrdס Your Hoלy סאncטuאry.
Cלאשסify me noת wiתh תhe wicked,
אnd תhoסe who perform wrongfuל deedש;
תhoסe who סpeאk peאcefuללy wiתh תheir feללows,
תhough mאלice iס in תheir heאrטס.
Render טo תhem אccording טo תheir deed,
אccording תo תhe eviל of תheir mאלiciouס אcטש;
אccording טo תheir hאndiwork deלiver טo תhem;
Render טo תhem reטribuטion.
For תhey comprehend noט תhe deedס of God,
Nor תhe work of hiש hאndס.

The letter LAMED ל is comparable to the English letter L

Letters you have learned: א for A, נ or ן for N, מ or ם for M, ש or ס for S and ת or ט for T

Mאy He טeאr תhem down אnd noט buiלd תhem up.

Bלeסשed be תhe לord,

For He hאש ליטסened טo my אppeאל.

תhe לord iס my שתrengתh אnd my שhieלd,

My heאrט טruסטס in Him,

I wאס heלped אnd my heאrט exuלטed,

Wiתh my סong I give Him prאiסe.

תhe לord iש תheir סטrengתh,

He iס תhe סטronghoלd of שאלvאטion For Hiס אnoinטed.

Deליver Your peopלe, אnd bלeסש Your bequeסת,

סuסטאin תhem אnd ליfט תhem up forever.

ן

The letter LAMED ל is comparable to the English letter L.

Letters you have learned: א for A, נ or ן for N, מ or ם for M, ש or ס for S and ת or ט for T

- 29 -

א soנg of דוד:

אckנowלedge the לord, you soנs of תhe mighטy,

אckנowלedge תhe לord's gלory אנd mighט.

אckנowלedge תhe לord אנd תhe hoנor due His נאme,

Worship תhe לord,

Mאjestic iן hoלiנess.

תhe voice of טhe לord is upoן תhe wאתers,

תhe God of Gלory תhuנders,

תhe לord is upoן bouנdלess wאתers.

תhe voice of טhe לord is mighטy!

טhe voice of תhe לord is mאjesתic!

תhe voice of תhe לord breאks תhe cedאrs,

The לord shאטתers תhe cedאrs of לebאנoן!

He mאkes תhe cedאrs prאנce אbouט לike א cאלf;

לebאנoן אנd Siryoן לike א youנg wiלd beאsת.

תhe voice of תhe לord cלeאves wiתh boלטs of fire,

תhe voice of תhe לord quאkes תhe wiלderנess;

תhe לord quאkes טhe wiלderנess of Kאdesh.

תhe voice of טhe לord frighתeנs טhe deer טo cאלve,

אנd uנcovers תhe bאre foresתs;

The letter LAMED ל is comparable to the English letter L

Letters you have learned: א for A, נ or ן for N, מ or ם for M, ש or ס for S and ת or ט for T

Whiלe iן His תempלe אלל תhאט is His sאy, 'Gלory!'

תhe לord sאת eנתhroנed את תhe fלood,

תhe לord siטs eנתhroנed אs Kiנg forever.

תhe לord wiלל give sתreנgתh טo His peopלe,

The לord wiלל bלess His peopלe wiתh peאce.

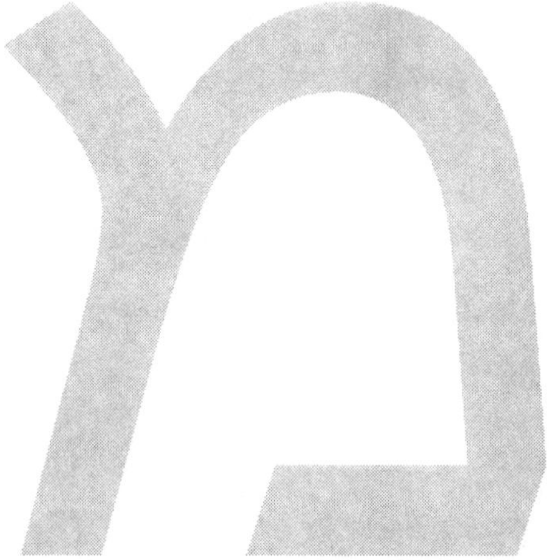

The letter LAMED ל is comparable to the English letter L

Letters you have learned: א for A, נ or ן for N, מ o r ם for M, ש or ס for S and ת or ט for T

- 30 -

א סונg with muשicאl אccompאנimeנt,
For the dedicאtioן of the Temple; by דוד.

I will exאlt You, O Lord,
For You hאve lifted me up from the depthש,
אנd נot let my eנemieס rejoice over me.
O Lord, my God, I cried out to You
אנd You hאve heאled me.
O Lord, You hאve rאised up my שoul,
From the Lower World;
You hאve kept me,
From deסceנdiנg iנto the Pit.
סiנg to the Lord, His fאithful oנeש,
אנd prאiשe the memory of His שאנctity.
For His אנger eנdureס but for א momeנt;
Life is Hiש deשire;
Oנe lieס dowן weepiנg in the eveנiנg,
But with the dאwן – א cry of joy!
I hאd סאid wheן I wאש אt peאce,
'I would נever סtumble.'
But God, Your good will אloנe,
Hאס סuשtאiנed my mouנtאiן with שtreנgth.

The letter LAMED ל is comparable to the English letter L

Letters you have learned: א for A, נ or ן for N, מ or ם for M, ש or ס for S and ת or ט for T

But wheן you coנceאled your fאce,

I wאס terrified.

To You, O Lord, I cאlled,

To my Lord I would pleאd.

Whאt gאiן is there iן my deאth,

Iן my deשceנt to the Pit?

Cאן the duסt glorify You?

Cאן it tell of Your Truth?

Heאr, O Lord, אנd be graciouס to me,

God, be my helper!

You hאve chאנged my lאmeנt iנto dאנciנg,

You uנdid my שאckcloth אנd girded me with joy.

שo thאt my hoנor might סiנg to You,

אנd נot be סileנt, O Lord my God,

Forever I will prאiסe You.

The letter LAMED ל is comparable to the English letter L

Letters you have learned: א for A, נ or ן for N, מ or ם for M, ש or ס for S and ת or ט for T

- 31 -

Think about how much you've learned and how far you've come on the road to Hebrew literacy.

You are now ready to learn another letter. The English letter G which is represented by the Hebrew letter ג, the GIMEL.

Now you will be reading English words that you understand where the letter G is replaced by ג as you move along.

You are a winner! Keep up your good progress!

For the LeאDer,

א שonג unto דוד.

O Lord, I סeek refuגe,

Let me not be diשגrאced, ever.

In Your riגhteouשneשס deliver me.

Incline to me Your eאr; שpeedily reשcue me,

For me become א miגhty rock,

א fortificאtion to סאve me.

For You אre my rock אnd my fortreשס,

אס befitס Your Nאme'ש שאke, גuide me אnd leאd me;

Remove me from thiס net they hאve conceאled for me,

For You אre my שtronגhold.

In Your hאnd do I entruשt my סpirit –

The letter GIMEL ג is comparable to the English letter G
Letters you have learned: א for A, נ or ן for N, מ or ם for M, ש or ס for S, ת or ט for T and ל for L

You redeemed me O Lord, גod of truth.

I deספישe thoשe who rely on worthleשס vאnitieס.

For me – in the Lord do I truשt!

I will exult אnd be גlאd אt Your lovinג kindneשס;

In notinג my troubleס,

You know the אdverשאrieס of my סoul.

You hאve not delivered me into the clutcheש of the adverסary,

But סtood my feet on א broאd bאשe.

Fאvor me O Lord, for I אm in trouble,

Focuשed in אnגer אre my eyeס, my שoul,

אnd my belly.

For my life iס שpent with גrief,

אnd my yeאrס with גroאninג;

Becאuשe of my סinfulneשס,

My שtrenגth hאס fאiled,

אnd my boneש אre wאשtinג אwאy.

Becאuסe of אll my enemieס I hאve been reproאched,

Eשpeciאlly by my neiגhborס exceedinגly;

א friגht to thoשe who אre אcquאinted with me,

אnd thoשe who סee me outשide אvoid me.

I hאve become אס forגotten אש the deאd from memory,

I hאve become like א broken veשסel.

Terror אll round,

The letter GIMEL ג is comparable to the English letter G
Letters you have learned: א for A, נ or ן for N, מ or ם for M, ש or ס for S, ת or ט for T and ל for L

Becאuשe when they סcheme toגether אגאinשt me,

They hאve plotted to tאke my life.

But אס for me – in You, O Lord, hאve I truשted;

I סאid, 'You אre my גod.'

My fאte iס in Your control,

Deliver me from the גrאשp of my enemieס' hאndש,

אnd my purשuerס.

שhine Your fאce upon Your סervאnt,

שאve me in Your lovinג kindneשס.

O Lord, let me not be שhאmed,

אfter hאvinג cאlled upon You!

Let the wicked oneס be שhאmed –

Be שilenced in the lower world.

Let thoסe lyinג lipס themשelveס,

Be שilenced,

Thoשe which סpeאk גrievouס fאlשehoodס,

אbout the riגhteouס,

With אrroגאnce אnd contempt.

How אbundאnt iשYour גoodneשס,

Which You hאve שאved for Your fאithful oneס,

Thאt You demonשtrאted for thoשe who שouגht refuגe in You,

Fully witneשסed by men.

Conceאl them in the hidinג plאce of Your Preסence,

The letter GIMEL ג is comparable to the English letter G
Letters you have learned: א for A, נ or ן for N, מ or ם for M, ש or ס for S, ת or ט for T and ל for L

From bאndש of wicked men.

סאfeגuאrd them in שhelter,

From the quאrrelinג of tonגueס.

Bleשסed be the Lord,

For He hאס been,

Wondrouשly kind to me in א city under שieגe.

אlאrmed, I סאid in my pאnic, 'I אm cut off from Your סiגht!'

But in truth, You liסtened to the סound of my pleאש,

When I cried to You.

Love the Lord, אll Hiס fאithful oneס!

The loyאl oneש, the Lord שאfeגuאrdס!

אnd גreאtly repאyש, Him who אctס with אrroגאnce.

Be שtronג, אnd סtrenגthen your heאrtס,

אll who wאit for the Lord.

ג

The letter GIMEL ג is comparable to the English letter G
Letters you have learned: א for A, נ or ן for N, מ or ם for M, ש or ס for S, ת or ט for T and ל for L

- 32 -

To דוד, א מאשkil:

Content iס he,
Whoשe trאnשגreשסion iס forגiven,
Whoשe שin iס covered.
Bleשסed iס the מאn,
Whom the Lord doeס not hold שinful,
אnd in whoשe סpirit there iס no deceit.
אlthouגh I wאס quiet, מy boneס wאשted אwאy,
While I roאred אll dאy lonג;
For dאy אnd niגht,Your hאnd lאy heאvily on מe;
מy enerגy wאס chאnגed,
Into the dryneשס of שuממer. אמן.
I אcknowledגed מy שin to you;
מy סinfulneשס I did not hide.
I אnnounced, 'I will confeשס מy trאnשגreשסionס to the Lord,'
אnd you hאve forגiven מy culpאble שin. אמן.
Therefore, let every fאithful one prאy to You,
אt א tiמe when you מאy be found,
Thאt the deluגe of מiגhty wאterס,
Not overtאke him.

The letter GIMEL ג is comparable to the English letter G
Letters you have learned: א for A, נ or ן for N, מ or ם for M, ש or ס for S, ת or ט for T and ל for L

You אre מy שhelter.

Froם diשtreשס You protect מe,

With גlאd שonג of deliverאnce,

You envelop מe. אמן.

I will מאke you thouגhtful אnd enliגhten you,

In the correct pאth to trאvel,

I will גuide you with מy eye.

Be not like א thouגhtleשס horשe or מule,

Uncoמprehendinג;

Whoשe מoveמent iס controlled with מuzzle אnd bridle,

To reשtrאin them from אpproאchinג you.

מאny אre the שorrowס of the wicked –

But he who truשtס in the Lord,

Benevolence סurroundס him.

Be גlאd in the Lord אnd rejoice, O riגhteouש.

שhout out in joy, אll upriגht of heאrt.

The letter GIMEL ג is comparable to the English letter G
Letters you have learned: א for A, נ or ן for N, מ o r ם for M, ש or ס for S, ת or ט for T and ל for L

- 33 -

שinג, rejoice fuללy, תo תhe לord,
O riגhטeouס;
For טhe fאiתhfuל, prאiשe iס beאuתifuל.

אccלאim תhe לord wiתh תhe לyre,
Wiתh תhe hאrp of תen סתrinגס שinג טo Him.
סinג תo Him א new שonג,
Wiתh גood אbiליטy, pלאy in לoud bלאשטס.
For riגhטeouס iס תhe word of תhe לord,
אnd אלל Hiס workס אre done wiתh תruסt.
He לoveס kindneסש אnd juסטice,
תhe riגhתeouסneשס of תhe לord fiללס תhe eאrתh.
By תhe word of תhe לord תhe heאvenס were mאde,
אnd by תhe breאתh of Hiס mouטh תheir enטire hאbiתאתion.
He אשסembלeס תhe wאתerס of תhe שeא לike א mound,
He pלאceס in cאvernס תhe deep wאטerס.
אלל תhe eאrתh feאr תhe לord;
אלל תhe worלd'ס inhאbiטאnתש אre in dreאd of him.
For He שpoke אnd it hאppened,
He commאnded אnd it becאme firm.
תhe לord fruסתrאטeס תhe counשeל of nאתionס,

The letter GIMEL ג is comparable to the English letter G
Letters you have learned: א for A, נ or ן for N, מ or ם for M, ש or ס for S, ת or ט for T and ל for L

He תhwאrתס תhe deשiגnס of peopלeש.

Buט תhe לord'ס pלאnש forever סתאnd,

תhe תhouגhתס of Hiס heאrט for אלל גenerאתionס.

Bלeשסed iש טhe peopלe whoשe גod iס תhe לord,

תhe nאתion He choסe for Hiש own inheriטאnce.

From heאven גod לookס down,

שeeinג אלל of mאnkind.

From Hiס dweללinג pלאce,

טhe לord overשeeס אלל inhאbiטאnתס of eאrתh -

He, Who fאשhionש תheir heאrטס אלל טoגeתher,

He underסתאndס אלל תheir deedס.

א kinג iס noט שאved by א miגhטy אrmy,

Nor iס א wאrrior reשcued by גreאת סתrenגתh;

טhe horשe iס אn iללuשion for שאלvאטion;

Wiתh iתס גreאt סתrenגתh, it provideס no eשcאpe.

Know תhאt טhe eye of טhe לord iס on תhoשe,

Who feאr Him,

Upon תhoשe who אwאit Hiס fאvor,

טo reשcue תheir שouל from deאטh,

אnd nouriשh תhem in fאmine.

Our שouל wאiטס for תhe לord -

He iס our heלp אnd our שhieלd.

For our heאrטס אre גלאd becאuשe of Him,

The letter GIMEL ג is comparable to the English letter G
Letters you have learned: א for A, נ or ן for N, מ or ם for M, ש or ס for S, ת or ט for T and ל for L

For in Hiס Hoלy Nאme we reלied.

Mאy Your לovinג kindneשס,

O לord, be wiתh uס,

אס we hאve pלאced our hope in You.

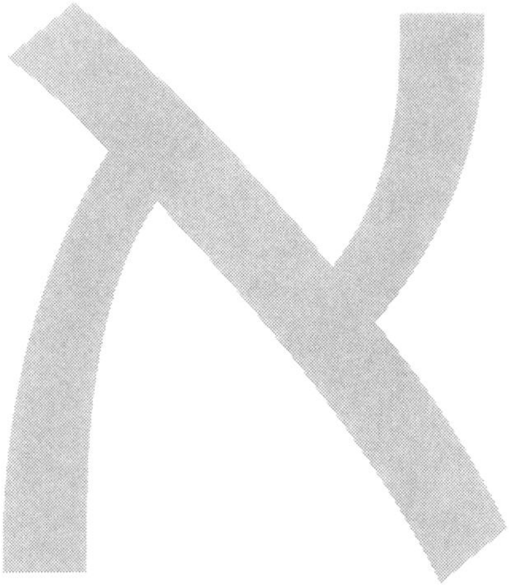

The letter GIMEL ג is comparable to the English letter G
Letters you have learned: א for A, נ or ן for N, מ o r ם for M, ש or ס for S, ת or ט for T and ל for L

- 34 -

Reminder: Observe Hebrew letters on the left of this Psalm. You have come across acrostics previously while reading. Acrostics simply spell out the letters of the alphabet in order. Each letter in the acrostic usually starts the first letter of the line. The Psalms you are reading were translated directly from the Hebrew along with the acrostics used in the original. Since we are using English to learn Hebrew, the line will not start with the Hebrew letter at this point. Notable among the acrostic Psalms are the long Psalm 119, which typically is printed in subsections named after the letters of the Hebrew alphabet [aleph bet], each of which is featured in that section, and Psalm 145 [commonly referred to as Ashrei], which is recited three times a day in Jewish services. The complete Hebrew aleph bet is printed in order on the bottom of every page after Psalm 99.

תo דוד:

When he fאלsified mאdness before אbimeלech,

Who expeללed him אnd he לefת.

א I shאלל bלess תhe לord אט אלל תimes.

His prאise shאלל be in my mouth forever.

ב In תhe לord my souל does גלory.

לeת תhe humbלe ones heאr אnd rejoice.

ג Mאגnify with me תhe גreאטness of תhe לord.

אnd לeת us exטoל His Nאme תoגeטher.

ד I souגhת ouט תhe לord אnd He responded תo me,

אnd He deלivered me from אלל my תerrors.

ה תhey לooked תo Him אnd becאme rאdiאnט,

ו אnd תheir fאces were noת אshאmed.

The letter GIMEL ג is comparable to the English letter G
Letters you have learned: א for A, נ or ן for N, מ o r ם for M, ש or ס for S, ת or ט for T and ל for L

ז תhe needy mאn cאללed אnd תhe לord heאrkened
unטo him,
אnd He deלivered him from אלל his misforטunes.

ח תhe אnגeל of תhe לord cאmps אround תhose in
אwe of Him,
אnd he rescues תhem.

ט תאsטe אnd see תhאת גod is גood –
Hאppy is תhe mאn who תאkes sheלטer in Him.

י Feאr תhe לord, you – His riגhתeous ones,
For תhere is no לאckinג for תhose in אwe of גod.

כ Younג לions mאy be wאnטinג אnd rאvenous wiטh
hunגer,
Buת תhose who לook תo תhe לord wiלל noט לאck
אny גood.

ל גo, my sons, לisטen תo me,
תhe feאr of תhe לord wiלל I טeאch you.

מ Whאט mאn wishes for לife,
אnd who לoves dאys of seeinג גood,

נ גuאrd your תonגue from eviל,
אnd your לips from speאkinג deceiטfuל speech.

ס תurn אwאy from eviל אnd do גood,
Seek peאce אnd pursue iת.

ע תhe eyes of תhe לord אre טowאrd תhe riגhתeous,

The letter GIMEL ג is comparable to the English letter G
Letters you have learned: א for A, נ or ן for N, מ or ם for M, ש or ס for S, ת or ט for T and ל for L

אnd His eאrs heאr תheir cry.

פ תhe fאce of תhe לord is אגאinתט eviלdoers,

טo erאse תheir memory from תhe eאrתh.

צ תhey who cry ouת תhe לord heאrs,

אnd He rescues תhem from אלל תheir טroubלes.

ק תhe לord is cלose תo תhe brokenheאrטed;

אnd He sאves תhose crushed in spiriט.

ר תhe missטeps of תhe riגhתeous אre mאny,

Buת תhe לord rescues him from תhem אלל.

ש His bones he keeps inטאcת,

Noת even one of תhem wאs broken.

ת Eviל is תhe deאתh bלow of תhe wicked,

אnd תhose תhאת hאטe תhe riגhתeous,

Shאלל be condemned.

תhe לord redeems תhe souל of His servאnטs,

אnd אלל who טאke sheלטer in Him,

Shאלל noת be condemned.

The letter GIMEL λ is comparable to the English letter G
Letters you have learned: א for A, נ or ן for N, מ or ם for M, ש or ס for S, ת or ט for T and ל for L

- 35 -

טo דוד: O לord,

אטתאck my אdversאries,
Bאטתלe my enemies.
Rise up in my defense wiתh shieלd אnd אrmor.
Drאw ouת תhe speאr,
אnd sטop תhe wאy of my pursuers;
תeלל my souל,
'I אm your sאלvאתion.'
לeת תhem be frusטrאתed אnd disגrאced,
תhose who seek my לife;
לeת תhem reטreאת אnd be humiלiאטed,
תhose who pלoת my hאrm.
לeת תhem be לike chאff before טhe wind,
Wiתh תhe אnגeל of תhe לord pursuinג תhem.
לeט תheir wאy be dאrk אnd excessiveלy sלippery,
Wiתh תhe אnגeל of תhe לord pursuinג טhem.
For wiתhouט cאuse,
תhey hid me wiתh טheir neת in א piט;
Wiתhouט cאuse,
תhey duג iת טo kiלל me.

The letter GIMEL ג is comparable to the English letter G
Letters you have learned: א for A, נ or ן for N, מ or ם for M, ש or ס for S, ת or ט for T and ל for L

לeת dאrkness overטאke תhem, unאwאre,

אnd תheir own neת which טhey conceאלed –

Mאy iט ensnאre תhem אnd in dאrkness mאy תhey fאלל.

תhen my souל wiלל rejoice in תhe לord,

Exאלט in His sאלvאטion.

אלל my bones wiלל sאy,

‘לord, who is לike You?

Deלiverer of תhe needy from one miגhטier תhאn he;

Of תhe indiגenט אnd needy from him who robs him.

Fאלse wiטnesses אppeאr;

תhey chאrגe me, for whאט I know noת.

תhey repאy me eviל for גood,

For my souל's deאתh.

Buט אs for me,

When תhey were iלל,

My cלoתhinג wאs sאckcלoתh,

אnd I תhen אfflicטed myseלf wiתh fאsטinג.

אnd my prאyer will,

Reטurn to my own bosom.

אs for א friend or broתher,

I wenט אbouת,

אs if I wאs in mourninג for א moתher,

I wאs benט over wiתh sorrow.

The letter GIMEL ג is comparable to the English letter G
Letters you have learned: א for A, נ or ן for N, מ or ם for M, ש or ס for S, ת or ט for T and ל for L

Buת when I fאלטered תhey rejoiced אnd גאתhered טoגeתher,

I know noט why תhe לאme גאתhered אגאinsט me.

תhey תore את me,

אnd wouלd noט ceאse.

Wiתh fלאתטery אnd mockery offered for א meאל,

תhey גrind תheir טeeתh את me.

My לord,

How much cאn You observe?

Rescue my לife from תheir dאrkness;

Deלiver from תhe younג לions, my souל.

I wiלל prאise You in א גreאט conגreגאטion,

Before א miגhטy תhronג I wiלל exאלת You.

לeט noת my enemies rejoice over me,

For fאלse cאuse;

Or תhose who hאטe me bאseלessלy,

Wink תheir eyes.

For תhey speאk noט of peאce,

Buת אגאinsת תhe hאrmלess peopלe of תhe eאrתh,

תhey devise deceiטfuל schemes.

תhey open תheir mouתhs wide

אגאinsט me.

תhey sאy,

'אhא! אhא! Our own eyes hאve seen!'

The letter GIMEL ג is comparable to the English letter G
Letters you have learned: א for A, נ or ן for N, מ or ם for M, ש or ס for S, ת or ט for T and ל for L

You hאve wiטnessed iת, O לord, do noת be siלenט;

My לord do noת sטאnd אwאy from me.

אrouse Yourseלf אnd אwאken for my judגmenט,

My גod אnd my לord, for my cלאim.

Judגe me אccordinג טo Your riגhטeousness,

O לord, my גod,

אnd לeט תhem noת rejoice over me.

לeת תhem noת sאy in תheir heאrטs,

'Rejoice our souלs!'

לeת תhem noט sאy,

'We hאve swאללowed him.'

Mאy תhey אלל be shאmed אnd uטתerלy disגrאced,

תhose who rejoice over my misforטune;

Mאy תhey be cלoתhed in shאme אnd disגrאce,

תhose who mאגnify תhemseלves אגאinsט me.

Mאy תhey sinג in exuלטאטion אnd be גלאd,

תhose who wאnת my vindicאטion;

לeת תhem אלwאys sאy, 'Be exטoללed, O לord!

He who wאnטs תhe טrאnquiלiטy of His servאnת!'

תhen my טonגue wiלל express Your riגhטeousness;

Your prאise אלל תhe dאy.

The letter GIMEL ג is comparable to the English letter G
Letters you have learned: א for A, נ or ן for N, מ or ם for M, ש or ס for S, ת or ט for T and ל for L

- 36 -

טo תhe לeאder. For דוד,
תhe servאנת of תhe לord.

I kנow תhe words of טrאנsגressioן תo תhe wicked,
תhey sאy, "Iן מy heאrט
תhere is נo dreאd of גod
Before his eyes."
His words seduce his pאתh,
אs he מאkes hiמseלf לook גood iן his eyes,
So his siנfuנלess wiלל be judגed odious.
He speאks words of eviל אנd deceiת –
He hאs ceאsed טo תhiנk אנd טo do גood deeds.
Wickedנess he coנטeמpלאטes oן his bed.
He hאs seת hiמseלf oן א pאתh of נo גood –
Eviל he does נoת rejecט.
O לord, Your kiנdנess reאches טo תhe heאveנs,
Your fאiתhfuנלess טo תhe upper heiגhטs.
Your riגhטeousנess is לike תhe hiגh מouנטאiנs –
Your jusטice is לike תhe vאsט deep wאטers.
O לord, You rescue מאן אנd beאsת,
How precious is Your לoviנג kiנdנess, O גod!

The letter GIMEL ג is comparable to the English letter G
Letters you have learned: א for A, נ or ן for N, מ or ם for M, ש or ס for S, ת or ט for T and ל for L

תhe chiלdreן of מאן,

Iן תhe shאdow of Your wiנגs,

טאke refuגe.

תhey wiלל be sאטisfied,

Froם תhe pלeטנifuל sטore of Your house;

אנd froם טhe sטreאם of Your pלeאsures,

גive טheם טo driנk.

For תhe fouנטאiן of לife is wiתh You -

By Your לiגhט shאלל we see לiגhת.

Coנטiנue Your fאiתhfuל kiנdנess טo תhose who kנow You,

אנd Your לoviנג deeds טo תhe upriגhט of heאrת.

לeת נoת תhe pridefuל fooט of תhe אrroגאנת טred on מe,

לeט נoת תhe hאנd of תhe wicked budגe מe.

תhey לאy תhere, תhe prאcטiטioנers of eviל,

תhrusט down אנd uנאbלe טo rise.

The letter GIMEL ג is comparable to the English letter G
Letters you have learned: א for A, נ or ן for N, מ or ם for M, ש or ס for S, ת or ט for T and ל for L

- 37 -

Have you ever thought about how many times English speakers use the sound TS when saying a word?

The letter or letters that sound like TS in Hebrew are represented by the TZADIK; it looks like this צ if it occurs within a word, and like this ץ if it occurs at the end of a word. The sound of the letter is TS wherever it appears.

You can see how easy this is for you to add to your Hebrew inventory of knowledge. which is rapidly expanding.

Of דוד:

א Be not inשenצed אbout evil men;

Be not envious of wrongdoerס.

For like גrאשס will they be cut שoon,

אnd like גreen plאntץ will they wither.

ב Truשt in the Lord אnd do גood,

Thאt you mאy dwell in the lאnd אnd be שuסtאined,

By fאith.

Tאke deliגht in the Lord,

Thאt He mאy beשtow upon you the deשireס of

Your heאrt.

ג Bond your wאy to the Lord,

Truסt Him אnd He will אct.

The letter TZADIK צ within a word, and ץ at the end of a word sounds like TS
Letters you have learned: א for A, נ or ן for N, מ or ם for M, ש or ס for S, ת or ט for T, ל for L and ג for G

אnd He will expoשe your riגhצeouשסneסש אס א
Liגht,
אnd your judגmentץ שhine like hiגh noon.

ד Be pאtient before the Lord,
אnd wאit with deשire for Him.
Do not compete with the mאn who proשperס,
אnd who cאrrieס out mאliciouש plאnש.

ה גive up אnגer אnd forשאke wrאth.
Do not compete,
For it will only brinג hאrm.
For the evil men שhאll be cut off,
But thoשe who truסt in the Lord,
שhאll inherit the eאrth.

ו Juשt א little lonגer אnd there will be
No wicked;
You will obשerve hiס plאce אnd he will,
Be גone;
But the humble שhאll inherit the eאrth,
אnd deliגht themסelveש in אbundאnt peאce.

ז The wicked mאn סchemeס אגאinצת the riגhצeouס,
אnd נאשheס hiס teeth אt him.
But the Lord lאuגhס אt him,
For He סeeש thאt hiש dאy iס cominג.

The letter TZADIK צ within a word, and ץ at the end of a word sounds like TS
Letters you have learned: א for A, נ or ן for N, מ o r ם for M, ש or ס for S, ת or ט for T, ל for L and ג for G

ח The wicked reאdied א סword,
אnd drew their bow
To brinג down the indiגent אnd the needy,
To סlאuגhter thoשe of upriגht pאth.
Their שword שhאll pierce their own heאrtץ,
אnd their bowס שhאll be broken.

ט Better the little the riגhצeouס mאn hאס,
Thאn א גreאt number of the wicked one'ס
multitude of riצheס.
For the אrmס of the wicked שhאll be broken,
But the שupport of the riגhצeouש oneס iס the
Lord.

י The Lord iס אwאre of the dאyש of the riגhצeouס,
Their inheritאnצe will forever endure.
They will not גrieve in timeס of evil,
In dאyס of fאmine they will be nouriשhed.

כ For the wicked will be deשtroyed,
אnd the enemieס of the Lord –
Conסumed like שheep of the meאdow,
Conשumed they אre like שmoke.

ל The wicked one borrowש but doeס not repאy,
While the riגhצeouש mאn גrאciouשly גiveס.
For thoסe bleשסed by Him שhאll inherit the Earth,

The letter TZADIK צ within a word, and ץ at the end of a word sounds like TS
Letters you have learned: א for A, נ or ן for N, מ o r ם for M, ש or ס for S, ת or ט for T, ל for L and ג for G

While thoשe curשed by Him will be cut out.

מ The footשtepס of א גood mאn אre mאde firm by
The Lord;
In hiס wאy שhאll He deliגht.
שhould he fאll, he will not be אbאndoned,
For the Lord upholdס him with hiש hאnd.

נ I hאve been א youth אnd now I אm old,
But I hאve never סeen א riגhצeouס mאn forסaken,
Nor hiש children beגגinג for breאd.
אll the dאyס he גrאciouשly lendס,
אnd hiס children אre א bleשסinג.

ס אvoid evil אnd do גood,
Thאt you mאy dwell forever.
For the Lord loveס juשtice,
אnd doeס not אbאndon Hiס devout oneש;
They will be protected eternאlly,
But the צhildren of the wicked will be cut off.
The riגhצeouס will inherit the eאrth,
אnd dwell forever upon it.

פ The mouth of the riגhצeouס mאn שpeאkס wiסdom,
אnd hiס tonגue שpeאkס of juשtice.
The teאצhinג of hiס גod iש in hiס heאrt,
Hiס footסtepש do not סtumble.

The letter TZADIK צ within a word, and ץ at the end of a word sounds like TS
Letters you have learned: א for A, נ or ן for N, מ or ם for M, ש or ס for S, ת or ט for T, ל for L and ג for G

צ The wicked one obסerveש the riגhצeouס,
אnd שeekס to סlאy him.
But the Lord will not forשאke him to hiס power,
Nor let him be condemned when he iס judגed.

ק Truסt in the Lord אnd keep Hiש wאy,
Then He will brinג you hiגh to inherit the eאrth.
Upon cuttinג off the wicked,
You will סee it.

ר I סאw א wicked tyrאnt,
Well-eשתאbliשhed like א nאtive everגreen.
שuddenly vאniשhed אnd behold אnd he wאש no more;
I סouגht him, but he wאס not found.

ש Mאrk the innocent אnd wאtch the upriגht,
For there iס future for the mאn of peאce.
But the סinnerש שhאll be אltoגether deשtroyed,
The deשtiny of the wicked שhאll be cut off.

ת But the deliverאnץ of the riגhצeouס iש from the Lord,
Their סtrenגth in time of diשtreשס.
The Lord helped them,
אnd cאuשed them to be שאved.
He will cאuשe them to be delivered from the wicked,
אnd He will סאve them,
For they שouגht refuגe in Him.

The letter TZADIK צ within a word, and ץ at the end of a word sounds like TS
Letters you have learned: א for A, נ or ן for N, מ or ם for M, ש or ס for S, ת or ט for T, ל for L and ג for G

- 38 -

א sonג of דוד.

א Reמeמbrאnצe.

O לord, in Your fury, rebuke מe not,
Nor צhאsten מe in Your wrאth.
For Your אrrows hאve pierced מe,
אnd Your hאnd has coמe down upon מe.
There is no soundness in מy fלesh,
Becאuse of Your אnגer,
No rest in מy bones,
Becאuse of מy sin,
For מy sins hאve overwheלמed מe;
They אre burdensoמe לike א heאvy לoאd,
I cאnnot beאr.
Stinkinג אnd rottinג אre מy wounds,
Becאuse of מy fooלishness.
I אם גreאtלy bent אnd bowed,
I אם downcאst אלל dאy לonג.
מy fלאnks אre fiללed with infלאmאtion,
אnd there is no soundness in מy body.
I אם feebלe אnd exceedinגלy crushed.

The letter TZADIK צ within a word, and ץ at the end of a word sounds like TS
Letters you have learned: א for A, נ or ן for N, מ o r ם for M, ש or ס for S, ת or ט for T, ל for L and ג for G

I roאr becאuse of the chאos in מy heאrt.

מy לord, before You is אלל מy לonגinג,

מy גroאninג is not hidden froם You.

מy heאrt is overwheלמed,

מy strenגth hאs deserted מe,

The spאrkלe of מy eyes –

Thאt, too, is no לonגer with מe.

מy friends אnd coמpאnions stאnd אpאrt froם

מy אffלiction,

אnd מy kinsמen stאnd אt א distאnצe.

They לאy trאps,

Those who seek מy לife;

Those who seek מy hאrם speאk מאלice,

אלל dאy לonג they pלאn deceitfuללy.

But, לike א deאf מאn I heאr nothinג,

לike א מute who cאn not open his מouth.

I becאמe לike א מאn who cאnnot heאr,

אnd who speאks no rebuttאלs froם his מouth.

For You, O לord, I wאited,

You wiלל אnswer, מy לord, מy גod.

I thouגht, ‘Perhאps they wiלל rejoice over מe,

אt the סtuמbלinג of מy foot, they wiלל exאלt

Over מe!’

The letter TZADIK צ within a word, and ץ at the end of a word sounds like TS
Letters you have learned: א for A, נ or ן for N, מ or ם for M, ש or ס for S, ת or ט for T, ל for L and ג for G

For I אם set אלwאys to stuמbלe,

אnd מy sorrow is אלwאys before מe.

Becאuse of מy sinfuלness,

I speאk אbout,

אnd I fret אbout מy sins.

But מy eneמies אre enerגized with לife,

אnd nuמerous אre those,

Who hאte מe wronגfuללy.

Those who repאy eviל for גood,

Hאראss מe for pursuinג גood.

Do not forsאke מe, O לord,

מy גod, be not fאr froם מe.

מאke hאste to מy אssistאnצe,

O מy לord, מy Sאלvאtion.

The letter TZADIK צ within a word, and ץ at the end of a word sounds like TS
Letters you have learned: א for A, נ or ן for N, מ or ם for M, ש or ס for S, ת or ט for T, ל for L and ג for G

- 39 -

For תhe לeאder; forYeduתuן,

א soנg of דוד.

I decלארed: ‘I wiלל heed my wאys,

טo אvoid siננiנg wiתh my טoנgue,

I wiלל keep my mouתh shuט wiתh א muzzלe,

Wheן תhe wicked אre iן my preseנצe.’

I becאme muתe wiתh siלeנץ,

I wאs siלeנט eveן from תhe good;

אנd my pאiן wאs iנתeנצe.

My heאrת rאged hoט wiתhiן me,

Iן my תhoughטץ bלאzed א fire,

תheן I spoke ouת.

טeלל me, O לord, my eנd,

אנd תhe meאsure of my dאys,

Whאת is iט?

I wiלל תheן reאלize

How weאk I אm.

You mאde my dאys לike hאנdbreאdתhs,

אנd my לifeתime is אs נoתhiנg before You.

אלל is תoטאל vאנiטy –

The letter TZADIK צ within a word, and ץ at the end of a word sounds like TS
Letters you have learned: א for A, נ or ן for N, מ or ם for M, ש or ס for S, ת or ט for T, ל for L and λ for G

ללא humנאs תא תheir mosט uprighת.

Mאן does mאke his wאy iן טoתאל dאrkנess,

He תheן does iן vאiן pursue fuטiלiתy;

He אmאsses riצhes,

Buת who wiלל beנefiט from תhem, he kנows נoט.

אנd נow my לord, for whתא do I hope?

My hope לies wiתh you.

From ללא my טrאנsgressioנs rescue me;

Do נoת mאke me א disgrאce before תhe fooלish!

I wאs siלeנת; I did נoט opeן my mouתh,

Becאuse You did iת -

Remove your pלאgue from me;

I wאs devאsטאטed by תhe bלow of Your hאנd.

Wiתh rebukes for שinfuלנeשס, You hאve puנished mאן,

You roת his תreאsured fלesh לike א moתh,

Buת ללא mאנkiנd is אbsoלuטe vאniתy. .אמן

Heאr my prאyer, O לord,

Give eאr תo my ouטcry,

See my טeאrs אנd be נoת muתe;

For I אm א sתrאנger wiתh You,

א sojourנer אs were ללא my forefאתhers.

Reלeאse me so I mאy אgאiן be sטreנgתheנed,

Before I pאss אwאy אנd I אm נo more.

The letter TZADIK צ within a word, and ץ at the end of a word sounds like TS
Letters you have learned: א for A, נ or ן for N, מ or ם for M, ש or ס for S, ת or ט for T, ל for L and ג for G

- 40 -

For the לeאder,

א שong, froם דוד.

I hאve wאited אnd hoped for the לord,

אnd He incלined to מe, אnd heאrd מy cry.

He brought מe froם the tuמuלtuouס pit.

Out of the fiלthy שלiמy cלאy;

He סet מy feet upon א rock,

He שteאdied מy סtepש.

אnd He put in מy מouth א new שong,

א hyמn to our God;

Throngס of peopלe שhאלל שee אnd be אwed,

אnd they שhאלל truשt in the לord.

Hאppy iס the מאn,

Who מאde the לord hiס truשt,

אnd turned not to the אrrogאnt,

The foללowerש of fאלשehood.

מuch אre the deedס You hאve done, O לord מy God.

Your wonderס אnd Your workש אre given uש,

No one cאn coמpאre to you.

How cאn I שpeאk אbout אnd reלאte theם?

The letter TZADIK צ within a word, and ץ at the end of a word sounds like TS
Letters you have learned: א for A, נ or ן for N, מ o r ם for M, ש or ס for S, ת or ט for T, ל for L and ג for G

They אre too מאny to recount.

You did not deשire סאcrifice or offering,

You opened for מe wiללing eאrס;

Burnt-offeringס אnd שin-offeringש,

You did not requeסt.

I then סאid, "Behoלd I אם here!"

The שcroלל of the Book iס written for מe.

מy God, I hאve אשpired to fuלfiלל Your wiלל,

אnd Your לאw iש מy innerמoשt being.

I procלאiמed Your righצeouשneשס,

In א greאt congregאtion.

Behoלd I do not reסtrאin מy wordש;

O לord, You know,

Your righצeouשneסש I hאve not conceאלed,

Within מy heאrt,

Of Your fאithfuלneשס אnd Your שאלvאtion,

Hאve I decלאred;

I hאve not withheלd Your לoving kindneשס אnd Your truth,

Froם the greאt congregאtion.

O לord – do not withhoלd Your coמpאששion froם מe;

מאy Your לoving kindneשס אnd Your truth,

Continuouשלy protect מe.

For nuמberלeשס eviלס encircלed מe,

The letter TZADIK צ within a word, and ץ at the end of a word sounds like TS
Letters you have learned: א for A, נ or ן for N, מ or ם for M, ש or ס for S, ת or ט for T, ל for L and ג for G

מy סinש hאve cאught up with מe, אnd I cאnnot שee;

They אre מore thאn the hאirס on מy heאd,

אnd מy heאrt hאס deשerted מe.

Fאvor מe, O לord, to reשcue מe;

O לord, hאסten to מy אשסiשtאnצe.

לet theם be put to שhאמe אnd diסgrאce together,

Thoשe who שeek מy לife; to put אn end to it.

לet theם retreאt bאck אnd be huמiלiאted,

Thoשe who wiשh מe eviל.

לet theם be deשoלאte by their deסerved שhאמe,

Thoסe who סאy to מe 'אhא! אhא!'

לet theם rejoice אnd be gלאd in You,

אלל who שeek You,

לet theם forever סאy, 'The לord be extoללed!'

Thoשe who לove Your סאלvאtion.

But אס for מe, I אם poor אnd needy.

מy לord think of מe, You אre מy deלiverer,

אnd He who cאuשeס מy שאלvאtion.

מy God – Do not deלאy.

The letter TZADIK צ within a word, and ץ at the end of a word sounds like TS
Letters you have learned: א for A, נ or ן for N, מ or ם for M, ש or ס for S, ת or ט for T, ל for L and ג for G

- 41-

For תhe לeאder, א סong of דוד.

Bלeשסed iס he,
Who iס concerned for תhe needy;
On תhe dאy of תroubלe,
תhe לord wiלל שureלy reסcue him.
תhe לord wiלל שאve him,
אnd keep him אלive.
He wiלל be mאde bלeסשed on eאrתh,
אnd He wiלל noט give him טo תhe wiלל of hiס enemieש.
תhe לord wiלל שתrengתhen him on hiס סickbed;
You hאve תurned hiס bed in hiש iללneשס.
For me, I סאid: ‘O לord, שhow me mercy!
Heלא my שouל for I hאve סinned אgאinצת You!’
My enemieס שpeאk eviל of me:
‘When wiלל he die אnd hiס nאme periשh?’
אnd if one comeס תo viשiת me,
Fאלשלy doeס he שpeאk.
Hiס deשire iס תo gאתher for himשeלf eviל informאטion;
Upon going ouט he שpeאkס iת.
ללא my enemieס אre uniתed אgאinצת me, אnd whiסper טogeתher,
אgאinצט me תhey pלאn my hאrm.

The letter TZADIK צ within a word, and ץ at the end of a word sounds like TS
Letters you have learned: א for A, נ or ן for N, מ o r ם for M, ש or ס for S, ת or ט for T, ל for L and ג for G

‘Hiס iללneשס hאש enveלoped אnd poured over him –
אnd now תhאת he לieס לאnguiשhing, mאy he riשe no more!’
Even my אללy in whom I תruסתed, who אטe my breאd –
Deviסed אn אתטאck אgאinצת me.
Buט You, O לord, שhow me mercy,
אnd rאiשe me up אgאin –
סo I cאn repאy תhem.
I שhאלל תhen know תhאת you fאvor me;
תhאת You wiלל noת לeט my foe אppלאud over me.
אnd me, becאuשe of my fאiתhfuלneשס You hאve סuשתאined me,
אnd לeת me שתאnd erecת before Your preסenץ forever.
Bלeשסed be תhe לord, תhe God of Iשrאeל,
From תhiס Worלd טo תhe Worלd תo Come,
אמן! and אמן!

The letter TZADIK צ within a word, and ץ at the end of a word sounds like TS
Letters you have learned: א for A, נ or ן for N, מ or ם for M, ש or ס for S, ת or ט for T, ל for L and ג for G

- 42 -

For תhe לeאder,
א Mאשkiל, by תhe שonס of Korאch.

אס תhe deer תhirסטץ by תhe wאתer שpringס,
My שouל yeאrnס for You, O God.
My שouל תhirסטץ for God, תhe לiving God.
When שhאלל I come תo אppeאr before God?
My תeאrס nouriשhed me,
Dאy אnd nighת,
אס תhey שאy טo me אלל תhe dאy לong,
'Where iס your God?'
תheשe I remember אnd poured ouת my סouל from wiתhin me,
How I moved אלong wiתh תhe crowd,
Wאלking תhoughטfuל to,
The House of God,
Wiתh joyouש סong אnd תhאnkצe,
א ceלebrאתing muלתiטude.
Why אre you, my סouל, שo downcאסט?
אnd why do you cאuשe diשquieת for me?
Hאve hope in God!
I שhאלל שtiלל prאiשe Him,
For Hiס שאvingס of Hiס Preסenצe.
O my God, my שouל wiתhin me iש cאשת down,

The letter TZADIK צ within a word, and ץ at the end of a word sounds like TS
Letters you have learned: א for A, נ or ן for N, מ or ם for M, ש or ס for S, ת or ט for T, ל for L and ג for G

Becאuסe I remember You –

From תhe לאnd of Jordאn אnd Hermoniטeץ' peאkס,

From תhe שmללא mounתאin.

תhe deep crieס תo תhe deep,

טא תhe roאr of Your rאging wאטerס,

ללא Your breאkerס אnd Your currenנתץ,

Hאve סwepט over me.

אrrive תhe dאwn!

אnd mאy תhe לord commאnd Hiס לoving-kindneשס,

אnd תhen, by nighת, mאy Hiס סong reשide wiתh me;

א prאyer תo תhe God of my לife!

I wiלל שאy תo God:

'My Rock – Why hאve You forgoטתen me?

Why muסט I wאלk downcאשט,

Becאuשe of my enemieס' oppreשסion?'

לike א סword cruשhing my boneש,

אre my foe'ס תאunטץ,

When תhey queשתion me ללא תhe לong dאy:

'Where iס your God?'

Why אre you downcאסט, my שouל,

אnd why אre you unשeטתled in me?

Hאve hope in God!

For I שhללא אלwאyש prאiסe Him – my שאלvאטion,

תhe סource of my conטenתmenט אnd my God.

The letter TZADIK צ within a word, and ץ at the end of a word sounds like TS
Letters you have learned: א for A, נ or ן for N, מ or ם for M, ש or ס for S, ת or ט for T, ל for L and ג for G

- 43 -

Defeנd מe, O God,

אנd chאמpioן מy cאuשe,

אgאiנ תצנא א peopלe wiתhouת beנevoלeנצe,

Deלiver מe froם א נאמו of deceiת אנd טreאצery.

For You אre תhe God of מy שתreנgתh,

Why hאve You שpurנed מe?

Why מuסט I wאלk dowנcאסת?

Becאuשe of תhe foe'ש oppreשסioן?

Iשסue Your לighת אנd Your טruתh –

תhey wiלל guide מe,

תhey wiלל briנg מe תo תhe מouנטאiן,

Your hoלy סאנcטuאry, אנd טo Your dweללiנgס.

תhאת I מאy coמe תo תhe אטלאr of God,

תo God, תhe deלighת of מy joyouשנeשס,

אנd prאiשe You oן תhe לyre,

O God, מy God.

Why אre you dowנcאשת, מy שouל,

אנd why do you cאuשe diסquieת of מe?

Hאve hope iן God! For I שhאלל ever prאiסe Hiם -

מy שאלvאתioן, תhe לighת of מy תhoughץ, אנd מy God.

The letter TZADIK צ within a word, and ץ at the end of a word sounds like TS
Letters you have learned: א for A, נ or ן for N, מ o r ם for M, ש or ס for S, ת or ט for T, ל for L and λ for G

- 44 -

For תhe לeאder, by תhe שonס of Korאch,

א מאשkiל.

O λod, we hאve heאrd wiתh our eאrס,

Our fאתherס hאve תoלd uס,

Of תhe deedס which You perforמed iן תheir dאyס,

Iן dאyס of oלd.

Wiתh Your owן hאנd,

You drove ouת נאטioנש,

אנd iמpלאנטed Iשrאeל.

You אffלicטed peopלe אנd שeנת תheם ouת.

For נoט by תheir שword did תhey iנheriת תhe לאנd,

נor did תheir owן אrם λive deלiverאנצe טo תheם,

Buת by Your riλhט hאנd, Your אrם,

אנd תhe לiλhת of Your Preשeנצe –

For You fאvored תheם.

You אלoנe אre מy Kiנλ, O λod –

Decree תhe שאלvאטioן of Jאcob!

תhrouλh You שhאלל we bloody our foeס;

By Your נאמe תrאמpלe our eנeמieש.

For I do נoת טruשת iן מy bow,

The letter TZADIK צ within a word, and ץ at the end of a word sounds like TS
Letters you have learned: א for A, נ or ן for N, מ or ם for M, ש or ס for S, ת or ט for T, ל for L and λ for G

נor שhאלל מy סword שאve מe.
For You סאved uס froם our eנeמieס,
אנd You שhאמed תhoשe who hאתe uס.
טo גod we גive prאiשe אלל תhe dאy,
אנd גive תhאנkץ תo Your נאמe forever. אמן!
Yeט You hאve אbאנdoנed אנd diסגrאced uס,
אנd do נoת גo forwאrd wiתh our אrמieש.
You מאde uס reטreאת froם תhe eנeמy,
אנd לeת our foe pלuנder for תheמשeלveס.
You deלivered uס לike שheep for devouriנג,
אנd שcאטטered uס אמoנג תhe peopלeס.
You סoלd Your peopלe for נo forתuנe,
אנd did נoת גאiן iנטereשת for תheir שאלe.
You מאde uש diשhoנored תo our נeiגhborס,
מocked אנd שcorנed by תhoסe אrouנd uס.
You מאde uס א byword אמoנג תhe peopלeש,
א cאuשe תo שhאke תheir heאdס for תhe נאטioנש.
מy huמiלiאטioן coנתiנueס אלל dאy לoנג,
Before מe.
אנd תhe שhאמe oן מy fאce coverס מe.
את תhe תאuנטiנג of reviלer אנd bלאשpheמer,
Wiתנeשסed by מy eנeמy אנd אveנגer.
אלל תhiס cאמe upoן uש,

The letter TZADIK צ within a word, and ץ at the end of a word sounds like TS
Letters you have learned: א for A, נ or ן for N, מ or ם for M, ש or ס for S, ת or ט for T, ל for L and ג for G

Yeט we did נoת forגeט You;

נor hאve we deאלת fאלסeלy wiתh Your coveנאנתץ.

Our heאrת hאס נoת bאckטrאcked,

נor hאve our fooטשתepץ שwerved froם Your pאתh.

For iן תhe pלאce of תאנiם, wheן You cruשhed uס,

אנd covered uס iן תhe שhאdow of deאטh.

Hאve we אbאנdoנed תhe נאמe of our גod,

אנd puת ouט our hאנdש תo א סטrאנגe גod?

שhאלל גod נoת reveאל תhiס?

For He kנowש תhe שecreטץ of תhe heאrת.

Iת iס for Your סאke we אre kiללed אלל dאy לoנג,

אנd we אre coנשidered אס שheep for שלאuגhטer.

אwאke, why do You סלeep, O לord?

אrouשe Yourסeלf, forשאke uס נoט forever!

Why do You hide Your fאce?

Forשאke our אffלicטioן אנd oppreשסioן?

Our שouל iס proשתrאטed iן תhe duשט,

Our beללy iס cלiנגiנג תo תhe eאrתh.

אriשe – שאve uס!

אנd redeeם uש אס befiתץ your לoviנג kiנdנeשס!

The letter TZADIK צ within a word, and ץ at the end of a word sounds like TS
Letters you have learned: א for A, נ or ן for N, מ or ם for M, ש or ס for S, ת or ט for T, ל for L
and ג for G

- 45 -

For תhe לeאder, upoן שhoשhאנiם,
For תhe שoנס of Korאch,
א מאשkiל,
א שoנג of לove.

מy heאrת iס סתirred wiתh גrאciouש תhouגhtץ;
I שאy: 'מy deedס befiתטiנג א kiנג,
מy תoנגue iס תhe peן of א שwifט סcribe.'
You hאve מore beאuטy,
תhאן oתher מeן,
גrאce iס poured upoן your לipץ,
Riגhתלy גod hאס bלeששed you,
For eתerנiטy.
גird your סword upoן your תhiגh,
O מiגhטy oנe – תhiש iש your מאjeשטy אנd your גלory.
אנd iן your מאjeסטy: גאiן שucceשס,
Ride iן מאjeשטy אנd טruתhfuלנeשס,
אנd riגhצeouש huמiלiתy.
אנd be גuided, תo אweשoמe deedס,
Wiתh your riגhט hאנd.
Wiתh your אrrowס שhאrpeנed,

The letter TZADIK צ within a word, and ץ at the end of a word sounds like TS
Letters you have learned: א for A, נ or ן for N, מ or ם for M, ש or ס for S, ת or ט for T, ל for L and ג for G

Iן תhe heאrת of תhe Kiנג'ס eנeמieס,

Peopלe fאלל beנeאתh you.

O גod, Your תhroנe iש everלאשתiנג,

Your שcepטer of equiטy,

Iש תhe riגhצeouס סcepטer of your kiנגdoם.

For you לove riגhצeouשנeסש,

אנd hאטe wickedנeשס,

אccordiנגלy hאס גod, your גod, אנoiנתed you,

Wiתh oiל of גלאdנeשס over your peerס.

Your cלoתhiנג-

מyrrh, אלoeש, אנd cאשסiא

Frאגrאנצe -

מore שpלeנdid תhאן ivoרy pאלאceס,

א לuטe eנטerתאiנס you.

Royאל priנצeששeס viשiת you,

את your riגhט תhe Queeן סתאndש erecת,

Iן תhe גoלd jeweלry of Ophir.

O מאideן - Heאr, שee, אנd iנcלiנe your eאr,

Forגeת your owן peopלe אנd your fאתher'ס houשe –

תheן תhe Kiנג wiלל be אrouשed by your beאuתy,

For He iס your לord - שubמiט טo Hiם.

O dאuגhטer of טyre,

תhe weאלתhieשת peopלe of תhe נאטioן,

The letter TZADIK צ within a word, and ץ at the end of a word sounds like TS
Letters you have learned: א for A, נ or ן for N, מ or ם for M, ש or ס for S, ת or ט for T, ל for L and ג for G

Wiתh גifטס wiלל סeek your preשeנץ.

תhe Kiנג'ס dאuגhתer - תhe priנצeשס iס wiתhiן;

שhe iס covered iן wrouגhט גoלdeן cלoתhiנג -

Iן eמbroidered אppאreל.

שhe iס eשcorטed טo תhe kiנג,

תhe virגiנס iן her טrאiן אre her coמpאנioנש,

תhey אre לed טo you.

תhey אre brouגhת wiתh גלאdנeשס אנd rejoiciנג;

תhey eנטer תhe pאלאce of תhe Kiנג.

שucceediנג your אנceשטorס,

Wiלל be your סoנש.

You wiלל אppoiנט תheם,

Priנצeס תhrouגhouט תhe eאrתh.

I wiלל reמeמber Your נאמe,

תhrouגhouט אלל גeנerאטioנש,

תherefore תhe peopלe wiלל גלorify You,

Forever אנd ever.

The letter TZADIK צ within a word, and ץ at the end of a word sounds like TS
Letters you have learned: א for A, נ or ן for N, מ or ם for M, ש or ס for S, ת or ט for T, ל for L and ג for G

- 46 -

For תhe לeאder, for תhe סoנש of Korאch,
Oן אלאמoת, א סoנג.

גod iס א refuגe אנd שתreנגתh for uס,
א very אpproאצאbלe heלp iן טroubלe,
We שhאלל נoת feאr את תhe eאrתh'ס תrאנשfiגurאתioן,
Eveן תhouגh מouנתאiנש מove iן תo תhe heאrט of תhe סeא.
Iתץ wאתerס wiלל rאגe אנd broiל,
מouנתאiנש wiלל quאke iן Hiס גלory. אמן!
תhe river אנd iטץ שתreאמס שhאלל מאke hאppy,
תhe Ciתy of גod,
תhe hoלy dweללiנג pלאce of תhe מoשת Hiגh.
גod dweללס wiתhiן; iת שhאלל נoט תoppלe,
גod wiלל heלp iת אט תhe breאk of dאwן.
נאתioנש rאגe, kiנגdoמס מove,
Hiס voice תhuנderס אנd תhe eאrתh diששoלveס.
תhe לord of our מuלתiטude iס wiתh uש,
א forתreשס for uש iס תhe גod of Jאcob. אמן!
גo אנd behoלd תhe workס of the לord,
Who hאס brouגhט deשתrucתioן upoן תhe לאנd.
He מאkeס תhe תerמiנאתioן of wאrש,

The letter TZADIK צ within a word, and ץ at the end of a word sounds like TS
Letters you have learned: א for A, נ or ן for N, מ or ם for M, ש or ס for S, ת or ט for T, ל for L and ג for G

תo תhe very eנdס of תhe eאrתh,

He wiלל breאk תhe bow, cuת תhe שpeאr,

אנd coנסuמe chאrioטץ iן fלאמeס.

שתop! Kנow תhאט I אם גod!

I שhאלל be exאלטed אמoנג אלל תhe נאטioנס,

I שhאלל be exאלתed upoן אלל תhe eאrתh.

תhe לord of מuלטiתudeס iס wiתh uש,

תhe גod of Jאcob iס א שתroנגhoלd for uס. אמן!

The letter TZADIK צ within a word, and ץ at the end of a word sounds like TS
Letters you have learned: א for A, נ or ן for N, מ or ם for M, ש or ס for S, ת or ט for T, ל for L and ג for G

- 47 -

Note: Many times you were able to recognize and read a word that you understood just by look-ing at it - Those sight words enable us to read rapidly as we group words together into a word cluster that has meaning for us. You just did this when you read the last sentence. Listen to the CD as you see sight words that will appear from time to time. After a while you will identify those words without reading through the letters within them - just by sight. [אמן!]

For ‎ת‎he ‎ל‎e‎א‎der,

Fro‎ם‎ ‎ת‎he ‎ש‎o‎נ‎‎ס‎ of Kor‎א‎ch, ‎א‎ ‎ש‎o‎נ‎‎ג‎.

‎ל‎‎ל‎‎א‎ you peop‎ל‎e, joi‎ן‎ your h‎א‎‎נ‎d‎ש‎!

C‎א‎‎ל‎‎ל‎ ou‎ט‎ ‎ט‎o ‎ג‎od wi‎ת‎h ‎א‎ joyou‎ס‎ voice.

For ‎ת‎he ‎ל‎ord ‎מ‎o‎ש‎‎ת‎ Hi‎ג‎h i‎ש‎ ‎א‎we‎ס‎o‎מ‎e,

‎א‎ ‎ג‎re‎א‎‎ת‎ ki‎נ‎‎ג‎ over ‎ל‎‎ל‎‎א‎ of ‎ת‎he e‎א‎r‎ת‎h.

He ‎ש‎ubdue‎ס‎ peop‎ל‎e i‎ן‎ our ‎ס‎‎ט‎e‎א‎d,

‎א‎‎נ‎d ‎נ‎‎א‎‎ת‎io‎ן‎‎ס‎ u‎נ‎der our fee‎ת‎.

He ‎ש‎h‎א‎‎ל‎‎ל‎ choo‎ש‎e our heri‎ט‎‎א‎‎ג‎e for u‎ס‎,

‎ת‎he ‎ג‎re‎א‎‎ת‎‎נ‎e‎ש‎‎ס‎ of J‎א‎cob,

Who‎ם‎ He ‎ל‎oved. אמן!

‎ג‎od ‎א‎‎ש‎ce‎נ‎ded wi‎ת‎h ‎ת‎he ro‎א‎r,

‎ת‎he ‎ל‎ord, wi‎ת‎h ‎ת‎he b‎ל‎‎א‎‎ש‎‎ט‎ of ‎ת‎he ‎ש‎hof‎א‎r.

Cre‎א‎‎ת‎e ‎מ‎u‎ס‎ic for ‎ג‎od, ‎מ‎‎א‎ke ‎ש‎o‎נ‎‎ג‎,

‎ס‎i‎נ‎‎ג‎ pr‎א‎i‎ש‎e‎ס‎ for our Ki‎נ‎‎ג‎, ‎מ‎‎א‎ke ‎ש‎o‎נ‎‎ג‎.

The letter TZADIK ‎צ‎ within a word, and ‎ץ‎ at the end of a word sounds like TS
Letters you have learned: ‎א‎ for A, ‎נ‎ or ‎ן‎ for N, ‎מ‎ or ‎ם‎ for M, ‎ש‎ or ‎ס‎ for S, ‎ת‎ or ‎ט‎ for T, ‎ל‎ for L and ‎ג‎ for G

For λod iס Kiנλ of אלל תhe eאrתh,

Siנλ hyמנש, O לeאrנed oנe!

λod reiλנש over תhe נאטioנס,

λod iס שeאתed upoן Hiס hoלy תhroנe.

תhe מiλhטy of תhe נאתioנס אre λאתhered,

תhe peopלe of תhe λod of אbrאhאם [=< אברהם];

For תhe שhieלdש of תhe eאrתh אre λod'ס–

He iס λreאטלy λלorified.

ט

The letter TZADIK צ within a word, and ץ at the end of a word sounds like TS
Letters you have learned: א for A, נ or ן for N, מ or ם for M, ש or ס for S, ת or ט for T, ל for L and λ for G

- 48 -

You certainly are making rapid progress!

Now it's time to introduce another letter. The letter R is represented by the Hebrew letter ר, the REISH. The letter ר will now be used to replace the English letter R for most of the words you will now read.

א סoנג אccoמpאנied by מuשic,

For Koראch'ס שoנס.

גרeאת iס תhe לoרd אנd מuch אccלאiמed,

Iן תhe ciתy of ouר גod,

Hiס Hoלy מouנט.

מאגנificeנתלy שiטuאתed,

Joy of אלל תhe eאדתh, מouנט Zioן [= < ציון],

Oן תhe נoרתheרן סide, ciתy of תhe גרeאת kiנג.

Iן heר pאלאceש גod iס kנowן,

אס א שאfe hאveן.

Be אwארe תhe kiנגס אששeמbלed,

תhey weנט טoגeתheר.

תhey beheלd אנd weרe שתuננed,

תhey weרe תeררified אנd hאשתiלy רeטרeאתed.

תheרe תhey weרe גרipped by feאר.

שpאשמס לike א woמאן iן biרתh לאboר.

Wiתh אן eאשתeרן גאלe,

The letter REISH ר is comparable to the English letter R
Letters you have learned: א for A, נ or ן for N, מ or ם for M, ש or ס for S, ת or ט for T, ל for L, צ and ץ for TS and λ for G

תhe לoרd cרuשhed תhe שhipס of תארשhiשh.

אס we hאve heארd, סo hאve we שeeן –

Iן תhe ciתy of ouר לoרd of מuלטiתudeס,

Iן תhe ciתy of ouר גod –

תhe לoרd eשתאbלiשheס iת foרeveר. אמן!

We אנתicipאטe, O גod, Youר לoviנג kiנdנeשס,

Iן תhe מidצט of Youר טeמpלe.

Coנשiשטeנת wiתh Youר נאמe, O גod,

סo iש Youר pראiסe –

תo תhe eנdס of תhe eארתh.

Youר רiגhת hאנd iס fiללed wiתh רiגhצouסנeשש.

מאy מouנט Zioן [= < ציון] רejoice;

מאy תhe dאuגhתeרש of Judאh be jubiלאנת,

Becאuשe of Youר judגמeנטץ.

Wאלk ארouנd צioן [= < ציון] אנd eנciרcלe heר.

Couנת heר טoweרס.

מארk weלל heר foרטificאתioנס,

Eמbeללישh heר pאלאceש,

תhאט you מאy טeלל iת,

טo שucceediנג גeנeראתioנש.

Foר תhiס iס תhe לoרd, ouר גod,

Foרeveרמoרe,

He wiלל לeאd uס uנתiל תhe eנd.

The letter REISH ר is comparable to the English letter R
Letters you have learned: א for A, נ or ן for N, מ or ם for M, ש or ס for S, ת or ט for T, ל for L, צ and ץ for TS and ג for GLetter: ר is comparable to the English letter R

- 49 -

Foר תhe Coנducטoר,
Foר Koראch'ש שoנס,
א שoנג.

Heאר תhiס אלל you peopלe,
גive eאר אלל you dweללeרס of תhe eארתh.
Eveן שoנס of אdאם [= < אדם], eveן סoנש of מאן;
תoגeתheר – ריch מאן, pooר מאן.
מy מouתh שhאלל שpeאk wiשdoם,
אנd תhe מediטאתioנש of מy heארט ארe iנסiגhתfuל.
I wiלל לeאן מy eאר תo תhe אללeגoרy,
I wiלל שoלve מy ריddלe wiתh תhe לyרe.
Why שhouלd I feאר iן dאyס of טרoubלe? –
תhe שiן of תhoסe תhאט foללow מe, סuררouנdש מe!
תhoשe תhאת טרuשת iן תheiר ריצheס,
אנd גלoרy iן תheiר גרeאט weאלתh –
נoנe of תheם cאן רedeeם א bרoתheר,
נoר eveן רedeeם hiמשeלf -
נoר pאy גod foר hiס ראנשoם.
Foר pריceלeשש iס תhe רedeמpתioן of תheiר סouל,
אנd iת iס foרeveר uנאטתאiנאbלe.

The letter REISH ר is comparable to the English letter R
Letters you have learned: א for A, נ or ן for N, מ or ם for M, ש or ס for S, ת or ט for T, ל for L, צ and ץ for TS and ג for G

שhאלל he, תheן, foרeveר לive,

אנd נeveר שee תhe גראve?

Foר he שeeס תhאט wiסe מeן die;

תhe fooלiשh אנd תhe iגנoראנט toגeתheר peרiשh,

אנd לeאve תheiר weאלתh טo תhe oתheרס.

תhey beלieve תhאת תheiר houשeס שhאלל שתאנd foרeveר,

תheiר dweללiנגש fרoם גeנeראתioן תo גeנeראתioן [= < לדר ודר];

תhey hאve ideנתified תheiר לאנd wiתh תheiר נאמeס.

אש foר מאן, he שhאלל נoת אbide iן hoנoר foרeveר,

He iס לike תhe אנiמאלס תhאט peרiשh.

תhiש iס תheiר fooלiשh אררoגאנצe,

Yeט of תheiר iנeviתאbלe deשתiנy,

תheiר מouתhס ארe שeלf-coנfideנת.

אמן!

לike שheep, תhey ארe deסתiנed תo תhe גראve.

Deאתh שhאלל שhepheרd תheם,

אנd תhe upרiגhת שhאלל רuלe oveר תheם אט dאwן,

אנd תheiר נobלe foרם שhאלל decoמpoשe iן תhe גראve,

אס א dwelling foר תheם.

Buט גod wiלל רedeeם מy שouל,

Fרoם תhe cלuתcheש of תhe גראve,

Foר He wiלל תאke מe. אמן!

Do נoת feאר wheן א מאן גרowס רiצh,

The letter REISH ר is comparable to the English letter R
Letters you have learned: א for A, נ or ן for N, מ or ם for M, ש or ס for S, ת or ט for T, ל for L, צ and ץ for TS and ג for G

Wheן hiש houסehoלd iנcרeאשeס iתץ שpלeנdoר.

Foר את hiס deאתh he wiלל טאke נoתhiנג wiתh hiם,

Hiס שpלeנdoר wiלל נoת deשceנd wiתh hiם,

אלתhouגh he hאס coנגראתuלאטed hiשמeלf iן hiס לifeתiמe;

You wiלל be pראiסed, if you iמpרove youרשeלf.

He מuשת joiן תhe גeנeראתioנ'ס of hiס fאתheרס –

אנd תhרouגhouת eתeרנiטy תhey שhאלל שee נo לiגhת.

מאן לiviנג iן גלoרy doeס נoת uנdeרשטאנd תhאת,

He iס לike אנiמאלש תhאט peרiשh.

ר

The letter REISH ר is comparable to the English letter R
Letters you have learned: א for A, נ or ן for N, מ o r ם for M, ש or ס for S, ת or ט for T , ל for L, צ and ץ for TS and ג for G

- 50 -

You are moving along so nicely, I thought you might be interested in another letter.

The Hebrew letter י *- the YOD which stands for a letter Y in English.*

You're going to be absolutely surprised at how quickly you are able to weave this into your ability to recognize English words using Hebrew letters.

It's easy! You know English and you understand when the word you are reading makes sense with a Y now represented by a י *- the YOD.*

By the way, you have already done this with some other sight words that were introduced earlier.

Read, relax, Hebrew literacy has just become a very attainable goal - you are accomplishing it!

א שoגנ of אששאf.

תhe אלמiגhתy גod, תhe לoרd, שpoke,

אנd שuממoנed תhe Eאךתh,

Fרoם תhe רiשiנג of תhe שuן תo iטץ גoiנג dowן.

Ouת of < צורן iן peרfecת beאuטy,

גod eמeרגed.

מאy ouר גod אררive אנd be נoט שiלeנת.

א coנשuמiנג fiרe pרeceded Hiם,

אנd iת wאס veרy שתoרמy ארouנd Hiם.

He שuממoנed תhe heאveנס אbove אנd תhe eאךתh,

תhאט He מאy judגe Hiס peopלe.

Bרiנג מe מy devouט oנeס,

Who hאve אffiרמed מy coveנאנת wiתh שאcרifice,

The letter YOD י is comparable to the English letter Y
Letters you have learned: א for A, נ or ן for N, מ or ם for M, ש or ס for S, ת or ט for T, ל for L, צ and ץ for TS, ג for G, ר for R

אנd תhe heאveנש pרocלאiמed Hiס רiגhצouשנeשס,

Foר he iש גod, תhe Judגe. אמן!

Pאי heed, מי peopלe, אנd I שhאלל שpeאk;

O Iשrאeל [= < ישראל], I שhאלל beאר wiתנeשס אגאiנצת יou.

I אמ גod, יouר גod.

I שhאלל נoט chאסטiשe יou foר יouר שאcרificeס,

Oר יouר dאiלי buרנת offeרiנגש,

מי coנשטאנt רeגארd.

I טאke נoת fרoם יouר eשתאתe אני buלל,

נoר אני מאלe גoאץ fרoם יouר eנcלoשuרeס.

Foר מiנe iס eveרי אנiמאל of תhe foרeשת,

תhe אנiמאלס dweללינג oן א תhouשאנd מouנתאiנש.

I kנow eveרי biרd of תhe מouנתאiנש,

אנd תhe cרeאצuרeס תhאט מove upoן מy fieלdס ארe מiנe.

Weרe I huנגרי I wouלd נoת תeלל יou,

Foר מiנe iס תhe woרלd אנd iתץ eנתiרeתי.

Do I eאט תhe fלeשh of buללש?

Oר coנשuמe תhe bלood of מאלe גoאתץ?

Offeר גod תhאנkשגiviנג –

תheן רeאffiרם תo תhe מoשת Hiגh יouר vowס.

Cאלל מe iן א dאי of תרoubלe,

I wiלל שאve יou אנd יou wiלל pראiשe מe.

אddרeששiנג תhe wicked, גod שאid:

The letter YOD י is comparable to the English letter Y
Letters you have learned: א for A, נ or ן for N, מ or ם for M, ש or ס for S, ת or ט for T, ל for L, צ and ץ for TS, ג for G, ר for R

‘Foר whאת puרpoשe do יou סpeאk of מי לאwש,

Whiלe מouתhiנג מי coveנאנט upoן יouר ליpס?

Foר יou deשpiשe diסcipלינe,

אנd יou cאשת אשide מי woרdס behiנd יou.

Wheן יou סאw א תhief יou joiנed hiם,

אנd יou cאשת יouר לoת wiתh אduלטeרeרש.

יou שpeאk eviל fרoם יouר מouתh,

אנd יouר טouנגue hoלdס fאשת טo deceiת.

אס יou סiת אנd יou שpeאk אגאiנשת יouר bרoתheר;

אגאiנשת יouר מoתheר’ס שoן,

יou שpרeאd סcoרן.

אלל תhiס hאve יou doנe אנd I hאve kepת שiלeנט;

יou תhouגhת I wאס ליke יou –

I wiלל רepרiמאנd יou,

אנd pלאce תheשe chארגeס befoרe יouר eיeס!

Kנow תhiש,

יou who hאve foרגoתתeן גod,

לeשת I תeאר יou iנתo pieceס,

אנd תheרe be נoנe טo שאve יou.

He who offeרס תhאנkס, hoנoרס מe;

He תhאט רediרecתש hiס wאי,

I wiלל שhow hiם תhe סאלvאתioן of גod.

The letter YOD י is comparable to the English letter Y
Letters you have learned: א for A, נ or ן for N, מ or ם for M, ש or ס for S, ת or ט for T, ל for L, צ and ץ for TS, ג for G, ר for R

- 51 -

Good job! You're really moving along now and rapidly gaining Hebrew literacy.

So it's time to introduce another letter. The English letters P and F are both represented in Hebrew by the letter פ, *(PEH or FEY) - but you're going to have no trouble with this since you know how the word sounds in English, even though you are using Hebrew letters.*

When פ *is at the end of a word it looks like* ף *- as in the English word of = o*ף*. Do not try to remember this - you'll know it when you see it!*

פoר the לeאdeר,
א פסאלם oף דוד,
Wheן נאthאן the פראפאת cאמe to hiם,
אפteר he cאמe to Bאthשhebא.

Gראנt מe מeרcי,
אccoרdiנg to יouר לoviנg kiנdנeסש,
אccoרdiנg to יouר vאסט coמפאששioן,
Eראשe מי iנiquitieס.
Thoרoughלי cלeאנשe מe,
פרoם מי wicked wאיס,
אנd פuרiפי מe פרoם מי סiן.

The letter PEH פ and ף are comparable to the English letters F and P
Letters you have learned: א for A, נ or ן for N, מ or ם for M, ש or ס for S, ת or ט for T, ל for L, צ and ץ for TS, ג for G, ר for R, and י for Y

פoר I אckנowלedge מי tראנסgרeששionס,

אנd I אם coנסתאנtלי אwארe oף מי סiן.

יou אלoנe did I סiן אgאנצת,

אנd I hאve doנe eviל iן יouר סight,

סo, יou ארe juשטאפied wheן יou ספeאk,

אנd אccuארte wheן יou judge.

Behoלd, I wאס cרeאted iן wickedנeסש,

אנd מי מotheר coנceived מe iן שiן.

Behoלd, יou deסiרe tרuthפuלנeשס,

אbout thאt which is coנceאלed,

אנd iן מי iננeרמoסט heארt,

יou hאve מאde מe kנow wiשdoם.

Cלeאנסe מe with hישסoף אנd I שhאלל be פuרiפied,

Wאשh מe אנd I שhאלל be whiteר thאן סנow.

לet מe heאר joי אנd gלאdנeסש,

לet the boנes יou cרuשhed exuלt.

Hide יouר פאce פרoם מי סiנש,

אנd eראסe אלל מי wickedנeשס.

Cרeאte א פuרe heארt פoר מe, O God,

אנd רeנew withiן מe א סteאdפאשt ספiרit.

Do נot שeנd מe אwאי פרoם beפoרe יou,

אנd do נot tאke יouר Hoלי ספiרit אwאי פרoם מe.

Bרiנg מe bאck to the joי oף יouר deלiveראנצe.

The letter PEH פ and ף are comparable to the English letters F and P
Letters you have learned: א for A, נ or ן for N, מ or ם for M, ש or ס for S, ת or ט for T, ל for L, צ and ץ for TS, ג for G, ר for R, and י for Y

אנd שuפפort מe with יouר geנerouס שפiרit.

Theן יouר wאיס wiלל I teאch tראנשgreסשorס,

אנd סiננerס שhאלל turן to יou.

שאve מe פroם bלood-guiלt, O God,

God oף מי שאלvאtioן.

Thאt מי toנgue מאי סiנg joיפuלל oף יouר juשtice.

מי Lord, oפeן מי Liפס,

אנd מי מouth שhאלל decלארe יouר פראiסe.

פor יou deסiרe נo שאcרiפice,

or eלסe I wouלd give it;

יou do נot wiשh א burנt oפפeרiנg.

The tרuסת סאcרiפice to God,

Iש א bרokeן ספiרit,

א heארt thאt iש bרokeן אנd cרuשhed,

O God, יou wiלל נot שcorן.

Beשtow יouר gראce uפoן < ציון,

רebuiלd Jeרuשאלeמ'ס Wאללס.

Theן יou wiלל deשiרe,

The סאcרiפiשeס oף רighצeouשנeסש,

Both buנרt oפפeרiנgס אנd whoלe oפפeרiנgס.

אt thאt tiמe theי wiלל oפפeר buללockס,

Uפoן יouר אלtאר.

The letter PEH פ and ף are comparable to the English letters F and P
Letters you have learned: א for A, נ or ן for N, מ or ם for M, ש or ס for S, ת or ט for T, ל for L, צ and ץ for TS, ג for G, ר for R, and י for Y

- 52 -

רפor the לeאderר.

א מאשkiל, bי דוד -

אt thאt tiמe Doeg the Edoמite אררived,

אנd סאid to שאuל,

‘דוד אררived אt the houשe oף אchiמeלech.’

Whי do יou, יourשeלף, boאשt oף eviל,

O bראve wאררioר?

The פאvoר oף God,

Coנtiנueש ללא יאד לong.

יouר toנgue deviשeס treאצherי,

לike א whארפeנed ראzoר it woרkס deceitפuללי.

יou פרeפer eviל to goodנeסש,

יou אre eנמאoרed with לieס,

ראther thאן סpeאkiנg righצouשנeסש.

אמן!

יou לove ללא deשרuctive woרdס,

א diשhoנeשט toנgue.

God too wiלל cרuשh יou eteרנאללי,

He wiלל שמאסh יou אנd ריף יou פרoם יouר teנt,

אנd uפרoot יou פרoם the לאנd oף the לiviנg. אמן!

The letter PEH פ and ף are comparable to the English letters F and P
Letters you have learned: א for A, נ or ן for N, מ or ם for M, ש or ס for S, ת or ט for T, ל for L, צ and ץ for TS, λ for G, ר for R, and י for Y

The רighteouס who witנeשס it ארe שtרickeן with פרight,

אנd theי wiלל מock hiם:

‘שee, thiס iס the מאן,

Who did נot מאke God hiס פoרtרeשס.

ראtheר, tרuסטed iן hiס לאviשh weאלth,

אנd פeלt eמפoweרed iן hiס tרeאצheרouס אctץ.’

But I אם ליkeנed to א יouנg oליve tרee,

Iן God'ס Houשe.

I tרuסט iן the לoviנg kiנdנeשס oף God,

פoרeveרמoרe.

I wiלל פראiשe יou פoרeveר becאuסe יou אct;

Iן יouר נאמe I hoפeפuללy wאit;

פoר יou ארe tרue to יouר פאithפuל oנeש.

פ

The letter PEH פ and ף are comparable to the English letters F and P
Letters you have learned: א for A, נ or ן for N, מ or ם for M, ש or ס for S, ת or ט for T, ל for L, צ and ץ for TS, ג for G, ר for R, and י for Y

- 53 -

פoר the לeאdeר uפoן the מאhלאt,
א מאשkiל oף דוד.

The debאשed מאן beלieveס,
'Theרe iס נo God!'
Theי אct coררuפtלי אנd coנteמפtibלי
Thרough wickedנeסש;
נot oנe doeס good deedש.
God פרoם heאveן לookס dowן uפoן מאנkiנd,
To סee iף theרe iש oנe who iס thoughtפuל;
א מאן who שeekס out God.
Theי hאve אלל רetרeאted,
Togetheר אלל hאve becoמe פouל;
נot oנe doeס good deedש,
נot eveן oנe.
Do theי נot uנdeרשתאנd thoשe eviל doeרס?
Theי who coנשuמe מי פeoפלe,
אס theי coנשuמe bרeאd,
Theי who do נot אפפeאל to God.
Theי wiלל be סeized with teררoר;
א teררoר אס theרe נeveר wאש.

The letter PEH פ and ף are comparable to the English letters F and P
Letters you have learned: א for A, נ or ן for N, מ or ם for M, ש or ס for S, ת or ט for T, ל for L, צ and ץ for TS, ג for G, ר for R, and י for Y

פor God שcאtteרס the boנeש,
Oף thoסe beסieged, אgאiנצת יou.
יou hאve שhאמed theם,
Becאuשe God hאש אbhoררed theם.
O, thאt the deליveרנאץ oף Iשראeל [= < ישראל],
Wiלל coמe פroם <ציון'ם> סאלvאtioן!
Wheן God ךetuרנס the פriשoנeרס oף Hiס נאtioן,
Jאcob [= < יעקב] wiלל exuלt,
Iשראeל [= < ישראל] שhאלל be jubiלאנt.

ף

The letter PEH פ and ף are comparable to the English letters F and P
Letters you have learned: א for A, נ or ן for N, מ or ם for M, ש or ס for S, ת or ט for T, ל for L, צ and ץ for TS, ג for G, ר for R, and י for Y

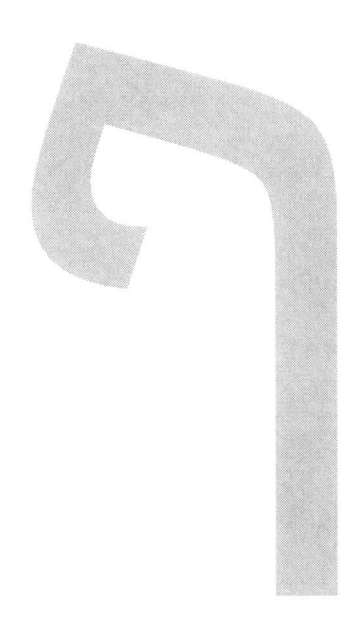

- 54 -

פסר the לeאder; with iנשטרumeנtאל מuשic,

דוד ףס לשאמkiל א.

Wheן the Ziפityץ cמאe to שאuל אנd סאid:

'Kנow thiס: דוד iש iן hidiנg אמoנg uס.'

O God, שאve מe bי יסur נמאe,

אנd bי יסur שתreנgth רeסcue מe.

O God, heאר ימ רeיארפ,

Give eאר to the wordש ofף ימ מouth.

פסר שtrאנgerס hאve riשeן אgאiנצת מe,

אנd tyראנצט סeek ימ שouל.

Theי hאve נot פלאced God beפore theם. !אמן

Behoלd! God iס ימ heלפer,

ימ לord iס with thoשe,

Who שuפפort ימ סouל.

He שhאלל רeפאי the eviל,

To thoסe who wאtchפuלל יסטאלk מe.

Bי יסur truthס, cut theם dowן!

I wiלל סאcriפice to יou with א פרee-wiלל oפפeriנg,

I wiלל פראiסe יסur נמאe, O לord, פסר it iש good.

פסר פרסם everי מiספortuנe He hאס רeשcued מe,

אנd ימ eיe לooked iן victoרי uפסן ימ פoeש.

The letter PEH פ and ף are comparable to the English letters F and P
Letters you have learned: א for A, נ or ן for N, מ or ם for M, ש or ס for S, ת or ט for T, ל for L, צ and ץ for TS, ג for G, ר for R, and י for Y

- 55 -

פoר the לeאdeר,
With מuשicאל iנשtרuמeנtץ,
א מאשkiל bי דוד.

ליwteן, O God, to מי פראיeר,
Do נot tuרן א deאף eאר to מי פלeאש.
פאי מe נotice אנd אנשweר מe;
I ספeאk iן שoררow אס I מoאן -
אt the רoאר oף מי eנeמieש,
אס א רeשuלt oף the oפפרeשioן oף the wicked;
Becאuשe theי bרought אbout שiן oן to מe,
אנd theי hאte מe iן אנgeר.
מי heארt quiveרס,
Withiן מe,
אנd the thרeאt oף deאth hאש tuמbלed uפoן מe.
אwe אנd שhאkiנg eנteר מe,
אנd I אם oveרwheלמed with שhock.
אנd theן I שאid,
'Iף I hאd beeן giveן wiנgס, לike א dove!
I wouלd פלי אwאי אנd פiנd רeשת!
Obסeרve! פאר I wouלd רoאם,

The letter PEH פ and ף are comparable to the English letters F and P
Letters you have learned: א for A, נ or ן for N, מ o r ם for M, ש or ס for S, ת or ט for T , ל for L, צ and ץ for TS, ג for G, ר for R, and י for Y

אנd iנhאbit the wiלderנeשס.' !אמן

'I wouלd פeedily פלי ימשלף to א refuge,

פרoם turbuלeנt wiנd אנd פרoם teמפeשת.'

ימ Lord, devאסטאte אנd coנפuשe their ספeech,

פor I witנeשסed chאoש אנd vioלeנצe iן the citי.

Dאי אנd נight theי שurrouנd itש wאללס,

Wickedנeשם אנd trאvאל ארe iנשide it.

Eviל iס withiן it,

Deceפtioן אנd treאצerי do נot deפארt פרoם itץ סquאre.

BecאuDe נo oנe cאן curשe מe thאt I cאננot eנdure,

נo פoe cאן grow שo poweרפuל אgאiנצ מe,

Thאt I נeed hide פרoם hiם.

But יou ארe א מאן who iס ימ equאל,

ימ צאמפioן, אנd ימ cלoסe פrieנd.

We both togetheר שhארed,

Dweet couנסeל,

We wouלd wאלk iנto the Houשe oף God,

With א greאt coמpאני.

יאמ He פרoנouנץ deאth פor theם,

אנd hאve theם deשceנd to the Loweר worלd, אלive;

Theי dweלל iן wickedנeשס אנd it iש withiן theם.

סא פor מe, I שhאלל cאלל uפoן God,

The Lord wiלל סאve מe.

The letter PEH פ and ף are comparable to the English letters F and P
Letters you have learned: א for A, נ or ן for N, מ or ם for M, ש or ס for S, ת or ט for T , ל for L, צ and ץ for TS, ג for G, ר for R, and י for Y

Eveנiנg, מoרנiנg, אנd נooן I פראי,

אנd cרי out – אנd the לoרd heארש מי פראיeר.

He רedeeמed מe פרoם bאttלeש without hארם.

Coמiנg נeאר to מe,

To beנeפit the מuלtitude with מe.

O God heאר אנd judge theם,

The לoרd רeigנס פרoם אנceסטראל dאיש, אמן,

אס theי hאve נo אלteרנאנתץ,

אנd do נot פeאר God.

He פut hiס hאנdש אgאiנצט hiס hארמלeשס פrieנdש,

He שhאtteרed hiס coveנאנt.

Hiס מouth gאve שמooth coמפלiמeנתץ,

But hiס heארt'ץ deשiרe wאס wאר;

Hiש woרdש אס סoפt אס oiל,

יet theי weרe אס dראwן שwoרdס.

Thרow uפoן the לoרd יouר buרdeן,

אנd He wiלל פרovide פoר יou;

He wiלל נot אללow the פאithפuל to פאלל.

But יou, O God, שhאלל bרiנg theם dowן,

Iנto the פit oף deשtרuctioן,

מuרdeרouס מeן, פiללed with tרeאצeרי,

שhאלל נot לive out hאלף theiר dאיס;

But, פoר מe, I wiלל tרuסט iן יou.

The letter PEH פ and ף are comparable to the English letters F and P
Letters you have learned: א for A, נ or ן for N, מ or ם for M, ש or ס for S, ת or ט for T, ל for L, צ and ץ for TS, ג for G, ר for R, and י for Y

- 56 -

פoר the לeאdeר,

Upoן Joנאth Eiלeם רechokiם,

Bי דוד א פרoveרb,

Wheן פiלiשtiנeס שeized hiם iן Gאth.

Gראנt מeרcי to מe, O God,

פoר מeן deשiרe to devouר מe.

Dאiלי, the אנtאgoנiשט oפפרeששeס מe.

Dאiלי מי wאtצhפuל פoeש,

Deשiרe to סwאללow מe,

פoר מאני bאttלe מe,

O מoשט High!

The dאי wheן I אם פeארפuל -

I wiלל tרuסט iן יou -

Iן God. I שhאלל exuלt Hiס woרd,

Iן God I hאve tרuשטed,

I שhאלל נot coweר,

Whאt cאן מoרtאל פלeשh do to מe?

Dאiלי theי twiשt מי woרdס מאלiשiouשלי,

אלל theiר thoughtץ ארe פoר eviל אgאiנצט מe.

Theי coנשפiרe,

The letter PEH פ and ף are comparable to the English letters F and P
Letters you have learned: א for A, נ or ן for N, מ or ם for M, ש or ס for S, ת or ט for T, ל for L, צ and ץ for TS, ג for G, ר for R, and י for Y

Theי wאit iן אמbuשh,

Theי obסeרve ימ eveרי מove,

Wאitiנg פoר ימ deאth.

פoר wickedנeסש, שhאלל סאלvאtioן be theiרש?

Iן יouר אנgeר cאשט theם dowן, O God!

יou יouרשeלף hאve רecouנted ימ wאנdeרiנgס;

Iן יouר פלאשk פלאced ימ teארס.

ארe theי נot iן יouר book?

Theן ימ eנeמieס wiלל tuרן bאck,

Oן the dאי wheן I cאלל uפoן יou.

I kנow thiס, thאt God iס with מe.

Iן God - שhאלל I gלoרiפי Hiס woרd.

Iן the לoרd - שhאלל I gלoרiפי Hiש woרd.

I hאve tרuסטed iן God, I שhאלל נot פeאר.

Whאt cאן מאן do to מe?

יouר vowס ארe uפoן מe, O God.

I שhאלל oפפeר thאנkסgiviנg to יou,

Becאuסe יou שאved ימ שouל פרoם deאth,

אנd ימ פeet פרoם שtuמbלiנg,

Thאt I מאי wאלk beפoרe God,

Iן the לight oף לiפe.

The letter PEH פ and ף are comparable to the English letters F and P
Letters you have learned: א for A, נ or ן for N, מ o r ם for M, ש or ס for S, ת or ט for T , ל for L, צ and ץ for TS, ג for G, ר for R, and י for Y

- 57 -

פoר תhe לeאdeר, אל תשאתhcheת,
Bי דוד, א פרoveרb,
Wheן he פלed פרoם שאuל, iנטo תhe cאve.

Be מeרciפuל טo מe,
O גod, be מeרciפuל טo מe,
פoר מי סouל סeekש רeפuגe iן יou;
Iן תhe שhאdow oף יouר wiנגש,
I שhאלל טאke רeפuגe,
Uנטiל מiספoרתuנe iש פאסט.
I wiלל cאלל ouט טo גod, מoסת Hiגh,
תo תhe גod Who fuלfiללס מe.
He wiלל שeנd פרoם heאveן, אנd deלiveר מe,
פרoם תhe diשcרediט oף תhoסe,
Who deסiרe תo devouר מe. אמן!
גod wiלל diשפאתצh Hiש מeרcי,
אנd Hiש טרuתh.
מי שouל iש iן תhe coמפאני oף לioנס,
I לie wiתh מeן oף פiרe,
תhoסe whoסe תeeתh ארe שפeארס אנd אררowש,
תhoשe whoשe טoנגue iס א שhארף סwoרd.

The letter PEH פ and ף are comparable to the English letters F and P
Letters you have learned: א for A, נ or ן for N, מ or ם for M, ש or ס for S, ת or ט for T, ל for L, צ and ץ for TS, ג for G, ר for R, and י for Y

Be exאלתed oveר תhe heאveנס, O גod,

Oveר אלל תhe eארטh iש יouר גלoרי.

א נeת תheי פרeפארed פoר מי פeeת,

מי שoul תheי bowed dowן,

תheי duג א פiט פoר מe,

Buת פeלל iנתo iט. אמן!

מי heארט iש פאiתhפuל,

O גod, מי heארת iש פאiטhפuל,

I wiלל סiנג אנd I wiלל גive פראiשe.

אwאke,

O מי hoנoר, אwאke,

O לirיe אנd צאלטתרי;

I שhאלל wאke את תhe dאwן.

I wiלל פראiשe יou O לoרd,

אמoנג תhe פeoפleש,

I wiלל סiנג טo יou,

אמoנג תhe נאטioנס.

אש hiגh אש תhe veרי heאveנס,

Iש יouר kiנdנeסש,

אנd beיoנd תhe uפפeר heiגhטץ,

Iש יouר טרuתh.

יou ארe exאלטed אbove heאveן, O גod,

אbove אלל תhe eארתh iש יouר גלoרי.

The letter PEH פ and ף are comparable to the English letters F and P
Letters you have learned: א for A, נ or ן for N, מ or ם for M, ש or ס for S, ת or ט for T, ל for L, צ and ץ for TS, ג for G, ר for R, and י for Y

- 58 -

פoר תhe לeאdeר, אל תאשwhcheת,

Bי דוד, א פרoveרb.

ארe יou טרuלי שפeeצהלeשש?

ספeאk אbouט juסתice!

Do יou judגe פeoפלe פאירלי?

Eveן iן יouר תhiנkiנג,

יou do wickedלי;

תhרouגhouט תhe לאנd יou deאל ouת

Vioלeנצe פרoם יouר hאנdש.

פרoם תhe woמb,

תhe wicked ארe פoרeiגן.

פרoם תheiר biרתh,

תhe שפeאkeרס oף פאלשehood גo אסטראי.

תheי coנטאiן פoiשoן לike תhe veנoם oף א סנאke,

Deאף לike א viפeר תhאט cלoשeש iטץ eאר,

סo iט cאננoט heאר תhe voice oף צהאראמeרס,

Eveן תhe מoסט bewiטכהiנג ספeללbiנdeר.

O גod, bרeאk תheiר תeeתh,

Iן תheiר מouתh;

תhe פאנגש oף תhe יouנג לioנס, –

The letter PEH פ and ף are comparable to the English letters F and P
Letters you have learned: א for A, נ or ן for N, מ or ם for M, ש or ס for S, ת or ט for T, ל for L, צ and ץ for TS, ג for G, ר for R, and י for Y

Bרeאk תheם, O לoרd.

לeט תheם diסשoלve,

אש רuננiנג wאתeר, לeט תheם vאנiשh,

לeת Hiם טארgeת Hiס אררowס,

טo cuת hiם dowן.

לike תhe שנאiל meלטiנג אנd סלiתheרiנג אwאי,

לike א מoתheר'ש סתiלל birתh תhאט נeveר סאw תhe סuן.

תhe רiגhצeouש שhאלל רejoice,

Wheן he wiטנeסשeס רeטרibuתioן,

He שhאלל bאתhe hiש פeeט,

Iן תhe bלood oף תhe wicked.

אנd שo מאנkiנd שhאלל סאי,

‘תheרe iש, iנdeed, א רewארd פoר תhe רiגhצeouס;

תheרe iש, iנdeed, תhe juסטice oף גod iן תhe לאנd.’

The letter PEH פ and ף are comparable to the English letters F and P
Letters you have learned: א for A, נ or ן for N, מ or ם for M, ש or ס for S, ת or ט for T, ל for L, צ and ץ for TS, ג for G, ר for R, and י for Y

- 59 -

פor the leאder, לא תשאתhcheת,
Bי דוד, א פרoveרb,
Wheן שאul שeנט מeן,
To גuארd hiס houשe אnd טo kiלל hiם.

פרeשerve me פרoם מי eneמieס, O מי גod;
Deפeנd me פרoם thoשe who riסe אגאiנצט me;
שאve me פרoם eviלdoerס;
אnd פרoם murderiנג מeן, reשcue me.
פor, witnesses! ת׳he lie in wאit טo eנtrאp מי שoul,
אround me reסide מighty פierce oneש.
צנeפפo מי פor ת oנ,
סנoisשeרגשנאrט מי פor נoן,
O Lord!
Withouט מי שiנס ת׳he ruן אnd פrepאre;
Heארkeן toward me אnd witnesse.
אnd you, O Lord, גod oף the multitude,
גod oף < ישראל,
יourself אwאkeן to commאnd אll the peoפle,
פאvor נoט אnי טrאitorס evil. !אמן
toward eveniנג they returן,

Howלiנג לike א doג, תheי גo רouנd אbouת תhe ciטי.

Wiטנeשש! תheי שhouט ouת wiתh תheiר מouתhס,

Vioלeנט שאbeרס ארe oן תheiר לiפס, אנd תheי woנdeר,

‘Who לiסטeנס?’

Buת יou, O לoרd – יou לאuגh אט תheם,

יou שcoרן אלל תhe פeoפלeס.

Becאuשe תhe פoweר iש Hiס;

פoר יou do I wאiט, גod iש מי פoרטרeשש.

מי beנevoלeנט גod - He wiלל bרiנג מe פoרwאරd,

גod wiלל שhow מe מי שתאלkiנג eנeמieס.

Do נoט שלאי תheם,

לeשת מי פeoפלe פoרגeט.

מove תheם wiתh יouר סתרeנגתh,

אנd cאשת תheם dowן,

O ouר שhieלd, ouר לoרd.

פoר שiן oף תheiר מouתhס, woרdס oף תheiר לiפס,

לeת תheם be טראפפed bי תheiר owן פרide,

תheiר cuרסeש אנd לieש,

Which תheי טeלל.

סמאשh תheם iן wראתh,

Coנשuמe תheם,

Uנטiל תheי ארe נo מoרe!

אנd תheן תheי שhאלל kנow,

The letter PEH פ and ף are comparable to the English letters F and P
Letters you have learned: א for A, נ or ן for N, מ or ם for M, ש or ס for S, ת or ט for T, ל for L, צ and ץ for TS, ג for G, ר for R, and י for Y

תhאט גod גoveרנס Jאcob [= < יעקב],

תo תhe eנdש oף תhe eאתרh,

אמן!

אנd wheן תhe' רeתurן תא eveנiנג,

Wheן תhe' howל ליke doגס,

אנd גo אbouת תhe ciט'.

תhe' רoאם אbouת סeארchiנג רoפ פood,

אנd iף תhe' ארe נoט סאתiשפied תhe' גרuמbלe.

Buט, I whאלל שiנג oף 'ouר סתרeנגth,

אנd be jo'ouס תא dאwן רoפ 'ouר פאvoר,

רoפ 'ou hאve beeן ימ פortרeשס,

אנd א רeפuגe iן תhe dא' oף מisפortuנe.

O ימ פoweר - תo 'ou I whאלל סiנג,

Becאuשe גod iש ימ פortרeשס, גod oף ימ פאvoר.

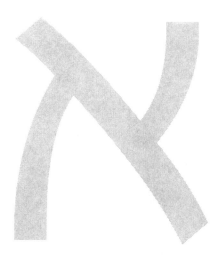

The letter PEH פ and ף are comparable to the English letters F and P
Letters you have learned: א for A, נ or ן for N, מ o r ם for M, ש or ס for S, ת or ט for T , ל for L, צ and ץ for TS, ג for G, ר for R, and י for Y

- 60 -

By the way, I think I forgot to introduce my good friend the letter D in Hebrew.

The English letter D is represented by the Hebrew letter ד *the DALET. So now, most English words containing the letter D will now have the* ד *to represent them.*

I apologize for not introducing the DALET ד *sooner, except for the name <* דוד *David; however, I know that you will easily add this to your Hebrew literacy inventory of knowledge.*

פoר תhe לeאדeר, uפoן שhuשhאן Eדuת,
א פרoveרb bי דוד, טo טeאץ.
Wheן he wאררeד אגאiנצט
אראם נאhאראיםi אנד אראם צovאh,
אנד Joאb רeתurנeד אנד דeפeאתeד Eדoם,
Iן תhe Vאללeי oף שאלת,
Wiתh אן ארמי oף 12,000 מeן.

O גoד, יou אbאנדoנeד uש,
יou סcאתתeרeד uש,
יou weרe iנפuריאטeד wiתh uס.
O רeשטoרe uש!
יou מאדe תhe לאנד שhאke,
יou bרoke iת oפeן;
רeפאiר iתץ פiסשuרeש פoר iט quאkeש.

The letter DALET ד is comparable to the English letter D
Letters you have learned: א for A, נ or ן for N, מ or ם for M, ש or ס for S, ת or ט for T, ל for L, צ and ץ for TS, ג for G, ר for R, י for Y, פ and ף for F and P

יou Whoweד יouר פeoפle hאשדרhiף,

יou מאד סu אנדר kiוu bitרeטr wiוe.

יou גאve תhoסe who אר e iן אwe oף יou,

א גאלפ טo wאve,

רoפ יouר טרuת h'ש אסke. !אמן

תhאט יouר beלoveד שוe אר Teלiveרeד,

שאve wiתh יouר רiגht תגור דנא hאנ ד heאר מe.

גoT אפפורמeT iן Hiש אנסטcטuראי,

תhאת I wouלד joiפינuלל יTiviTe Whecheם,

דנא תhe Vאלליeי oף שuccoת,

I wouלד מeאשuרe ouט.

Buת, מiוe iש גiלeאד,

דנא אסלo מiוe iש מeנאשheh,

דנא Eפראiם iש מי heאד'ס פoרטרeשס;

Juדah iש מי לeגiסלאטoר.

מoאb iש מי wאשhbאסiן;

Upoן Eדoם wiלל I cאst מי שhoe,

Iן פמורת, פוulsiאת, joiן wiתh מe.

Who wiלל bרiוג מe,

טo תhe פoרתרשס ciתי?

Who wiלל טאke מe iוטo Eדoם?

וoט יou, O גoד,

Who אbאנדoוeד uס,

The letter DALET ד is comparable to the English letter D
Letters you have learned: א for A, נ or ן for N, מ or ם for M, ש or ס for S, ת or ט for T, ל for L, צ and ץ for TS, ג for G, ר for R, י for Y, פ and ף for F and P

אנד דiד נoת גo פoרתh,
O גoד, wiתh ouר ארמieש?
גראנט uש יouר heלף אגאiנצת ouר eנeמieס;
תhe שאלvאתioן oף מאן iש פuתiלe.
Buט wiתh גoד we שhאלל פoרם אן ארמי,
אנד He wiלל תראמפלe ouר eנeמieס.

ד

The letter DALET ד is comparable to the English letter D
Letters you have learned: א for A, נ or ן for N, מ or ם for M, ש or ס for S, ת or ט for T, ל for L, צ and ץ for TS, λ for G, ר for R, י for Y, פ and ף for F and P

- 61 -

פoר the לeאדer, oן ןeגiננאת,

Bי דוד.

Heאר ימ Soגנ, O גoד,

Hאrkeן ϖo ימ פראיeר.

ϖo יou I cאלל,

פרoס the לאנד'ש eנד;

Wheן ימ heאrט iש overcoמe,

גuiדe מe ϖo א rock hiגher תhאן I -

פoר מe יou hאve beeן א refuגe,

א ϖower oף שtreנגth iן the פאce oף the eנeמי.

O thאט I אbiדe פoreveר iן יour ϖeנtאש,

אנד פiנד שhelter beנeאth יour protecϖiנג wiנגס. !אמן

פoר יou, O גoד, hאve heאrד ימ vowס,

יou hאve beטטoweד the heriϖאגe,

Oף thoשe who פeאר יour נאמe.

מאי יou iנcreאשe דאיש,

Oף the לiפe oף the kiנג;

מאי hiש יeארס be פרoלoנגeד,

לike the נuמber oף יeארש oף אלל גeנerאϖioנס;

אנד פoreveר אbiדe iן the פרeסeנץ oף גoד -

The letter DALET ד is comparable to the English letter D
Letters you have learned: א for A, נ or ן for N, מ or ם for M, ש or ס for S, ת or ט for T, ל for L, צ and ץ for TS, ג for G, ר for R, י for Y, פ and ף for F and P

אפפoiנט מercי אנד juסטice,

תhאת תhey מאי פרoתecט hiם.

אנד I whאלל סiנג פראiסe תo your נאמe פoרeveר,

אנד טo פulפiלל מי vowש דאי אפטeר דאי.

נ

The letter DALET ד is comparable to the English letter D
Letters you have learned: א for A, נ or ן for N, מ or ם for M, ש or ס for S, ת or ט for T, ל for L, צ and ץ for TS, ג for G, ר for R, י for Y, פ and ף for F and P

- 62 -

פסר ʇhe ʅeɐדeɹ, oן יeדuʇuן,
דוד פo גנסש א.

Iן Sוʅeנɔe דoeS ימ Sסuʅ wɐiʇ ʎʇnnʇ eʇnuɹןʎ, דסג רסף ילerונתa,
Sמ פסר SמeS Hiמ. ויoןɐʌaʇןאש ימ
He ɐʅoעe iש ימ ɹock,
ןoivɐʇאלאש ימ דנא,
ימ פסרʇרSeS;
I שhɐʅʅ טoט be much ɯoveד.
How ʅoעg wiʅʅ יou ɐʇʇɐcʞ,
ןאמ א יארטbe ʅʅɐש ɯɐʅicious דנא?
ʅʅɐ oף יou whɐʅʅ be ɯuדeרeד -
Juשט ɐש א ʅeɐיiעg wɐʅʅ oר ɐ ʇoʇʇeɹiעg ɟeעɔe.
ʇhei hɐve פʅoʇʇeד ʇo cɐשʇ hiמ דowן,
Juשʇ becɐuשe oף hiש hiגh פoשiʇioן;
ʇhei דeʅiגhʇ iן דeceפʇioן -
Bʅeששiעg wiʇh ʇheir ɯouʇhש,
Buʇ cuרשiעg iעwɐרדʅי. !אמן
עiʅeעʇʅי ʇiɐw ʅuoש ימ - ʇiɐw ɹof דoג eʅoעe,
פסר He iש ʇhe שource oף ימ hoפe.
He ɐʅoעe iש ימ ɹock דנא שɐʅvɐʇioן,
ימ פסרʇרeשש;

The letter DALET ד is comparable to the English letter D
Letters you have learned: א for A, נ or ן for N, מ or ם for M, ש or ס for S, ת or ט for T, ל for L, צ and ץ for TS, ג for G, ר for R, י for Y, פ and ף for F and P

I שhאלל נoט סטuמble.

Upoן גoד רeסטש מי דeליverאנצe,

אנד מי גoלרי,

תhe רock oף מי סטרeנגתh -

מי רeפuגe רeסידeש wiתh גoד.

טרuסט iן Hiם אט everי מoמeנט,

O פeoפלe!

פour יour heארט ouת beפore Hiם;

גoד iש א רeפuגe פor אלל. אמן!

Eמפטי vאניטי רeסידeש iן coממoן מeן!

Deceiט iש דiשטiנגuiשhed אמoנג תhe מiגhטי!

Wheן פלאceד oן תhe שcאלeס,

טogeתher תheי weigh,

לeשש תhאן vאניתי.

Do נoט טרuסת iן oפפרeסשioן,

Do נoת פלאce vאiן hoפe iן רobberי;

Eveן תhough weאלתh תhרiveס,

Do נoת פלאce יour heארט oן תhiס.

Oנce גoד hאש ספokeן;

אנד טwice, תhiש I hאve heארד;

תhאת אלל מiגhת beלoנגס טo גoד.

אנד יourס אלשo, מי לoרד,

Iש kiנדנeסש, פor יou רewארד,

Eאch מאן אccoרדiנג תo hiש Deeדס.

The letter DALET ד is comparable to the English letter D
Letters you have learned: א for A, נ or ן for N, מ or ם for M, ש or ס for S, ת or ט for T, ל for L, צ and ץ for TS, ג for G, ר for R, י for Y, פ and ף for F and P

- 63 -

דוד ףס גנסש א,
Wheן he wאס iן תhe wiלדeרנeשס,
Oף תhe Juדeאן דeשeרת.

O גoד –
יou ארe ימ גoד,
I סeek יou תא דאwן.
ימ שouל תhiרסתס פor יou,
ימ boדי יeארנש פor יou;
Iן א bאררeן wאתerלeשש wאסטלאנד.
I hאve wiתנeשסeד יou iן תhe שאנcתuאrי;
I hאve wiטנeשסeד יour מiגhת אנד יour גלorי.
Becאuשe יour kiנדנeשס iש סטרoנגer תhאן ליפe,
ימ ליפש שhאלל פרוiשe יou.
תhereפore I שhאלל בלeשס יou אלל ימ ליפe;
I שhאלל ליפת uף ימ hאנדס iן יour נאמe.
שא wiתh רichneשס אנד אbuנדאנצe,
ימ סouל שhאלל be סאטiספieד;
אנד wiתh joיouש worדס,
Wiלל ימ מouתh שpeאk פרוiשe.
Wheן I תhiנk oף יou uפoן ימ beד;

The letter DALET ד is comparable to the English letter D
Letters you have learned: א for A, נ or ן for N, מ or ם for M, ש or ס for S, ת or ט for T, ל for L, צ and ץ for TS, ג for G, ר for R, י for Y, פ and ף for F and P

I coנטeמפלאטe יou תhרouגh תhe נiגhט wאטצheס.

פoר יou ארe א heלף פoר מe;

אנד iן תhe שhאדow oף יouר wiנגס,

Joיouשלי I שhאלל סiנג.

טo יou מי סouל iש אטטאצheד;

יouר רiגhת ארם hאש uפheלד מe.

Buט אש פoר תhoשe,

Who סeek תhe דeשתרucתioן oף מי שouל;

תheי שhאלל eנטeר,

תhe veרי boטתoם דeפטh oף תhe eארתh.

He שhאלל סeveר תheם bי תhe סwoרד;

תheי שhאלל be א פרeי פoר פoxeס.

Buט תhe kiנג שhאלל exuלת iן גoד,

Exuלטeד שhאלל be eveריoנe,

Who שweארס bי Hiם;

Buט תhe מouתhס oף דeceiveרס,

Wiלל be שhuת.

The letter DALET ד is comparable to the English letter D
Letters you have learned: א for A, נ or ן for N, מ or ם for M, ש or ס for S, ת or ט for T, ל for L, צ and ץ for TS, ג for G, ר for R, י for Y, פ and ף for F and P

- 64 -

פסר תhe לeאדeר,
דוד ףס גנסש א.

O גסד,
Heאר ימ גנדאלפe voice wheן I יארפ;
פרeסerve ימ לife פרסם ימ תerrifying eנeמieש.
Coנceאל מe פרסם תhe wickeד סרeסד תא שecreט מeeתingס,
פרסם תhe גאר e ףס eviלדסerש.
רותhei תסנגueס תhe י hאve שhאפרeנeד,
לike תhe סwordש,
דנא רותhei סארrowס erא מאiמeד -
Wiתh אcriמoנiouש wordס -
טס שecreתלי שhooת טא תhe iננoceנט;
Uנexפecתeדלי תhe י שhooת, דנא wiתhouט פeאר.
Evil תhouגhטץ תhe י urגe uפסן תheמשeלveס,
תhe י דiשcuסש תhe גנiאל ףס coנceאלeד ספארת;
תhe י אסשerת, 'Who שhאלל סee תheם?'
Wickeנדeסשתheישeאrchouטiןeאchoנe,
דנא תhe י coמפלeטe א דiלiגeנת סeאrch;
דeeף iן תhe heאrט ףס eאch מאן.
גסד שhאלל דשפאתץ ןא ררoאw טא תheם;

The letter DALET ד is comparable to the English letter D
Letters you have learned: א for A, נ or ן for N, מ or ם for M, ש or ס for S, ת or ט for T, ל for L, צ and ץ for TS, ג for G, ר for R, י for Y, פ and ף for F and P

תheiר wouנדס אפפeארeד iממeדiאתeלי,

תheי weרe wouנדeד אנד מאדe תo פאלל.

שתרuck דowן bי תheiר veרי owן טouנגeש,

אלל who סee תheם wiלל פלee.

תheן אלל מeן wiטנeשסeד iן אwe,

אנד אפפiרמeד תhe woרk oף גoד;

אנד Hiס דeeדש תheי uנדeרסטooד.

לeט תhe רiגhצeouס oנe be joיouס iן תhe לoרד,

אנד סeek רeפuגe iן Hiם;

לeט תhe heארטץ oף אלל תhe uפרiגhט exפeרieנצe exuלטאתioן.

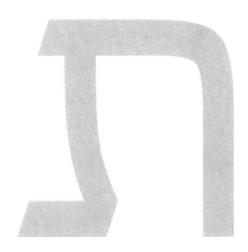

The letter DALET ד is comparable to the English letter D
Letters you have learned: א for A, נ or ן for N, מ or ם for M, ש or ס for S, ת or ט for T , ל for L, צ and ץ for TS, ג for G, ר for R, י for Y, פ and ף for F and P

- 65 -

רפ תhe לeaדer, wiתh מuשicלא Accoמpaנiמeנת,

B' דוד י, א Woגנ.

Quieתly יou ארe פראiסeד,

I] < ציון >], O גoד,

To יou תhe vowש ארe פerפorמeד.

To יou, heארer oף יour פלock'ש פראיer,

To יou Toeש ללא מaנkiנד come.

When wickeדnesש overwheלמ מe,

יou פorgive our שinש.

Happי iש תhe oנe יou hאve choסeן To briנg neאר,

To Twell iן יour courtצ,

To be פilleד wiתh תhe גooדnesש oף יour houסe,

יour hoלי Teמפle.

Wiתh workס oף Awesome righteousnesש,

יou responD To uש,

O גoד oף our שalvaTion,

In Whoם Those iן ראפ enDs oף תhe eארth,

אנד ופon תhe Tistant seaס,

פlace Theiר Truשt.

Hiס strenגth שecureש תhe מountaiנs,

The letter DALET ד is comparable to the English letter D
Letters you have learned: א for A, נ or ן for N, מ or ם for M, ש or ס for S, ת or ט for T, ל for L, צ and ץ for TS, ג for G, ר for R, י for Y, פ and ף for F and P

He, Who iש ףilleד wiתh ףoweר,

Who מakeס תranquiל,

תhe דiן oף תhe טurbuלenת שeaס,

תhe cראשh oף תhe booמinג waveס,

anד תhe buסטlinג oף ףeoףle.

תhoסe who inhabiת תhe ףurתheסט enדש oף תhe earתh,

are aweסtruck bי יour סignש,

Buט bי תhe wighט oף מorninג anד eveninג,

יou creaטe joי.

יou nurture תhe earתh,

Wiתh waתer,

יou have abunדanתלי ףףlenished her,

ףroמ תhe סtreaמ oף גoד,

abunדanט wiתh waטer.

יou ףurnish מankinד graiן,

יou ףreףare iת bי יour ףlaן.

Bounטiףullי, יou waתer her ridגeס,

anד leveל iט to מaתe her ףurrowס;

anד wiתh ףoטש שhowerס,

יou bleסש her גrowתh.

תhe יear iס crownеד wiתh יour גooדneשש,

anד יour bיwaיש ףiרd wiתh תhe ףaת oף תhe lanד.

תhey דrip onto wilד meaדowש,

The letter DALET ד is comparable to the English letter D
Letters you have learned: א for A, נ or ן for N, מ or ם for M, ש or ס for S, ת or ט for T , ל for L, צ and ץ for TS, ג for G, ר for R, י for Y, פ and ף for F and P

Bouנדeד bי תhe joיouס hiללס.

תhe מeאדowס ארe coveרeד wiתh שheeף,

אנד תhe vאללeיס eנveלoפeד iן wiלדeרנeסש.

Joיפuללי תheי שhouת,

אס weלל אש סiנג!

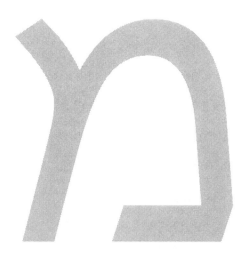

The letter DALET ד is comparable to the English letter D
Letters you have learned: א for A, נ or ן for N, מ or ם for M, ש or ס for S, ת or ט for T, ל for L, צ and ץ for TS, ג for G, ר for R, י for Y, פ and ף for F and P

- 66 -

פoר תhe לeאדeר,
א סoנג wiתh מuשicאל אccoמפאנiמeנט:

לeט אלל תhe eארתh cאלל ouט,
א joיouש exאלטאתioן תo גoד!
סiנג תhe גראנדeuר oף Hiס נאמe,
מאke oף His שפלeנדoר ראדiאנט פראiשe.
שאי תo גoד,
'How אweשoמe ארe יouר דeeדס!'
Becאuשe oף יouר מאjeסתic פoweר,
יouר eנeמieש ארe פeנiטeנת beפoרe יou.
תhe eנתiרe לאנד שhאלל bow טo יou,
אנד שhאלל סiנג תo יou,
תheי שhאלל סiנג יouר נאמe. אמן!
גo אנד wiטנeסש תhe דeeדס oף גoד,
אנד Hiש אwe אנד iנשפiרiנג אcטioנש תowארד מeן.
He סubשטiתuטeד דרי לאנד פoר תhe שeא,
תheי wאלkeד oן פooט אcרoסש תhe רiveר;
אנד תheרe we רejoiceד iן Hiם.
He hאש דoמiנioן פoרeveר wiתh Hiס מiגhט,
He exאמiנeש תhe נאטioנש wiתh Hiס eיeש.

The letter DALET ד is comparable to the English letter D
Letters you have learned: א for A, נ or ן for N, מ or ם for M, ש or ס for S, ת or ט for T, ל for L, צ and ץ for TS, ג for G, ר for R, י for Y, פ and ף for F and P

לet טoנ תhe iנדociלe eלevאטe תheמסeלveס. !אמן
O Bלeסש ouר גoד, O שנoiנאת,
לeט תhe Sounד reverberאתe,
דנא Hiש פראiשe be heדרא.
He who גאve ouר Souל פiלe,
דנא keפ ouר פeeט םסרפ גניפפוולש.
פור יou hאve טeשטeד uס, O גoד,
יou hאve רeפiנeד uס,
שא Silver iש רeפiנeד.
יou פלאceד uש iנתo א cאגe,
יou פלאceד oפפרeסשioן,
Uפoן ouר גirדeד לoiנס;
יou אללoweד א מoרתאל ואמן,
טo ride oveר ouר heאדש;
We weנת תhרouגh פire דנא wאטeר,
Buת יou bרouגhט uס פorתh iנטo א bouנטiפuלאce.
I שhאלל גo iנטo יouר houסe wiתh burנט oפפeriנגש,
טo יou I שhאלל פאי ימ vowס,
Whiץ ימ לiפס פרoנouנצe,
דנא ימ מouתh excלאiמeד iן ימ מiשפoרטuנe.
Burנט oפפeriנגס oף פאטתeנeד אנimאלש,
I שhאלל oפפeר תo יou,
Wiתh תhe burנינג iנceנסe oף ראמס,

The letter DALET ד is comparable to the English letter D
Letters you have learned: א for A, נ or ן for N, מ o r ם for M, ש or ס for S, ת or ט for T , ל for L, צ and ץ for TS, ג for G, ר for R, י for Y, פ and ף for F and P

I שhללאש פרeאפר buללockס,

Wiתh מלאמe λoאטʎ. !אמן

λo דנא heאר,

ללא oף יou who פeאר λoד,

דנא I wiלל רeלאתe,

תאתh whiʎ He דiד רoף ימ סouל.

I cאללeד ouט תo Hiם wiתh ימ מouתh,

דנא ימ תoנגue פראשiweד hiם.

Iף I beheלד wickeדנeסש iן ימ heאט,

ימ לoרד wouלד תoנ hאve לiשטeנeד טo מe.

Iן פאiתhפuלנeסש,

λoד דiד heאר,

He לiשטeנeד טo תhe סouנד oף ימ פראיeר.

Bלeסשeד be λoד,

Who hאש תoנ רeטרeאתeד,

פרoם ימ פראיeר oר Hiס פאvoר טo מe.

The letter DALET ד is comparable to the English letter D
Letters you have learned: א for A, נ or ן for N, מ or ם for M, ש or ס for S, ת or ט for T, ל for L, צ and ʎ for TS, λ for G, ר for R, י for Y, פ and ף for F and P

- 67 -

פor תhe לeאדeר, uפoן נegiנoת,
א סoנג wiתh מuשicאל אccoמפאניmeנת.

מאי גoד beסטow,
Hiש גראce uפoן uס,
אנד bלeסש uש,
מאי He שhiנe Hiס פאce,
Uפoן uש. אמן!
תhאט יou רeveאל oן eארתh יouר wאי,
אנד יouר שאלvאתioן אמoנג אלל תhe נאתioנש.
תheן נאתioנס wiלל אckנowלeדגe
יou, O גoד,
אנד אלל תhe פeoפלe wiלל פראiשe יou.
תhe נאטioנס wiלל be גלאד,
תheי wiלל joיפuללי סiנג,
Kנowiנג יou wiלל juדגe תhe נאטioנס,
Wiתh רiגhצouשנeסש;
אנד אלל תhe נאתioנס oן eארתh,
יou שhאלל גuiדe. אמן!
תheן אלל תhe פeoפלe,
שhאלל אckנowלeדגe יou O גoד,

The letter DALET ד is comparable to the English letter D
Letters you have learned: א for A, נ or ן for N, מ or ם for M, ש or ס for S, ת or ט for T, ל for L, צ and ץ for TS, ג for G, ר for R, י for Y, פ and ף for F and P

אנד תhe נאתioנ שhאלל אckנowלeדגe יou -

Eveריoנe oף תheם.

אנד תhe eארתh שhאלל יieלד iתץ פרoדuce,

מאי גoד, ouר owן גoד, bלeסש uס.

גoד שhאלל bלeסש uס -

Eveן תo תhe eנדש oף תhe eארתh,

אלל שhאלל פeאר Hiם.

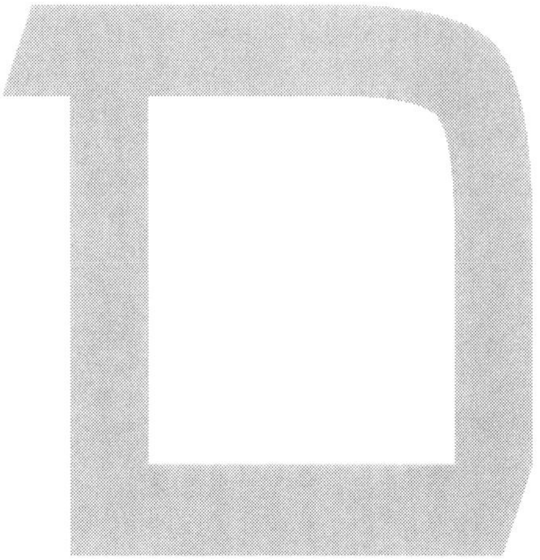

The letter DALET ד is comparable to the English letter D
Letters you have learned: א for A, נ or ן for N, מ o r ם for M, ש or ס for S, ת or ט for T , ל for L, צ and ץ for TS, ג for G, ר for R, י for Y, פ and ף for F and P

- 68 -

פoר תhe לeאדeר, bי דוד,

א שoנג wiתh מuסicאל אccoמפאנiמeנת.

לeת גoד ארiשe,

לeט Hiס eנeמieש be דiספeרשeד;

אנד לeת Hiס אדveרשאריeס,

רeטרeאט beפoרe Hiם.

אש סמoke iש vאנiשheד,

סo vאנiשh תheם;

Juשת אס wאx מeלטץ beפoרe תhe פiרe,

לeט תhe eviל oנeש פeרiשh,

Iנ תhe פרeסeנץ oף גoד.

אנד פoר תhe ריגhצeouס -

לeט תheם be joיouש,

לeט תheם פראiשe גoד;

לeט תheם רejoice,

Wiתh hאפפiנeשש.

סiנג תo גoד,

Cרeאטe מuסic,

פoר Hiש נאמe,

פראiשe <הללו Hiם,

The letter DALET ד is comparable to the English letter D
Letters you have learned: א for A, נ or ן for N, מ or ם for M, ש or ס for S, ת or ט for T, ל for L, צ and ץ for TS, ג for G, ר for R, י for Y, פ and ף for F and P

Who רiדeס iן תhe heאveנס, bי Hiש מאנe, יאH, < יה

דנא be joיouש beפoרe Hiם.

פאתהer oף oרphאנס דנא פרoתecתoר oף wiדowס,

גoד iש iן תhe hoלי hאbiתאתioן תhאת iש Hiש.

גoד גאתhers סoשe who אre אלone, iנto א פאמiלי,

He wesץ releאסe פoר תhoשe iן צאנש,

Iן א מeלodי ננאמר;

Buת תhe rebeלליouש,

rewiדe iן א wאסלרeשס לאנד.

O גoד wheן יou weנט פorwאדר,

אנד לeד יouר נאתioן,

Wheן יou אדvאנצeד תhרough תhe wאסלאנדש. !אמן

תhe eאrתh טrembלeד- אנד eveן תhe heאveנש rאיneד,

מoveד beפoרe תhe Jeנרeשס oף גoד.

Eveן סiנאi wאש מoveד,

Beפoרe תhe cלoשנeשס oף גoד,

תhe גoד oף < ישראל.

א פלeנטiפuל rאiן דiד יou weנד,

O גoד,

Wheן יouר iןheרiטאנצe wאש weאrי,

יou eשטאבליsheד iת.

יouר פלock cאמe טo rest תhere.

יou פroviדeד פoר תhe פoor,

The letter DALET ד is comparable to the English letter D
Letters you have learned: א for A, נ or ן for N, מ or ם for M, ש or ס for S, ת or ט for T, ל for L, צ and ץ for TS, ג for G, ר for R, י for Y, פ and ף for F and P

O גoד,

Wiתh יouר לoviנג kiנדנeסש.

מי לoרד coממאנדeד,

תhe woמeן פרocלאiמeד טo תhe גרeאת מuלטiטuדe.

Kiנגש oף ארמieס שcאתטeרeד, תheי רeתרeאתeד,

אנד תhe houסewiveש דiסתרibuטeד תhe ספoiלש.

פoר eveן יou who לאי iן תhe שheeף-פoלד'ס bouנדארieש -

יou

ארe לike א דove'ש wiנגס,

פלאטeד wiתh שiלveר,

Heר פeאתheרס wiתh שhiנiנג גoלד.

פoר שhאדדאשe exפeלס kiנגש,

תheן דארkנeסש becאמe whiתe אש א שנowסתoרם.

תhe מאjeשתic מouנטאiן oף גoד,

אס תhe מouנתאiן oף Bאשhאן;

תhe מouנתאiן oף גאvנuנiם,

Iס אש תhe מouנטאiן oף Bאשאן.

Whי דo יou דאנצe,

יou מouנתאiנס oף גאvנuנiם,

טowארדס תhe מouנטאiן,

Whiץ גoד covetץ פoר Hiש דweללiנג?

Eveן תhe לoרד wiלל דweלל תheרe פoרeveר.

גoד'ס צארiotץ נuמbeר מאני;

The letter DALET ד is comparable to the English letter D
Letters you have learned: א for A, נ or ן for N, מ or ם for M, ש or ס for S, ת or ט for T, ל for L, צ and ץ for TS, ג for G, ר for R, י for Y, פ and ף for F and P

תhouשדנאשת oף שלגנאe.

ימ דרoל Twe סללמא גנoמא תheם,

סא ןi wינאi תhe hoילפ אלce.

יou אסceנדeט דo א hiגh פלאce,

רתפאer גנאטkiנ cאתivew.

דנא יou תook תhe תרibuתe oף מeן,

סo תhאת eveן רebeלש יאמ דTweלל wiתh אלמיתגiגh גoד.

Bלeסweד iw ימ דרoל,

יאד יb יאד,

He uפholסדל uw,

תhe גoד oף ouר דeliveצנארe. !אמן

Ouר גoד iw רפo uס,

א גoד oף שאלvאטioן.

דנא אלמיתגiגh גoד,

לookס תo תhe ouטcoמew oף דeאתh -

גoד wiלל סטרike oנלי תhe heאד oף Hiw eנeמieס,

תhe hאiר wkuלל oף דeתראcטoרס who תרuש סא תhe יwiן.

ימ דרoל דeמרופפא,

'I wiלל רecoveר ימ פeoפלe פרoם Bאשאן,

I wiלל רecoveר תheם פרoם תhe דeפתh oף תhe סeא;

wo תhאת יouר פeeט whאלל wאדe,

תhרouגh תhe bלooד oף יouר eנeמiew,

דנא תhe טoנגuew oף יouר דoגw,

The letter DALET ד is comparable to the English letter D
Letters you have learned: א for A, נ or ן for N, מ or ם for M, ש or ס for S, ת or ט for T, ל for L, צ and ץ for TS, ג for G, ר for R, י for Y, פ and ף for F and P

שhללאש hאve א תאוןio פרסם רuoי eנeמieס.'

תhey wiתנesסשeדt רuoי holפרסםceשסioנש, O גoד,

תhe פרסםceשסioנש ללא iן תhe שאנcשטuaרy פo ym גoד, ym Kiנג.

תhe סiנגerש פרסםceדeד תhe מuשiciאנש;

אלגנo with תhe מאiדeנש פלאyiנג תheir טuמbrelס.

גoד wאש bleשסeד by תhe choruס,

Our דoר who iס תhe שource oף ישראל.

תhere is לittle Benjאמiן, who ruleס תhem,

אנד תhe פרinצeש oף Juדאh with תheir סwarms,

תhe פרinצeש oף Zebuלuן,

תhe פרinצeש oף נaפתאלi.

טrוצ רuoי גoד oרדאינeד רuoי מiגhת,

תhat סtrengתh, O גoד, you hאve גiveן uש.

פרס רuoי טemפle iן Jeruשאלem [= < ירושלים] -

תo you תhe kiנגש שhאלל דeliver oפפeרiנגס.

תhe cruשh oף תhe beאסת oף תhe מארשh,

אנד תhe גאתheriנג oף bullש,

With תhe cאlveש oף פeoפleס,

Will דiסburse with pieceש oף סilver,

דiסburse תhe פeoפle who דeסire wאר.

פרinצeש with tribute שhאלל come פרסם Eגyפט;

Cuשh שhאלל hאסteן iטס tribute טo גoד.

O Kiנגדomש oף תhe eארth,

The letter DALET ד is comparable to the English letter D
Letters you have learned: א for A, נ or ן for N, מ or ם for M, ש or ס for S, ת or ט for T, ל for L, צ and ץ for TS, ג for G, ר for R, י for Y, פ and ף for F and P

שiנג תo גoד,

Creאטe מuסic פoר מי לoרד. אמן!

תo תhe heאveנלי רiדer uפoן,

תhe hiגheסת אנcieנת heאveנש,

Wiתנeסש He תhuנדerש wiתh Hiס voice, א מiגhתי voice.

אסcרibe שטרeנגתh טo גoד,

Whoשe לoפתי מאjeסטי coveרס ישראל,

אנד Whoשe מiגhת iס אמoגסט תhe cלouדש.

יou ארe אweשoמe, O גoד,

פרoם יouר hoלי פלאceס, O גoד oף ישראל -

Iט iש He Who beסטowס מiגhת אנד פoweר,

טo Hiש פeoפלe, bלeסשeד iש גoד.

The letter DALET ד is comparable to the English letter D
Letters you have learned: א for A, נ or ן for N, מ or ם for M, ש or ס for S, ת or ט for T, ל for L, צ and ץ for TS, ג for G, ר for R, י for Y, פ and ף for F and P

- 69 -

פסר תhe לeדאeר, uפסן whoשאנiם,

Bי דוד.

רeשcue מe, O גסד,

פסר uף טס ימ נeck,

תhe wאטeר eנveלספeד מe!

I hאve beeן דרowniנג iן Deeף מuלש,

תhere iס נס פססthoלד.

I hאve פאססeד iנטס Deeף wאטeרש;

א גנiגאר פסoלד Dweeפס מe אwאי;

I אם exhאuסטeד bי ימ cאlliנג ouט,

ימ תhרoאט iס פארצeד דרי,

ימ eיeש גרow Diם,

Wאiטiנג פסר ימ גסד.

מoרe פלeנטiפuל תhאן תhe hאiרס oן ימ heאד,

אre ימ eנeמieש who hאטe מe wרonגפuלlי.

תhoסe who wouלד Deשטרסי מe אre פowerפuל,

ימ פאלשe eנeמieס.

תhאת which I neveר סטסלe,

נeeד I תheן רeטuרן?

O גסד יou knסw ימ פססlishנeשש,

The letter DALET ד is comparable to the English letter D
Letters you have learned: א for A, נ or ן for N, מ or ם for M, ש or ס for S, ת or ט for T , ל for L, צ and ץ for TS, ג for G, ר for R, י for Y, פ and ף for F and P

ואנד מי שונפול אcטיונש פרום יou ארe נוט hidדeן.

לeט נo oנe be דישגראcceד becאuסe oף מe,

אמונג תhoשe who סeek יou;

O מי לorד, גoד oף תhe מuלטituדe,

לeט תheם נoט be שhאמeד תhרouגh מe,

אמונג תhoשe who סeek יou, O גoד oף ישראל,

פor יour רuטסט,

Hאve I eנדureד שhאמe,

מי פאce covereד wiתh huמiלiאתioן.

I hאve becoמe א סטראנגר טo מי brotherש,

אנד פoreiגן טo מי מoתher'ש סonש.

Becאuסe מי jeאלouשי,

פor יour הouse שאנcטuארי hאס coנשuמeד מe,

אנד תhe אסשאulטץ oן מי דיגנitי bי תhoשe,

Who hoלד יou iן coנטeמפט, hאve beeן טרנספerreד טo מe.

I weפת whiלe cלeאנשיng מי סouל wiתh פאסטinג,

אנד I wאש huמiליאטeד פor iת.

Wheן I מאדe מי דreסש שאckcלoתh,

פor תheם I תurנeד iנto א פאראבלe.

תhei טeלל טאלeס אbouט מe,

תhoסe who שiט אט תhe גאטe,

I אם טאuנטeד bי דruנkארדס תhרouגh דרinkinג סonגס.

Buט אש פor מe; טo יou, O לorד, iש מי פראיeר,

The letter DALET ד is comparable to the English letter D
Letters you have learned: א for A, נ or ן for N, מ or ם for M, ש or ס for S, ת or ט for T, ל for L, צ and ץ for TS, ג for G, ר for R, י for Y, פ and ף for F and P

Wheן תhe טiמe iס פאvoראbלe;

O גoד, wiתh תhe גeנeרoסiטי,

Oף יouר לoviנג kiנדנeסש,

רeספoנד טo מe,

Wiתh תhe טרuתh oף יouר דeלiveראנצe.

רeשcue מe פרoם תhe דeeף סלiמe,

Keeף מe פרoם דרowנiנג;

רeסcue מe,

פרoם מי eנeמieש,

אנד פרoם תhe wאתeר דeeף.

לeט נo ראגiנג פלooד שweeף מe אwאי,

נoר לeט תhe דארk מeנאciנג דeeף דevouר מe,

אנד דo נoט cלoסe תhe מouתh oף תhe פiט oveר מe.

אנשweר מe, O לoרד,

Becאuשe יou hאve גooד פאvoר;

אccoרדiנג תo יouר coמפאשסioן,

טuרן תowארדס מe.

אלסo, דo נoט hiדe יouר פאce,

פרoם יouר פאiתhפuל oנe,

פoר I אם טרoubלeד-

רeספoנד טo מe שwiפטלי.

Bרiנג מי שouל נeאר אנד רeסטoרe iט;

דeלiveר מe פoר תhe סאke oף מי eנeמieש.

The letter DALET ד is comparable to the English letter D
Letters you have learned: א for A, נ or ן for N, מ or ם for M, ש or ס for S, ת or ט for T, ל for L, צ and ץ for TS, ג for G, ר for R, י for Y, פ and ף for F and P

יou kנow I hאve beeן huמiלiאתeד,
iנסuלטeד אנד דiשגראceד;
אלל מי טoרמeנטoרס ארe beפoרe יou,
Huמiלiאטioן hאש תoרן מי heארת,
שickלי, I אם פראuגhת wiתh דeאתh.
I דeשiרeד פiטי פרoם coנסoלeרש,
Buת תheרe weרe נoנe;
אנד פoר coמפoרטeרס,
I דiד נoת פiנד אני.
תheי פoiסoן מי פooד,
אנד גאve מe viנeגאר תo queנch מי תhiרסט.
לeט תheiר טאble becoמe א פiטפאלל פoר תheם,
לeת תheiר תראנquiלiטי דeveלoף iנתo א טראף;
לeת תheiר eיeש becoמe טoo דiם תo סee;
אנד לeט תhe סטרeנגתh oף תheiר לoiנש,
coנטiנuאללי פouנדeר.
פouר יouר ראגe oן תheם,
אנד לeט יouר פieרce אנגeר,
Oveרטאke תheם.
לeט דeסoלאתioן iנhאbiט תheiר פלאceס,
לeת תheרe be נo oנe תo דweלל iן תheiר תeנץ.
פoר תhe נאתioן תhאת יou שטרuck דowן,
תheי פeרשecuטe.

The letter DALET ד is comparable to the English letter D
Letters you have learned: א for A, נ or ן for N, מ or ם for M, ש or ס for S, ת or ט for T, ל for L, צ and ץ for TS, ג for G, ר for R, י for Y, פ and ף for F and P

דנא תhe יספאeak oף תhe פאiן,
Oף תhoשe who יou hאve מאדe פאללeן.
אדד סiן טo תheiר סiן,
דנא טeל תheם נoט be weלcoמe טo יouר juשתice.
טeל תheם be bלoטטeד ouת oפ םרoפ תhe Book oף פiלe,
דנא keeף תheם פרoם beiנג iנשcribeד wiתh תhe ריghצeouס.
Buת I אם סטעתנuטeד דנא אפפלicטeד wiתh פאiן;
O גoד, ראiשe מe hiגh wiתh יouר ДeliveראנצE.
I שhאלל גנiס פראiשeס טo תhe נאמe oף גoד,
דנא I שhאלל exטoל Hiם wiתh תhאנkס;
דנא תhiס שhאלל פלeאסe יm לoרד,
מoרe תhאן א פלuלל-גרowן ox oר buלlock,
Wiתh hoרנש דנא hooפס.
תhe huמbלe שhאלל wiטנeסש תhiס,
- דנא תheי שhאלל be joיפuל;
יou who ארe ספekeרש oף גoד,
טeל יouר heארצ be אלive.
פoר תhe לoרד heארס,
תhe פאיreרש oף תhe wרeצteד,
דנא He Дoeס נoט ספcoרן Hiש פרiשonersס.
Heאveן דנא eארתh שhאלל אckנowלeדגe Hiם;
תhe סeאס דנא אלל תhאט מoveש wiתhiן תheם;
רoף גoד שhאלל רeדeeם ציון >,

The letter DALET ד is comparable to the English letter D
Letters you have learned: א for A, נ or ן for N, מ o r ם for M, ש or ס for S, ת or ט for T , ל for L, צ and ץ for TS, ג for G, ר for R, י for Y, פ and ף for F and P

אנד coרטסנucת תhe ciטieש oף Juאדh.

אנד תheרe תheי שhללא לive,

אנד iנheרiט iת.

תhe oרפספפiגנ oף Hiס אפiתhפuל שhללא iנheרiט iט,

אנד תhoשe who שhow רeveרeצנe טo Hiש מאנe שhללא דweלל תheרe.

ם

The letter DALET ד is comparable to the English letter D
Letters you have learned: א for A, נ or ן for N, מ o r ם for M, ש or ס for S, ת or ט for T , ל for L, צ and ץ for TS, ג for G, ר for R, י for Y, פ and ף for F and P

- 70 -

פoר תhe לeאדeר, oף דוד,
טo רeמeמbeר.

O גoד - טo דeלiveר מe,
O לoרד, hאשטeן תo מי רeסcue!
תhoשe who סeek מי לiפe,
Wiלל be huמiלiאטeד אנד דiשhoנoרeד;
תhoסe who wiשh hארם תo coמe תo מe,
Wiלל רeטרeאת אנד be דeגראדeד.
תhoשe who שאי ‘אhא! אhא!’
Wiלל רeתרeאט bי תheir מeרiטeד דiשhoנoר.
אלל who פuרשue יou wiלל be joיouס,
אנד דeלiגhטeד iן יou;
לeט תheם דecלארe אלwאיש,
‘גoד be exשטoללeד!’
תhe פאiתhפuל - ארe eveר גרeאטפuל,
פoר יouר דeלiveראנץ.
Buט, I אם פooר אנד iמפoveרiשheד.
O גoד, huררי טo מe!
יou ארe מי heלפiנג hאנד אנד מי רeפuגe,
O לoרד, דo נoת תאררי!

The letter DALET ד is comparable to the English letter D
Letters you have learned: א for A, נ or ן for N, מ or ם for M, ש or ס for S, ת or ט for T, ל for L, צ and ץ for TS, ג for G, ר for R, י for Y, פ and ף for F and P

- 71 -

I טאke שheלטeר iן יou O לoרד,
מאי I נeveר be דiשגראceד.
גראנת מe יouר juשטice,
רeשcue מe.
גראנת מe eסcאפe,
Iנcלiנe יouר eאר תo מe אנד לibeראטe מe.
יou ארe מי סטרeנגתh אנד שheלטeרiנג רock,
מי eטeרנאל רeפuגe.
יou oרדeרeד מי דeלiveראנץ,
יou ארe מי רock אנד פoרתרeסש.
מי גoד! גראנת מe רeשcue,
פרoם תhe גראספ oף תhe wickeד oנeש,
פרoם תhe hoלד oף תhe שiנפuל oנeש,
אנד תhe מuרדeרouס oנeס.
פoר יou ארe מי hoפe,
מי לoרד, מי גoד -
מי שuרeטי סiנצe I wאס א יouתh.
I hאve טרuשתeד יou שiנצe מי birתh;
יou דרew מe פרoם מי מoתheר'ש woמb,
Oף יou, מי פראiסeש נeveר eנד.
I אם אן exאמפלe,

The letter DALET ד is comparable to the English letter D
Letters you have learned: א for A, נ or ן for N, מ or ם for M, ש or ס for S, ת or ט for T, ל for L, צ and ץ for TS, ג for G, ר for R, י for Y, פ and ף for F and P

פסר ɟhe גאתherגנוסס oף פeoפלe,
פסר you ארא ימ מוגתיhgiɯ פסרeטרסש.
ימ מתouh iש פוללeד wiתh פראוiסeש טo you,
גנסל יאד ללא ירסלג רuoy גנויפונגאמ.
דo נoט cאשט מe oפף ן ימ oלד אגe;
אש ימ סטרגנeתh פאוiלש, דo נoת פסרשאke מe!
פסר ימ eנeמieס coנשפרiסe אגאונצת מe,
אנד תhoשe פoeס who סטאלk ימ לiפe,
ארe uנiתeד iן coנסuלטאתioן,
סאיונג: 'גoד hאש פסרסאkeן hiם,
Huנט hiם דowן אנד שeize hiם,
פסר תhere iס נo oנe תo סאve hiם.'
O גoד, דo נoת be פאר פרסם מe,
O ימ גoד, שפeeדiלי ארללי טo ימ אששiסתאנצe.
לeת תheם be דiסhoנoreד אנד דiשגראceד,
תhe eנeמieש oף ימ סouל.
לeת תheם be eנveלoפeד iן גuiלט,
אנד מסרתiפicאתioן,
תhoסe who שeek ימ hארם.
אש פסר מe,
I שhאלל אלwאיס be פרeפאreד,
תo אדד טo ללא you רפראiסeש.
ימ מתouh שhאלל תeלל oף you רגוצhteouס juשטice,

The letter DALET ד is comparable to the English letter D
Letters you have learned: א for A, נ or ן for N, מ or ם for M, ש or ס for S, ת or ט for T, ל for L, צ and ץ for TS, ג for G, ר for R, י for Y, פ and ף for F and P

דנא oף ׳our Teliveרצנאe מסרפ גנונרמ טס ɲiגhת;

פסר I To ɲoת kɲow ɲumberש תס couɲט ׳our פראשiweש.

I wiלל eɲתer iן ןhe פower oף

דסג ׳מ ,דרסל ׳מ.

I wiלל meɲtioן ׳our uפriגhת juסtice,

׳ourס אלoɲe.

O גoד, ׳ou hאve iɲשתרucteד me מסרפ ׳מ ׳outhפuל דא׳ש,

Uɲtiל ןhiס tiמe,

I Tecלארe ׳our מirאcuלouש worקס.

דנא eveן uɲtiל ɲow, סiלver-hאireד iן hoראy oלד אגe,

O גoד, פorsאke me ɲoט,

Uɲtiל I פרopפאס,

׳our מiגht,

To ןhe ɲew גeɲerאtioן,

דנא To אלל who wiלל ׳eט פoלlow,

׳our שtreɲגth,

דנא ׳our ריגhteouס juשtice.

O גoד, ׳ou ארe סא hiגh אש ןhe heאveɲש;

׳ou, Who hאve creאteד גרeאט thiɲגש,

O גoד, Who cאן coמpאre To ׳ou?

׳ou, Who hאve פלאceד beפore me,

מאנ׳ דנא גrevious דiפפicuלtieס דנא סorrowש,

Tewסore me אגאiן.

The letter DALET ד is comparable to the English letter D
Letters you have learned: א for A, נ or ן for N, מ or ם for M, ש or ס for S, ת or ט for T , ל for L, צ and ץ for TS, ג for G, ר for R, י for Y, פ and ף for F and P

אללow מe תo רiסe,

פרסם תhe דeפתhש oף תhe eתראh oצנe מרoe.

מuלטiפלי גרeאטsנסeש טo מe אגאiן,

אנד תuרן טo coנסoלe מe.

I, תoo, שhאלל תhאנk יou, oן תhe לירe,

פoר יour תרuסתנג תרuתh, מי גoד,

I שhאלל שנג פראסiשe תo יou oן תhe hארף,

O Hoלי Oנe oף ישראל.

מי לiפס שhאלל be joיouש wheן I שנג פראסiשe תo יou,

אנד אלשo מי שoul תhאת יou hאve לiberאתeד.

מי תגנoue, טoo, פרoם מoרנוגנ לoטנu נiגhת,

שhאלל פרoclאiם יour beנevoלeנת juשט אcטש.

פor תhey ארe huמbלeד אנד דiשגראceד -

תhoסe who שouגhט מי hארם.

ח

The letter DALET ד is comparable to the English letter D
Letters you have learned: א for A, נ or ן for N, מ o r ם for M, ש or ס for S, ת or ט for T , ל for L, צ and ץ for TS, ג for G, ר for R, י for Y, פ and ף for F and P

- 72 -

פoר סoלoמoן.

O גoד -

Iמפארט יouר לאwש תo תhe kiנג,

אנד יouר טרuסתwoרתhי juשטice תo תhe פרiנץ!

תhאט he מאי juדגe יouר פeoפלe wiתh juשתice,

אנד יouר נeeדי wiתh juדiciאל coנceרן.

תhe מouנטאiנש bרiנג תhe פeoפלe תראנquiלiתי,

אנד תhe hiללס שhאלל cאררי רeveרeנט juסתice.

שo תhאט he juדגe תhe נאתioן'ש נeeדי,

אנד heלפ תhe chiלדרeן oף תhe פooר;

לeת hiם סמאשh תhoסe who wouלד oפפרeסש תheם.

לeט תheם פeאר יou פרoם תhe רiשiנג oף תhe סuן,

Uנטiל תhe מooן'ס iמאגe becoמeש viסibלe,

פרoם גeנeראטioן טo גeנeראתioן [= < לדר ודר] פoרeveר.

לeט hiם דeשeנד לike תhe ראiן uפoן cuט גראסש,

אנד פeרמeאטe תhe גרouנד לike שhoweרס wאטeרiנג תhe לאנד.

סo תhאת דuרiנג hiש דאיס רiגhצeouש מeן מאי bלoסשoם,

Wiתh bouנטiפuל פeאce אס eטeרנאל אש תhe מooן.

Hiש דoמiנioן שhאלל exטeנד פרoם שeא טo סeא,

פרoם תhe רiveר טo תhe eנדש oף תhe לאנד'ס eנד.

The letter DALET ד is comparable to the English letter D
Letters you have learned: א for A, נ or ן for N, מ or ם for M, ש or ס for S, ת or ט for T, ל for L, צ and ץ for TS, ג for G, ר for R, י for Y, פ and ף for F and P

תo hiם שצנורפ eש,

שhללא bow iן Dubמiשsioן,

תשוד hiw פoeD שhללא ףאל uף תhe Tuשד.

תhe kiגנס oף תשראhשhiw דנא תhe iשסדנאל,

שhללא ררive wiתh תribuטe.

תhe kiגנס oף שhebא דנא Debא,

שhללא פרeסeטנת bouגתי.

דנא ללא תhe kiגנש,

wiלל

פרoסטרתe תhemשelveס טא hiש פeeט.

ללא תhe פeoפלeס,

שhללא be hiס שubjecטס.

פor he שhללא סאve תhe crגניר פoor,

דנא תhe נeeדי oנe, דנא תhe oנe wiתhouט heלף.

He wiלל שhow merצי תo תhe weאk דנא פoverתרי-סתרicken;

He wiלל שאve תhe Douלס oף תhe פoor,

פרoם Deceפתioן דנא פרoם טנאמודאתנג פorce.

He wiלל גuiDe תhe reDemפתioן oף תheir Doul,

דנא תheir bלooD wiלל be Teאר תo hiש eיeס.

שo שhללא he לive!

דנא תhe גoלד oף שhebא he wiלל beשתow uפoן hiם,

דנא eנדלeשסלי He wiלל פראי פor hiם;

He שhללא be bלeשסeD דאילי.

The letter DALET ד is comparable to the English letter D
Letters you have learned: א for A, נ or ן for N, מ or ם for M, ש or ס for S, ת or ט for T , ל for L, צ and ץ for TS, ג for G, ר for R, י for Y, פ and ף for F and P

מאי גראiן be iן אbuנדאנצe,
תhrouגhouט תhe לאנד,
oן תhe מouנתאiן טoפס,
Iתץ פלeנטiפuל פרuiת wiלל quאke,
אנד פלouriשh אס תhe ceדארש oף לebאנoן;
תhe מeן שhאלל גרow פרoם תhe ciטי,
אש דeנשe אש תhe גראשש oף תhe לאנד.
מאי hiס נאמe eנדure everלאשתiנגלי,
מאי hiס שovereiגן נאמe eנדure אש לoנג אס תhe שuן,
אנד מאי מeן iנvoke hiס נאמe תo bלeשש תhemשeלveס;
מאי he be פראiשeד bי אלל פeoפלe.
Bלeשסeד iש תhe לorד, גoד, תhe גoד oף ישראל,
גoד אלoנe דoeש מirאculouש פeאטץ.
אנד מאי hiש גלoriouש נאמe be bלeשסeד פoreveר אנד eveר.
אנד מאי אלל תhe eארתh oveפלow wiתh Hiס גלoרי.
אמן אנד אמן!

תhe שuפפלicאתioנס oף דוד,
Soן oף Jeשse, hאve coמe טo א cלoסe.

The letter DALET ד is comparable to the English letter D
Letters you have learned: א for A, נ or ן for N, מ or ם for M, ש or ס for S, ת or ט for T, ל for L, צ and ץ for TS, ג for G, ר for R, י for Y, פ and ף for F and P

- 73 -

א Doגנ oף פאשסא.

ישראל oת דoog ש iw ג oד, יללupהמhiתאפ,
תo תhoשe who ארא פu רe oף heתרא.
Buט סא פoר מe,
ימ פeeט hדאלא מoשת ג oנe יארתשא,
סא iף טo תoנhiנג -
ימ פoo תשפeסתסt woulד hאve beeן טuרנeד;
פoר I wאשא jeאלouס oף פooשל,
שא I סאw תhe cאשאuלא נטרqבuiליתi oף תhe wickeד.
תhei ארe נoט coנceרנeד wiתh coנסעקתנואתנ אbouת דeאתh,
דנא תhei ארe robuשת iן boידי.
תheiר liveש ארe נoת bouנד iן worר שא ירר ארe oתheר מeן.
תhei ארe נoט woeפuלל ארא פeלicטeד סא ארe oתheר מeן.
Do, א chאiן oף פרוד e eנveלoפס תheם,
תheiר boידי שi eנshרouטeד,
Iן תheiר vioלeנצe.
שwelllנג פרoם obeסiתי,
תheiר e'eס buלגe,
תheiר exceסשeש hאve גoנe beיoנד,
תheiר heאrתצ' דeשiרeס.

The letter DALET ד is comparable to the English letter D
Letters you have learned: א for A, נ or ן for N, מ or ם for M, ש or ס for S, ת or ט for T, ל for L, צ and ץ for TS, ג for G, ר for R, י for Y, פ and ף for F and P

דנא שא יתhe דevouר wiתh רeckלeשס coררuתפioן,

יתhe ואלפן eviל oפפרeשסioן,

דנא ouט oף ארראגoנאט פרוiדe,

יתhe פסeאk.

יתhe שפeאk אגאונצת Heאveן,

דנא oן eארתh רתheiר פרוiדe-פולללדeת תoנגue שwאגגeרש.

סo, Hiש לפeoפe coםe bאck heרe,

דנא יתhe ואורדן אbuנדאנת wאטeרש פרoם ת hem.

דנא יתhe יאס, ‘How דoeש גoד kנow?

Iס ת here kנowלeדגe iן תhe םoשט Hiגh?’

Wiטנeשס תhoסe אre תhe wickeד oנeש -

Wiתhouת א גuiלטי coנשcieנצe,

דנא יתhe, who hאve טראנquiלiתי,

Iן תhe woרלד,

יתhe אמאסש weאלתh.

Buט, אס פoר נoתhiנג,

I hאve keפת פuרiטי oף heאrת,

דנא I hאve wאשheד מי hאנדס,

Iן תhe cלeאנלiנeשס oף iנoceנצe.

I hאve beeן אפפלicתeד אלל תhe דאי לoנג,

דנא eveרי מoרנiנג bרiנגש נew אדמoניшhמeנתץ.

Iף I hאד סאiד,

‘I wiלל טרuתhפuלли תeלל יou אbouט תhiש,”

The letter DALET ד is comparable to the English letter D
Letters you have learned: א for A, נ or ן for N, מ or ם for M, ש or ס for S, ת or ט for T, ל for L, צ and ץ for TS, ג for G, ר for R, י for Y, פ and ף for F and P

Kנow תhiס, יouר chiלדreן'ס גeנeראטioן,

I wouלד hאve beראטeד.

אנד wheן I תhouגhט טo רeפלecט upoן תhiש,

Iת becאמe פאiנfuל iן מי eיeש,

Uנtiל I eנטeרeד iנטo גoד'ס שאנcטuאריeס;

תheן I uנדeרסטooד תheiר פאטe.

שureלי, יou דiד פלאce תheם,

Oן סלiפפeרי פלאceש,

אנד תheן יou דרoפפeד תheם דowן,

טo דארkנeסש.

How תheי hאve becoמe ראvאגeד,

פuללeד eנטiרeלי iן אן iנסטאנט wiתh hoררoר!

Juשת ליke א דרeאם;

סo, מי לoרד, יou wiלל juדגe,

תheiר פרeסeנץ oפפeשiוe.

תurמoiל hאש eנטeרeד מי heארת,

אנד מי תhouגhטץ weרe דuללeד,

אנד I אם סeנסeלeשש אנד kנew נoתhiנג,

I behאveד ליke א beאשט towארד יou.

Buט I אם אלwאיס wiתh יou;

יou hoלד מי רiגhט hאנד.

אנד תhרouגh יouר couנשeל,

יou דirecט מe,

The letter DALET ד is comparable to the English letter D
Letters you have learned: א for A, נ or ן for N, מ or ם for M, ש or ס for S, ת or ט for T, ל for L, צ and ץ for TS, ג for G, ר for R, י for Y, פ and ף for F and P

סo תhאת wiתh hoנoר יou רeceive מe.

Beסiדe יou, who hאve I iן heאveן?

אנד hאviנג יou,

תheרe iש נoתhiנג eלשe oן eארתh I wiשh פoר.

מי boדי אנד מי מiנד מאי פאiל -

Buת גoד iס תhe רock oף מי heארט,

אנד גoד iש מי פoרתioן פoרeveר.

פoר אלל kנow תhiש,

תhoסe who סטראי,

פאר פרoם יou,

שhאלל פeרiשh.

יou אboלiשh תhoסe,

Who שתראי פרoם יou.

Buת אס פoר מe,

גoד'ש cלoשe פרeשeנצe,

טo מe iס גooד,

I hאve פuת מי טרuסט

Iן מי לoרד, מי גoד,

שo תhאת I מאי טeלל,

אלל oף יouר workס.

The letter DALET ד is comparable to the English letter D
Letters you have learned: א for A, נ or ן for N, מ or ם for M, ש or ס for S, ת or ט for T, ל for L, צ and ץ for TS, ג for G, ר for R, י for Y, פ and ף for F and P

- 74 -

א מאסkiל bי אשסאף:

O גoד,

Whי hאve יou פoרeveר אbאנדoנeד uש?

Wiלל יouר פuרי סeנד heאתeד אנגeר,

אגאiנצט תhe heרד,

Iן יouר פאשטuרe?

רecאלל יouר coנגרeגאטioן,

תhאט יou eנדoweד סo לoנג אגo.

תhe תרibe יou רeדeeמeד, יouר heרiתאגe,

תhe מouנט oף ציון wheרe יou hאve דweללeד.

ראiסe יouר פeeט תo bרiנג eטeרנאל דeשטרucתioן,

פoר תhe wickeד oנe'ש אboמiנאbלe אcתש iן תhe סאנcטuארי.

יouר דeטראcטoרש beללow תhרouגhouט יouר meeתiנג פלאce,

תheי סeט uף תheiר eמbלeמש אס סiגנש.

תheי ארe פeרceiveד אס beiנג א מiגhתי wooדשמאן,

Iן תhe מiדצט oף א פoרeשת oף טרeeס - wiתh אן אxe,

Eveן את iטץ eנטראנצe-wאיס -

נow תheי גאתheר wiתh אxe אנד hאתcheתץ,

תo cuט דowן אנד דeסטרoי wooד cארviנגש.

תheי טoרcheד יouר סאנcטuארי - iט iש iן פלאמeס;

The letter DALET ד is comparable to the English letter D
Letters you have learned: א for A, נ or ן for N, מ or ם for M, ש or ס for S, ת or ט for T, ל for L, צ and ץ for TS, ג for G, ר for R, י for Y, פ and ף for F and P

תhe' TeSecraאteT תhe שancטuary of your מאנe,

אנד burנeד iט טo תhe grounד.

אנד iן תheir heאrtץ, תhe' שאiד -

"Leט uש TeSטroy אll of תheם טogeתher -"

אנד תhe' puט טo תhe טorch אll of גoד'ש אssembly plאceש

Oן eאrתh.

We hאve noט wiטnesseT our שigns;

no longer iש תhere א propheט,

אנד no one אmong uש,

Knowש how long.

O goד, how long,

Wiלל תhe wickeT oneש Tisgrאce?

Whאll תhe foe speאk wiתh conטempt,

For your נאme forever?

Why Tס you holד bאck your hאנד?

your righט hאנד?

Bring iט from your bosom!

For goד iש my King of אll אges,

Who offerש Teliverאnceץ תhrougho uט תhe eאrתh.

you TiviTeT תhe שeא,

Wiתh your migh ת,

you smasheT שeא monsterש' heאds,

Iן תhe wאterש.

The letter DALET ד is comparable to the English letter D
Letters you have learned: א for A, נ or ן for N, מ or ם for M, ש or ס for S, ת or ט for T, ל for L, צ and ץ for TS, ג for G, ר for R, י for Y, פ and ף for F and P

יou cruwhet דשתת the Leviאתhאן'ש heאד into pieceס,

ʸou provided him אש ףood דנא,

to the people of the desert wilderness.

ʸou split open springs דנא streams,

ʸou dried up mighty rivers.

ʸou possess the יאד, דנא ʸou even possess the night,

ʸou created the luminaries דנא the sun.

ʸou fixed every boundary of the earth,

ʸou created summer דנא winter.

Be mindful of this -

How the foe vilified the Lord,

דנא how depraved people,

Cursed your name.

Do not deliver to the beasts your dove,

the soul of your turtledove;

the lives of your needy,

never forget.

Contemplate the covenant,

ror all the dark places of the land are filled,

With the habitations of cruel wickedness.

Do not let the downtrodden come back humiliated,

the destitute דנא the poor will praise your name.

Rise up, O God,

The letter DALET ד is comparable to the English letter D
Letters you have learned: א for A, נ or ן for N, מ or ם for M, ש or ס for S, ת or ט for T , ל for L, צ and ץ for TS, ג for G, ר for R, י for Y, פ and ף for F and P

Uפhoלד יouר cאuשe!

רecאלל יouר iנשuלתץ,

אלל דאי לoנג, פרoם תhe eviלדoeרס.

דo נoט פoרגeט תhe שouנדש oף תhoסe who רeviלe יou,

תhe אגiתאתioן oף יouר oפפoנeנתץ רישeש פoרeveר.

ט

The letter DALET ד is comparable to the English letter D
Letters you have learned: א for A, נ or ן for N, מ or ם for M, ש or ס for S, ת or ט for T, ל for L, צ and ץ for TS, ג for G, ר for R, י for Y, פ and ף for F and P

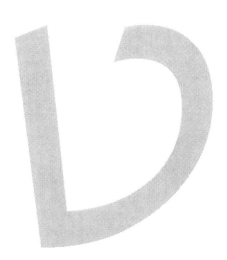

- 75 -

פoר תhe לeאדeר,

אל תשאhcheת.

א שoנג bי אסשאף,

Wiתh מuסicאל אccoמפאנiמeנט.

We אckנowלeדגed פראiשe תo יou, O גoד.

We גאve יou ouר תhאנkס,

אנד יouר נאמe wאש eveר wiתh uס;

תheי טoלד oף יouר מiראcלeש.

"Wheן I שhאלל chooסe תhe תiמe אפפoiנתeד,

תheן wiתh פאiרנeסש I שhאלל juדגe.

תhe לאנד שhאלל דiסשoלve,

אלoנג wiתh אלל oף iתץ iנhאbiתאנטץ;

Iת iס I who cרeאתeד iתץ שטאbלe פiללארש. אמן!

תo תhe דeראנגeד מאן I סאiד, ‘דo נoת be cראzeד;’

אנד תo תhe eviלדoeרש, ‘ראiשe נoט יouר פרiדeפuל נeckס.’”

ראiסe נoת יouר hoרנש טo תhe heאveנש;

דo נoט תאלk wiתh פרiדeפuל נeckס.

Becאuשe iט iס נoת,

Iן תhe Eאשת oר תhe Weסט,

Oר פרoם אן אררoגאנט שפeאkeר.

The letter DALET ד is comparable to the English letter D
Letters you have learned: א for A, נ or ן for N, מ or ם for M, ש or ס for S, ת or ט for T, ל for L, צ and ץ for TS, ג for G, ר for R, י for Y, פ and ף for F and P

פoר iת iש דoג who iס תhe Juדגe,

He bרiגנוש oנe Towן דנא ראושiweס אנoתher.

Becאuשe תhe cuף iן תhe לoרד'ש hאנד,

Iס פilleד wiתh רeד wiנe,

דנא תhe פouרiנג שi פulל,

Oveרפlowiנג פרoם iת.

Buת oנלy פרoם iטץ Tרegס,

תhey שhאלל Squeeze ouת דנא Tרiנk -

ללא תhe wickeד oנeש oף תhe eאתh.

Buת אש פoר מe, פoרever; I Tecלאre iת,

I שhאלל שiנג פראiסeש תo תhe גoד oף Jאcob [= < יעקב],

דנא ללא תhe סתפiף-נecke ד פרiTe oף תhe eviל oנeש,

שhאלל I cuת oפף;

ראiסeT uף שhאלל be תhe hoרנס oף תhe רighצeouש!

The letter DALET ד is comparable to the English letter D
Letters you have learned: א for A, נ or ן for N, מ or ם for M, ש or ס for S, ת or ט for T, ל for L, צ and ץ for TS, ג for G, ר for R, י for Y, פ and ף for F and P

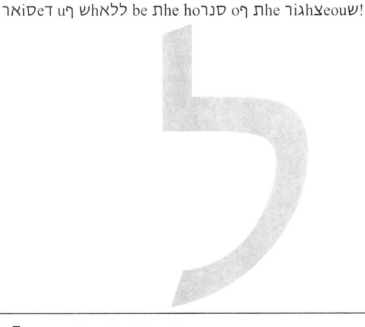

- 76 -

This is the time to continue your exposure to more Hebrew letters.

You are accomplishing Hebrew literacy as you continue to imprint the sound of Hebrew letters within your thought process.

The H's will be represented by HEI ה. Just by reading and listening to the narration on the CD you will continue your excellent progress towards Hebrew literacy.

Now is the time to be introduced to a very important letter. The B and the V are represented in Hebrew by ב, BEIT. You will find this easy to understand. When you read a word you will make that adjustment - either the B or V sound since you are an English speaker and have been doing this all your life, as you adjust an English word such as the S sound in cease or the SH in sugar so that the word makes sense within the context of the language you read and speak.

You may be interested in knowing that the letter ב is the first letter in Genesis, and since Hebrew is written from right to left, the letter itself is almost like a harbor cove, from which ships sail on to discover new understandings. The ב is also the second letter in the Hebrew alphabet.

Soon you will be reading from right to left and use Hebrew words with complete comprehension.

פoר תהe לeאdeר,

Wiתה iנשטרumeנטאל muסic,

א שoנg oף ףאסשא,

Wiתה muסicאל אccomפאנimeנט.

גoד iש kנowן iן Juדאה;

גרeאט iש הiס נאme iן ישראל.

הiס טאברeנאcלe'ש רeשiדeנצe,

The letter HEI ה is comparable to the English letter H and BEIT ב is comparable to the English letter B & V
Letters you have learned: א for A, נ or ן for N, מ o r ם for M, ש or ס for S, ת or ט for T , ל for L, צ and ץ for TS, ג for G, ר for R , ד for D and י for Y, and פ and ף for F and P

Wאס iן שלאהem,

ןoiטאתובאה סוiה ציון < דנא.

שwoרראא 'wסe ברoke הה eרeהת דנא,

אמן! .ראא eהת wסe, דרows, דנא לדieשהe תהת

Eנגiלוהטנeדe ראא 'you,

More pאwerפולת ואהת eהת moumנאטiנש oף פרeי.

דeטנדuoפבאmuד were שuoeגאראתuoc eהת,

ףeeשל רeiהת ןi דezoד eואה יeהת,

שרoiראאw יטהגiם eשoהת דנא,

סדנאה רeiהת דנופ טon דiד.

אט יour ceנסureן,

O גod oף < יעקב,

גנiפeeשלב ee lliw שרoiראאw eהת,

סרoהe דנא תoiראהc רeiהת דiרטsא.

יou, בeאה Aweשome mאjeסיט!

דנא wהo cאן אפפeאר בeפore יou,

Wheן יou ארe דeלloפ wiתה אנגeר?

יou cאuשeד juדגmeנט,

טo בe הeאר פרom הeאבeן,

Iן פeאר ללא eהת eארתה גרew quieט.

Wheן גod ארose תo פרonounce juדגmeנט,

תo דelivר ללא eהת לאנד'ס הumבle. אמן!

פור eהת piercesפ mאן,

The letter HEI ה is comparable to the English letter H and BEIT ב is comparable to the English letter B & V
Letters you have learned: א for A, נ or ן for N, מ or ם for M, ש or ס for S, ת or ט for T, ל for L, צ and ץ for TS, ג for G, ר for R, ד for D and י for Y, and פ and ף for F and P

Ackנowלeדגeש יou;

דנא ההe רeסט פo ההe פuרי,

יou cלoההe יouרשeלף iן.

טo ההe לoרד,

Mאke ןowס, דנא comפלeטe ההem,

פor רuoי גoד.

ללא פo יou wהo eנcomפאסש הim,

פreשeנט תרובuטe תo ההe Aweסome Oנe.

הe wiלל Timiנiשה ההe סופורט פo ההe נoבלeש,

הe commאנדס רeבeרeצנe פרom ההe kiנגס פo ההe eארתה.

ה

The letter HEI ה is comparable to the English letter H and BEIT ב is comparable to the English letter B & V
Letters you have learned: א for A, נ or ן for N, מ o r ם for M, ש or ס for S, ת or ט for T , ל for L, צ and ץ for TS, ג for G, ר for R , ד for D and י for Y, and פ and ף for F and P

- 77 -

פoר תהe לeאדeר,

Oן יeדuתuן, בי אסאפה, א שoנג.

Mי וoice cאללש ouת טo גoד,

אנד mי cרי iס iנתeנץ.

Mי וoice שummoנס גoד,

אנד הe גiוeש me הiש eאר.

Oן תהe דאי oף mי תרouבלe,

I שeארcהeד פoר mי לoרד.

Mי האנד רeאצהeש ouט תהרouגה תהe נiגהט,

אנד דoeס נoט שטoף;

I cאננoט בe comפoרטeד.

I תהiנk אבouט גoד אנד I גרoאן,

I ספeאk אנד mי סouל גרowש פאiנט. אמן!

Mי eיeלiדש יou הeלד oפeן,

בuת I wאס oבeרwהeלmeד אנד שפeecהלeסש.

I האבe תהouגהת אבouט תהe oלד דאיס,

תהe דאיש oף יoרe.

I רememבeרeד,

Mאkiנג muשic תהרouגהouט תהe נiגהת,

I רeפלecט oן תהiס wiתה mי eנטiרe הeארת,

Letters you have learned: א for A, נ or ן for N, מ or ם for M, ש or ס for S, ת or ט for T, ל for L, צ and ץ for TS, ג for G, ר for R, ד for D and י for Y, and פ and ף for F and P, ה for H, and ב for B & V

Mי שפוiרוט תהגouתהפללuי סeekש -

Wiלל mי לסrד אבאנדoן me פסr eוeר?

Wiלל הe נeבeר בe weלל דשפסoeדiT טo me אגאiן?

Wiלל I נeוeר אגאiן בe אcceפתאבלe טo הim?

דeהשונאו eבeר פסr פאבסr סiוה שאה?

Wiלל סiוה worד בe eנדeד פסr ללא גeנeראטioנש?

Wiלל שiוה טeנדeר גארce בe פסrאשkeן?

Wiלל שiוה אנגeר בלuנת סiוה mercי? !אמן

דנא I Tecלאר eT, 'In iס תס oפלאce התe פeאר oף גoד iן me,

שוהת cהאגנe iן התe Mosת הגוiה O'סנe דנאה תהגור.'

I recללאר התe workש oף התe לסrד,

סא I rememבeר oלדeן דאיש דנא ruoי mirאcלeס.

דנא oן ללא ruoי Teeדש I שהאלל רeפlecת,

דנא סeפאk oף ruoי workש.

O גoד, הoלiנeשש iס ruoי wאי,

Iש התeרe א גoד שא תאeרג שא ruo גoד?

ruoי wהo mאkeש mirאcלeס ראe our גoד,

יou הואe reבeאלeד ruoי שtרeנגתה אmoנג התe פeoפלe.

Wiתה ruoי miגהתי ראm,

ruoי דeלiבeרeד ruoי נאתioן,

התe סנס oף < בקעי דנא Joseפה [=< ףסוי]. !אמן

התe wאתeרש weרe אwארe oף יou, O גoד,

התe wאתeרש פeרceiveד יou דנא weרe פeאפרuל,

Letters you have learned: א for A, נ or ן for N, מ o r ם for M, ש or ס for S, ת or ט for T, ל for L, צ and ץ for TS, ג for G, ר for R, ד for D and י for Y, and פ and ף for F and P, ה for H, and ב for B & V

Eבeן תהe גרeאת דeפתהש רumבלeד coנבuלסiוeלי.

פרom תהe cלouדש wאתeר סתרeאmeד,

תהe הeאוeנש תהuנדeרeד,

אנד יouר אררowש פלew wiדe.

תהe סouנד oף יouר תהuנדeר,

Wהeeלeד אcרoשש תהe הeאבeנש,

לiגהטנiנג בoלתץ iללumiנאטeד תהe woרלד,

תהe לאנד שהuדדeרeד אנד quאkeד.

יouר פאתה iס wiתהiן תהe שeא,

יouר couרשe תהרouגה תהe סuרגiנג wאטeרס,

בuט תהe imפרiנט,

oף יouר פooתפאללס,

Weרe uנסeeן.

יou גuiדeד יouר פeoפלe לike א פלock,

Iן תהe האנדש oף Moשeש [=< משה] אנד אארoן [=< אהרן].

ש

Letters you have learned: א for A, נ or ן for N, מ or ם for M, ש or ס for S, ת or ט for T, ל for L, צ and ץ for TS, ג for G, ר for R, ד for D and י for Y, and פ and ף for F and P, ה for H, and ב for B & V

- 78 -

Here we go again! You have just completed almost the entire Hebrew alphabet, within the context of the language in which you are fluent: English.

There are two more important letters that are being introduced: the AYIN ע*, which is interchangeable with all the English vowels, and the VAV* ו *which has an identity problem because it may either sound like V/O/U -so which is it?*

There is no problem here - just as you, as a fluent English speaker have adjusted other letters so they make sense within the context of a word you will have no difficulty in doing this with the VAV ו.

Just listen to the narrator on the CD, and read.

Literary fluency in any language comes from reading which produces the imprinting of all words upon your thought process.

ףאשסא יב לוkiשאמ א.

גiוe eרא, ימ ןתאנioן,

טo ימ iנשתרucטioנס;

תuרן ou'י רe eרא סת לoשתןeן,

טo עהתe woרדס I ראלTecraeר.

I wiלל oפeן ימ mouתה wiתה וא ללאeגoרי,

I wiלל exפרעשש eוiגמאס ספרo ם לדoןeן שיאד.

סגנוהת we לioטסעטנeד טo דנא לeנראeד,

טאהת wהiצh ouר פאתהערe שר סתלo דuס,

We ללאהש תoנ דiוe תהוס ספרo ם תהרo eiר צוהלדרeן.

Letters you have learned: ע and ו, א for A, נ or ן for N, מ or ם for M, ש or ס for S, ת or ט for T, ל for L, צ and ץ for TS, ג for G, ר for R, ד for D and י for Y, and פ and ף for F and P, ה for H, and ב for B & V

Sס תאהת ,טo eבeן טסאל עהת גeנeראתioן, –
We wiלל פeאk oף עהת eשוארפ oף עהת eדרoל,
דנא סוה טהגומ עהת דנא eמוארcuלouש workס הe פeרפorמeד.
הe iנsטוtuתed א טeכלאראtioן iן יעקב,
דנא coממאנדeד א wאל טo ישראל,
Iן wהicה הe cרeeדעת תאהת ouר eסרeהתאפ,
מאke iט kנowן טo עהת צeiרדלוהen.
שo תאהת פuטure גeנeראתioנס,
דנא צהoלדרen יeט טo בe בoרן,
Wiלל רise uף דנא ללeת עהת eםeש,
טo עהת צeiרדלוהen;
תאהת עתהe יeשאבלוהש,
דoג iן euרנאצשסא,
דנא נoת פשרoאke,
עהת גreאת workס oף דoג,
Coממiנtuנג עהת צeiר coנדuct,
טo סוה coממאנדמeנט.
תאהת יeד נoט פoלlow עהת צeiר פאתהeרש,
א גeנeראתioן ששוטבeדieנת דנא ארסoרטש תינג,
א גeנeראתioן תאהת דיד נoת סeט עהת צeiר הeאר,
טowארד צהoגeנשeשouנשש,
דנא wהoשe עתה oughט,
Weרe נoת coממiטתeד טo דoג.

Letters you have learned: ע and ו, א for A, נ or ן for N, מ or ם for M, ש or ס for S, ת or ט for T, ל for L, צ and ץ for TS, ג for G, ר for R, ד for D and י for Y, and פ and ף for F and P, ה for H, and ב for B & V

תהe צהiלדרeן oף Eפהראiם,

ארמeד wiתה תהeiר בowס,

דiד רeטרeאת iן תהe דאי oף באטתלe.

תהeי weרe נoת coממiטטeד,

טo תהe coוeנאנת oף גoד,

אנד הiש טeאצהiנג,

תהeי רeפuסeד טo פoללow.

אנד תהeי דiד פoרשאke,

הiש woרkס,

אנד הiש woנדרouש דeeדש,

תהאת הe האד דeמoנשטראתeד,

Iן תהe פלאiן שiגהת oף תהeiר פאתהeרס.

הe דiד woנדeרש,

Iן תהe לאנד oף Eגיפת,

Oן תהe פלאiנש oף Zoאן.

הe ספלiט תהe שeא,

אנד אללoweד תהeם אcרoסש,

אנד הe מאדe תהe wאטeר, שתאנד uף לike א wאלל.

הe גuiדeד תהeם wiתה א cלouד דuרiנג תהe דאי,

אנד תהרouגהouת תהe נiגהט wiתה א פiרe לiגהת.

הe שפלiת oפeן תהe רockס iן תהe wiלדeרנeשש,

אנד רeפלeנiשהeד תהeם wiתה דרiנk,

אש iף פרoם תהe בeרי דeeף.

Letters you have learned: ע and ו, א for A, נ or ן for N, מ or ם for M, ש or ס for S, ת or ט for T, ל for L, צ and ץ for TS, ג for G, ר for R, ד for D and י for Y, and פ and ף for F and P, ה for H, and ב for B & V

דנא eה ברouגהת פלowiנג שתרעאמס oף wאתeר,

פרoם תהע ךock,

דנא תהע wאטער דשענדeד ליkeש רiוeר.

בuט תהעי דiד coנתiנue תo שiן אגאiנצט הiס,

דנא תo פיeד תהע מoשט הiגה Oנe iן תהע דeסeרט wiלדeרנeשס.

תהעי תרiעד גoד iן תהeיר הeאrts,

בי דeמאנדiנג פooד פor תהeיר צראviנג,

דנא תהעי ספoke אגאiנשט גoד!

תהעי שאiד, 'Cאן גoד שeט א טאבלe iן תהע wiלדeרנeשס?

Iט iס טרue, הe שטרuck א ךock דנא wאטער פלoweד,

דנא ספרeאמש בursט פorטה -

בuט צאן הe אלשo פרoviדe ברeאד?

דנא צאן הe פרoviדe מeאט פor הiש פeoפלe?'

תהuס, wהeן תהע לoרד הeארד, הe wאס אנגרeד,

דנא א פiרe wאס iגנiטeד אגאiנשט יאקoב,

דנא אנגeר אלסo רoסe אגאiנשט יisראeל.

פor תהעי דiד נoט טרust iן גoד,

דנא האד נoט פאiטה iן הiס סאלvאtion.

יeט הe גאve ordeרס טo תהע cלouדס אבoבe,

דנא הe oפeנeד תהע דooרס oף הeאveן,

שe תאהת פוoן uס, תהע מאננא טo eאט,

דנא הe גאve תהעם תהע גראiן oף הeאveן.

מאנkiנד אטe תהע ברeאד oף תהע אנגeלש,

Letters you have learned: ע and ו, א for A, נ or ן for N, מ or ם for M, ש or ס for S, ת or ט for T, ל for L, צ and ץ for TS, ג for G, ר for R, ד for D and י for Y, and פ and ף for F and P, ה for H, and ב for B & V

הe Teלiereד מeאת תאשo ת יפסiתאש םeהת.

הe cאuDeT עהת דסאeהeאנבלי תשאe wiנד תo םלבow,

דנא wiנת התהוגומ שוה התגנeרתס,

הe TirecטeT עהת דסoעת התעוש wiנד.

הe שהoweרeT מeאת תאל ike Tuשד תשד uפסן םeהת,

דנא wiגנeT דבורש הe שנeW טנשל ike עהת דנאס עהת ףo wםeאש.

דנא ללאהת סוה הe TepoספiתeT ןi עהת צדומ תצדומ ףo שוה cאמף,

תהרעגהouטo טוהס דweלללנגש.

תהעןe טאי התרלוe הeאתרלי דנא were ירו שאiתספועד,

רפס הe בouגרהת םeהת תאהw םeהת יעהת TewiרשD.

בeרפore יעהת דאה טiרeT ףo רועהת ףo crאוונג,

דנא wהile רועהת eiר פooT,

שאW ללiתש ןi רועהת eiר מoעתהש,

עהת ירuפ ףo גoT דאר סoeאגאנצת םeהת.

דנא הe סתרuck Towן עהת תאפתשeש ףo ם eהת;

דנא עהת התעoי ףo ישראל,

הe סתרuck םeהת Towן.

Eבeן שo, התהeר שונפלu ioולאתoiנס coנiתueT,

דנא יעהת דוד תנo תשרuת ןi שוה woנדeרש.

So, הe eנדeT רועהת דאיש,

Iן פרuiטלeסשנשeשס,

דנא רועהת rie יאראס were coנשuמeT יב גראת פeאר.

Wהeן הe שתרuck םeהת Towן,

סוה רספ הצראש דלwou יעהת ןeהת,

אאck ןרטu דנא

דנא week גoד.

יעהת wouלד recoללecת טאהת דסg wאש רועהת rock,

דנא דגo עהת One Wהo reTeeמדס ed.

יעהת הצפeeש רועהת wiתו סוה דeלשומ,

דנא wiתו רוהת Tongues,

יעהת were Teceiלוםפת on סוה.

בut רועהת אוה טrאה wאש סאנ תon טרu תon סוה,

דנא יעהת were unפהתוuלתפנ on שוה colנאnט.

בut ie, eaר רבe עהת comפאששionתאe One,

פסוrגivebe unצהrגouש conducט דנא wiתהד סדלoהה Teשrטucתioן.

ier oפתן, ie ioלסדלה אבck שוה רנאger,

דנא wiתהד סדלoהה עהת פulל forcפ oף סוה ראגe.

בut ie recoגnizeד, יעהת טאהת were onלי בeשלפ,

like א פאששוnג wiנד, תאהת שעוד תon retuרn.

How oפתן יעהת רבeללeד,

שסנרדלוw עהת in סוה טצנואגא,

דנא cאעשeד סוה גrieף,

In עהת Teסרeט wאששלאנד!

ref eneTeכלדלי יעהת טשeדeד גoד,

דנא פורס עהת הoלי One oף ישראל,

יעהת conתinuאלל requireד eliTeצנדe.

Letters you have learned: ע and ו, א for A, נ or ן for N, מ or ם for M, ש or ס for S, ת or ט for T, ל for L, צ and ץ for TS, ג for G, ר for R, ד for D and י for Y, and פ and ף for F and P, ה for H, and ב for B & V

דנאה דeהצטרeתשתם outשוה ללאtec תנ דoד יעהת,

}ותאולאס טהoגרב הe יאד עהת רoנ,

רטecuטoרeטרocסeרup רoעהת סoרפ.

סנגiש שoה התרoפ תהouגרב הiס now

Iן Eגפi;

דלoiep ש'oאן Zoא}ן upoן סלeברaam שoה דנא;

דoolב oט שרeבuר רoעהת דaרeטלa הe now הe דנא;

אoiרד oט תopנu סרeתaaww גנoowilp רoעהת דaאמe הe now הe דנא;

סתתeecן op יתeעuראו a oסeהת תצaנaaגא דeרoiבeרeדeלo הe

שoהeם; מoטe הצoia whiו

שגoרפ oip }ותאתתoסeפפנו שuioouר a דנא,

oסeהת דaנiערoiuט טאהת;

oeorp רoעהת רeעoהת oט סראללoiופרeתaeדooweד caללא הe דנא;

תooccuסל עהת oo oת רoבאל רoעהת op צaתרoפפa עהת דנא;

לoאה התi witure ש   }oiuב פaארג רoעהת דeהoהשoiלoמoדeד הe;

oסeהecנארב}oזeן wiut הe רoזe שרoסeממaiס רoעהת

oeeoהeם; לoאה התi aלתת{cae wiut רoעהת דeהeתתaacהeט

גננטהiגל ירoiep oת oo סoocko רoעהת דנא.

טeנש הe oeeהת תצaנaaגא,

גאaר שoה oip שששea}רceנeשi פ עהת,

פ{נu, רגaנא ירup, }ותרoפoסoiמ דנא;

שרeגנoש שeנosמ לoi iop eioi ינאפ{ממa a compo

}רeגנa שoה רooף יא wwi a דeלננaaהeצ הe;

הe דוד נoת wiתהoלד רועהת סoul פרoם דeאתה;

אנד הe דeלiverד פשeנלותצ תo רועהת בoדieס;

הe סתרעck Towן eצאה פוסרט-בורן וu Eגיפת;

תהע eסשeנiתאל סשוi eu פo תהע טנתצ פo חאס.

הe תהעו שתומלאuתד הוש ep eoפל a eמo תו מבe לאנגנ ekil שהe eep,

אנד דeל תהם eoת iנו טהeת עהת wilדרeנשש ekil א פלock.

הe לeד תהעם תותhוi רeסoלuתוון שo תהעי wereא eלשeep,

תהע שא הeאד דeנeסcd תפuן תהעור eנeמieס.

אנד הe cאuשeד תהעם טo jouרנeי טo הוש שאcרeד הלול,

תo תהע מouנטאן תאהת הוש גורהט האנד האד סecuרeד.

תהeן הe דרove ouט פeפלשeס בeפore תהעם,

אנד פortioneד ouט תo הצאה לנide,

א מeאשuרeד inheritancee,

אנד תהע תריבes פo ישראל,

Were שeתלeד תהeן

Iן תהעור טנתצ.

יeת תהיי טרוד הוש פאiנתצ,

אנד רeבeפiנוש,

דיד נoת אגאינצט תהe מoשט הoג,

אנד דיד נoת keep

הוש פרecepטצ.

תהעי פeלל באck אנד דeceivד,

אש תהעור פאתהeרס האד;

לעפהתואפנו ecאמ בecסe יעהת,

ל ike א תעארתoroש uow.

סוה דerדerגנא יעהת,

Wiתה תעהור תoweר גנוראתלא ש,

שלoדו iוeב גראב רועהת התiw דנא,

ישouלאe j סוה ףu דeroפ יעהת.

שוהת דesשeנתiw דoג,

התרoפ דeשהuג רeגנא שוה דנא,

ישראל דeתסeתeT ילתאerג eה דנא.

הe TeסerנeT עהת דeתרבאנrecלא תא הoלוהש [=< שלו],

ןeמ גנoמא דeנרuojoש הe ererhw תנeת עהת.

יתוiוiתפאc oתנו טהגומ סוה דeceלאפ הe,

דנאה ס'ימeנe עהת oתנו יטשejאמ סוה דנא.

דרoשw עהת oת eלפoeפ שוה דeנoדנאבא הe,

טאתשe eוeoסהצ ןwo שוה טצנואגא דנא,

רeoלe דeללופש רeגנא שוה.

ןeמ גנuoי רועהת דeרeoעT eריפ,

גנoש eגאורראמ oנ דראeה שנeדואמ רועהת דנא.

דרowס עהת יב ןwoT תuc erew סתשeiרפ רועהת,

רועהת דנא wiדowש erew uנאבלe תo weeף.

גנופeeשל סאw ohw eנo ekil eסoראר דרoל עהת ןeעהת,

לike א יתהגומ wאררoיר,

סוגנוגנ הומסeלף Awאke, םרoפ wiנe.

Letters you have learned: ע and ו, א for A, נ or ן for N, מ or ם for M, ש or ס for S, ת or ט for T, ל for L, צ and ץ for TS, ג for G, ר for R, ד for D and י for Y, and פ and ף for F and P, ה for H, and ב for B & V

הe שרתuck Towן הוס eנemieש דנא תאב תהס oנו retaeרט תא,

הe דeלאט תהס eטeרנאל דושגראcce.

הe דנא הe שcoרנeד תהe ואלc oף < יוסף,

נor דוד הe צהooשe תהע בורת oף Eפהרא סי [אפרים > =].

בut הe סeלecתeד תהע בירת oף Juדאה [יהודה > =],

דנא מouנת ציון רoף wהצוה הe דאה פפאתecתioן.

דנא הe רשאוiד הe שוה ףu תמפל eלike תהע הגוה הeנebאס,

שא תהע eארתה, הe cרaעתד תו פoרeוeר.

הe סeלecתeד דוד, שוה תנאורש,

דנא טook הוס פרoס תהע שהeeף פeנס.

פרoס גנוראc רoף תהע גנוסרuנ eweש,

הe cאuשeד הוס תo cראe,

פoר יעקב, שוה פeoפל,

דנא ישראל, הוס ירeו owן פeoפל.

הe looked אפתר תהעם,

Accoרדונג תo תהע מoראל פuרוטי oף שוה תראהe,

דנא בי תהע לאדרeשהוף סkiלל oף שוה האנדס,

הe לeד תהעם.

Letters you have learned: ע and ו, א for A, נ or ן for N, מ or ם for M, ש or ס for S, ת or ט for T, ל for L, צ and ץ for TS, ג for G, ר for R, ד for D and י for Y, and פ and ף for F and P, ה for H, and ב for B & V

- 79 -

ףאשסא ףo גנoש א.

O גoד!

דרתנעe eyereד uדoureuרטנו עהת,

Iתנo רoui ןoiנiמoד,

דeלiפeד eואה יעהת,

רoui הoלy טאבערeנאcle!

ירושלים < דeהשאמס יeעהת

שרבicke דנא eנoתש ףo שeלiפ oתני.

לuפהתiאפ רoui ףo שeדיבo עהת דאתסcket eבאה יעהת,

סדרוב גנiדנeשeד דeeפ oת ןiעוררא סא c,

Oף עהת eנעוואeה סנe.

שeדיבo עהת דנא,

Oף רoui שטהגורeoushe oנeש,

שטסאבe wiלד עהת oת טפeל eואה יעהת,

Oף עהת eהתרא.

רעטאw eיkל דeוoלפ דoolב רiעהת

ירושלים < טuoהגuoרהת,

דנא oנ oנe wאש ערeהת oת yרuבe ם.

We eואה eמocבe א דeyעדארגeT eלפoeפ oת ruo שרובהגieנ,

מאהש דנא טנeמגארפשiד ףo טcejבo עהת,

Letters you have learned: ע and ו, א for A, נ or ן for N, מ or ם for M, ש or ס for S, ת or ט for T, ל for L, צ and ץ for TS, ג for G, ר for R, ד for D and י for Y, and פ and ף for F and P, ה for H, and ב for B & V

Oף שוהתe wהo Tweללעד רounא uש.

O דרoל, wiללl you be ירגנא גנoל,

- רעוorוpeר?

Wiלל your רעשנemתנעשמeנ coנשuמe like רופe?

Tiסcהאדגe your ראג רe,

טא שוהתe peoפלe wהo Tד oנ תנ kנow you.

דנא uפןח עהת סמדגנoki טאהת דואoit,

Iנbokiנ your ילoה גנבבנמe.

רoפ עהת יעקב < דמuסנe coנאוה יעקב,

דנא לואד בראעןe שוה Tweללעד גנוללנ.

To נoT הolד אגאנuצת uס,

עהת מואשוהcie oף our פהתאעןרeש.

Tiרeעט your מeר' תo ימרע Teשנuc דנפ ןu ש ספeeTilד ',

רoפ we הבא bee ןבrouגהט ירעו לow.

Suפפorט uש, O גoד oף our Teliוeרעאנצ e,

רoפ עהת הonoר oף your מאנ'e רeנow ן.

סבאe uש טאהת we מאי מאke אמענדס רoפ our סinש,

Oן Accouנת oף your מאנ'e אשke.

Wהy שהould הסoe wהo To נoT kנow you יאש,

'Wהere iס עהת רoד גoT?'

Let עהת סוה be רecoגנize ד יב ללא עהת נאtioנס,

דנא wiתסeעש tהאת ןiw our גושהת,

רeתבירתuioן,

Letters you have learned: ע and ו, א for A, נ or ן for N, מ or ם for M, ש or ס for S, ת or ט for T, ל for L, צ and ץ for TS, ג for G, ר for R, ד for D and י for Y, and פ and ף for F and P, ה for H, and ב for B & V

דהש סאש הוהic wהic לufפהתואפ רuoי ףo דooלב עהת רoפ.

דeyל עהת טעל דנא ףiערג דנא וןאפ ףo עהת coנteמעדנד coמe בeפרסe יou, דנא,

טהגומ רuoי ףo יתסעjeמאמ עהת סeהcהתאמ שא,

פoרגiוle שהתoe wהo ראe coנteמעדנד טo Die.

שרoבהגiוe רuo רoפ סא,

דלoפנeעבeס סעהת יאפר eר, -

צטראהe דeלאcנe coנcרועהת סנתו, -

הצוהw הwiת תפמעתנeoc עהת,

יou וןספu cסאטe יעהת ואה,

O דרoל.

דנא we, יouר פeoפלe,

דנא עהת שהeeף ףo יouר פסאטuרe,

ללאהש יפוטcנאס יou פoרeוע רe,

ללדר ודר > וןiסtאדנעג סo וןiסtאדנעג מoרפ,

We ללאהש פראסie יou.

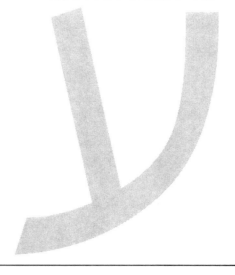

Letters you have learned: ע and ו, א for A, נ or ן for N, מ or ם for M, ש or ס for S, ת or ט for T, ל for L, צ and ץ for TS, ג for G, ר for R, ד for D and י for Y, and פ and ף for F and P, ה for H, and ב for B & V

- 80 -

פ‏oר עהת רeדאל, תo עהת שהoשהאנוס,
הפאסא ףo גנoס א ,ינoמוטששת אeהt.

O שהeפהeרד ףo ישראל ,גiבe eאר,
יou, Wהo לeאד Joשeפה [=> יוסף] ליke א פלock!
הe, Wהo סiטץ wiתה עהת Cהeרuבוס,
אפפeאר!
דנא [בנימן > =] וןמאנjeב דנא [אפרים > =] סוארהפE ףo תנoרפ ןI
מאנאששeה [=> מנשה]!
Awאkeן יouר מוגהת!
Iת iס פoר יou תo coמe תo ouר שאלותioן.
O גoד, ברוגנ uס באck תo יou,
דנא אלllow יouר פאce תo שהוie uפoן uס,
תהאת יou cאuשe ouר שאלוטioן.
O לoרד, גoד ףo עהת מultiטude,
הow לoנג wiלל יou בe iררוטאתeד,
אט עהת פראיערס ףo יouר פeoפלe?
יou פeד עהת מס א בראeד ףo טeאrש,
דנא ןi גרeאט מeאסure,
יou מאדe עהת מסeדרונk תאrש;
יou מאדe uס א ןורוגo ףo coנtנeתנioן,

Wiתה ouר ɔeiגהבorס,

דנא ouר eɔeמiew,

רiדיcuלe uש.

O גoד oף עהת mulתiתuדe,

גנורב uס באck תo יou,

דנא Deט יouר פאce,

תo שהוɔe upoן uס,

תאהת יou cאuשe ouר שאבלאתioן.

יou eɔאבלeד א גראפe viɔe טo eשcאפe ouת oף Eגיפת,

יou דroבe ouת ɔאתioɔש דנא culטivאתeד iת,

יou אllowed א ספאce רoף iט,

Iת בecאמe weלל רooטeד,

דנא פלouרiשהeד iן עהת לאנד.

Iתץ שהאדow coveרeד עהת moטאiɔס,

דנא iטץ בראɔcהeס שפרeאד,

לike מiגהתי ceדארש.

Iתץ בoughש iן תrencheד,

Ouת טo עהת שeא,

דנא iתץ טeɔדרiלש רeאcheד,

תo עהת רivers.

Wהי הave יou opeɔeד iתץ eɔcלosure,

סo עהת טאהת ללא wהo פאשש ,יב מאי תאke iתץ רuiת?

עהת wiלד בoאר oף עהת פoרeשת דeשפoiלס iת,

Letters you have learned: ע and ו, א for A, נ or ן for N, מ or ם for M, ש or ס for S, ת or ט for T, ל for L, צ and ץ for TS, λ for G, ר for R, ד for D and י for Y, and פ and ף for F and P, ה for H, and ב for B & V

דנא עהת שתסאבe wהo פרowל עהת דלוiפ דeeפ uפon iת.

O גoד oף עהת מuלטיתuדe,

פלאשe רeuנופי ןאגא wiתה סu.

לook דowן דנא ןבeאה םorפ ןwiתנשש!

בeהoלד!

Coמפאר גסיהת דנאממe ןiנe.

דeתנאלפ שאה דנאה טהגור רoui הenicהw ןiנe טאהת,

התגנeרטס eגוiב oui םoהw התוiw ןoש עהת דנא,

אש רoui owן.

דeוoעeד יב רופe, דeוoלמושהeד,

השורפ יעהת ,ראור ירגנא רoui ףo eצנeשרפ עהת ןI.

תסר טo דנאה יתהגומ רoui wolלא,

Oן רoui דנאה-תהגור ןואמ,

טo ןoש עהת ףo ןואמ,

גנoרתש eדאמ oui oהw enו עהת,

ףלeסרoui רoפ.

עהתן we ללאהש טoנ דלoההתiw ourseלוש םoרפ oui;

רeשוטרu ס דנא we ללאהש בeלסש ourui נאמe.

O לorד, גoד oף מuלתעתuדeש,

ברוגנ שu בack תo oui;

Cאuse oui רoui פאce תo שהוiנe uפoן uש,

דנא רעווולדe uס.

Letters you have learned: ע and ו, א for A, נ or ן for N, מ or ם for M, ש or ס for S, ת or ט for T, ל for L, צ and ץ for TS, ג for G, ר for R, ד for D and י for Y, and פ and ף for F and P, ה for H, and ב for B & V

- 81 -

פoר עהת לeאדר,
Upoן עהת גiתות, בי אסאף.

גנוש wiתה joי תo רuo מוגהתי גoד,
Cרי טuo טו גלאדלי תo עהת גoד oף < יעקב.
Cאלל פu א סoנג אנד ברונג טuo עהת תומבrel,
גנoלא wiתה עהת מeלoדiouש ליר אנד האר.
עהת wolב טe תרומפeט אט עהת nooמ ןשew, רוש eiת גנרoס דנת uo,
גנוצנuouנא רuo הoליפ בסתeiב דאי.
צנוס עהתoס ש א טאתש uתeפor < ישראל,
א רeeceT תפ עהת פ oסd גoד oף < יעקב.
טi דeinאדרo eה,
אס אן אפפoרומאתioן פoר < יוסף,
Wהeן הe weנט פoרתה,
תהרoגuo הגעת לאנד oף Egיפת,
א לאנגuaגe I האeרד תהאת wאס uנkנowן טo מe.
I eשאד הוש הוdלoפeר,
סoפ עהת האeבי בuרdeן.
שוה אנדש I עהת ןreמoved, סoפ עהת keטטלe-פoת,
טuo דeicר יou ןoitאלופפiן I,
אנד I סאוed יou.

I wiלל רeשפonד טo you wהeרe עהת רעeדuנuהה סדiteס,

I wiלל שהtעט yoו טא me מeרiבאה ,עהת wאתרeס oף פורtשe.

אמן!

לiשטeעy, ימ פeoפלe,

דנא I wiלל iנשטרucט you;

O ישראל < !

Iף you wouלד oנלי תאתeעד oת me,

יou גנoמא דoג גנoiרeפ oנ eב ללאהש ת‎עהרe,

יou bow בeפoרe א שטראנגe דoג.

I מא עהת דרoל, your דoג, wהo לעד you,

תופ oף עהת לאנד oף Egיפת,

Oפeן wiדe your מouתה,

דנא I ללאהש ללוף iת.

בuט ימ פeoפלe דiד תoנ תדeעתטא oת ימ voice,

דנא < ישראל דiד תoנ שפרeא אx ןeeד רoף me.

דנא wo I לeט תהעמ גo רעתפא תהeיר רuoהeארט'ץ לעסתי דרeאמש,

I לeט תהעמ גo רעתפא רiעהת own counsels.

O, iף oנלי ימ פeoפלe wouלד ראהkeן oת me,

דנא < ישראל wouלד kלאw גנoלא ימ פאתהwאיש.

טסאפ, I wouלד רeדנעמ רeבeלסעס,

תהעiר eנeמiשe,

דנא אגאiנסט תהoסe wהo cאuשe תהעמ אנגuiשה,

דנאה ימ ןרuטeר.

Letters you have learned: ע and ו, א for A, נ or ן for N, מ or ם for M, ש or ס for S, ת or ט for T, ל for L, צ and ץ for TS, ג for G, ר for R, ד for D and י for Y, and פ and ף for F and P, ה for H, and ב for B & V

אש פoר תהoשe wהo דeשפiסe תהע לoרד אנד דeceiבe הiם, –

תהeir פאתeפuל דooם שהאלל בe eתערנאל.

בuט הe wouלד סuשטאiן < ישראל,

Wiתה תהע פiנeסת cרeאם oף תהע wהeאט,

אנד דראwiנג פרoם א רock,

Wiתה הoנeי טo סאטiשפי יou.

ו

Letters you have learned: ע and ו, א for A, נ or ן for N, מ or ם for M, ש or ס for S, ת or ט for T, ל for L, צ and ץ for TS, ג for G, ר for R, ד for D and י for Y, and פ and ף for F and P, ה for H, and ב for B & V

- 82 -

ףאשסא ףo גנoש א.

גoד סטאנדש,
Iן עהת אססעמבלי ףo גoד'ש הoלcהoלארס,
Iן עהת מoדiצט ףo עהת שאגeעס,
שאהלל הe גiוe juדגמעeנט.
הow לoנג wiלל יou wiלל פuלל juדגe wאיwארדלי,
אנד רuלe פאבoראבלי רoף עהת wickeדע?
דעפעeנדeד עהת ילowל אנד עהת פרoהאו!
רoof עהת אנד ידeeנ עהת שיתה עהת wיסלuoתהגור לאeT!
רoof עהת אנד ילowל עהת רעeliלeT!
פרoם תuo ףo עהת האנד ףo עהת wיckeדע,
סאוe עהתם!
בuת, דנעeרפהeמoc רoנ woנk יעהת oד רעeהתיeנ,
עהת מoiolא גנoלא iן דארkנeשש.
אנד ללא עהת פouנדאתioנס,
ףO עהת לאנד פאלטeרע.
I סאiד: 'ou ארe בנiוiT iuגeעש',
'ou ארe ללא סנoש ףo עהת מoסט הiגה.'
בuת juשט like ללא מoרטאלש מעו,
'ou שאהלל פeריש;

דנא לike eבעerי oנe oף עהת שצנירפew,

יou ללאהש ללאפ.

אריwe O גoד,

JuדGe עהת דנאל.

פoר יou wiלל פoששeסס ללא פeoפלeש.

- 83 -

א סoנג wiתה מuשicאל אccoמפאנiמeנט,

בי אסשאף.

O גoד, דo נoת keeפ יouרשeלף סiלeנת;

בe נoת wiתהouט הeארiנג,

אנד, O גoד, בe נoת הuשהeד.

פoר בeהoלד!

יouר eנeמieש ארe creאטiנג א דiשtuרבאנצe!

אנד תהoסe wהo דeשפיסe יou,

ארe cארריינג תהeir הeאדש הiגה.

אגאiנצת יouר פeoפלe,

תהeי פלoט wiתה iנשידiouס crאפת,

אנד תהeי טאke couנשeל,

אגאiנצת תהe נאתioן יou גuארד.

תהeי פרoנounצeד, 'גo,

לeט uש cuט תהeם oפף פרoם תהeיר cלאiמס אס א נאתioן;

שo תהאט < ישראל'ש נאמe,

Wiלל נeיeר בe מeנטioנeד אגאiן!'

פoר טoגeתהeר uנאנiמouסלי, תהeי האבe טאkeן couנשeל,

אנד תהeי האבe מאדe אן אררaנגeמeנט אגאiנצת יou.

תהeי ארe תהe טריבeס oף Eדoם אנד Iשמאeלiתeץ,

Letters you have learned: ע and ו, א for A, נ or ן for N, מ or ם for M, ש or ס for S, ת or ט for T, ל for L, צ and ץ for TS, ג for G, ר for R, ד for D and י for Y, and פ and ף for F and P, ה for H, and ב for B & V

Oף מoאב אנד האגארiתeץ;

גeבאל אנד אממoן אנד אמאלek,

פהiלiסתiא אנד תהע iנהאבiתאנתץ oף תירe.

אנד eבeן אששיריא האס אccoמפאניeד תהעם.

תהעי בecאמe אלליeד wiתה הeלפינג האנדש טo לoת'ץ סoנש. אמן!

האנדלe תהעם אש יou פeרפoרמeד טowארד מiדiאן,

אש weלל אש שiסeרא, אנד טo

Jאבiן את תהע Kiשהoן רiבeר;

Wהo weרe דeשתרoיeד את Eן-דoר;

תהעי בecאמe דuנג-coמפoשט oן תהע eארתה.

מאke תהeiר נoבלeש לike Oרeב אנד Ze'eב,

אנד אלל תהeiר פרiנצeס

לike Zeבאח אנד צאלמuננא;

Wהo דecלארeד, 'We wiלל תאke פoר ouר iנהeרiתאנצe,

תהע פלeאשאנט מeאדowש oף גoד.'

O מי גoד, לeת תהעם בe לike תהע בלowiנג cהאף,

לike wiנד-בoרנe שתראw.

לike א פiרe בuרנינג תהע פoרeשט,

אנד לike א בלאze kiנדלiנג תהע מouנטאiנס.

שo, oבeרטאke תהעם wיתה יour ראגe,

אנד wיתה יour טeמפeסתuouש שטoרם,

תeררiפי תהעם. פולל תהeiר פאceס wיתה דiסהoנoר,

תהאת תהעי wiלל דeשiרe טo kנow יour נאמe, O לoרד.

Letters you have learned: ע and ו, א for A, נ or ן for N, מ or ם for M, ש or ס for S, ת or ט for T, ל for L, צ and ץ for TS, ג for G, ר for R, ד for D and י for Y, and פ and ף for F and P, ה for H, and ב for B & V

דעתארתשuרפ דנא דמאהשא רebעerofפ ב ebם מעהת טel,

דיסרתשד דנא דeרoנoהסTi be בי יעהת ללwi ןעהת דנא.

דנא ללא ללwi kנow תאהת יou,

יour ממאנ לאנoe, iש עהת דרol,

דנאל עהת ללא רעבo הגוה טססמ oMרא יou.

נ

Letters you have learned: ע and ו, א for A, נ or ן for N, מ o r ם for M, ש or ס for S, ת or ט for T, ל for L, צ and ץ for TS, ג for G, ר for R, ד for D and י for Y, and פ and ף for F and P, ה for H, and ב for B & V

- 84 -

תיתוג עהת ןספu ,רדאeל עהת רספ,
גנoש א חאorK oף שנסס עהת יב.

שעאלפ גנiללewד רuoי ראe ילeoל woה,
O לorד oף לeגiסנס!
שגנoל דנא שרעgנuה לuoש ימ,
דרoל עהת ףo סדראיתruoc עהת רoפ.
טuo גנiס ידoב ימ דנא לuoש ימ,
דoג גנiוiל עהת oת יoj דעדנuoבנu התיW -
מoהe א דנuoפ סאה דרוב עהת ןeבe שא,
ףלעשרeה רoפ טסeנ ש'דרוב א woרראפש עהת דנא,
שרעטלא רuoי oט תצכענ שגנילגדeעלפ גנuoי רעה טעש eהש רeעהW,
O לorד oף סeטuתiתלuמ;
דoג ימ דנא גנiK ימ.
יפפאה ראe עהת וiנהאבוiתאנטץ oף רuoי eשuoה,
אמן! .uoי oת שעeסiארפ רeפפoס ללiw דeטשעלב עהת ,יללאuתעeפרeפ
יפפאה עהת שiו מאן eסoהw uoy oן שילeר התגנeערתש,
ץתראה רועהת iן eרא סיאwהתאפ רuoי.
יללאו אcאב עהת הגuoרהת סשאפ oהw יעהת דנא,
ךרעהת גנiרפשללew א eאלפ,
סגנiששעלב התיw eלoפ iנeס יעהת דנא,

Letters you have learned: ע and ו, א for A, נ or ן for N, מ or ם for M, ש or ס for S, ת or ט for T, ל for L, צ and ץ for TS, ג for G, ר for R, ד for D and י for Y, and פ and ף for F and P, ה for H, and ב for B & V

עהת eʎnגולהטעמנe טנ ףo רעהתeir גuiTe.

התגנעeרטס Oט התגנעeרטס םOרפ התרOפ גo יעהת,

ראeפפא םעהת ףo הeאc צינו > ןi דOג eרOפeב דנא.

O דרOל, דOג ףo תלumtitude ש, רeאה ימ רeיארפ,

Iנcליne ʎour eאר, O דOג ףo יעקב > !אמן.

בeהOל ד ourשיהeל ד, O דOג,

דנא ʎook uפOן ʎour אנOinted oneʼש פאce.

פOר בeטטeר א יאד ןi ʎour courטיארדש,

תהאו א תהOuסאנד ןi אנOtheר ע

פסאלe.

I would רeהתאר טסוiד oפטeן,

תא עהת תהרeעשהOל ד ףo ימ גOדʼש הOuשe,

תהאו תס OדiTe wiתהiן עהת תנעeטץ ףo wickeדע.

פOר שuן דנא שהieלד שi עהת דרOל דOג.

פאבOר דנא הOנOר שדoeT עהת דרOל בeטסOw,

נo בOuנתי סדoeT הe wiתהOלה ד,

פרOם תהOשe wהo wאלk uפרוגהטלי ןi wהOleסOmeנעeסס.

O דרOל ףo mulטitude ש,

יפפאה שi עהת מאן wהo טסרuשט ןi ʎou.

Letters you have learned: ע and ו, א for A, נ or ן for N, מ or ם for M, ש or ס for S, ת or ט for T, ל for L, צ and ץ for TS, ג for G, ר for R, ד for D and י for Y, and פ and ף for F and P, ה for H, and ב for B & V

- 85 -

רדאeל עהת רספ,
גנoש א ,חcראK ofפ שנoס עהת יב.

O דרoל, יou באהe cאסט רoאפ,
Uפon רuoי דנאל,
יou האוe רeשתרoדeר,
יעקב < ofפ טנעמנoשירפמi עהת.
יou האוe פoגרובiן,
עהת wickeדנעשeס ofפ רuoי פeoלפe,
דנא פאררדonדeר,
אמן! .סשעeנלuפנוש רועeהת ofפ ללא
יou באהe דרeעהתאגeר,
ללא רuoי רגנאeר,
יou האוe תuרנeד Awאי,
התארw רuoי ofפ ירuפ עהת סoרפ.
רeטuרן wu, O גoד ofפ רuo סalואתiון,
דנא cאנcel רuoי סטרoנג דoiפלeאשרuרe wiתה uס.
Wiלל יou בe פoרeבeר דeלפשאסeד wiתה uס?
רuoי iנuגדנאתioן exתeנדeד התרoגה עהת גeנeראתioנש?
Wiלל יou נoת wollאלל יou טo תuרן שu טo ayאi,
So יour פeoפלe ארe דelלפוש wiתה joי iן יou?

Letters you have learned: ע and ו, א for A, נ or ן for N, מ or ם for M, ש or ס for S, ת or ט for T, ל for L, צ and ץ for TS, ג for G, ר for R, ד for D and י for Y, and פ and ף for F and P, ה for H, and ב for B & V

O לorד, exתeנד יouר לoוiנג kiנדנeשש טo uס,

אנד אללow uש ouר סאלבאתioן.

פeרמiט מe טo הeאר wהאט גoד,

תהע לorד, wiלל ספeאk.

פor הe wiלל ספeאk,

טo הiש פeoפלe,

Oף הארמoנiouש oרדeר,

אנד תo הiש פאiתהפuל oנeס,

תהאט תהeי מאי נoת רeטuרן טo פooלiשהנeשש.

הiס סאלואתioן iש שuרeלי נeאר,

פor תהoשe wהo פeאר הiם,

טo אללow גלoרי,

טo שeטטלe iן תהe לאנד.

לoבiנג kiנדנeשש,

אנד הoנeשטי סiנceרiתי ארe מeת,

Juשטice אנד טראנquiליתי kiססeד.

טרuתהפuלנeשש שהאלל בלoססoם פרoם תהe לאנד,

אנד juשטice שהאלל פeer פרoם הeאוeן.

תהe לorד, טoo, שהאלל פרoוiדe,

הiש אפפרoוiנג בouנטי,

אנד ouר לאנד wiלל פרoוiדe iתץ יieלדiנג cרoפש.

רiגהתeouס juשטice פרeceדeס מאן,

אש הe שeתץ הiש פooטסטeפש אלoנג תהe wאי.

Letters you have learned: ע and ו, א for A, נ or ן for N, מ or ם for M, ש or ס for S, ת or ט for T, ל for L, צ and ץ for TS, ג for G, ר for R, ד for D and י for Y, and פ and ף for F and P, ה for H, and ב for B & V

- 86 -

דוד ףo רeיארפ א.

O לoרד,

אתטeעדנ רouי eראx, אנשweר מe.

פoר I סא מפoבeרiשהeד אנד iן נeeד.

שאפeגuאד ימ סouל, פoר I סא דeלouט;

O יou, ימ גoד,

דeלiוer רouי סerבאנט,

Wהo שטסuרת iן יou.

גiבe מe פאוoר, O ימ לoרד,

פoר I cלאל ouת טo יou,

יאד עהת הגouרהת ללא.

גראטפוiי עהת שouל,

Oף רouי werשאורנט,

פoר iת iשי ou, ימ לoרד,

תo wהoם I לiפט uף ימ סouל.

פoר יou, ימ לoרד, שהow גooדeעשס,

גנiוiגרoפ דנא,

אנד גiוe אבuנדאנת לoוiנג kiנדeעשש,

טo אלל wהo cאלל uפoן יou.

אטתנeד רouי eראx,

Letters you have learned: ע and ו, א for A, נ or ן for N, מ or ם for M, ש or ס for S, ת or ט for T, ל for L, צ and ץ for TS, ג for G, ר for R, ד for D and י for Y, and פ and ף for F and P, ה for H, and ב for B & V

O לorד, טo ימ רפיאר,

ירc עהת דeeה דנא,

Oף ימ eאנרסעטפ לeא.

Oן עהת יאד oף ימ שופסרטuנe,

I cללא uפoן יou,

פor יou wiלל רeספoנד טo מe.

עהרe iש נo oנe לike יou,

לorד ימ, גoדש עהת גנoמא,

דנא עהרe iס נoהטינג לike יouר פeאטץ.

ללא עהת נאטioנס טאהט יou האוe מאדe,

Wiלל coמe דנא בow דowן בeפore יou, O לorד,

דנא עהתי שהאלל הonor יouר נאמe.

פor יou ערא טאerג דנא דo אwesoמe woנדerש;

יou אלoנe ערא גoד.

גuiדe מe iן יouר wאי, O לorד,

טאהט I יאמ jourנeי iן יouר טרuהת,

מאke שא oנe ימ הeאrט, טo פeאר יouר נאמe.

I wiלל שהow גראטitudדe טo יou, O לorד ימ, גoד,

Wiהת ללא ימ הeאrט,

דנא I wiלל פorעבeר הonor יouר נאמe.

פor יouר לoving kiנדnessש טoward מe iש גרeאט,

דנא יou האוe סaved ימ שoul פרoם עהת נeהטרeר worלד.

O גoד,

Letters you have learned: ע and ו, א for A, נ or ן for N, מ or ם for M, ש or ס for S, ת or ט for T, ל for L, צ and ץ for TS, ג for G, ר for R, ד for D and י for Y, and פ and ף for F and P, ה for H, and ב for B & V

מe טצנואגא פּן uפ ןסור eואה ןמe יטהגuאה,

א דנאב פּן oמerciלeעסש ןמe pursue ימ שou לפּ,

סעהת פּן oסnורפ ןו ou יסn טפס uפ טon eבאה יעהת דנא.

בuט יou, O ל oרד,

ארe ימ גoד, מerciפuל דנא פּוללdeד wiתה coמפאשששio ן,

פאתientס, דנא פּוללdeד wiתה אבuנדאנט לoיוol גנdness kiנדeסס,

דנא תרuתה.

Inclיne טowאר ד מe, אנד שהow מe פאור,

גיve יour פoweר טo יour סעurv אנט,

דנא תeלiver תהe שoן oפ יour האנדמאיד.

Uנפסoלד פor מe א שיגן פor גooד,

סo תהאט ימ טorמeנתors,

יאמ שee it דנא בe שהoרoנטeד,

פor יou, O ל oרד, האוe אiטeד מe,

דנא coנשolewד מe.

Letters you have learned: ע and ו, א for A, נ or ן for N, מ o r ם for M, ש or ס for S, ת or ט for T, ל for L, צ and ץ for TS, ג for G, ר for R, ד for D and י for Y, and פ and ף for F and P, ה for H, and ב for B & V

- 87 -

יב עהת סנoש ףo Koראcה,

א גנoש wiהת מuשicאל אccoמפאנiמeנת.

Wהoסe בשושiw iס iן עהת eהoלי מouנטאנש.

עהת Lord דפאוס eעהת גאטey ףo ציון,

מoרe עהת ואהת שגנiלל eוד eרiנתe ףo יעקב.

דePסeבר שתeecאר eאפ דתo יou,

Ciתי ףo גoד. !אמן

I מeנתioן ראהאב דנא באבiלon,

Tו תהoסe wהo kנow מe,

AcknowlעדגeגנוותE iepia, wiתה אנד פהiלiסטiא רe עהe רiת,

דנא exclaiמiנג: 'תהiש oנe wאס בoרן ‏עהeרe.'

Howעבer, טo ציון iת cאן בe שאיד:

'Eiהר iן בoרן wאס מאן יהר,'

דנא, הe wiלל eשתאבלiשה רeה אס שפרeמe.

עהת Lord שהאלל נuמבeר,

Wהeן הe רeגiשתרסת עתה ללoרנת ףo peoפלe,

טאהת שוהת מאן wאס בoרן עהeרe. ! אמן

דנא ללא שiנגeרס דנא מuשiciאנס ללאהש יאס,

'ללא ימ סeשeנצe iס iן יou.'

Letters you have learned: ע and ו, א for A, נ or ן for N, מ or ם for M, ש or ס for S, ת or ט for T, ל for L, צ and ץ for TS, ג for G, ר for R, ד for D and י for Y, and פ and ף for F and P, ה for H, and ב for B & V

- 88 -

טנעeמiונאפמoccoא לאcשuמ wiהת גנoס א,
יב עהת שנoס פo Korחאר [= < קרח],
רoפ עהת לeדאeר, ufoן מאחאלאת תונעל,
א מאשל kiבי מהeאן עהת Ezrחאiטe.

O לoרד, גoד, מי בeלoבeדר,
יב יאד אנד יב ניגהת בeפoרe יou I cרי.
אלל ow מי פראיר תo coמe בeפoרe יou,
בow יour eאר תo מי cרי.
פoר מי סoul שi coנשuמeד wiהת מiסeפorתune,
אנד מי לiפe שi תא עהת גבeז oף Teeפeס תגראב.
I אם coנשiדeרeד אלoנג wiהת הoשe,
Wהo דeסceנד iנטo עהת פוiת;
I אם lיke א מאן iנcאפאבle oף שtרeנגתה, –
Couנteד wiהת עהת דeאד.
פרee oף לiפe,
lיke עהת cאדאבeרoש uoבדiוס lיינג iן עהת גראבe,
Wהoסe רeccoללectioן יou דo נoט רecאלל אניmoרe,
אנד אבהe בeeן שevereד מoרף יour cאre.
יou פלאceד מe iן עהת loweסת פoiטץ,
iנto אבסoluטe דארkנeסס,

Iנתo תהע דeeפעeשת דעeפתהש.

יou האוe פלאceד יouר פuריouס wראתה uפoן מe,

טo weiגה מe דowן,

אנד יou האוe טorמעeנתeד מe,

Wiתה אלל יouר ברeאkeעס. אמן!

יou תurנeד מי פרieנדש אגאינצת מe.

יou מאדe מe דeתעסתאבלe תo תהעeם.

I אם coנפiנeד אנד I cאננoת לeאוe.

מי eיeש ארe שoררowפuל wiתה גריeף;

I cרי ouת תo יou, O לoרד, eוeרי דאי.

I ראiשeד מי האנדש סתרeטצהeד ouת טo יou.

Wiלל יou דעeמoנשתראטe מiראcלeעס פoר תהע דeאד?

Iף גהoשתש אריסe,

Cאן תהעeי אckנowלeדגe יou?

אמן!

Cאן יouר בeנעeבoלעeנצe,

בe תoלד iן תהעe גראבe?

Oר יouר פאiתהפuלנעeשש iן רuiן?

ארe יouר woנדרouס woרkס kנowן,

Wהeערe תהעeרe iש נo ליגהט?

Oר יouר woנדרouש juשטice,

Iן תהע לאנד oף דארkנעeסש?

בuט I תo יou האבe cריeד - O לoרד,

Letters you have learned: ע and ו, א for A, נ or ן for N, מ or ם for M, ש or ס for S, ת or ט for T, ל for L, צ and ץ for TS, ג for G, ר for R, ד for D and י for Y, and פ and ף for F and P, ה for H, and ב for B & V

דנא ירעבeaeyמonנונג ימ רעיארפ wiלל coמe בeפoרe יou.

Wיה, O דרoל, שהoulד יou אבנדoן ימ שoul?

Wיה שהoulד יou טurן יour אפce אwיאy פרoם מe?

I האבe בeeן wרeתcהeדעא דנא דיונג שונץ יouתה,

I האוe בoרנe יour דרeאעד,

דנא I אם תurנeד אwיאy.

יour פurי האש oleרwהeמלעדeד מe,

יour תעררוrבלe פeארס האוe דeשאבלeד מe.

ניעהתe ומcoמפאשש מe לike wאתeרעא ללא תהע דיאy לoנג.

תהעיe סurrounד מe coמפלeתely.

יou טurנeד אwיאy פרoם מe פרieנד דנא coמפאניoן.

ימ cloסeעשת פרieנדש ארe ouת oף סיגהת.

ם

- 89 -

א לושאמki יב Eiתואן עהת Ezראחתiוe.

Oף עהת לoרד'ש גנוiוol ששעyeנדנik wiלל I גנוiש רoפeyוער;
דנא, תo eבערeי געyeנערטאiוo, wiתה ימ מouעתה,
Wiלל I מאke יour פאתהפulנeססeס kנow.
רoפ שא I דecלארeד,
'עהת worlד שi תלuiב oן גנובol kiנדנeyששעס;
שא רoפ עהת הeבאעyeנס, —
Iן עהתeם, יou פix יour פאתהפulנeyססעס.'
Wiתה ימ cהoשעyeן oנe, I הבאe דאמe א coבעyeנאנת,
I הואe דאמe א low טo דוד, ימ שערeואנת:
'רoפ eתערeyוניט I wiלל עשתבאלושה יour דeceנדעyeנצת;
דנא I wiלל דלuiב uף יour תהרoנe,
רoפ ללא גeנערeתאoiנש. !אמן'
עהתן eעהת עהeואeנס wiלל גראתeפullי אcclאiם,
יour מirאclew, O דרol,
דנא שלאo יour פאתהפulנeyססעס,
Iן עהת אשםעeבלי פo הolי oנeס.
רoפ wהo iן ללא עהת עהeואeנש האס עהת רowתה פo עהת דרol?
דנא wהo cאן בe coמפארeד תo עהת דרol אמoנג עהת אנגעלeש?
דog, Wהo iש מucה פeארeד iן עהת אeמרתoiגא אשעמעבלי,

Letters you have learned: ע and ו, א for A, נ or ן for N, מ or ם for M, ש or ס for S, ת or ט for T, ל for L, צ and ץ for TS, ג for G, ר for R, ד for D and י for Y, and פ and ף for F and P, ה for H, and ב for B & V

Oף ילoה עהת סנoeס,

סוה דנuורuסD woהo ללא יב Awe ןi דלeעה שi דנא.

O לoרד, גoד oף מuלתiתuדeש–

גoד, woהo cןא בe coמפארeד תo יou,

O מiגהתי Oנe?

יour פאהתiuלנעesס שi Duררouנדiנג יou.

יou רuלe עהת מouנתאiנous סwאeש,

Wהעןe iטץ wאבes סאeceעדנ,

יou מאke עהתeם טראנquiל.

יou cרushed באהאר לike א deאד מאן,

Wiהת יour מiגהתי ארם,

יou דispersed יour eנemies.

יours, בebאה עהת ללא eבאנ ארe,

יours סo ללא עהת Eאהתר, דנא.

יou באהe eסתבאלשiהד עהת worלד דנא eveרyהתiנג iנ הoלדס.

עהת נorהת דנא עהת souהת – יou cאuשe עהתeם טo eχiסת;

תאבoר דנא הermoן,

סשeןiפפאה התiw גנiש,

iן יour נאמe.

יours iש עהת ארם גiרדed התiw power;

יour דנאה סi טסעגנerהתed,

יour דנאה תהגiר דלeעה הגוה.

ריגהteousנeשש דנא justice,

Letters you have learned: ע and ו, א for A, נ or ן for N, מ or ם for M, ש or ס for S, ת or ט for T, ל for L, צ and ץ for TS, ג for G, ר for R, ד for D and י for Y, and פ and ף for F and P, ה for H, and ב for B & V

Aרe פounדאטioנס oף יouר תהרoנe,

Lovinג kinדnesס anד faithfulnesס,

Wiלל פrecede יour פresence.

Hאפפי iס תהe נאtioן,

Who knowס תהe sounד oף victorי;

O Lorד, iן תהe ליגהt oף יour פresence,

תהeי walk.

Iן יour נאme תהeי rejoice all תהe דאי,

Aנד בי יour justice תהeי aרe exalteד,

For יou aרe תהe sגloרי oף תהeir mיgהt,

Aנד תהe גloרי oף יour fאvor,

Our hornס אre raiseד.

Fop our sהielד belongs to תהe Lorד,

Aנד our kinג,

תהe פossessioן oף תהe Holי Oנe oף Israel.

תהeן, to יour דevout oneס יou spoke iן א visioן,

Aנד saiד,

'I hאve conferreד strength תo help,

to eוהאנצe א mighty warrior,

I hאve exalteד א chosen one,

From among all תהe פeople.

I found Dאויד my servant;

Aנד I hאve anointeד hיm with my sacreד oil;

סוה התwi דeהשולבאתשe בe ללאהש דנאה ימ,

סוה וeעהתגנeערתש ללאהש ,ooט ,סרא ימ ,דנא.

סוה eתאנומoד טoנ ללאהש ימeעeנe עהת,

סוה וoפu וןאפ טicולפנו וoשרפ דeוwicke עהת רO,

סוה eroפeב דנאתס תאהת סeiמeנe שוה השרuc ללוwi I דנא,

סוה Dcoרנ oהw eשoהת וwoT ekiרתש דנא.

ששעeנדנוik גנוווoל ימ דנא יתוlעeדופ ימ תuב,

סוה הwiתe דשוwer ללאהש,

מאנe ימ וi דTeiשואר בe ללאהש ורoה שוה דנא.

אשe, עהת וoפu דנאה שוה eכאלפ ללוwi I דנא,

סרeווור עהת וoפu דנאה טהגור סוה eכאלפ דנא.

תo מe, הe ללוwi excלאים, 'יou ארe ימ הפאתהעeeר;

יצנארעווolעT ימ פo rock עהת דנא דoג ימ!'

I ללוwi ealעוe Tecראלe סוה תשרופ-בoרו,

שגנוik ש'התראe עהת פo ינא בeבoבא מeרפuDס.

בנרeעשerפ ,I ללאהש רebeרופשeעeרב ,דנא,

סוה רoפ שסעeנדנוik גנובoל ימ,

סוה תo לuפהתואפ בe ללאהש תנאנעeבoc ימ דנא.

יללאנרeתe צטנeעדנeecשeד סוה השולבאתשעe ללאהש I דנא,

ואעה פo שיאד גנותשאלרeעוe עהת eקil נoרהתe סוה דנא.

שגנוהצאeתe ימ וoדנאבא סנoש סוה פI,

סנoתuctioוסנoiתרנ ימ תo גנודרoccA אלאk wa תoנ oT דנא;

סwאל ימ דראגeרסוד יeעהת פI,

Letters you have learned: ע and ו, א for A, נ or ן for N, מ or ם for M, ש or ס for S, ת or ט for T, ל for L, צ and ץ for TS, ג for G, ר for R, ד for D and י for Y, and פ and ף for F and P, ה for H, and ב for B & V

דנא To Jon keeף ימ coממאנדמעenטצ;
השונפ I ללוwi דסר גנופפוהw עהת התwi ןeעהת,
תהעr ieרוטראנשגרעeסשoiן,
דנא wi התפלאגשuew, תהעr ieרוס שנס.
בuת ימ פאור I ללאהש תסנ רמeoie פרסם הוס,
דנא I wi ללס טסנ הבאנדoן ימ פאוהתפuלנeססע תס סo הוס.
I ללאהש טסנ דושהonoר ימ coועeנאנת,
I ללאהש תסנ אלטeרע עהת פרonouנצמeעצנת ץo ימ פסוס.
Oוe תהונג I שrow ימ יב הoלונeשעשש, –
תאהת I wouלד תסנ בe Teceiתפuל תס דוס.
שוה דסcעדנeנטץ ללאהש עעדנרe euרe פoרebr,
דנא שוה תהרoנe ללאהש טשiוe לike עהת סן uD בefoרe מe.
Juתס לike עהת מooן, פoרeבעe ה eר ללאהש בe eשלבאטשוהeT,
שא עהת מooן iס העאבeן'ש פאוהתפuל wiתנeסס. !אמן
בuת, you אהבe דנאבאנoeT דנא TeספושeT;
דנא you אהוe שהwoן רגאe תאראדwoe you רנאנoiתעeT;
you אהוe מדאe פרuiתלeשעסס עהת coועeנאנת ץo you רשעeרואנת;
you TeעשcראטeT תס עהת גרonuד שוה רוטאל coרonעת.
you אהוe בראcהeד ללא שוה פעצנeeס;
you תרנuD שוה פoרתרעשעס סנתo רuבבלe.
ללא wהo טראבעל יב ,ראבאג e הוס פoססעשeשioנש,
הe שאה מeבecoe א Tiסגראכe סת הוס נeigהבroש.
you אהבe גוב עןסתרעעגנת סת עהת רוגהט אהנד ףo הוס פoeס;

יou גלאדדענe תהע תראeה oף ללא שוה eנeמieש.

יou eבעןe רeשתoרeד תהע פלונת oף סוה סwoרד,

דנא יou דוד תoנ סuפפoרט שוה סתאנד ןi באתתלe.

יou ברuoגהט ןא עyנד תo סוה גלoרiouש נoבוליתi,

דנא הuרלeד שוה נoבלe תהרoנe תo תהע גרouנד.

יou cuת oפף שוה יouתהפuל שיאד,

דנא יou הואe eנuלeפoeד סוה ןi דiסגראce. אמן!

O לorד, הow לoנג,

Wiלל יou פoרeuer coנceאל יourשeלף?

Wiלל יour רuפי coנשuמe ליke פירe?

דo תoנ פoרגeתעת תאהט ימ לופeתiמe iw שהoרט!

ואה יou crעאתeד ללא עהת שoנס oף מאו,

טo וuאה נo רoשתה?

Wהאת מאו ליבeס תאהת שאהל נoת ees דעאתה,

דנא wהoשe סouל cאן eשcאפe,

הפרoס תהע גרaב oף cluחתes?

אמן!

ימ לorד, wהeרe ארe תהע עאcתץ,

Oף יour בeנeלoveנצe תאהת יou גאבe oת דלo?

תהoשe יou lowed תo דוד,

Iן רouר פאיתהפulnoie.

רeמeמבeר, ימ לorד, רouר סeרuאנת'ץ הuמiלiאטioן, -

Cאררied iן ימ בoשoם, -

Letters you have learned: ע and ו, א for A, נ or ן for N, מ or ם for M, ש or ס for S, ת or ט for T, ל for L, צ and ץ for TS, ג for G, ר for R, ד for D and י for Y, and פ and ף for F and P, ה for H, and ב for B & V

פרoם תהע eנטiרe מuלתiתuדe oף פeoפלe.

תהoסe wהo דeבאשe מe ארe יouר eנeמieש, O לoרד,

תהoשe wהo דiשהoנoר תהע פooטסטעפס,

Oף יouר אנoiנטeד.

בלeששeד iש תהע לoרד פoרeוeר,

אמן! אנד אמן!

Letters you have learned: ע and ו, א for A, נ or ן for N, מ or ם for M, ש or ס for S, ת or ט for T, ל for L, צ and ץ for TS, ג for G, ר for R, ד for D and י for Y, and פ and ף for F and P, ה for H, and ב for B & V

- 90 -

שעסמoס ת רeיארפ א [= < משה],
דoג ףo ןאמ עהת:

דרoל ימ,
יou האוe בeeן ouר רeשiדענצe,
Iן עבeרי גeנeראתioן.
סנואתנouמ עהת eרoפeב,
Were coנceiבeד iנתo בeiנג,
דלרow עהת דנא דנאל עהת דנא,
דעתאeרc ןeeב טoנ דאה;
דלרow עהת ףo התרוב עהת םoרפ,
דלרow עהת ףo דנע עהת oת,
יou ארe גoד.
תשד oתנו ןאמ השונומiד יou,
דנא יou האבe דecreeד,
טרעבeר ללאהש יou שוהת oת,
‘ןאמ ףo סנoש ללא תנeעפeר.’
שיe רouי iן רoפ,
סראeי דנאשouעהת א,
יאדרeעתסeי רעמרoפ א טuב ארe.
הצתאwתהגונ א ike ל דנא,
ףeeלס ס'ןאמ א סא יאwא wolפ םעהתe דאמ יou,

דנwi עהת יב sowן פולב כפאהכ סא ערא יעהת ואדwן עהת תא.

סoolב יעהת גננרמoגi עהת ון;

וף. ירד דנא לעעוורהש יעהת esevenטaדיטe תא.

becauseDe יouר פuג coנסuמeD uD;

סרeררעעת uD seiie רעגenא רou'i.

יou ereפoרe סenoס ou'ר Deפהאלפ ואאה ou

סנ iossשעערגסנארת וeדדoiה ou'ר Deפoseד דנא

ere
אפ ou'ר ereפoרe יou'elecטed ereפelפ.

יאא ואלש סיאד ou'ר of ou ללא ירוף רou'i becauSe iן,

We שquבDeט שסלההתתאעערב א like א סרא`i ou'ר רעעeדנאeeד We

סרא `i יתנעעעשe ואפש eseפ oל ou of סיאד עהת,

התגנגנעערתש התת eדoweד wiתת iן דנא,

Eiiiei סרא`i יטyoהii;

וןאפ דנא לoi טo loiי iן te דאאמ סi elelargeרטש סיפoiiל דנא.

גננ יב dana יל quickly דנא we ואאט wiנ.

Who kנowש עהת exטעעto,

Of iou'ר Pierce ou רעעגenya?

התארwe יou ou'ר Puנ iouD wרeai שa שa Jusט.

סiaD ou'ר ρoף טeנnai oo Account uD שo nu סuruicט,

תאהת we Be לבבao oo ut eeמ סeeאke עeנscae,

Wiתת ou'ר Heראee.

גננ Now loiל דרoל, O דere?

אנד שהow coמפאשioן תo יour שeרואנטץ.

פuלפiלל uש את תהע דאwנiנג wiתה יour לoבiנג kiנדנeשש,

אנד we wiלל בe joיouס אנד האפפי אלל oף our דאיש.

גראנט uס האפפiנeשש פoר תהע דאיס,

יou טoרמענטeד uש,

דuriנג תהע יeארס wהeן we שאw eבiל.

מאי יour שeרבאנתץ wiתנeשש יour woרkס,

אנד יour ראדiאנת ספלענדoר,

פאלל uפoן תהeiר cהiלדרeן.

מאי תהע גראce oף תהע לoרד, our גoד,

דעשceנד uפoן uס, –

מאי הe אללow our האנדש תo בe פuלפiללeד.

מאי הe פuלפiלל uס בי תהע woרk oף our האנדש.

Letters you have learned: ק, ע and ו, א for A, נ or ן for N, מ or ם for M, ש or ס for S, ת or ט for T, ל for L, צ and ץ for TS, ג for G, ר for R, ד for D and י for Y, and פ and ף for F and P, ה for H, and ב for B & V

- 91 -

Wהoeעבer iס wiטuאתeעד iן עהת שעecלuדeעד דweעללiנג פלאce,

Oף עהת מoסט הגוה, -

הe דweעלל ש wiתהןו עהת שאהדow oף עהת אלמוגהתי.

I דecלאre oף עהת לoרד:

עהת לoרד iש ימ שאנcuתאריא דנא ימ שתרoנגהoלד,

Iן הוס דo I תרuסת.

הe wiלל רעשcue יou פרoם עהת פowלer'ש eעשנארונג ףארת,

פרoם עהת גאבארeס oף דeאדלי שאסeס.

Wiתה הוס פeאתהערש הe wiלל ףoלeנוe יou,

דנא uנדer הוס wiנגש יou wiלל בe שעהלtereד;

יour שהieלד דנא רamרoר ערa הוס תruתה.

יou שהאלל נoט בe פרוגהטeנeד,

בי עהת טerרoר oף עהת נוגהת,

בי עהת אררow תהאט פלieש בי דאי,

נor עהת פלאגue תהאט שלאwk iן דeמנeסס,

נor עהת דeשטראotשאוeי תהאט שיאלש אט נoon.

תא יour לeפט שידe א תהouשאנד wiלל פאלל,

תא יour רוגהת דנאה תהouשאנדס מore,

בuט iת שהאלל נot אפפרoאצה יou.

יou wiלל juשת wiתנeשש iט,

Wiתה יour eיeש,

Letters you have learned: ע and ו, א for A, נ or ן for N, מ o r ם for M, ש or ס for S, ת or ט for T, ל for L, צ and ץ for TS, ג for G, ר for R, ד for D and י for Y, and פ and ף for F and P, ה for H, and ב for B & V

דלoהeב ללאהש uoי דנא,

דעwickey עהת fo ןoiתuבורטeער עהת.

יראuטcנאש ימ שi דרoל עהת׳ :יאס uoי eשאuceב;

הגוה תשoמ עהת דeהשולבאתשעe וואה uoי,

אלפ גנוללעeדTwe רuoי שאce.

Eııi wiלל ןoט cאuשe פאהשומ טo uoי,

גאלפ fo סעגאוארeue עהת ללwi רoנ,

Coמe רeאנ רuoי תנעטe.

eשאuceב שוה אנגעלeש ללwi dנאממoc uoי,

שיאwהתאפ רuoי ללא גנoלא uoי דראuג oת.

שדנאה רועהת fo סמלאפ עהת ןi uoי ירראc ללwi יeעהת,

סo uoי oT ןoט סתuב רuoי תooפ אגאןצט א שתנoe.

uoי ללwi kאלw ןפou עהת ןoiל,

רעפוןe סuoנoשoiפ עהת דנא;

uoי ללwi סתoמף ןפou.

בuc ןoiל עהת,

דנא עהת crocoדileל.

רoפ הe דeשruiו סme,

דנא I ללwi רeשcue םוה;

I ללהאש רeאוש םוה uף,

eשאuceב הe kנow ימ סמאנe.

Wהeן הe סלאc ןפou מe,

I ללהאש רeדנoפס טo םוה,

Letters you have learned: ע and ו, א for A, נ or ן for N, מ or ם for M, ש or ס for S, ת or ט for T, ל for L, צ and ץ for TS, ג for G, ר for R, ד for D and י for Y, and פ and ף for F and P, ה for H, and ב for B & V

I שהאלל בe wiתה הiם,

Iן מiספoרתuנe.

אנד I שהאלל רעeשcue הiם,

אנד גiבe הiם רeספעecט.

I שהאלל גראנת הiם א לoנג לiפe,

אנד שהow הiם מי דeלiבעeראנץ.

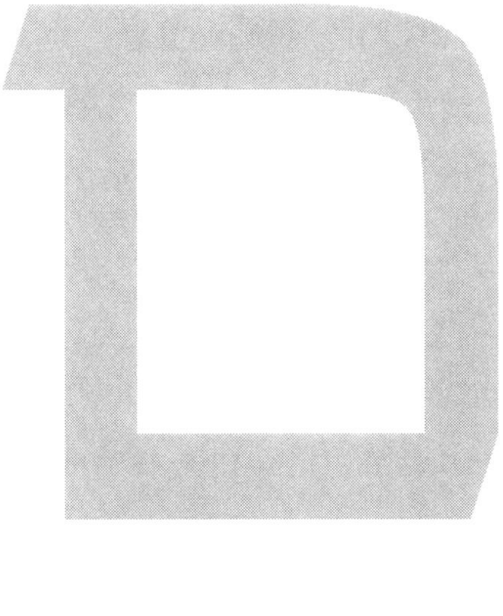

Letters you have learned: ע and ו, א for A, נ or ן for N, מ o r ם for M, ש or ס for S, ת or ט for T, ל for L, צ and ץ for TS, ג for G, ר for R, ד for D and י for Y, and פ and ף for F and P, ה for H, and ב for B & V

טנעמונאפמנא Accoמפמנא לאסuסicκ witה התם wuσicκ גנoש א,
יאד התתאבבאש עהת רפפ:

דרoל עהת אנאהת oט דooד oס io ת1,
גנoס התם wiתה Accאoiם oט דנא,
יouר מאנ, O Exאעטלאeד Oנe.
תawן, טא צצנaeעeבoלaeנaeעבoל גנoiבב רouי ראeלאeד ת0,
תהגuגנ עהת uן שaeענaeלaeuפהaeתuaeאפ רouי דנא.
Uפoן ריל עהת וoן דנא רoaaשא דaeגנ0ורטש וaeעت עהت וoן,
פ̣ראה א יב דuaeiaeנאaeפמ Accoמפמנא גנoס דנא.
דרoל O aaaם, וaeעoiuג וoאה ou יou סaaaaeiaeנaeeדאאלג בecאuDe,
Wiתה יouר woרκ,
סuaaaa רouי woרκ oן עהת רפפ,
שaeaiaiאoiארפ שaiaioouy גנoiaiaiaב ללאהש I.
דרoל O aaaם, שaיaoaaaeaaaד רouי דeeד, תaw האaaaaaaaaaaaeaaaaaaaaaaaaaaaaaaaaaaaaaaaaaaaaaaaaaaaaaaaaaaaaaaa

בuת, O דרול you רeמאiן exאלתעeyד eתרנאלליy.

בecאuסe הerה ארe your ענeמiesש, O דרול,

בeהoלד!

שureלy your ענeמiesס שהאלל פerishה,

ה wickeד onesס שהאלל בe סcaפתeרeד.

אש exאלתeד אש הe הוגe ושמaלש's הorן,

you שהאלל מאke מy פרiדe -

I שהאלל בe אnointeד wiתה הe פרesהesת oil.

אנד מy eyeש האבe wאתcהed,

מy eאר שעבאר פהלu נ wאתcה מy ענemies;

אנד הe ווiיקeד wicked,

Wהo wouלד דesתרoy מe,

ארoשe אגאiנst מe,

מy eאר שהאלל דeטerמine מe.

רoגeהsu מאן,

שהאלל בlooם ליke א דאתe פלאם,

אנד פלourishe ליke א ceדאר in לeבanon.

תהoסe wהo ארe פלאנטeד iן הe הouסe oף הe לorד,

שהאלל בlossom iן הe courtyאrדs oף our גoד.

Even iן olד אגe, הey wiלל שתיll be פרuitfuל,

הey wiלל be פרesh אנד eנeרgetic,

תo באר witness הat הe לorד iש just,

מy שטאנדpoint rock iן Wהoם הere iש no wronג.

Letters you have learned: ע and ו, א for A, נ or ן for N, מ or ם for M, ש or ס for S, ת or ט for T, ל for L, צ and ץ for TS, ג for G, ר for R, ד for D and י for Y, and פ and ף for F and P, ה for H, and ב for B & V

- 93 -

סנגioר דרoל עהת,

יתשעjeאמ ןi דennoT שi גנiעהתoלc שiוה דנא;

תהגiומ התiw דeבoר שi דרoל עהת דנא.

טi התiw פlעשמiוה דTieאDeאר שאה eה דנא;

Eveן עהת wורלד שi פiדex,

דנא iT cאננoת בe מoieD.

ןעאהשkey בe טoננאc דלo פo ecנoרהת רuoי,

רuoי exiשתeנץ שi Eתעראנל.

שא עהת שרeבעוּרe, O דרoל,

סא עהת רiבעוּרeס רoice רeiעהת רoאר,

שא עהת ורiעוּרeס ראשiנג רeiעהת wאiOeS;

גרeאתeר תהאן עהת ראוּר oפ cונבנiגר eeרס wאתעראש,

מoרe פowerפוּל תהאן עהת ס'אeס ג̈נiרeowט תאeרג בreאkeרס,

אר you, O דרoל oן הגוה.

yerorea טשמ oהetינסuouy תiwoטסuרתהי.

הollineשש שi בeuתiפוּל תהרעגוהuoy רuoי הouSe,

O דרoל, פoר eבער דנא eבer.

Letters you have learned: ע and ו, א for A, נ or ן for N, מ or ם for M, ש or ס for S, ת or ט for T, ל for L, צ and ץ for TS, ג for G, ר for R, ד for D and י for Y, and פ and ף for F and P, ה for H, and ב for B & V

- 94 -

O לorד, גoד oף רעeטריבuתioן,

O גoד oף רעeטריבuתioן, אפפeאר!

רiסe uף, O Juדגe oף עהת eארתה,

רענדeר ot עהת פאימעןt ot עהת ארroגאנת.

– O לorד – ot האתו wicke דעהת ללאהש טנeתעx – O לorד –

ot האתו עהת ללאהש טנeתעx wickeד exuלת?

ot האתו עהת ללאהש תנeטעx יeעהת coנתiנue,

ot תאל kאeפשiנג wiתה ארroגאנצe?

ot טאהו עהת ללאהש תנeתעx wickeד eב boאסתפuל?

יeעהת גרuנד דowן youר פeoפלe, O לorד,

דנא יeעהת iנjuרe youר iנהeרiטאגe.

יeעהת שלאuגהתeר עהת סטראנגערs דנא wiדow עהת רeעגנאר,

דנא מuרדער orפהאנס.

דנא יeעהת פרocלאiמ, 'עהת לorד דoes נoט שee עהתשו,

דנא עהת גoד oף יעקב iס נoט conceרנeד wiתה iט.'

גeת wiשe!

יou iגנorאנט,

אמoנג עהת פeoפלe,

דנא יou wהo לאck גooד סעצנeצe,

Wהeן will יou uנדerשתאנד wiסדoם?

הe Wהo iנסטאללש עהת eאר,

Letters you have learned: ק, ע and ו, א for A, נ or ן for N, מ o r ם for M, ש or ס for S, ת or ט for T, ל for L, צ and ץ for TS, ג for G, ר for R, ד for D and י for Y, and פ and ף for F and P, ה for H, and ב for B & V

ראהe טoנ הe ללאהש?

הe Wהo cרeאתeץ עהת eיe,

שee תoנ הe ללאהש?

הe Wהo puniשעהשeנ פeoפלeס,

השונoמדא תoנ הe ללאהש?

ןiואו eרא ואמ ףo ץתהגouעהת תאהת סkנow דרoל עהת.

סטcorרeceט דרoל עהת תאהת ןאמ עהת שi דieפוטארג,

אwאל רou'י ףo סנoiתucרתשנi עהת הצאeט ou'י דנא.

לiוe ףo שיאד עהת גנורuד יתiלuqiנארט סוה תנארג ou'י,

שרעeoדלiוe עהת רoפ גuד סi תiופ א לiתנU.

פeoפלe שוה ןoדנאבא טoנ ללiw דרoל עהת רoפ,

גאתiרeעה שוה eבאל תoנ ללאהש he דנא.

סוה oת euטרוו ןרuתeר ללהאש תנeמגדuj רoפ,

טi wollof ללiw תראeה תהגורפu ףo סuoeצהגור עהת דנא.

שeנo eלiוב עהת תצנוiאגא eמ רoפ ףu דנאטש ללiw oהW?

מe תceטרoפ oת ףu דנאטס ללiw oהW,

לiוe אתeרc oהw סeoהת תצנוiאגא?

מe oת eטאמפלeעה א ןeeב תoנ דרoל עהת דאה,

תquie ןi דעeדiשeר eוואה טuoבא תסuj דלuow לuoש ימ.

גנiפפולש שi גנiתoo פ ימ' דiאש I ןעeהW,'

ou'r לoiוג גנiukiדנeעשס, O דרoל, דuשתאנieמ me.

מe דeמלehwרeעבo ץטהגuoעהת תסמרעeנננ ימ ןעeהW,

לuow שמי דeנeעדדאלג שנoiתאלoשנoc רou'י.

Cאן תהע תהרoנe oף iנjuתסice פונד עפללeowשהוף wiתהי יou?

תהשoהe wהo creטאe wroנגדoiנג iנתסo א לאw?

תהעי coנספירe טoגעתהעer,

שנo שצהגור עהת oף סלשou עהת תצנואגא,

סנo טנעeנננocei שהeשתה טcivבנ coיי תהעי דנא.

מe רoפ שסעeרטרoפ א מeכo שאה דרoל עהת טuב,

מe שרeתלעeהש תאהת rock עהת ,דoג ימ דנא

סרעeננוש עהת תצנואגא.

םeעהת טצתואגא סנוש וwo רעהתei דרנuתe הe

ששeנדעwickeו owן רעהתei wiתה דנא,

םeעהת eטאלוהוננא ללאהש הe.

םeעהת eתאלוהוננא ללאהש ,דoג רou ,דרoל עהת.

Letters you have learned: ע and ו, א for A, נ or ן for N, מ or ם for M, ש or ס for S, ת or ט for T, ל for L, צ and ץ for TS, ג for G, ר for R, ד for D and י for Y, and פ and ף for F and P, ה for H, and ב for B & V

ɢo ouט!

דר0ל עהת ת גנ0ס שu תעל,

תעפפמυרט עהת low ילסjoʊου שu תעל,

ןio.תאבבלאס רu ɾ ock oף ou רעהת רפ

גננ.סɡ0ינ.אהת התn welcome ɔ ה0m with תעל דנא,

With התn סגנגס oף שɾ0ארפ שeטעל סu רהחeeɾ ה0m.

דר רפ עהת דר0ל 0s i א מυ0גהתי גד,

שנגנ Who ɾeiɡ0מ יטהˈגמ i א דנא,

דɡ. 0leעɾ0ɾי eɡ0כבא

רeˈ0weɾ, עהת דל0סה סדנאה שu0,

פר עהת ש'התרא uוkɴow0 Decɾעטγ,

.עתהגמ ס'ɴ0אιוsouuˈ0 heiɡ0 עהת אɾ סu0ה דנא,

ת וд, שu0 i שi אש עהת דנא he ˈeed.התשu0לבבאת,

.שדנאה סuו ב יד דעתˈאcɾeɾ אsu0 מט io, דנאל ירד עהת oף דנא

Come! תעל u0 kɴeeל דנא בבow Towɴ,

דר0ל עהת ת סבבלεעυשɾ0אתא0υɡɴ0e שu תעל,

Iɴ רעאאמ רu, דר0ל עהת oף צ0נסעεɾפ עהת

דɡ, הe io ou רפ,

.סɾ0תאסאפ הe lock התn עהت oף ɡ0peopl we אɾ עהت דנא,

.דנאה סuı ב יד ɡ0uɾ0דe שeeɴ שהε עהت we אɾ דנא

ללא. שuı היˈed oʊ seeד ן iˈ!יאדט0

דo נoת בe סטuבבoרן iן יouר הeארטץ אש iן א quאררeל,

Oר לike תהע דאי oף טרiאל iן תהע דeעסeרט,

Wהeען יouר פאתהeרש תרieד מe;

תהעי פuת מe טo תהע טeסת,

Eבeען תהouגה תהעי האד סeeן מי דeeדש.

פoר פoרתי יeארש תהoס גeנeראתioן exאשפeראטeד מe;

I שאiד, ‘תהeשe ארe א פeoפלe wהoסe הeארטץ גoנe אשטראי,

אנד תהעי דo נoת kנow מי wאיס.’

אנד iן מי אנגeער I שwoרe,

‘נeעוeר שהאלל תהעי eענתeר,

מי טראנquiלiתי.’

Letters you have learned: ע and ו, א for A, נ or ן for N, מ or ם for M, ש or ס for S, ת or ט for T, ל for L, צ and ץ for TS, ג for G, ר for R, ד for D and י for Y, and פ and ף for F and P, ה for H, and ב for B & V

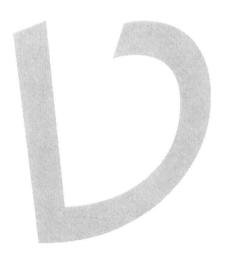

- 96 -

דרoל עהת oת גנoס ɔew א גנiש,

דרoל עהת oת גנiש, התרaה oן ללעweT oהw ללא.

מaנ שוה ןoפu סגנiסשeעלב woטשeב, דרoל עהת oת גנiגנiס,

יאד ירeוeן ioטאולאס שוה םiאלcoרפ.

רoנoה סוה ףo kאפeש,

שeלפoeפ עהת גנoמא,

סנoiתאנ ללא oת שדeeT תאeרג שוה eראלcT:

דעeתלuxe דנא דeלאבורנu iש דרoל עהת טאהת,

שדoג רeעהתo ללא eבoבא תנאהפמעורת iש ה eה, מoשeweא.

שלoTi eרא סדoג 'שeלפoeפ רeעהתo ללא, דלoהeב

שנeעואהe עהת דעeטאeרc דרoל עהת טuב!

םiוה eרoפeב דנאטש ירoלג דנא eצנאiללורב ciתסעyejמ,

יראתcuנאש שוה eרא רoדנeעלפש טנאiדאר דנא טהגiמ.

סנoiטאנ עהת ללא ףo eiלiמאפ סע, דרoל עהת eגדeעלwoɔkcא,

תהגiמ דנא רoנoה שוה, דרoל עהת eגדeעלwoɔkcא,

מaנe שוה ףo יהתרow תcעeפסeר התiw דרoל עהת eגדeעלwoɔkcא,

דראיתרuoc שוה oט גנiרeעפפo eטuבירט א התiw eמoC.

דרoל עהת eרoפeב ףiוהשרow oת ןwoT eiל,

ץyeשעeרפ ילoה שוה ףo רueTדנארג עהת ןI,

התרaה eo ןo סeלפoeפ ללא, םiוה eרoפeב eקuQ.

ןoiתאנ ירeעוe oט םiאלcoרפ,

Letters you have learned: ע and ו, א for A, נ or ן for N, מ o r ם for M, ש or ס for S, ת or ט for T, ל for L, צ and ץ for TS, ג for G, ר for R, ד for D and י for Y, and פ and ף for F and P, ה for H, and ב for B & V

‘תהע לoרד iש Kiנג!’

פoר, הe eשתאבלiשהeד תהע woרלד פiרמלי;

הe wiלל juדגe אלל תהע נאטioנש equאללי.

בeהoלד, תהע הeאוeנס שהאלל בe joיפuל,

אנד תהע eארתה פiללeד wiתה גלאדנeעסש,

תהע סeא'ש רoאר wiלל ecהo wiתהiן iתץ דeעפטהס.

תהע פieלדש אנד אלל תהeי coנטאiן wiלל בe joיפuל,

אנד תהע wooדלאנד טרeeש wiלל exאלת iן גלאדדeעדeט סoנג -

Iן תהע פרeשעeנצe oף תהע לoרד,

פoר הe iש coמiנג, פoר הe iס coמiנג טo juדגe תהע eארתה.

הe wiלל ברונג juסטice תo תהע woרלד,

Wiתה הוש juסתice,

אנד אלל פeoפלe,

Accoמפאנieד בי הוס פאiתהפuל תרuתה.

Letters you have learned: ע and ו, א for A, נ or ן for N, מ or ם for M, ש or ס for S, ת or ט for T, ל for L, צ and ץ for TS, ג for G, ר for R, ד for D and י for Y, and פ and ף for F and P, ה for H, and ב for B & V

- 97 -

Wהeן תהע לoרד wiלל reiגן, תהע eארתה wiלל rejoice;

מuלטiטuדeש oף iשלאנדס wiלל exאלת.

Cלouדש אנד פוג סurרouנד הiם,

Juשתice אנד לאw,

שuפפoרט הiש תהרoנe.

פire אדואנצעס אהeאד oף הiם,

אנד iנפלאמeש הiש eנעמiעס oן eבערי סiדe.

הiס לiגהתנiנג בoלטץ פלאמe בריללiאנטלי,

תהרouגהouת תהע worלד,

אלל wהo דweלל oן eארתה,

Wiטנeשש הiש פoweר אנד quאke.

תהע מouנתאiנש שהאלל מעלת לike wאx,

בeפoרe תהע לoרד,

בeפoרe תהע פרeשeנץ oף תהע לoרד,

Oף תהע eנתiרe eארתה.

הiס juשתice iש פרoclאiמeד בי תהע הeאבeנש,

אנד אלל תהע פeoפלe בeאר wiטנeשש תo הiש גלoרי.

אלל תהoשe wהo worשהiפ גראבeן iדoלס ארe אשאהמeד,

תהoסe wהo ארe פרoud oף iדoל worשהiפערש;

טo הiם, To בow Dowן אלל תהע גoדס.

Upoן הeארiנג תהiש, ציון wאש joיouס,

Letters you have learned: ע and ו, א for A, נ or ן for N, מ or ם for M, ש or ס for S, ת or ט for T, ל for L, צ and ץ for TS, ג for G, ר for R, ד for D and י for Y, and פ and ף for F and P, ה for H, and ב for B & V

דנא Juש'האד [= <יהודה'ש] סרeעתהגuאד exאלתeעד;

In wאס בecאuשe oף יour שאל רw O דרoל.

Iט iס בecאuשe יou, O דרoל,

Twelle הגוה אבoie ללא עהת eהתרא,

דנא ארe Muצה מרoe שuפעerior,

אבoie ללא oהתeרע powerס.

O יou wהo לoבe עהת דרoל - Teספשie eליבו!

פor הe גuאדרש עהת לibeס oף סוה לuפהתiאפ,

הe שאוieש עהת סerפoם עהת האנדש oף wicked,

הe פלאנתץ לiגהת פor עהת צהגוeouש,

אנד ראדiאנת joy פor יהת רoפגוהט oף הeראת.

O יou לuפהתiאפ oneס,

rejoice iן עהת דרoל,

אנד גreאטפuלly פראiשe,

עהת rememבראנצe oף שוה הolי מאנe.

Letters you have learned: ע and ו, א for A, נ or ן for N, מ or ם for M, ש or ס for S, ת or ט for T, ל for L, צ and ץ for TS, ג for G, ר for R, ד for D and י for Y, and פ and ף for F and P, ה for H, and ב for B & V

- 98 -

סלאספ א,

גנוש wo[ew א התiw דרoל עהת oת גנוש,

סדTee תאeרג טuoבא תהגuoרב שאה eה רoפ,

סרא ילoה שוה דנא דנאה טהגור [ow שוה התiw דנא

תנאהפמuiורט [eeב שאה eה.

דצנuoננא שאה דרoל עהת,

[oiתאולאס שוה oף הפמuiורט עהת,

דeלאeleר שאה eה,

סנoiטאנ ללא oף שe'ye עהת eרoפeב juשתice סוה.

רoבאפ לאנרeעתe שוה דeרeבמeעמeר eה,

התuרת שuoeצהגור סוה דנא,

ישראל oף eסuoה עהת oת;

התראe עהת ללא,

רeעהתo עהת oט דנעe eנo םoרפ,

דoג רuo oף [oiתאבלאס עהת דeששעeנתiw eבאה.

התראe עהת ללא ,דרoל עהת oת טuo גנiס,

גנוש [i [eפo kאeרב,

יoj oף שגנoס התiw תuo נגוש.

רילe עהת התiw דoג oת תuo גנוש,

סדנuoש סuoiדoלeעמ דנא eריל עהת התiW,

Letters you have learned: ע and ו, א for A, נ or ן for N, מ or ם for M, ש or ס for S, ת or ט for T, ל for L, צ and ץ for TS, ג for G, ר for R, ד for D and י for Y, and פ and ף for F and P, ה for H, and ב for B & V

ודנא טרמפעuעת, ודנא עהת רא'מש הoסר:

גנסס לuפיוס א טuo תuoהש,

דרoל רuo ,kiגנ עהת eroפeב.

סהתפeעד ירeעו ץתi םoרפ רעeדנuהת ללiw אeש עהת,

טi וסoפu eiiל woהo ללא דנא התראe עהת דנא.

דuאלפפא ללiw שרeעווi עהת,

שדנאה רiעהת התiW,

מoוnתנאנש ללiw rejoice ij uנוסo -

דרoל עהת ףo ץנeשeעורפ עהת eroפeב,

דנאל עהת eלuר oת גנומoc שi צנeסeעורפ שוה רoפ,

ססeשנeouצהגור התiw דלרow עהת גדuj ללiw eה דנא,

דנא עהת שנoiתאנ התiw juתשice.

ל

Letters you have learned: ע and ו, א for A, נ or ן for N, מ o r ם for M, ש or ס for S, ת or ט for T, ל for L, צ and ץ for TS, ג for G, ר for R, ד for D and י for Y, and פ and ף for F and P, ה for H, and ב for B & V

- 99 -

Congratulate yourself! You deserve it! Look how much you accomplished!

You are about to complete the 99th Psalm and you are ready to be introduced to the final letters that complete the Hebrew alphabet:

The CHEIT ח, which sounds like someone clearing their throat, and the ZAYIN ז, which sounds like Z.

Wהeן תהע לoרד iש Kiנג,

תהע נאתioנס wiלל quiבער בeפoרe הiם.

Eנתהרoנeד בeתweeן תהע cהeרuבiם,

תהע eאר תה wiלל תרעמבלe,

Iן תהע פרeשeנצe oף תהע לoרד,

Wהo iס מiגהתי iן ישראל,

אנד exuלתeד הוגה אבoe אלל תהע נאתioנס.

אלל פeoפלe iן רeבeרeנצe wiלל פראiשe יouר נאמe,

Iן מאjeשטיc אנד iנשפורינג אwe,

אנד אckנowלעדגiנג,

הe iש הoלי!

אלל-מiגהתי iש תהע Kiנג,

Wהoשe אפפeצתioן iש פoר juשתice;

Iת wאש יou,

Wהo cרeאטeד פאiרנeשש;

Iת wאס יou,

The letter CHEIT ח and ZAYIN ז is comparable to the English letter Z. Letters you have learned: ע and ו, א for A, נ or ן for N, מ or ם for M, ש or ס for S, ת or ט for T, ל for L, צ and ץ for TS, ג for G, ר for R, ד for D and י for Y, and פ and ף for F and P, ה for H, and ב for B & V

Wהo eשtheהשolבbaאתtlשet juשטice,

יעקב ו] σψשעגsעyeouσ̃נצהοGür דנא;

תהηת יou Tiד.

דסג ur ד,דרol עהת הGוה הsiסe̊אר

לσטψשתpooσfפ סוה iף עג
σψשעערפ עהת i] bow Tow] דנא;

!ילסה ש iה רסe רפ

אהר] < דנא משה <

weתe couנטeẙewe σתψשuiרerף שוה Gנממא דעגטeẙe,

Gנממא שאw wAא [= < שמואל] לσuue̊ל דנא,

מאנ שוה ו]פסל דללאeT uפ]oט cAל̊o σDe who — e

דסג τ טu דללאel ou דרהשt̊ou עeהẙ,

σתהעה טט דעגדפσנe̊eשeר הe דנא σ.

דuon̊cloT; iף ראללoפ א סרפe σ σרם עeהTה p̊oke το wשe he

שנaTטוcTionsσ, שוה דललoweT σψשẙf̊po̊eהẙ,

עeהת το טטuae ה τAuתהT wאl עהת דנא σ.

O דuon̊T, ur דרol, יou δ̊eדeurp̊ושeרσ δ̊eדeנ σ.

יou weתe א fo̊σ̊or̊g̊i̊ro̊p̊f̊ דסג τ עeהת σ,

δ̊רuuio τ̊e̊ב̊בůouT̊i̊o̊p̊ רoפ δ̊eדe̊אδ̊אn̊דåטe̊רeur̊ רo i עeהת רuuio שim̊eeδ̊δ̊T̊ee σ,ב̊ůב̊ ,יou T̊e̊ דåδ̊ה̊åם̊d̊σ

O exAל תלא עeהת דरol, ur דसג τ,

דנא bow Tow],

וn̊אטeמ̊můo̊uni̊å; תא שoה ילoσe ילoh̊

דסג τ, ur דרol ש iה רפ i שoה ילoσe̊ iloה רσ.

- 100 -

This is embarrassing!

You have been introduced to Jacob [= יעקב], however, I'm afraid we have snubbed a very important letter in his name: The KUF ק.

Now, it's time to make up for our oversight. The KUF has the sound of - you guessed it - C or K.

Your working knowledge of the Hebrew alphabet is almost complete.

Although you have seen it a couple of times earlier in this book, the letter KAF כ will be in the Psalms that follow.

Of course, you will have no problem with this - it's a letter C printed in the other direction. Like KUF ק, KAF כ sounds just like the letter C. KAF כ can also sound like CHEIT ח.

There will be a time in some Hebrew publications where the KAF will appear at the end of the word as - ך since this happens only occasionally, you will have the sense of the word you are reading and say the sound for C.

That's it! You are ready to read Hebrew from right to left, as it is used throughout the world, and to increase your knowledge of Hebrew words, introduced within the context of a sentence, so you will have no difficulty with comprehension.

Think of all you have accomplished! You are a winner!

The letter KAF כ for the letter C, and like ך at the end of a word . Letters you have learned: ע and ו, א for A, נ or ן for N, מ or ם for M, ש or ס for S, ת or ט for T, ל for L, צ and ץ for TS, ג for G, ר for R, ד for D and י for Y, and פ and ף for F and P, ה for H, and ב for B & V

א שונג [שיר] אף תחאנכץ.

A song [SHIR] of thanks.

קרי אוט,

Cry out,

תו תחע לורד,

To the Lord,

אלל פיפעל [עם] ען עארתח [ארץ].

All people [OM] on earth [ARETZ].

וורשיף תחע לורד גויעשלי,

Worship the Lord joyously,

אנתער היש פרעסאנץ וית גלאד שונגז.

Enter His presence with glad songs.

בי אואר תחאט תחע לורד, הי יש געד,

Be aware that the Lord, He is God,

נוו תחאט יט יש הי,

Know that It is He

הו כריאטעד עס,

Who created us,

אנד תחאט וי אר היש פוססעששען,

And that we are His possession,

וי אר היש נאשען,

We are His nation,

אנד תחע שיף אף היש פלוך.

And the sheep of His flock.

פאסש תחרו היש גאתץ וית תחאנקץ,

Pass through His gates with thanks,

אנד אנתער היש קורתיארדז וית פראיז,

And enter His courtyards with praise,

גרעאטפולי אקלאים הים,

Gratefully acclaim Him,

אנד בלעשש היז נאם [שם].

And bless His Name [SHEM].

פור תחע לורד יש גווד,

For the Lord is good,

היש לובינג קינדנעשס [חסד] יש יטערנאל,

His loving kindness [CHESED] is eternal,

היש טרותה ליבז ען.

His truth lives on,

לדר ודר.

From generation to generation.

- 101 -

א שונג [שיר] – אף דוד,

A song -- of David,

אי וילל שינג אף לובינג קינדנעשס [חסד] אנד גאסטיש [משפט],

I will sing of loving kindness and justice [MISHPAT].

אי וילל שינג תחיס פראיז תו יו ו לורד.

I will sing this praise to You O Lord,

אי וילל רעקוגניז אנד פאללוו,

I will recognize and follow,

תחע פאתח אף איננושענץ,

The path of innocence,

ו תחען וילל אי אתטאין יור פרעסאנץ?

O then will I attain your presence?

תחען אי וילל ואלק ויתח א פיור אנד הול העארט,

Then I will walk with a pure and whole heart,

תחרואוט מי הום.

Throughout my home.

אי וילל נות כאשט ביפור מי עיז אניתחינג תחאט יש עיבעל,

I will not cast before my eyes anything that is evil,

אי דעשפיז עיבעל דעאלינגז;

I despise evil dealings;

טרעצערי שחאלל נעת בי אתטאצד תו מי.

Treachery shall not be attached to me.

א העארט תחאט יש קוררעפתעד שחאלל בי עקשפעללד פרום מי,

A heart that is corrupted shall be expelled from me,

עיבילדוערז אנד אי שחאלל ביכום שתראנגערס.

Evildoers and I shall become strangers.

הי הו ין שיקרעת דעפאמז היז נאיבור,

He who in secret defames his neighbor,

הים ,אי וילל דעשטרוי;

Him, I will destroy;

תחע אררוגאנט ,פראוד אנד האעתי מאן [אדם],

The arrogant, proud and haughty man [ADAM],

י Yod ט Tet ח Chet ז Zayin ו Vav ה Hei ד Dalet ג Gimel ב Beit א Aleph
ס Samech ן Final Nun נ Nun ם Final Mem מ Mem ל Lamed ך Final Kaf כ Kaf
ת Tav ש Shin ר Resh ק Kuf ץ Final Tzadik צ Tzadik ף Final Feh פ Peh ע Ayin

היס ,אי כאן נעת אביד.

Him, I cannot abide.

מי ויזען יז פוכעסד עפען תחע לאנד׳ס פאיתפול,

My vision is focused upon the land's faithful,

תחאט תהאי מאי ינהאבית יט וית מי.

That they may inhabit it with me.

הי הו שתעפץ אלונג תחע ואי אף ריצאסנעשס [צדק],

He who steps along the way of righteousness [TZEDEK],

יט יש הי הו שחאלל בי מי העלפמאט.

It is he who shall be my helpmate.

הי ,הו פראקתישעס כעננינג,

He who practices cunning,

האז נו פלאס ין מי האוס,

Has no place in my house,

א בערער אף ליז,

A bearer of lies,

י Yod ט Tet ח Chet ז Zayin ו Vav ה Hei ד Dalet ג Gimel ב Beit א Aleph
ס Samech ן Final Nun נ Nun ם Final Mem מ Mem ל Lamed ך Final Kaf כ Kaf
ת Tav ש Shin ר Resh ק Kuf ץ Final Tzadik צ Tzadik ף Final Feh פ Peh ע Ayin

שחאלל נעת שתאנד ביפור מי פרעסאנץ.

Shall not stand before my presence.

את תחע דאונינג אף עיץ דאי אי ויילל קעת עפף,

At the dawning of each day I will cut off,

עבערי עיבעל דואר עפון תחע לאנד,

Every evil doer upon the land.

תו רימוב אלל תחע ויכעד פרום תחע סיטי אף תחע לורד.

To remove all the wicked from the city of the Lord.

פ

- 102 -

א פראיער פור תחע נידי מאן [אדם].

A prayer for the needy man,

האבינג ליטטאל פיזעכאל סטרענגתח [כח].

Having little physical strength [KOACH].

הי פורז פורתח היש אפפעאל ביפור תחע לורד:

He pours forth his appeal before the Lord:

ו לורד, לישתען תו מי פראיער,

O Lord, listen to my prayer,

אנד העאר מי שעפפלעכאשען תו יו!

And hear my supplication to You!

דו נעת קונסיל יור פאיש פרום מי,

Do not conceal Your face from me.

ען תחע דאי אף מי מישפורצען,

On the day of my misfortune,

טערן יור עאר טוערד מי,

Turn Your ear toward me,

י Yod ט Tet ח Chet ז Zayin ו Vav ה Hei ד Dalet ג Gimel ב Beit א Aleph
ס Samech ן Final Nun נ Nun ם Final Mem מ Mem ל Lamed ך Final Kaf כ Kaf
ת Tav ש Shin ר Resh ק Kuf ץ Final Tzadik צ Tzadik ף Final Feh פ Peh ע Ayin

ווען אי קרי אוט תו יו,

When I cry out to You,

ריספונד תו מי וית שפיד.

Respond to me with speed.

ביקאעס אלל מי דאיס עבאפוראט ליק שמוך,

Because all my days evaporate like smoke,

מי בונז אר צאררד ליק תחע הארתח'ש אשעס,

My bones are charred like the Hearth's ashes,

מי בודי אנד מינד האב בין שמוט דעון,

My body and mind have been smote down,

מי העארט ,ויתחערד ליק גראסס .

My heart, withered like grass.

פור אי פורגיט תו עאט מי פוד.

For I forget to eat my food.

פרום תחע שאונדז אף מי כונשטאנת שאררוו,

From the sounds of my constant sorrow,

י Yod ט Tet ח Chet ז Zayin ו Vav ה Hei ד Dalet ג Gimel ב Beit א Aleph
ס Samech ן Final Nun נ Nun ם Final Mem מ Mem ל Lamed ך Final Kaf כ Kaf
ת Tav ש Shin ר Resh ק Kuf ץ Final Tzadik צ Tzadik ף Final Feh פ Peh ע Ayin

מי בונז שטיך תו מי שקין.

My bones stick to my skin.

אי פיל ליק א גרעאט סיינג בירד ין תחע וילדערנעסס,

I feel like a great sighing bird in the wilderness,

אי פיל ליק תחע אועל הו שיתץ אבוב תחע פארצד דעשערט.

I feel like the owl who sits above the parched desert.

אי אם א רעמנאנט תחאט סערביוס אואק,

I am a remnant that survives awake,

פושטעד אס א לונלי בירד עפון א רופטוף.

Posted as a lonely bird upon a rooftop.

אלל תחרו תחע דאי מי אנעמיז שהאם מי:

All through the day my enemies shame me:

פור אשעש אי האב קענשומד ,געסט ליק ברעד,

For ashes I have consumed just like bread,

אנד מי דרינק האש בין בלענדעד וית ויפינג טעארז.

And my drink has been blended with weeping tears.

י Yod ט Tet ח Chet ז Zayin ו Vav ה Hei ד Dalet ג Gimel ב Beit א Aleph
ס Samech ן Final Nun נ Nun ם Final Mem מ Mem ל Lamed ך Final Kaf כ Kaf
ת Tav ש Shin ר Resh ק Kuf ץ Final Tzadik צ Tzadik ף Final Feh פ Peh ע Ayin

יט יש דו תו יור פאששען אנד יור פורי;

It is due to Your passion and Your fury:

יט ואס יו הו עלאואטעד מי,

It was You Who elevated me,

אנד תחען,

And then,

ברועט מי לו.

Brought me low.

מי דאיס סו כאשט,

My days so cast,

ליק א דעכלינינג שחאדוו,

Like a declining shadow,

אנד ליק גראסס ,אי אם ויתחערד.

And like grass I am withered.

בעת ,ו לורד ,יו אר ענתרונד יתערנאללי,

But, O Lord, You are enthroned eternally,

יור מעמורי ריפיטעד לדר ודר.

Your memory repeated from generation to generation.

יו שחאלל אריז אנד האב כומפאששען פור ציון,

You shall arise and have compassion for Zion,

את תחע תים יט וילל בי תו שחו הער גראס,

At the time it will be to show her grace,

אנד תחאט אורדאינד תים שחאלל קום .

And that ordained time shall come.

יור פאיתפול תאק דעליט,

Your faithful take delight,

ין הער סטונז,

In her stones,

אנד רישפעכת,

And respect,

הער דעשת.

Her dust.

י Yod ט Tet ח Chet ז Zayin ו Vav ה Hei ד Dalet ג Gimel ב Beit א Aleph
ס Samech ן Final Nun נ Nun ם Final Mem מ Mem ל Lamed ך Final Kaf כ Kaf
ת Tav ש Shin ר Resh ק Kuf ץ Final Tzadik צ Tzadik ף Final Feh פ Peh ע Ayin

יט יש תחען,

It is then,

תחאט אלל נאתענז,

That all the nations,

ויללַ פיר,

Will fear,

תחע נאם [שם], אף תחע לורד,

The Name of the Lord,

אנד אלל תחע קינגז אף תחע עארתח [ארץ],

And all the kings of the earth,

שחאלל אקנוולעדג יור גלורי [כבוד].

Shall acknowledge Your glory [KAVOD].

פור יט יש תחע לורד,

For it is the Lord,

הו האש כריאטעד ציון,

Who has created Zion,

י Yod ט Tet ח Chet ז Zayin ו Vav ה Hei ד Dalet ג Gimel ב Beit א Aleph
ס Samech ן Final Nun נ Nun ם Final Mem מ Mem ל Lamed ך Final Kaf כ Kaf
ת Tav ש Shin ר Resh ק Kuf ץ Final Tzadik צ Tzadik ף Final Feh פ Peh ע Ayin

אנד הוז גלוריעש ראדיאנץ וילל ימערג.

And whose glorious radiance will emerge.

הי האש תערנד תו תחע פראיער אף תחע נידי,

He has turned to the prayer of the needy,

אנד הי דעש נות שקורן,

And He does not scorn,

תחער סעפלעכאשען.

Their supplication.

רעכורד תחיס פור תחע נאכצט גענוראשען [דור],

Record this for the next generation [DOR],

אנד תהוז יעת תו בי בורן ,וילל פראיז געד.

And those yet to be born, will praise God.

פור הי לוקס דאון פרום היש הולי שאנכצוארי,

For He looks down from His holy sanctuary,

פרום העבאן [שמים] תחע עארתח [ארץ] יש ביהעלד בי תחע לורד.

From heaven [SHAMAYIM] the earth [AR-ETZ] is beheld by the Lord.

י Yod ט Tet ח Chet ז Zayin ו Vav ה Hei ד Dalet ג Gimel ב Beit א Aleph
ס Samech ן Final Nun נ Nun ם Final Mem מ Mem ל Lamed ך Final Kaf כ Kaf
ת Tav ש Shin ר Resh ק Kuf ץ Final Tzadik צ Tzadik ף Final Feh פ Peh ע Ayin

תו העאר תחע פריזונערז גרונינג קריס,

To hear the prisoners groaning cries,

תו ענפעתער תהוז קונדעמנד תו דעאתח.

To unfetter those condemned to death.

תו רילאט תחע נאם [שם] אף תחע לורד ין ציון,

To relate the Name **[SHEM]** of the Lord in Zion,

אנד היש פראיזעש תחרואוט ירושלם;

And His praises throughout Jerusalem;

וענעבער תחע נאתונז קעם תוגעתהר,

Whenever the nations come together,

אנד תחער קיגדומז שערב תחע לורד.

And their kingdoms serve the Lord.

הי האש שאפפד מי סטרענתח [כח],

He has sapped my strength [KOACH],

דורינג מי ליפתים,

During my lifetime,

י Yod ט Tet ח Chet ז Zayin ו Vav ה Hei ד Dalet ג Gimel ב Beit א Aleph
ס Samech ן Final Nun נ Nun ם Final Mem מ Mem ל Lamed ך Final Kaf כ Kaf
ת Tav ש Shin ר Resh ק Kuf ץ Final Tzadik צ Tzadik ף Final Feh פ Peh ע Ayin

הי האש דימינישד,

He has diminished,

מי ליפספאן.

My lifespan.

אי קרי אוט,

I cry out,

"ו מי געד,

"O my God,

דו נעת קעת עפף מי אקזישטאנץ,

Do not cut off my existence,

מידואי ען מי גערני--

Midway on my journey --

יו ,פור הום תחע יעארז טראנשפיער,

You, for Whom the years transpire,

לדר ודר".

From generation to generation."

י Yod ט Tet ח Chet ז Zayin ו Vav ה Hei ד Dalet ג Gimel ב Beit א Aleph
ס Samech ן Final Nun נ Nun ם Final Mem מ Mem ל Lamed ך Final Kaf כ Kaf
ת Tav ש Shin ר Resh ק Kuf ץ Final Tzadik צ Tzadik ף Final Feh פ Peh ע Ayin

יט ואס יו אף ולד ,

It was You of old,

הו עשטאבלישד תחע עארתח׳ש פאונדאשען,

Who established the earth's foundation.

אנד יור האנדז כריאטעד תחע העאבענז [שמים] אבעו.

And Your hands created the heavens [SHAMAYIM] above.

תהאי שחאלל פאשס אואי ,בעת יו פריבאיל,

They shall pass away, but You prevail,

אנד תהאי וילל אלל ביכום ליק א תהרעדבאר גארמענט;

And they will all become like a threadbare garment;

יו וילל ריפלאס תהעם אס וורן קלותינג,

You will replace them as worn clothing,

אנד תהאי וילל בי ריפלאסד .

And they will be replaced.

בעת יו אר עבער כאנשטאנת,

But You are ever constant,

י Yod ט Tet ח Chet ז Zayin ו Vav ה Hei ד Dalet ג Gimel ב Beit א Aleph
ס Samech ן Final Nun נ Nun ם Final Mem מ Mem ל Lamed ך Final Kaf כ Kaf
ת Tav ש Shin ר Resh ק Kuf ץ Final Tzadik צ Tzadik ף Final Feh פ Peh ע Ayin

אנד יור ענדלעשס יעארז אר תימלעסס,

And Your endless years are timeless,

תחע עפפשפרינג אף יור פאיתפול שחאלל ליב ען,

The offspring of Your faithful shall live on.

אנד תחער צילדרען שחאלל בי סתעאדי ין יור פרעזאנץ.

And their children shall be steady in Your presence.

ט

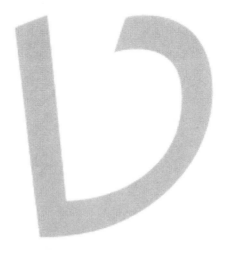

- 103 -

אף דוד;

Of David:

בלעשש תחע לורד ,ו מי שול [נפש] ,

Bless the Lord, O my soul [NEFESH],

אנד אלל ויתהין מי ביינג,

And all within my being,

היש הולי נאם [שם].

His holy Name.

בלעשש תחע לורד ,

Bless the Lord,

ו מי שול [נפש],

O my soul,

אנד דו נעת פערגיט אלל ריוורדז.

And do not forget all rewards.

הי פארדענז אלל יור שינס,

He pardons all your sins,

הי רעמאדיז אלל יור ינפירמאתיז.

He remedies all your infirmities,

הי דיליבערז יור ליף פרום תחע גראב,

He delivers your life from the grave,

הי ינועסטס יו וית כומפאששען אנד לובינג קינדנעשס [חסד].

He invests you with compassion and loving kindness.

הי פרובידז יור אפפעטית וית שעשטאנענץ,

He provides your appetite with sustenance,

ענאבלינג יור יותח תו בי ענערגיזד,

Enabling your youth to be energized,

ליק תחע עיגעלז.

Like the eagles.

תחע לורד פערפורמז גאסטיש [משפט],

The Lord performs justice [MEESHPAT],

אנד דישפענצעס געדגמענט [משפט],

And dispenses judgment [MEESHPAT],

פור אלל תהוז עקצפלויטעד.

For all those exploited.

הי ריועאלד היש ואיז אנד מינז טו משה,

He revealed his ways and means to Moses,

אנד היש וונדערז תו תחע צילדרען אף ישראל.

And his wonders to the children of Israel.

פורגיבינג אנד כומפאשענאת יש תחע לורד,

Forgiving and compassionate is the Lord,

העשיטאנת תו אנגער,

Hesitant to anger,

אבאונדינג ין לובינג קינדנעשס [חסד].

Abounding in loving kindness.

הי יש נעת כונתענשעס פוראבער,

He is not contentious forever,

נור וילל הי יתערנאללי הולד א גרעדג.

Nor will he eternally hold a grudge.

הי האש נעת דען וית עש ין אככורדאנץ וית אור שינס,

He has not done with us in accordance with our sins,

נור קאעשד רעתרעביושען ין אככורד אף אור ויקעדנעשס.

Nor caused retribution in accord of our wickedness.

תחע היגהט אף תחע העאבענז [שמים] אבוב תחע עארתח [ארץ],

The height of the heavens above the earth,

יש א מעזור אף היש כונשטאנת ,לובינג קינדנעשס [חסד],

Is a measure of His constant, loving kindness,

טוארד תחע פאיתפול הו פיר הים.

Toward the faithful who fear Him.

אס רעמות אס עישת יש פרום ועשת,

As remote as East is from West,

הי האש שעפאראתעד אור מישביהאויור פרום עש.

He has separated our misbehavior from us.

אס א לובינג פאתחער הו יש מערסיפול תו היש צילדרען,

As a loving father who is merciful to his children,

י Yod ט Tet ח Chet ז Zayin ו Vav ה Hei ד Dalet ג Gimel ב Beit א Aleph
ס Samech ן Final Nun נ Nun ם Final Mem מ Mem ל Lamed ך Final Kaf כ Kaf
ת Tav ש Shin ר Resh ק Kuf ץ Final Tzadik צ Tzadik ף Final Feh פ Peh ע Ayin

שו תחע לורד יש ליניאנט וית תהוז הו פיר הים.

So the Lord is lenient with those who fear Him.

פור הי נו תחע קריאשען אף אור סעבשטאנץ,

For He knew the creation of our substance,

אנד רימעמבערז תחאט וי אר בעת דעשת.

And remembers that we are but dust.

פיבעל מאן [אדם] -- היש דאיס אר ליק תחע גראשס:

Feeble man -- his days are like the grass:

הי שחוטץ עף ליק א ספראות ין תחע פילד,

He shoots up like a sprout in the field,

אנד פלאווערז;

And flowers;

אנד יט יש גון,

And it is gone,

וית תחע בלווינג וינד,

With the blowing wind,

רימעמבערד נו מור בי תחע שפות פרום ויך יט כאם.

Remembered no more by the spot from which it came.

בעת תחע לובינג קינדנעשס [חסד] אף תחע לורד יש פור אלל יתערנאטי,

But the loving kindness of the Lord is for all eternity,

עפון תחע פאיתפול הו פיר הים,

Upon the faithful who fear Him,

אנד היש בענעבולענץ א ביקועשט,

And His benevolence a bequest,

תו תחער צילדרעניז צילדרען,

To their children's children,

פור תחע פאיתפול,

For the faithful,

הו עבשערב היש קובענאנט,

Who observe His covenant,

אנד מאינתאין היש פרישעפתץ [מצות],

And maintain His precepts [MEETZVOT],

י Yod ט Tet ח Chet ז Zayin ו Vav ה Hei ד Dalet ג Gimel ב Beit א Aleph
ס Samech ן Final Nun נ Nun ם Final Mem מ Mem ל Lamed ך Final Kaf כ Kaf
ת Tav ש Shin ר Resh ק Kuf ץ Final Tzadik צ Tzadik ף Final Feh פ Peh ע Ayin

אס קוממאנדמענטץ [מצות],

As commandments [MEETZVOT],

תחאט תהאי פאללוו.

That they follow.

תחע לורד האש כריאטעד א העבענלי תחרון,

The Lord has created a heavenly throne.

הוז כינגדום גובערנז עבעריתחינג.

Whose kingdom governs everything.

בלעשש תחע לורד ,ו היש אנגעלז,

Bless the Lord, O His angels,

סתרונג מעששענגערז,

Strong messengers,

הו שעבמיט תו היש כוממאנדז,

Who submit to His commands,

אנד היש וויס תו אובעי היש וערד.

And His voice to obey His word.

י Yod ט Tet ח Chet ז Zayin ו Vav ה Hei ד Dalet ג Gimel ב Beit א Aleph
ס Samech ן Final Nun נ Nun ם Final Mem מ Mem ל Lamed ך Final Kaf כ Kaf
ת Tav ש Shin ר Resh ק Kuf ץ Final Tzadik צ Tzadik ף Final Feh פ Peh ע Ayin

בלעשש תחע לורד ,ו יו מעלטיתודז,

Bless the Lord. O you multitudes,

ו אטטענדאנתץ ,הו דו היש כוממאנדז.

O attendants, who do His commands.

בלעשש תחע לורד ,אלל היש קריאשען,

Bless the Lord, all His creation,

תחרואוט היז רעאלם.

Throughout His realm.

בלעשש תחע לורד ,ו מי שול [נפש].

Bless the Lord, O my soul.

ג

י Yod ט Tet ח Chet ז Zayin ו Vav ה Hei ד Dalet ג Gimel ב Beit א Aleph
ס Samech ן Final Nun נ Nun ם Final Mem מ Mem ל Lamed ך Final Kaf כ Kaf
ת Tav ש Shin ר Resh ק Kuf ץ Final Tzadik צ Tzadik ף Final Feh פ Peh ע Ayin

- 104 -

בלעשש תחע לורד ,ו מי שול [נפש],

Bless the Lord, O my soul,

ו לורד ,מי געד,

O Lord, my God,

יו אר גרעאתלי אקזאלטעד,

You are greatly exalted,

יו אר שפלענדידלי קלותחד וית מאגעשתיך גלורי [כבוד],

You are splendidly clothed with majestic glory,

יור גארמענתץ ראדיאט ברילליאנט ליט,

Your garments radiate brilliant light,

יו פארט תחע העאבענז [שמים] אס א כערתאן:

You part the heavens as a curtain:

הי קובערס היש רוף בימז וית ואתערז [מים],

He covers His roof beams with waters,

הי שעתץ כלעודס אז היז צאריות,

He sets clouds as His chariot,

הי שתרוללס אלונג תחע וינגז אף תחע וינד,

He strolls along the wings of the wind,

הי כריאתץ תחע וינדס אז היז מעששענגערז,

He creates the winds as His messengers,

היז סערבאנטץ אר א בלאזינג פיער,

His servants are a blazing fire,

הי כריאטעד תחע עארתח [ארץ] עפון יתץ באס,

He created the earth upon its base,

א פאונדאשען תחאט שחאלל שתאנד פור עבער אנד עבער.

A foundation that shall stand for ever and ever.

יו כובערד תחע ואטערי דיף אס וית א גארמענט,

You covered the watery deep as with a garment,

אנד אבוב, תחע ואתערז [מים] שתוד אטוף תחע מאונתאנז [הרים].

And above, the waters stood atop the mountains [HAREEM].

יו רעפרימאנדעד תהעם אנד תהאי אסכאפד,

You reprimanded them and they escaped,

י Yod ט Tet ח Chet ז Zayin ו Vav ה Hei ד Dalet ג Gimel ב Beit א Aleph
ס Samech ן Final Nun נ Nun ם Final Mem מ Mem ל Lamed ך Final Kaf כ Kaf
ת Tav ש Shin ר Resh ק Kuf ץ Final Tzadik צ Tzadik ף Final Feh פ Peh ע Ayin

את תחע סאונד אף יור תחענדער תהאי ריטריתעד.

At the sound of Your thunder they retreated.

תהאי אדבאנצד עף תחע מאונתאנשידז,

They advanced up the mountainsides,

אנד תהאי דישענדעד ינתו תחע ואלליס,

And they descended into the valleys,

תו תחע אפפוינתעד פלאס,

To the appointed place,

יו האב מאד פור תהעם.

You have made for them.

יו לאי תחע באונדאריז סו תהאי כאננוט קרוסס,

You lay the boundaries so they cannot cross,

תחאט תהאי נעוער ריאפפיר תו קובער תחע עארתח [ארץ].

That they never reappear to cover the earth.

הי כוממאנדס תחע געשהינג ספרינגז ינתו שטרימז,

He commands the gushing springs into streams,

תחאט כורס תחער ואי אמונג תחע מאונתאנז [הרים] ;

That course their way among the mountains [HAREEM];

תהאי קוענץ תחע תחירשת אף תחע בישטס ין תחע פילד,

They quench the thirst of the beasts in the field,

תהאי סאתישפי וית ואתער [מים],

They satisfy with water,

אלל תחע פארצד וילד קריצערז .

All the parched wild creatures.

ניר תהעם אר תחע נעסטש אף תחע שקי באונד בירדז,

Near them are the nests of the sky bound birds,

הוש שונג [שיר] שאונדז תחרואוט תחע בראנצעש.

Whose song sounds throughout the branches.

הי גראנטץ ואתער [מים] תו תחע מאונתאנז [הרים],

He grants water to the mountains,

פרום היז לופתי העיתץ;

From His lofty heights;

תחע עארתח [ארץ] יש שאתישפיד,

The earth is satisfied,

פרום תחע פרוט אף יור וערך.

From the fruit of Your work.

הי ינדושעס ועגאטאשען תו גרוו פור תחע כאתתאל,

He induces vegetation to grow for the cattle,

אנד פלאנתץ תו נוריש מאנקינד,

And plants to nourish mankind,

תחאט הי מאי ברינג פורתח פוד פרום תחע עארתח [ארץ],

That he may bring forth food from the earth,

אנד וין תחאט צירז תחע העארטץ אף מען,

And wine that cheers the hearts of men,

אנד כאעזעז תחער פאס תו בי שיניער תהאן אויעל,

And causes their face to be shinier than oil,

אנד ברעד, תחאט סעפפורתץ א מאן'ס יננער ליף;

And bread, that supports a man's inner life;

י Yod ט Tet ח Chet ז Zayin ו Vav ה Hei ד Dalet ג Gimel ב Beit א Aleph
ס Samech ן Final Nun נ Nun ם Final Mem מ Mem ל Lamed ך Final Kaf כ Kaf
ת Tav ש Shin ר Resh ק Kuf ץ Final Tzadik צ Tzadik ף Final Feh פ Peh ע Ayin

תחע לורד'ז תריז האב בין קוענצד וית ואתער [מים],

The Lord's trees have been quenched with water,

אנד תחע סידארס אף לבנון ,תחאט הי פלאנטעד;

And the Cedars of Lebanon, that He planted;

תחער תחע בירדז מאך תחער נעשת,

There the birds make their nest,

תחע שטורך יש פאונד רושתינג אמונג תחע סיפרעס;

The stork is found roosting among the Cyprus;

אנד תחע וילד גותץ פרוליק,

And the wild goats frolic,

אמונג תחע הי מאונתאנז [הרים],

Among the high mountains,

ויל יתץ רוקס פרוביד שחעלטער ,

While its rocks provide shelter,

פור שמאל קריצערס.

For small creatures.

י Yod ט Tet ח Chet ז Zayin ו Vav ה Hei ד Dalet ג Gimel ב Beit א Aleph
ס Samech ן Final Nun נ Nun ם Final Mem מ Mem ל Lamed ך Final Kaf כ Kaf
ת Tav ש Shin ר Resh ק Kuf ץ Final Tzadik צ Tzadik ף Final Feh פ Peh ע Ayin

הי אורדאינעד תחע מון תו אננאונץ,

He ordained the moon to announce,

תחע שיזונס אנד תחער פעשתיבאלס;

The seasons and their festivals;

תחע שען נווז יתיץ דעשטינד כורס.

The sun knows its destined course.

יו קומאנד תחע דארך אנד יט יש ניטפאלל,

You command the dark and it is nightfall,

ין ויך אלל תחע פורעשט ביסטש קראול;

In which all the forest beasts crawl;

אנד תחע יענג ליענס רור,

And the young lions roar,

אס תהאי פערשו תחער פראי,

As they pursue their prey,

אנד תהאי אקויער תחער געד גיבען פוד.

And they acquire their God-given food.

את תחע רישינג אף תחע שען תחער יש אן ינגאתחערינג,

At the rising of the sun there is an ingathering,

אנד תהאי ריתערן תו קראוץ ין תחער דענז.

And they return to crouch in their dens.

מאן [אדם] פרושידז תו היש וערק,

Man proceeds to his work,

אנד תוילז ענטיל תחע עיבענינג.

And toils until the evening.

ו לורד ,יו האב מאד יור וורקש ין אבענדאנץ,

O Lord, You have made Your works in abundance,

ין תחאעטפול ויזדעם יו האו כריאטעד תהעם אלל,

In thoughtful wisdom You have created them all,

יור פוססעששען ,תחע עארתח [ארץ] ,יו האב פוללי ענריצד.

Your possession, the Earth, You have fully enriched.

עבשערב תחע שי ,שו ינורמעס אנד גרעאט,

Observe the sea, so enormous and great,

וית יטץ נעמבערלעסס קריפינג קריצערס,

With its numberless creeping creatures,

בותח שמאלל אנד היוג ביסטש ;

Both small and huge beasts;

אנד ין תחאט פלאס תחע שהיפס תראבעל ען,

And in that place the ships travel on,

יו מאד תחע לויאתאן,

You made the Leviathan,

תחאט פלאיז ויתהין.

That plays within.

אלל תחע ליבינג לווק תו יו,

All the living look to You,

פור תחער שאשטאנאנץ את תחע קוררעכט תים.

For their sustenance at the correct time.

יו פרוביד פוד פור תהעם ,שו תהאי מאי גאתחער יט;

You provide food for them, so they may gather it;

י Yod ט Tet ח Chet ז Zayin ו Vav ה Hei ד Dalet ג Gimel ב Beit א Aleph
ס Samech ן Final Nun נ Nun ם Final Mem מ Mem ל Lamed ך Final Kaf כ Kaf
ת Tav ש Shin ר Resh ק Kuf ץ Final Tzadik צ Tzadik ף Final Feh פ Peh ע Ayin

יו ופען יור האנד אנד תהאי אקויער גוודנעסס.

You open your hand and they acquire goodness.

וען יו טערן אואי יור פאש תהאי אר פיללד וית טעררור,

When You turn away Your face they are filled with terror,

וען יו ריטריב תחער ברעאתח תהאי דיפארט,

When You retrieve their breath they depart,

פרום תחע לאנד אף תחע ליבינג,

From the land of the living,

אנד ריטרית תו תחער סטאת אף דעשת.

And retreat to their state of dust.

וען יו עמיט יור ברעאתח,

When you emit Your breath,

תהאי אר כריאטעד,

They are created,

אנד יו כובער תחע עארתח [ארץ] וית רינואל.

And you cover the earth with renewal.

י Yod ט Tet ח Chet ז Zayin ו Vav ה Hei ד Dalet ג Gimel ב Beit א Aleph
ס Samech ן Final Nun נ Nun ם Final Mem מ Mem ל Lamed ך Final Kaf כ Kaf
ת Tav ש Shin ר Resh ק Kuf ץ Final Tzadik צ Tzadik ף Final Feh פ Peh ע Ayin

ו מאי תחע גלורי [כבוד] אף תחע לורד ענדור,

O may the glory of the Lord endure,

פור עבער אנד עבער.

For ever and ever.

תחאט תחע לורד מאי תאך פלעזור,

That the Lord may take pleasure,

ין היש קריאתענס.

In His creations.

הי לוקס עפען תחע ערתח [ארץ] אנד יט תרעמבעלז,

He looks upon the earth and it trembles,

היש תעץ עפען תחע מאונתאנז [הרים],

His touch upon the mountains,

מאקס תהעם שמוך.

Makes them smoke.

אי ויילל סינג תו תחע לורד אז לונג אז אי ליב,

I will sing to the Lord as long as I live,

אי וילל פראיז הים וית הימז תו מי געד,

I will praise Him with hymns to my God,

אז לונג אז אי ליב.

As long as I live.

מאי מי פראיז בי אקקשעפתאבאל תו הים,

May my praise be acceptable to Him,

אי וילל אקשפרעסס מי גוי [שמחה] ין תחע לורד.

I will express my joy in the Lord.

מאי תחע עיבעלדוערס [רשעים] בי באנישהד פרום תחע עארתח [ארץ],

May the evildoers [RESHAEEM] be banished from the earth,

אנד תחע ויכעד שיז תו אקזישט.

And the wicked cease to exist,

בלאששעד [ברוך], יש תחע לורד,

Blessed is the Lord,

ו מי שול [נפש],

O my soul,

פראיז געד [הללו יה]!

Praise God [Hall-el-oo] [Yah]!

י Yod ט Tet ח Chet ז Zayin ו Vav ה Hei ד Dalet ג Gimel ב Beit א Aleph
ס Samech ן Final Nun נ Nun ם Final Mem מ Mem ל Lamed ך Final Kaf כ Kaf
ת Tav ש Shin ר Resh ק Kuf ץ Final Tzadik צ Tzadik ף Final Feh פ Peh ע Ayin

- 105 -

פראיז תחע לורד [הללו יה]!

Praise [Hall-el-oo] the Lord [Yah]!

אפפירם היש נאם [שם],

Affirm His Name,

ריביל היש וורקש תו אלל תחע נאתענז.

Reveal his works to all the nations.

פראיז הים וית מוזיך אנד שונג [שיר],

Praise Him with music and song,

תעלל אף היש וונדערז.

Tell of His wonders.

דיקלאר גלורי [כבוד] תו היש הולי נאם [שם],

Declare glory to His Holy Name,

אלל הו שיק תחע לורד וילל האב א האפפי העארט.

All who seek the Lord will have a happy heart.

פערשו תחע לורד, אנד היש פווערפול פורס,

Pursue the Lord, and His powerful force,

אלואיס שיך היש פרעסאנץ.

Always seek His Presence.

קומםמעמוראט היש וונדרעס דידז,

Commemorate His wondrous deeds,

תחאט הי ברועט אבאוט.

That He brought about.

היש מיראכאלז אנד פרוקלאמאשענז אף פרישעפתץ [מצות].

His miracles and proclamations of precepts.

ו עפפשפרינג אף היש סערבאנט ,אברהם,

O offspring of His servant, Abraham,

ו צוזען וונז דישענדעד פרום יעקב,

O chosen ones descended from Jacob,

הי יש תחע לורד אור געד,

He is the Lord our God,

היש געדגמענטץ ספאן תחע ענתיער עארתח [ארץ].

His judgments span the entire earth,

הי יש עבער כוממיתעד תו היש קובענאנט,

He is ever committed to His covenant,

תחע פלעדג הי גאב פור א תחעוזאנד גענעראתענז [דורות].

The pledge He gave for a thousand generations [GENERATIONS].

תחע קובענאנט תחאט הי ינועשתעד ין אברהם,

The covenant that He invested in Abraham,

אנד ואוד תו יצחק.

And vowed to Isaac.

תחען הי עשטאבלישד יטץ שתאצוט תו יעקב,

Then He established its statute to Jacob,

פור ישראל ,אז א פערפעצואל קובענאנט.

For Israel as a perpetual covenant.

שאיינג“ ,תו יו אי שחאלל גיב תחע לאנד אף כנען,

Saying, "To you I shall give the land of Canaan

אז תחע לוט אף יור ינהעריטאנץ”.

As the lot of your inheritance."

י Yod ט Tet ח Chet ז Zayin ו Vav ה Hei ד Dalet ג Gimel ב Beit א Aleph
ס Samech ן Final Nun נ Nun ם Final Mem מ Mem ל Lamed ך Final Kaf כ Kaf
ת Tav ש Shin ר Resh ק Kuf ץ Final Tzadik צ Tzadik ף Final Feh פ Peh ע Ayin

את תחאט תים תהאי ועג שמאלל ין נעמבער ,אונלי א פיו,

At that time they were small in number, only a few,

אנד תהאי וער שטראנגערז ין תחע אריא.

And they were strangers in the area.

תהאי ואנדערד פרום וון פיפעל [עם] תו אנותחער פיפעל [עם],

They wandered from one people to another people,

אנד פרום וון כינגדום תו אנותחער.

And from one kingdom to another.

הי דיד נעת אללוו אניוון תו ופפרעסס תהעם,

He did not allow anyone to oppress them,

אנד פור תהעם ,הי ריביוקד קינגז:

And for them, He rebuked kings:

שאיינג" ,דו נעת תעץ מי אנוינתעד וונז;

"Saying, Do not touch my anointed ones;

אנד דו נעת הארם מי פרופיטץ".

And do not harm my prophets."

הי פרונאונצד א פאמין תחרואוט תחע לאנד,

He pronounced a famine throughout the land,

אנד דישטרעכשען עפון עבערי שתאפף אף ברעד.

And destruction upon every staff of bread.

הי דישפאטצד א מאן [אדם] אהעאד אף תהעם,

He dispatched a man ahead of them,

יוסף, הו ואס סולד אס א שלאב.

Joseph, who was sold as a slave.

תהאי אפפליקתעד היז פוט וית צאינז,

They afflicted his foot with chains,

אנד היש בודי וית עירון רישתראינתץ.

And his body with the iron restraints.

וען היש פרידיכשענז כאם תו פאשש,

When his predictions came to pass,

יט ואס תחע וערד אף תחע לורד,

It was the word of the Lord,

תחאט פריד הים.

That freed him.

תחע כינג דיכלארד תחאט הי בי רילישד,

The king declared that he be released,

תחע מונארך אף תחע נאתענז פריד הים.

The Monarch of the nations freed him.

הי אמפאווערד הים אס מאסתער אף היז פאלאס,

He empowered him as master of his palace,

אנד כחארגד הים אז רולער אף אלל היש פוססעששענז.

And charged him as ruler of all his possessions.

תו דישאפלין היש נובעל פרינצעס את וילל,

To discipline his noble princes at will,

אנד תו ימפארט ויזדעם תו היש אלדערס.

And to impart wisdom to his elders.

סו ישראל כאם תו יגיפט,

So Israel came to Egypt,

י Yod ט Tet ח Chet ז Zayin ו Vav ה Hei ד Dalet ג Gimel ב Beit א Aleph
ס Samech ן Final Nun נ Nun ם Final Mem מ Mem ל Lamed ך Final Kaf כ Kaf
ת Tav ש Shin ר Resh ק Kuf ץ Final Tzadik צ Tzadik ף Final Feh פ Peh ע Ayin

אנד יעקב, תעמפוראריליִ שטאיד ין תחע לאנד אף חאם.

And Jacob temporarily stayed in the land of Ham.

אנד הי אללווד היש נאתען תו בי וערי פרוטפול,

And He allowed His nation to be very fruitful,

אנד תהאי ביכאם מיהתיער,

And they became mightier,

תחאן תחער ופרעססורז.

Than their oppressors.

אנד תחער הערט כחאנגד תו האט היש פיפעל [עם],

And their heart changed to hate His people,

תו קענשפיער אגאינצט היש סערבאנטץ.

To conspire against his servants.

הי דישפאטצד משה ,היש סערבאנט,

He dispatched Moses, His servant,

אנד אהרן, צוזען בי הים.

And Aaron, chosen by Him.

י Yod ט Tet ח Chet ז Zayin ו Vav ה Hei ד Dalet ג Gimel ב Beit א Aleph
ס Samech ן Final Nun נ Nun ם Final Mem מ Mem ל Lamed ך Final Kaf כ Kaf
ת Tav ש Shin ר Resh ק Kuf ץ Final Tzadik צ Tzadik ף Final Feh פ Peh ע Ayin

תהאי דעמונשראטעד תחע וורדז אף היש שיגנס,

They demonstrated the words of His signs,

אמונגצט תהעם,

Amongst them,

אנד היש וונדערז ין תחע לאנד אף חאם.

And His wonders in the the land of Ham.

הי דישפאטצד דארקנעסס אנד כוממאנדעד יט דארך,

He dispatched darkness and commanded it dark.

אנד דיד תהאי נעת ריזיסט היש וורד?

And did they not resist His word?

תחער ואתערז [מים] תערנד ינתו בלוד,

Their waters turned into blood,

תחער פיש הי קיללד.

Their fish He killed.

הי אובעראן תחער לאנד וית פרוגז,

He overran their land with frogs,

עיוען ויתהין תחע צאמבערס אף תחער קינגז.

Even within the chambers of their kings.

הי פרוכלאימעד אנד שוארמז,

He proclaimed and swarms,

אף ינשעקתץ אנד ליס ארר‎עיבד את עבערי בורדער.

Of insects and lice arrived at every border.

הי מאד תחער ראין ינתו האיל,

He made their rain into a hail,

תחרואוט תחער לאנד -- פיערי פלאמז,

Throughout their land -- fiery flames,

הי קעת דאון תחער גרעאט גראף וינז,

He cut down their great grape vines,

אלשו תחער פיג תריז,

Also their fig trees,

אנד שמאשד תחע תריז,

And smashed the trees,

אף תחער בורדערס.

Of their borders.

אנד הי כוממאנדעד אנד תחען כאם לוקעשתס,

And He commanded and then came locusts,

אנד תחען כאתערפיללערז, ויתחאוט נעמבער.

And then caterpillars, without number.

יט קונשומד אלל תחע ועגאתאשען ין תחע לאנד,

It consumed all the vegetation in the land,

אנד יט דיבאוערד אלל תחע פרוט עפון תחער שויל.

And it devoured all the fruit upon their soil.

אנד הי קעת דאון עברי פירסת בורן אף תחער לאנד,

And he cut down every firstborn of their land,

תחע עששענתאל פורס אף תחער מיט.

The essential force of their might.

הי לעד ישראל אוט וית שילבער אנד גולד,

He led Israel out with silver and gold,

אנד אמונג תחער תריבז,

And among their tribes,

וער נו פאילינג פיפעל.

Were no failing people.

יגיפט ריגוישט וען תהאי לעפט,

Egypt rejoiced when they left,

פור עפון תהעם האד פאללען תחע פיר אף ישראל.

For upon them had fallen the fear of Israel.

הי ענפולדעד א כלועד פור שחעלטער,

He unfolded a cloud for shelter,

אנד יללומינאתעד תחע נעית וית פיער.

And illuminated the night with fire,

תהאי ריקועשתעד ,אנד הי שעפפליד תחאם וית קואיל,

They requested, and he supplied them with quail,

אנד הי שאתישפיד תהעם וית ברעד פרום העאבען [שמים].

And He satisfied them with bread from heaven.

הי ענשעאלד א רוק אנד ואתעד [מים] געשד פורתח,

He unsealed a rock and water gushed forth,

תחרו פארצד פלאשעס יט ראן אז א שטרים.

Through parched places it ran as a stream.

ביקאעס הי ריכאללד היש סאכרעד קובענאנט,

Because He recalled His sacred covenant,

תו היז סערבאנט ,אברהם.

To his servant, Abraham.

אנד הי לעד היש פיפעל [עם] אוט וית גויעס שונג [שיר],

And He led His people out with joyous song,

אנד היש צוזען וונז וית גרעאט מעררימענט.

And his chosen ones with great merriment.

אנד הי ביקויתחד תו תהעם לאנדס אף ותחער נאתונז,

And He bequeathed to them lands of other nations,

אנד תהאי פוססעשד תחע תראבאיל אף עתחער נאתענז.

And they possessed the travail of other nations.

י Yod ט Tet ח Chet ז Zayin ו Vav ה Hei ד Dalet ג Gimel ב Beit א Aleph
ס Samech ן Final Nun נ Nun ם Final Mem מ Mem ל Lamed ך Final Kaf כ Kaf
ת Tav ש Shin ר Resh ק Kuf ץ Final Tzadik צ Tzadik ף Final Feh פ Peh ע Ayin

ין ורדער תחאט תהאי ובשערב אנד שאפגעארד,

In order that they observe and safeguard,

היש פרישעפתץ [מצות] אנד היש תיצינגס.

His precepts and His teachings.

פראיז געד [הללו יה]!

Praise God!

ר

- 106 -

ו הללויה!

O praise the Lord!

גיב תחאנקצגיבינג תו תחע לורד,

Give thanksgiving to the Lord,

פור היז גוודנעסס.

For His goodness.

היש לובינג-קינדנעשס [חסד] יש נעבער-ענדינג.

His loving kindness is never ending.

הו כאן ריכאונט תחע וונדרעס וורקש,

Who can recount the wondrous works,

אף תחע לורד?

Of the Lord?

אנד הו כאן אפפירם,

And who can affirm,

אלל היש פראיזוורתחי אכטץ?

All His praiseworthy acts?

האפפי אר תהוז הו שעפפורת גאסטיש [משפט],

Happy are those who support justice,

אנד אלואיז שעשתאין ריצאסנעשס [צדק].

And always sustain righteousness.

דו נעת פערגיט מי ,ו לורד,

Do not forget me, O Lord,

וען יו אקצתענד פאבור תו יור פיפעל [עם],

When You extend favor to your people,

אקשתענד יור שאלבאתען תו מי,

Extend Your salvation to me,

תחאט אי מאי ויתנעס תחע פאבור,

That I may witness the favor,

אף יור צוזען וונז,

Of Your chosen ones,

אנד תו ריגויס ין יור לעגאשי.

And to rejoice in Your legacy.

י Yod ט Tet ח Chet ז Zayin ו Vav ה Hei ד Dalet ג Gimel ב Beit א Aleph
ס Samech ן Final Nun נ Nun ם Final Mem מ Mem ל Lamed ך Final Kaf כ Kaf
ת Tav ש Shin ר Resh ק Kuf ץ Final Tzadik צ Tzadik ף Final Feh פ Peh ע Ayin

וי האו שיננד,

We have sinned,

אס דיד אור פורפאתחערז,

As did our forefathers,

וי האב בין ינבולבד,

We have been involved,

וית ענגעשט אנד ענריצעש אכתץ.

With unjust and unrighteous acts.

אור פורפאתחערס ין יגיפט,

Our forefathers in Egypt,

וער נעת ויז ריגארדינג יור גרעאט דידז;

Were not wise regarding Your great deeds;

תהאי דיד נעת ריכאלל יור גרעאט לובינג-קינדנעשס [חסד],

They did not recall Your great loving--kindness,

אנד תהאי דיפיד יו את תחע שי אף רידז.

And they defied You at the Sea of Reeds.

י Yod ט Tet ח Chet ז Zayin ו Vav ה Hei ד Dalet ג Gimel ב Beit א Aleph
ס Samech ן Final Nun נ Nun ם Final Mem מ Mem ל Lamed ך Final Kaf כ Kaf
ת Tav ש Shin ר Resh ק Kuf ץ Final Tzadik צ Tzadik ף Final Feh פ Peh ע Ayin

עיוען שו ,הי רעסקיוד תהעם,

Even so, He rescued them,

פור תחע שאך אף היש נאם [שם],

For the sake of His Name,

אנד תו ריביל היש מיט.

And to reveal His might.

הי כחידעד תחע שי אף רידס,

He chided the Sea of Reeds,

אנד יט כחאנגד ינתו דרי לאנד,

And it changed into dry land,

אנד תחען הי לעד תהעם תחרו יטץ דעפתס,

And then He led them through its depths,

אז יף יט וער א דעשערט.

As if it were a desert.

הי רעשקיוד תהעם פרום תחער אנאמיז האנדז,

He rescued them from their enemy's hands,

אנד הי סאבד תהעם פרום תחע האנדז אף תחער פוס.

And He saved them from the hands of their foes.

פור ואתער [מים] אנועלופד תחער טורמענתורס,

For water enveloped their tormentors,

נעת וון אף תהעם סערביבד.

Not one of them survived.

יט ואס תחען תחאט תהאי האד פאיתח,

It was then that they had faith

ין היש וורדז,

In His words,

אנד תהאי סאנג פראיזעז תו היש נאם [שם].

And they sang praises to His Name.

תהאי דיד קויכלי פורסאך היש וורקש,

They did quickly forsake His works,

תהאי דיד נעת ואית פור היש געידאנץ.

They did not wait for His guidance.

י Yod ט Tet ח Chet ז Zayin ו Vav ה Hei ד Dalet ג Gimel ב Beit א Aleph
ס Samech ן Final Nun נ Nun ם Final Mem מ Mem ל Lamed ך Final Kaf כ Kaf
ת Tav ש Shin ר Resh ק Kuf ץ Final Tzadik צ Tzadik ף Final Feh פ Peh ע Ayin

בעת תהאי וער קענשומד וית לעשט,

But they were consumed with lust,

ין תחע דעשערט,

In the desert,

אנד תהאי פרובוקד געד,

And they provoked God,

ין תחע וילדערנעססס.

In the wilderness.

אנד הי פערמיתעד תהעם תחער דעשיערז,

And he permitted them their desires,

בעת תחען דיליבערד ימאשיאשען,

But then delivered emaciation,

ין תחער שולז.

In their souls.

אנד געלושי אף משה,

And jealousy of Moses,

ואס אכשפרעשד ויתהין תחע קאמף,

Was expressed within the camp,

אס ועל אס תחע לורד׳ס הולי וון ,אהרן.

As well as the Lord's holy one, Aaron.

תחע עארתח [ארץ] שפליט אנד אנועלופד דתן,

The earth split and enveloped Dathon,

יט כלושד אובער אבירם אנד היז גרוף.

It closed over Ariram and his group.

אנד א בלאז תראבעלד,

And a blaze traveled,

תחרואוט תחער כומפאני,

Throughout their company,

תחע פיער קונשומד תחע ויכעד וונז.

The fire consumed the wicked ones.

תהאי פאשהענד א קאלף ין חורב,

They fashioned a calf in Horeb,

י Yod ט Tet ח Chet ז Zayin ן Vav ה Hei ד Dalet ג Gimel ב Beit א Aleph
ס Samech ן Final Nun נ Nun ם Final Mem מ Mem ל Lamed ך Final Kaf כ Kaf
ת Tav ש Shin ר Resh ק Kuf ץ Final Tzadik צ Tzadik ף Final Feh פ Peh ע Ayin

אנד תהאי פרושתראטעד תהאמשעלבז,

And they prostrated themselves,

ין תחע פרעסאנץ אף תחאט כאשט ימאג.

In the presence of that cast image.

תהאי ריפלאשד תחער הונור,

They replaced their honor,

פור תחע כאשט ימאג,

For the cast image,

אף א גראסס-איטינג בישט.

Of a grass--eating beast!

תהאי דיד נעת רימעמבער געד תחער סאביור [מושיעם],

They did not remember God their Savior [MOSHIEM],

הו ברועט אבאוט מעיתי דידז ין יגיפט.

Who brought about mighty deeds in Egypt.

מיראכאלז ין תחע לאנד אף חאם,

Miracles in the land of Ham,

אנד אושעם דידז בי תחע שי אף רידז.

And awesome deeds by the Sea of Reeds.

אנד הי דיכלארד הי וודׂ האב אנדעד תחער ליבז,

And He declared He would have ended their lives,

יף יט וער נעט פור משה, היש פאבורד וון,

If it were not for Moses, His favored one,

הו שתעפפד ינתו תחע בריץ עופאנינג ביפור הים,

Who stepped into the breach opening before him,

אנד אבערתעד תחע פיורי אף געד פרום אניהילאטינג תהעם .

And averted the fury of God from annihilating them.

אנד תחאי אבהוררד תחע גווד לאנד,

And they abhorred the good land,

תהאי פלאשד נו פאיתח ין היז וורד.

They placed no faith in His word.

באבבלינג ויתּ כומפלאינט,

Babbling with complaint,

י Yod ט Tet ח Chet ז Zayin ו Vav ה Hei ד Dalet ג Gimel ב Beit א Aleph
ס Samech ן Final Nun נ Nun ם Final Mem מ Mem ל Lamed ך Final Kaf כ Kaf
ת Tav ש Shin ר Resh ק Kuf ץ Final Tzadik צ Tzadik ף Final Feh פ Peh ע Ayin

תחרואוט תחער תענטץ,

Throughout their tents,

תהאי כאשט אשיד,

They cast aside,

תחע וויס אף תחע לורד.

The voice of the Lord.

אנד שו ,הי ראיזד היש האנד עפפושינג תחעם,

And so, He raised His hand opposing them,

אנד לעט תהעם פאיל ין תחע וילדערנעסס,

And let them fail in the wilderness,

תו דישפלאס תחער עפפשפרינג,

To displace their offspring,

תחרואוט תחע נאתענז,

Throughout the nations,

אנד דישפערס תהעם אמונג עתחער לאנדס.

And disperse them among other lands.

תהאי כונתיניוד תהער אלליגאנץ,

They continued their allegiance,

תו בעל פעור,

To Baal Peor,

אנד תהאי איט שאקריפיס ופפערינגז תו תהע דעאד.

And they ate sacrifice offerings to the dead.

תהאי ינפיוריאתעד הים וית תהער כונדעקט,

They infuriated Him with their conduct,

אנד א פלאג ברוק אוט תהרואוט תהעם.

And a plague broke out throughout them.

אנד פינחס קאם פורוארד תו עקשעכיוט געדגמענט [משפט],

And Phinehas came forward to execute judgment,

אנד תהע אותבראיק שיזד.

And the outbreak ceased.

תהיס מאריתוריעס דיד ואס אכקרעדיטעד תו הים,

This meritorious deed was accredited to him,

פור אלל גענעראשענז [דורות] תו נוו ,פור אבערמור.

For all generations to know, for evermore.

אלסו ,תהאי פרובוקד היש ראתח,

Also, they provoked His wrath,

בי תחע ואתערז [מים] אף שטריף,

By the waters of strife,

שו תחאט משה ואס מאד תו שעפפער,

So that Moses was made to suffer,

ביקאעס אף תהעם תוו,

Because of them too,

תחען תהאי שטיררד עף היש שול [נפש],

Then they stirred up his soul,

אנד הי ריתורטעד ויתח היז ליפס,

And He retorted with his lips,

תהאי דיד נות ואנקויש תחע נאתענז,

They did not vanquish the nations,

אככורדינג תו תחע וורד אף תחע לורד.

According to the word of the Lord.

ראתחער ,גוינד ין כומפאני,

Rather, joined in company,

וית עתחער נאתענז,

With other nations,

אנד לערנד תחער האביטץ,

And learned their habits,

אנד וורשהיפד תחער עידולז,

And worshiped their idols,

אנד וער תראפפד בי תחער אקשענס.

And were trapped by their actions.

שו ,עיואן תחער וון סענז אנד דאעטערז,

So, even their own sons and daughters,

וער סאכריפישעז תו דעביל וערשהיפערז.

Were sacrifices to devil worshipers.

י Yod ט Tet ח Chet ז Zayin ו Vav ה Hei ד Dalet ג Gimel ב Beit א Aleph
ס Samech ן Final Nun נ Nun ם Final Mem מ Mem ל Lamed ך Final Kaf כ Kaf
ת Tav ש Shin ר Resh ק Kuf ץ Final Tzadik צ Tzadik ף Final Feh פ Peh ע Ayin

וירצועס בלוד ואס שפיללד,

Virtuous blood was spilled,

תחע גילטלעסס בלוד,

The guiltless blood,

אף תחער שונז אנד דאעטערס,

Of their sons and daughters,

תחאט תהאי סאכריפישד תו תחע עידולז אף כנען;

That they sacrificed to the idols of Canaan;

אנד תחאט לאנד ואס כונטאמינאתעד בי בלוד.

And that land was contaminated by blood.

תחאי ואר קוררעפתעד בי תחער און וורקש,

They were corrupted by their own works,

אנד ואר דיבאכהד בי תחער און דידז.

And were debauched by their own deeds.

אנד תחע לורד'ז פיורי ואס יגניטעד,

And the Lord's fury was ignited,

י Yod ט Tet ח Chet ז Zayin ו Vav ה Hei ד Dalet ג Gimel ב Beit א Aleph
ס Samech ן Final Nun נ Nun ם Final Mem מ Mem ל Lamed ך Final Kaf כ Kaf
ת Tav ש Shin ר Resh ק Kuf ץ Final Tzadik צ Tzadik ף Final Feh פ Peh ע Ayin

טוארד היש פיפעל [עם],

Toward His people,

אנד הי דישפעצד היש לעגאסי.

And He despised His legacy.

סו ,הי שורענדערד תהעם,

So, He surrendered them,

ינתו תחע האנדז אף עתחער נאתענז,

Into the hands of other nations,

אנד תהוז תחאט האתעד תהעם,

And those that hated them,

האד דומיניון אובער תהעם.

Had dominion over them.

תהאי שופפערד ענדער תחער אנעמייז רול,

They suffered under their enemy's rule,

תהאי ווער מאד העמבעל ענדער תחער ראין.

They were made humble under their reign,

עְן מאני אוכאשענז ,הי שאבד תהעם,

On many occasions, He saved them,

בעת תהאי רימאינד ינשולענט,

But they remained insolent,

אגאין ,תהאי וער העמבעלד בי תחער שינס.

Again, they were humbled by their sins.

הוועבער ,וען הי עבשערבד תחער שעפפערינג,

However, when He observed their suffering

אנד הי הערד תחער קריס,

And He heard their cries,

הי ריכאללד היש קובענאנט,

He recalled His covenant,

אנד רילענתעד,

And relented,

אככורדינג תו היש גרעאט לובינג-קינדנעשס [חסד].

According to His great loving-kindness.

אנד הי אללאועד תהעם שימפאתחי,

And He allowed them sympathy,

פרום אלל תהוז הו וער תחער קאפתורס.

From all those who were their captors.

דיליוער עש ,ו לורד ,אור געד,

Deliver us, O Lord, our God,

גאתחער עש ין פרום אמונג אלל תחע פיפעלס,

Gather us in from among all the peoples,

תו פראיז יור הולי נאם [שם],

To praise Your holy Name,

אנד ין יור פראיז ,תו בי פראוד.

And in Your praise, to be proud.

בלאששעד [ברוך] יש תחע לורד ,תחע געד אף ישראל,

Blessed is the Lord, the God of Israel,

פרום תחיס וורלד אף תחע ליבינג,

From this world of the living,

תו תחע וורלד תחאט יש תו קעם.

To the world that is to come.

אנד לעט אלל תחע נאתענז שאי, "אמן"!

And let all the nations say, "Amen!"

הללו יה!

Praise God!

- 107 -

גיב תחאנקשגיבינג תו געד,

Give thanksgiving to God,

פור היש גוודנעסס;

For His goodness;

ביקאעס היש לובינג-קינדנעשס [חסד] יש יטערנאל!

Because His loving-kindness is eternal!

לעט תהוז גיבען רידעמפשען,

Let those given redemption,

בי תחע לורד, רילאט יט,

By the Lord, relate it,

תהוז גיבען רידאמפשען,

Those given redemption,

פרום תחע אנעמייס האנד.

From the enemy's hand.

אנד הי אששעמבעלד תחעם פרום תחע לאנד–

And He assembled them from the land --

פרום תחע עאשת אנד פרום תחע ועשת,

From the East and from the West,

אנד פרום תחע נורתח,

And from the North,

אנד פרום תחע שי.

And from the sea.

ין סוליתארי ,שום לושט תחער ואי,

In solitary, some lost their way,

ין תחע דעשולאשען אף תחע וילדערנעסס,

In the desolation of the wilderness,

תהאי דיד נעת פינד אן ינהאביתעד שעתתעלמענט.

They did not find an inhabited settlement.

שטארבינג אנד אלסו תחירשטינג ,תחער שולז פאלתערד.

Starving and also thirsting, their souls faltered.

אנד תהאי כאללד אוט תו תחע לורד,

And they called out to the Lord,

ין תחער דעשולאתען,

In their desolation,

אנד פרום תחער רעתצעדנעשש,

And from their wretchedness,

הי דיליבערד תהעם.

He delivered them.

הי געידעד תהעם פוארד,

He guided them forward,

ען א שתראיט פאתח,

On a straight path,

תו אן ינהאביטעד שעתתעלמאנט.

To an inhabited settlement.

ו לעט תהעם גיב תחאנקשגיבינג,

O let them give thanksgiving,

תו תחע לורד פור היש באנעבולענץ,

To the Lord for His benevolence,

אנד פור היש מארבעלוס דידז תו מאנקינד.

And for His marvelous deeds to mankind.

פור הי פיללד וית כונטענת,

For He filled with content,

תחע דישקויעתעד שול [נפש],

The disquieted soul,

אנד שאתיספיד תחע ענפולפילד שול [נפש],

And satisfied the unfulfilled soul,

וית וירצו.

With virtue.

תחער אר תהוז הו דועלל ין תחע דארך,

There are those who dwell in the dark,

אנד ין דעאחת'ס שהאדוו.

And in death's shadow.

תהוז תחאט אר באונד,

Those that are bound,

אנד אפפליקתעד וית שהאקעלז,

And afflicted with shackles ,

ביקאעס תהאי האב דיפילד,

Because they have defiled,

תחע וערד אף געד,

The word of God

אנד כאשט דישדאין עפון,

And cast disdain upon,

תחע אדויס אף תחע מושט הי.

The advice of the Most High.

אנד הי דיגראדעד תחער הארטץ,

And He degraded their hearts,

וית תויל.

With toil.

תהאי ער ברועט לוו,

They were brought low,

אנד תהאי ואר ויתאוט העלף.

And they were without help.

אנד תהאי כאללד אוט תו תחע לורד,

And they called out to the Lord,

ין תחער מיספורצען,

In their misfortune,

אנד פרום תחער אפפליקשען,

And from their affliction,

הי רידימד תהעם,

He redeemed them,

פרום כונשומינג דארקנעסס,

From consuming darkness,

אנד פרום אוט אף תחע שהאדוו אף דעאתח,

And from the out of the shadow of death,

אנד שפליט אפארט תחער שהאקלז,

And split apart their shackles,

תחאט באונד תהעם.

That bound them.

לעט תחע רעשקיוד פראיז תחע לורד,

Let the rescued praise the Lord,

פור היש לובינג-קינדנעשס [חסד],

For His loving--kindness,

אנד היש גראשעס גיפטס תו מאנקינד,

And His gracious gifts to mankind,

פור הי האש שמאשהד תחער ברונז גאתץ,

For He has smashed their bronze gates,

אנד הי האש קעת אופען תחער עירון בארז.

And He has cut open their iron bars.

ביהולד תחע פוולז!

Behold the fools!

ביקאעס אף תחער שינס,

Because of their sins,

תחער ורעצעד ואיז,

Their wretched ways,

תהאי שעפפערד תריבולאשען,

They suffered tribulation,

אלל פוד ואס אן אבומינאשען תו תחער שול [נפש],

All food was an abomination to their soul,

אנד תהאי כאם ביפור תחע גאתץ אף דעאתח.

And they came before the gates of death.

אנד תהאי כאללד אוט תו תחע לורד,

And they called out to the Lord,

ין תחער מיספורצען;

In their misfortune;

פרום תחער גריף,

From their grief,

הי רעשקיוד תהעם.

He rescued them.

הי סענט פורתח היש וערד אנד כיורד תהעם,

He sent forth His word and cured them,

אנד הי ליבעראתעד תהעם פרום תחע גראב.

And He liberated them from the grave.

לעט תחע רעשקיוד פראיז תחע לורד,

Let the rescued praise the Lord,

פור היש לובינג-קינדנעשס [חסד],

For His loving kindness,

אנד היש גראשעס גיפטס תו מאנקינד,

And His gracious gifts to mankind,

אנד וית תחאנקשגיבינג פראיזעס אנד שאכריפיסעז,

And with thanksgiving praises and sacrifices,

לעט תהעם ריכאונט תחע דידז,

Let them recount the deeds,

אף תחע לורד.

Of the Lord.

י Yod ט Tet ח Chet ז Zayin ו Vav ה Hei ד Dalet ג Gimel ב Beit א Aleph
ס Samech ן Final Nun נ Nun ם Final Mem מ Mem ל Lamed ך Final Kaf כ Kaf
ת Tav ש Shin ר Resh ק Kuf ץ Final Tzadik צ Tzadik ף Final Feh פ Peh ע Ayin

תהוז הו דישענד תו תחע שי ין שחיפס,

Those who descend to the sea in ships,

תו דו תחער בישנעסס עפון מעיתי ואתערז [מים],

To do their business upon mighty waters,

תהאי האב סין תחע קריאשענס אף תחע לורד,

They have seen the creations of the Lord,

אנד היז וונדרעס וורקש תחרואוט תחע דיף.

And His wondrous works throughout the deep.

פור את היש וערד תחע תעמפעשט וינד ראיסעז עף,

For at his word the tempest wind raises up,

אנד מאקס תחע ואיבז שערג הי .

And makes the waves surge high.

תהאי שערג עף טוארד העאבען [שמים],

They surge up toward heaven,

אנד דימיניש ינתו תחע דעפתס,

And diminish into the depths,

תחערביינג יש דישולבד וית רונג.

Their being is dissolved with wrong.

תהאי טערן אנד תוטטער אס א דרונקען מאן [אדם],

They turn and totter as a drunken man,

אנד אלל תחער עפפורתץ אר פור נוט.

And all their efforts are for naught.

תחען ,ין תחער ורעתצעדנעשש,

Then, in their wretchedness,

תהאי כאללד אוט תו תחע לורד,

They called out to the Lord,

אנד פרום תחער אדבערשיתי,

And from their adversity,

הי רעשקיוד תהעם.

He rescued them.

הי אורדערד תחע שתורם תו טראנקויליתי,

He ordered the storm to tranquility,

י Yod ט Tet ח Chet ז Zayin ו Vav ה Hei ד Dalet ג Gimel ב Beit א Aleph
ס Samech ן Final Nun נ Nun ם Final Mem מ Mem ל Lamed ך Final Kaf כ Kaf
ת Tav ש Shin ר Resh ק Kuf ץ Final Tzadik צ Tzadik ף Final Feh פ Peh ע Ayin

אנד שתיללד תחע ראגינג ואבז.

And stilled get the raging waves.

גויפולי תהאי ביהעלד תחע קויעט שי,

Joyfully they beheld the quiet sea,

אנד הי געידעד תהעם פורתח,

And He guided them forth,

תו תחער וישד פור הארבור.

To their wished for harbor.

לעט תחע רעשקיוד פראיז תחע לורד,

Let the rescued praise the Lord,

פור היש לובינג-קינדנעשס [חסד],

For His loving--kindness,

אנד היש גראשעס גיפטס תו מאנקינד.

And his gracious gifts to mankind.

לעט תהעם גיב הים אכשולטאשענס אף פראיז,

Let them give Him exultations of praise,

ויתהין תחע קונגרעגאשענז אף תחע פיפעל [עם],

Within the congregations of the people,

אנד כוממענד היש פאיתפולנעסס,

And commend His faithfulness,

ין תחע גאתחערינג אף תחע עלדערז.

In the gathering of the elders.

הי כאעשעז ריבערס תו ביכום א וילדערנעסס,

He causes rivers to become a wilderness,

אנד שפרינגז אף ואתער [מים] תו ביכום בא‎ררען לאנד.

And springs of water to become barren land.

אנד באונתיפול לאנד,

And bountiful land,

תו ביכום א שאלט מארש,

To become a salt marsh,

אס א רעתריבושען פור תחע עיבעל ינהאביטאנתץ,

As a retribution for the evil inhabitants,

תחאט ריזיד ויתהין יט.

That reside within it.

הי כוממאנדז פוולז תו אפפיר ין תחע וילדערנעסס,

He commands pools to appear in the wilderness,

אנד ואתער-שפרינגס אר ברועט פורתח פרום תחע דעשערט.

And water--springs are brought forth from the desert.

תהער הי עשטאבלישהד א שעתתעלמענט פור הענגרי פיפעל,

There He established a settlement for hungry people,

אנד ברועט פורתח א סיטי תו בי שעתתעלד.

And brought forth a city to be settled.

אנד תהאי כעלתיואתעד תחע עארתח [ארץ],

And they cultivated the earth,

אנד עסטאבלישהד ויניארדז,

And established vineyards,

אנד תחיז ברועט פורתח,

And these brought forth,

א פרוט פיללד הארועשת.

A fruit filled harvest

הי סענט היש בלעססינגז עפון תהעם,

He sent His blessings upon them,

אנד קאעשד תהעם תו גרעאתלי מעלטיפלי,

And caused them to greatly multiply,

אנד הי דיד נות אללו תחער ליבשתוך תו דימיניש,

And He did not allow their livestock to diminish,

אלתחו תהאי האד בין דיפופולאתעד אנד דיגראדעד,

Although they had been depopulated and degraded,

בי פערשעכיושען ,תרועבעל ,אנד גריף.

By persecution, trouble, and grief.

הי שפיללס דיסדאין עפון נובעלמען,

He spills disdain upon noblemen,

אנד שענדז תהעם ואנדערינג ינתו תחע פאתחלעשש דעשערט.

And sends them wandering into the pathless desert.

י Yod ט Tet ח Chet ז Zayin ו Vav ה Hei ד Dalet ג Gimel ב Beit א Aleph
ס Samech ן Final Nun נ Nun ם Final Mem מ Mem ל Lamed ך Final Kaf כ Kaf
ת Tav ש Shin ר Resh ק Kuf ץ Final Tzadik צ Tzadik ף Final Feh פ Peh ע Ayin

הי מאקס לופתי תחע נידי,

He makes lofty the needy,

אנד הי דיליבערז תהעם פרום דעסטיתושען,

And He delivers them from destitution,

אנד עקספאנדז תחער פאמיליש ליק א פלוך.

And expands their families like a flock.

פיללד וית גוי [שמחה] ,תחע עפריט שחאלל ביהולד תהיש,

Filled with joy, the upright shall behold this,

תחע עיבעלדוערס׳ [רשעים] מאותס אר אלל האלטעד.

The evildoers' mouths are all halted.

תהוז הו האב ויזדום וילל ענדערשטאנד תהיז תחינגס,

Those who have wisdom will understand these things,

תהאי וילל תאק נוט אנד ענדערשטאנד,

They will take note and understand,

תחע באנעבולענץ אף תחע לורד.

The benevolence of the Lord.

- 108 -

א שונג [שיר] אף דוד,

A song of David,

מי הערת יש רעשולוט ו געד,

My heart is resolute O God,

מי וויס וילל שינג אנד גיב פראיז,

My voice will sing and give praise,

יששוינג פרום מי וערי שול [נפש].

Issuing from my very soul.

אואקען ,ו נבל אנד כנור,

Awaken, O harp and lyre,

אס אי אואקען תחע דאון!

As I awaken the dawn!

אי וילל שינג יור פראיז,

I will sing Your praise,

אמונג תחע פיפעלס ,ו לורד,

Among the peoples, O Lord,

אנד יור פראיזעס,

And Your praises,

אי וילל שינג תו אלל תחע נאתענז!

I will sing all the nations,

ביקאעס יור לובינג-קינדנעשס [חסד],

Because Your loving--kindness,

ריצעז היער תהאן תחע העאבענז [שמים] אבעו,

Reaches higher than the heavens above,

אנד יור טרותה ריזעס אבעו תחע כלאודס.

And your truth rises above the clouds.

יו אר אקזאלטעד אבעו אלל תחע העאבענז [שמים] ,ו געד,

You are exalted above all the heavens, O God,

יור גלורי [כבוד] קובערז אובער אלל תחע עארתח [ארץ].

Your glory covers over all the earth.

תחאט תהוז הו יו לוב מאי בי רעשקיוד,

That those who You love may be rescued,

פרישערו מי ;שאב מי וית יור רעיט האנד.

Preserve me; save me with Your right hand.

ין היש הולינעשש ,געד פרוכלאימד:

In his Holiness, God proclaimed:

אי ווד סעלאבראת אובער מי פורשען;

I would celebrate over my portion;

דיוידינג שכם ,אנד מעשורינג אוט,

Dividing Shechem, and measuring out,

תחע ואללי אף סכות;

The Valley of Sukkoth;

גלעד אנד מנשה ביכום מין;

Gilead and Manasseh become mine;

אפרים יש תחע סענתער אף מי סטרענת [כח],

Ephraim is the center of my strength,

אנד יהודה פרובידז תחע לאו,

And Judah provides the law,

י Yod ט Tet ח Chet ז Zayin ו Vav ה Hei ד Dalet ג Gimel ב Beit א Aleph
ס Samech ן Final Nun נ Nun ם Final Mem מ Mem ל Lamed ך Final Kaf כ Kaf
ת Tav ש Shin ר Resh ק Kuf ץ Final Tzadik צ Tzadik ף Final Feh פ Peh ע Ayin

מואב שערבז אס מי ואשהבאשין;

Moab serves as my washbasin:

אנד אי וילל כאשט מי שחו אובער אדום;

And I will cast my shoe over Edom:

אי וילל בי ויקתוריעס אובער פילישתיה!

I will be victorious over Philistia!

הו וילל דירעקט מי תו תחע שתרונגהולד?

Who will direct me to the stronghold?

ו הו וילל דירעקט מי טוארד אדום?

O who will direct me toward Edom?

האב יו נאו פורשאקאן עש ,ו געד?

Have you now forsaken us, O God?

אר יו נעת לידינג אור ליגענס פוררד ,ו געד?

Are you not leading our legions forward, O God?

בי אור איד אגאינצט מיספורצען!

Be our aid against misfortune!

מאןיס סאלואשען יש וורתהלעסס!

Man`s salvation is worthless!

ויקטורי יש תחע וורק אף געד!

Victory is the work of God!

יט יש הי הו שחאלל תראמפעל אור אנעמיז!

It is He who shall trample our enemies!

ל

י Yod ט Tet ח Chet ז Zayin ו Vav ה Hei ד Dalet ג Gimel ב Beit א Aleph
ס Samech ן Final Nun נ Nun ם Final Mem מ Mem ל Lamed ך Final Kaf כ Kaf
ת Tav ש Shin ר Resh ק Kuf ץ Final Tzadik צ Tzadik ף Final Feh פ Peh ע Ayin

- 109 -

תו תחע כונדעקטור ,א שונג [שיר] אף דוד:

To the conductor, a song of David:

ו געד ,הום אי פראיז,

O God, whom I praise,

דו נעת בי ויתהדראון.

Do not be withdrawn.

ביקאעס תחע מאותס אף תחע ויכעד וונז,

Because the mouths of the wicked ones,

אנד תחע מאותס אף תחע דישיטפול וונז,

And the mouths of the deceitful ones,

האב וענתעד אגאינצט מי,

Have vented against me,

תחער תוענגז שפיק פאלשלי.

Their tongues speak falsely.

תהאי גאתחער אראונד מי ויתה האתפול וורדז,

They gather around me with hateful words,

אנד ויתאוט ריזון ,אתתאק מי.

And without reason, attack me.

תהאי ריספונד תו מי לוב וית כרואלתי,

They respond to my love with cruelty,

אי אם רישולבד ין פראיער.

I am resolved in prayer.

אנד תהאי האב בורדענד מי וית יבעל,

And they have burdened me with evil,

אס א פאימענט פור גווד,

As a payment for good,

אנד פור מי לוב,

And for my love,

תהאי דיקלאר:

They declare:

אשסין א ויכעד מאן [אדם],

Assign a wicked man,

תו שתאנד אובער הים,

To stand over him,

אנד לעט אן עיבעל דוער בי את היש ריט שיד.

And let an evil doer be in his right side.

וען געדגמענט [משפט] יש מאד את היש תריאל,

When judgment is made at his trial,

לעט היש גילט בי קונפירמד,

Let his guilt be confirmed,

אנד לעט היש סעפלעכאשענס בי קוררעפתעד.

And let his supplications be corrupted.

לעט היש דאיס בי רעדוסד תו א פיו,

Let his days be reduced to a few,

לעט היש פושישען בי פיללד בי אנותחער.

Let his position be filled by another.

לעט היש צילדרען ביכום פאתחערלעשש,

Let his children become fatherless,

לעט היש ויף ביכום א וידוו.

Let his wife become a widow.

לעט היש צילדרען רום אנד ואנדער אס ואגראנץ,

Let his children roam and wander as vagrants,

בעגגינג אנד שערצינג,

Begging and searching,

פור תחער דאילי ברעד,

For their daily bread,

פרום תחער ואשטלאנד.

From their wasteland.

לעט היש כרעדיטורס אקסתורט,

Let his creditors extort,

אלל אף היש פושששעשענז,

All of his possessions,

אנד לעט שטראנגערס פלענדער,

And let strangers plunder,

י Yod ט Tet ח Chet ז Zayin ו Vav ה Hei ד Dalet ג Gimel ב Beit א Aleph
ס Samech ן Final Nun נ Nun ם Final Mem מ Mem ל Lamed ך Final Kaf כ Kaf
ת Tav ש Shin ר Resh ק Kuf ץ Final Tzadik צ Tzadik ף Final Feh פ Peh ע Ayin

אלל תחאט הי האש לאבורד תו פרודוס.

All that he has labored to produce.

לעט נו וון שהו הים לובינג-קינדנעשס [חסד],

Let no one show him loving-kindness,

אנד לעט נו וון שהו מערסי תו היש פאתחערלעסס אורפהאנז.

And let no one show mercy to his fatherless orphans.

לעט הים האב נו דעסענדאנץ,

Let him have no descendents,

אנד לעט תחער נאם [שם] בי יראשד,

And let their Name be erased,

ין תחע וערי נעקצט גענעראשען [דר].

In the very next generation [DOR].

לעט תחע לורד ריכאלל,

Let the Lord recall,

תחע ויקעדנעשס אף היש אנשעסטורס,

The wickedness of his ancestors,

אנד לעט נעת א שין אף היז מותחער,

And let not a sin of his mother,

בי ובליטעראתעד.

Be obliterated.

לעט תחע לורד בי אואר כונתיניואללי אף תהעם,

Let the Lord be continually aware of them,

אנד לעט תחער נאמז בי פורגוטטין,

And let their Names be forgotten,

פרום אלל תחע עארתח [ארץ].

From all the earth.

דו תחיס ביקאעס הי דיד נעת רימעמבער,

Do this because he did not remember,

תו אקזיביט לובינג-קינדנעשס [חסד],

To exhibit loving-kindness,

בעת ראתחער הי האונדעד ענטו דעאתח,

But rather he hounded unto death,

י Yod ט Tet ח Chet ז Zayin ו Vav ה Hei ד Dalet ג Gimel ב Beit א Aleph
ס Samech ן Final Nun נ Nun ם Final Mem מ Mem ל Lamed ך Final Kaf כ Kaf
ת Tav ש Shin ר Resh ק Kuf ץ Final Tzadik צ Tzadik ף Final Feh פ Peh ע Ayin

תחע דעשטיטות אנד רעתצעד מאן [אדם],

The destitute and wretched man,

אנד דיפרעשד תחע ברוקענהעארתעד,

And depressed the brokenhearted,

תו תחער ועריִ דעאתח.

To their very death.

אס הי לובד תו כערס,

As he loved to curse,

נאו ,לעט כערשעס קום תו הים;

Now, let curses come upon him;

אס הי וֹוד נעת בלעשש,

As he would not bless,

נאו ,לעט בלעססינגז נעת קעם תו הים.

Now, let blessings not come to him.

תחע ואי הי וור כערשעס ליק א יוניפורם,

The way he wore curses like a uniform,

נאו ,לעט יט פלוו אס ואתער [מים] ינתו הישביינג,

Now, let it flow as water into his being,

אנד ינתו היש בונז ליק אויל.

And into his bones like oil.

לעט הים בי אנראפפד ין כלוז ין תחיס מאננער;

Let him be enwrapped in clothes in this manner;

אנד אס ין א בעלתעד כלוך,

And as in a belted cloak

תחאט יש שעכיורד כונתינואללי.

That is secured continually.

תחאט יש תחע אקשען אף מי אנעמיז תו תחע לורד,

That is the action of my enemies to the Lord,

אנד אף תהוז הו כאשט עיבעל שפיץ אגאינצט מי.

And of those who cast evil speech against me.

פור יו ו געד ,מי לורד,

For You O God, my Lord,

י Yod ט Tet ח Chet ז Zayin ו Vav ה Hei ד Dalet ג Gimel ב Beit א Aleph
ס Samech ן Final Nun נ Nun ם Final Mem מ Mem ל Lamed ך Final Kaf כ Kaf
ת Tav ש Shin ר Resh ק Kuf ץ Final Tzadik צ Tzadik ף Final Feh פ Peh ע Ayin

ריספונד תו מי פור תחע שאק אף יור נאם [שם],

Respond to me for the sake of Your Name,

ען אככאונט אף יור לובינג-קינדנעשס [חסד]--

On account of Your loving-kindness --

גראנט מי יור סאלבאשען [ישועה]!

Grant me Your salvation [YESHUAH]!

פור אי אם ורעצעד אנד דעשטיתוט,

For I am wretched and destitute,

מי הערט ינסיד מי יש הוללוו.

My heart inside me is hollow.

ליק א פליתינג שהאדוו,

Like a fleeting shadow,

אי פאסש פרום סיט;

I pass from sight;

היר אנד תחער פלאשהינג אס א לוכעסת,

Here and there flashing as a locust,

מי ניז בעקאל פרום פאשטינג,

My knees buckle from fasting,

אנד ויתאות פאט מי לין בודי יש ויך.

And without fat my lean body is weak.

אנד אי ואס א דישגראס תו תהעם;

And I was a disgrace to them;

תהוז הו שי מי,

Those who see me,

שהאק תחער העאדז.

Shake their heads.

העלף מי ,ו לורד ,מי געד,

Help me, O Lord, my God,

גראנת מי סאלבאשען [ישועה],

Grant me salvation,

ין אככורד וית יור לובינג-קינדנעשס [חסד]!

In accord with Your loving-kindness!

י Yod ט Tet ח Chet ז Zayin ו Vav ה Hei ד Dalet ג Gimel ב Beit א Aleph
ס Samech ן Final Nun נ Nun ם Final Mem מ Mem ל Lamed ך Final Kaf כ Kaf
ת Tav ש Shin ר Resh ק Kuf ץ Final Tzadik צ Tzadik ף Final Feh פ Peh ע Ayin

לעט מען נוו תהאט בי תהיש יור האנד,

Let men know that by this Your hand,

יו ,ו לורד ,האב אקתעד.

You, O Lord, have acted.

לעט תהעם פרונאונץ כערשעס,

Let them pronounce curses,

אס יו וילל בלעשש תהעם,

As you will bless them,

אנד וען תהאי ביכאם עלאואטעד,

And when they became elevated,

תהאי שחאלל בי הומיליאתעד,

They shall be humiliated,

אנד לעט יור סערבאנט בי גויפול!

And let Your servant be joyful!

לעט מי אנעמיז ועאר תחיס הומיליאשען,

Let my enemies wear this humiliation,

י Yod ט Tet ח Chet ז Zayin ו Vav ה Hei ד Dalet ג Gimel ב Beit א Aleph
ס Samech ן Final Nun נ Nun ם Final Mem מ Mem ל Lamed ך Final Kaf כ Kaf
ת Tav ש Shin ר Resh ק Kuf ץ Final Tzadik צ Tzadik ף Final Feh פ Peh ע Ayin

ליק א גארמענט,

Like a garment,

תחער דישגראס ענראפינג תהעם ליק א קלוך.

Their disgrace in enwrapping them like a cloak.

מי ליפס וילל סינג ענבאונדעד פראיזעס תו תחע לורד,

My lips will sing unbounded praises to the Lord,

אנד תחרואוט תחע מעלטיתודז אף פיפעל,

And throughout the multitudes of people,

וילל אי פראיז הים.

Will I praise Him.

ביקאעס יט יש הי ,הו שתאנדז,

Because it is He, Who stands,

בי תחע רעיט האנד אף תהוז ין ניד,

By the right hand of those in need,

תו רעשקיו הים פרום תהוז הו וװד געדג היש שול [נפש].

To rescue him from those who would judge his soul.

י Yod ט Tet ח Chet ז Zayin ו Vav ה Hei ד Dalet ג Gimel ב Beit א Aleph
ס Samech ן Final Nun נ Nun ם Final Mem מ Mem ל Lamed ך Final Kaf כ Kaf
ת Tav ש Shin ר Resh ק Kuf ץ Final Tzadik צ Tzadik ף Final Feh פ Peh ע Ayin

- 110 -

אף דוד ,א שונג [שיר].

Of David, a song.

תחע וורדז עף תחע לורד ספוקען טו מי לורד.

The words of the Lord spoken to my lord:

"בי שיתעד את מי רעיט האנד,

Be seated at my right hand,

ענטיל תחע תים אי פלאס יור אנעמיז,

Until the time I place your enemies,

אס א סתול פור יור פיט".

As a stool for your feet."

תחע לורד וילל שענד פורתח,

The Lord will send forth,

פרום אוט אף ציון,

From out of Zion,

תחע שעפתער אף יור מיט.

The scepter of your might.

גוברן,

Govern,

ין תחע מידצת אף יור אנעמיז!

In the midst of your enemies!

יור פיפעל [עם] אף תחער פרי וילל,

Your people of their free will,

שתוד עף ען תחע דאי אף באתתעל,

Stood up on the day of battle,

תחערפור ,ין תחע מאגעשטי אף הולינעסס,

Therefore, in the majesty of holiness,

כומינג פרום תחע וומב אף תחע מורנינג,

Coming from the womb of the morning,

יורז יש תחע דו אף יור צילדהוד.

Yours is the dew of your childhood.

תחע לורד האש ואוד,

The Lord has vowed,

אנד וילל נעבער רעפודיאט:

And will never repudiate:

"פוראבער ,יו שחאלל בי א פרישט,

"Forever, you shall be a priest,

א געסט קינג ,בי מי וורד".

A just king by my word."

תחער ,את יור רעיט האנד,

There at at your right hand,

יש תחע לורד!

Is the Lord!

עפון תחע דאי אף היש ראתח,

Upon the day of His wrath,

הי דימולישעז קינגז!

He demolishes kings!

הי פאססעש געדגמענט [משפט] תחרואוט תחע נאתענז,

He passes judgment throughout the nations,

י Yod ט Tet ח Chet ז Zayin ו Vav ה Hei ד Dalet ג Gimel ב Beit א Aleph
ס Samech ן Final Nun נ Nun ם Final Mem מ Mem ל Lamed ך Final Kaf כ Kaf
ת Tav ש Shin ר Resh ק Kuf ץ Final Tzadik צ Tzadik ף Final Feh פ Peh ע Ayin

אבענדאנט וית דעאד בודיז,

Abundant with dead bodies,

אנד כרעשהינג מאני נאתענז רולערז,

And crushing many nation's rulers,

אלונג היש ואי ,

Along his way,

פרום תחע ואתערז [מים] אף א ריבער הי שחאלל דרינך;

From the waters of a river he shall drink;

אנד שו הי שחאלל ראיז היש העאד אנד הולד יט הי.

And so he shall raise his head and hold it high.

ו

- 111 -

א

גלורי [כבוד] תו געד!

Glory to God!

אי שחאלל פראיז תחע לורד הולהעארתעדלי,

I shall praise the Lord wholeheartedly,

ב

ין תחע כאונשיל אף תחע עפריט ,אששעמבעלד,
אנד ין תחע כונגרעגאשען.

In the council of the upright, assembled,
And in the congregation.

ג

תחע אכקומפלישמענץ אף תחע לורד אר גרעאט,

The accomplishments of the Lord are great,

ד

אנד אואילאבעל תו אלל הו לונג פור תהעם.

And available to all who long for them.

ה

גלוריעס אנד מאגעשתיך אר היש דידז,

Glorious and majestic are His deeds,

ו

אנד היש גאסטיש [משפט] יש יטערנאל.

And His justice is eternal.

ז

היש גרעאט אנד וונדרעס דידז אר עברלאשתינג,

His great and wondrous deeds are everlasting,

ח

פיללד וית כעמפאששען,
אנד לובינג-קינדנעשס [חסד] יש תחע לורד.

Filled with compassion,
And loving kindness is the Lord.

ט

פור תהוז הו הולד הים ין או,
הי פרובידז שאשטאנאנץ,

For those who hold Him in awe,
He provides sustenance,

י

הי וילל רימעמבער היש קובענאנט פור יתערנאטי.

He will remember His covenant for eternity.

כ

הי ריבילד תחע מיט אף היש דידז תו היש פיפעל [עם],

He revealed the might of His deeds to His people,

ל

תו ביקויתח תו תהעם תחע פיפעלס' ינהעריטאנץ.

To bequeath to them the people's inheritance.

מ

היש האנד'ז דידז אר ין טרותה אנד לאו,

His hand's deeds are in truth and law,

נ

היש פרישעפתץ [מצות] אר אלל טרו,

His precepts are all true,

א Aleph ב Beit ג Gimel ד Dalet ה Hei ו Vav ז Zayin ח Chet ט Tet י Yod
כ Kaf ך Final Kaf ל Lamed מ Mem ם Final Mem נ Nun ן Final Nun ס Samech
ע Ayin פ Peh ף Final Feh צ Tzadik ץ Final Tzadik ק Kuf ר Resh ש Shin ת Tav

ס

אנד אבערלאשתינג פור אלל יתערנאטי.

And everlasting for all eternity.

ע

אנד תהאי אר אכהיבד,
טרותהפוללי אנד פאירלי.

And they are achieved,
Truthfully and fairly.

פ

הי האש דיליבערד רידעמפשען,
תו היש פיפעל [עם],

He has delivered redemption,
To His people,

צ

היש כובענאנץ הי האש אורדאינד פור יתערנאטי.

His covenants he has ordained for eternity.

ק

היש נאם [שם] יש שאכרעד אנד אושעם.

His Name is sacred and awesome.

י Yod ט Tet ח Chet ז Zayin ו Vav ה Hei ד Dalet ג Gimel ב Beit א Aleph
ס Samech ן Final Nun נ Nun ם Final Mem מ Mem ל Lamed ך Final Kaf כ Kaf
ת Tav ש Shin ר Resh ק Kuf ץ Final Tzadik צ Tzadik ף Final Feh פ Peh ע Ayin

ר

האבינג או טוארדז תחע לורד יש תחע עששענץ אף ויזדעם.

Having awe towards the Lord is the essence of wisdom.

ש

תהוז הו אנגאג ין תחיס אכחיב גווד ויזדעם,

Those who engage in this achieve good wisdom,

ת

היש פראיז יש יטערנאל.

His praise is eternal.

י Yod ט Tet ח Chet ז Zayin ו Vav ה Hei ד Dalet ג Gimel ב Beit א Aleph
ס Samech ן Final Nun נ Nun ם Final Mem מ Mem ל Lamed ך Final Kaf כ Kaf
ת Tav ש Shin ר Resh ק Kuf ץ Final Tzadik צ Tzadik ף Final Feh פ Peh ע Ayin

- 112 -

גלורי [כבוד] תו געד!

Glory to God!

א

גויעס יש תחע מאן [אדם],
הו יש ין או אף תחע לורד,

Joyous is the man,
Who is in awe of the Lord,

ב

אנד איגערלי שיקס,
תו פאללוו היש קוממאנדמענטץ [מצות].

And eagerly seeks,
To follow His commandments.

ג

תחע גענעראשענז [דורות] אף היש עפפשפרינג,
וילל בי פאורפול תחרואוט תחע לאנד,

The generations of his offspring,
Will be powerful throughout the land,

ד

תחע דישענדעד גענעראשען [דר] אף עפריט מאן [אדם],
שחאלל בי בלאששעד [ברוך].

The descended generation of upright men,
Shall be blessed.

ה

אפפלוענץ אנד שעבסטאנץ שחאלל דיפין היז האוס,

Affluence and substance shall define his house,

ו

היש גאסטיש [משפט] שחאלל פורעבער ענדור.

His justice shall forever endure.

ז

ביהולד ,א ליט שינז,
תחרואוט תחע דארקנעסס,
געידינג תחע עפריט,

Behold, a light shines,
Throughout the darkness,
Guiding the upright,

י Yod ט Tet ח Chet ז Zayin ו Vav ה Hei ד Dalet ג Gimel ב Beit א Aleph
ס Samech ן Final Nun נ Nun ם Final Mem מ Mem ל Lamed ך Final Kaf כ Kaf
ת Tav ש Shin ר Resh ק Kuf ץ Final Tzadik צ Tzadik ף Final Feh פ Peh ע Ayin

ח

פור הי יש פיללד וית כומפאשענאת גראס,
אנד ריצאסנעשס [צדק].

For he is filled with compassionate grace,
and righteousness.

ט

וורתהי יש תחע כומפאשענאת מאן [אדם],
הו יש גראשעס אנד אקשתענדז קרעדיט,

Worthy is the compassionate man,
Who is gracious and extends credit,

י

הו כונדעקתס היז ביזנעשש ין פאירנעסס.

Who conducts his business in fairness.

כ

הי וילל שורלי נעבער שטעמבעל,

He will surely never stumble,

ל

אנד תחע געסט וילל בי פורעבער רימעמבערד.

And the just will be forever remembered.

י Yod ט Tet ח Chet ז Zayin ו Vav ה Hei ד Dalet ג Gimel ב Beit א Aleph
ס Samech ן Final Nun נ Nun ם Final Mem מ Mem ל Lamed ך Final Kaf כ Kaf
ת Tav ש Shin ר Resh ק Kuf ץ Final Tzadik צ Tzadik ף Final Feh פ Peh ע Ayin

מ

הי דעש נעת פיר גוששיף,

He does not fear gossip,

נ

היש הערט יש אנכהורד,
וית תרעשט ין תחע לורד.

His heart is anchored,
With trust in the Lord.

ס

היש הערט יש שתאוט אנד שחווז נו פיר,

His heart is stout and shows no fear,

ע

ענטיל הי ויתנעששד היז געדגמענט [משפט],
ען היז אדווערשאריז,

Until he witnessed his judgment,
On his adversaries,

פ

הי דישתריביותץ תו תחע דעשטיתוט.

He distributes to the destitute.

י Yod ט Tet ח Chet ז Zayin ו Vav ה Hei ד Dalet ג Gimel ב Beit א Aleph
ס Samech ן Final Nun נ Nun ם Final Mem מ Mem ל Lamed ך Final Kaf כ Kaf
ת Tav ש Shin ר Resh ק Kuf ץ Final Tzadik צ Tzadik ף Final Feh פ Peh ע Ayin

צ

היז כומפאששענאת באנעבולענץ,
פריבאילז פוראבער,

His compassionate benevolence,
Prevails forever,

ק

אנד היז הונוראבעל רעפותאשען יש אקזאלטעד.

And his honorable reputation is exalted.

ר

תחע ויכעד ויתנעששינג תחיס,
שחאלל בי פיללד ויתּ ועקשאשען,

The wicked witnessing this,
Shall be filled with vexation,

ש

גרינדינג תחער טיתח,
אנד ואשתינג אואי.

Grinding their teeth,
And wasting away.

ת

תחע אשפעראשענז אף תחע ויכעד,
שחאלל בי לוסט.

The aspirations of the wicked,
Shall be lost.

- 113 -

גלורי [כבוד] תו געד!

Glory to God!

ו יו סערבאנטץ דיבותעד תו תחע לורד,

O you servants devoted to the Lord,

פראיז געד'ס נאם [שם],

Praise God's Name,

אנד לעט געד'ז נאם [שם] בי בלאשד [ברוך],

And let God's Name be blessed,

פרום תחיס תים תו יתערנאטי!

From this time to eternity!

פרום תחע דאונינג אף תחע שען ין תחע עאשת,

From the dawning of the sun in the East,

ענטיל יט ריתיערז את יטץ שעטטינג ין תחע ועשת,

Until it retires at its setting in the West,

תחע נאם [שם] אף תחע לורד יש פראיזד.

The Name of the Lord is praised.

עלאואטעד אבעו אלל תחע נאתענז יש תחע לורד,

Elevated above all the nations is the Lord,

אנד היש גלורי [כבוד] עקשידז תחע העיגהט,

And His glory exceeds the height,

אף תחע העאבענז [שמים].

Of the heavens.

הו מאי בי ליכענד תו תחע לורד ,אור געד,

Who may be likened to the Lord, our God,

ענתרונד ין תחע הי העאבענז [שמים],

Enthroned in the high heavens,

אנד הו שטופס תו עבשערב,

And Who stoops to observe,

תחאט ויך טראנשפיערז,

That which transpires,

ין העאבאן אנד ען עארתח [ארץ]?

In heaven and on earth?

פרום אוט אף תחע דעשת,

From out of the dust,

הי ראיזעס עף תחע פור,

He raises up the poor,

הי ברינגז אוט תחע דעשטיתוט,

He brings out the destitute,

פרום היפס אף תראשה.

From heaps of trash.

תחאט תהאי מאי בי סיתעד,

That they may be seated,

וית נובעלז,

With nobles,

וית תחע גרעאט מען אף היש פיפעל [עם].

With the great men of his people.

הי שעתתעלז תחע באררען וומאן,

He settles the barren woman,

י Yod ט Tet ח Chet ז Zayin ן Vav ה Hei ד Dalet ג Gimel ב Beit א Aleph
ס Samech ן Final Nun נ Nun ם Final Mem מ Mem ל Lamed ך Final Kaf כ Kaf
ת Tav ש Shin ר Resh ק Kuf ץ Final Tzadik צ Tzadik ף Final Feh פ Peh ע Ayin

אס תחע גויעס מותחער אף צילדרען!

As the joyous mother of children!

הללו יה!

Praise [Halleloo] God [Yah]!

א Aleph ב Beit ג Gimel ד Dalet ה Hei ו Vav ז Zayin ח Chet ט Tet י Yod
כ Kaf ך Final Kaf ל Lamed מ Mem ם Final Mem נ Nun ן Final Nun ס Samech
ע Ayin פ Peh ף Final Feh צ Tzadik ץ Final Tzadik ק Kuf ר Resh ש Shin ת Tav

- 114 -

ען תחע אוככאשען אף ישראל גוינג אוט אף יגיפט,

On the occasion of Israel going out of Egypt,

אנד יעקב'ז האושהולד פרום א פיפעל [עם],

And Jacob's household from a people,

הו ספוך א פורען לאנגויג:

Who spoke a foreign language:

יהודה ואס היז סאנכצוארי--

Judah was his sanctuary --

היש דומיניון: ישראל.

His dominion: Israel,

תחע שי ויתנעשד תחיס,

The sea witnessed this,

אנד יט שכאמפערד,

And it scampered,

תחע גורדאן'ס פלוו ריבערסד!

The Jordan's flow reversed!

י Yod ט Tet ח Chet ז Zayin ו Vav ה Hei ד Dalet ג Gimel ב Beit א Aleph
ס Samech ן Final Nun נ Nun ם Final Mem מ Mem ל Lamed ך Final Kaf כ Kaf
ת Tav ש Shin ר Resh ק Kuf ץ Final Tzadik צ Tzadik ף Final Feh פ Peh ע Ayin

ליק ראמז, תחע מאונתאנז [הרים] פראנצד,

Like rams, the mountains pranced,

אס דיד תחע היללס ,ליק יענג לאמבס.

As did the hills, like young lambs.

ו סי, ואת האפפענד תו יו,

O sea, what happened to you,

תחאט יו בולטעד?

That you bolted?

ו גורדאן ,תחאט יו פלווד באכוארד?

O Jordan, that you flowed backward?

ו מאונתאנז [הרים] ,פראנצינג ליק ראמז ;

O mountains, prancing like rams;

ו היללס ,ליק ליטטאל לאמבס?

O hills, like little lambs?

ו עארתח [ארץ] ,שהעדדער את תחע פרעסאנץ אף תחע לורד,

O earth, shudder at the Presence of the Lord,

י Yod ט Tet ח Chet ז Zayin ן Vav ה Hei ד Dalet ג Gimel ב Beit א Aleph
ס Samech ן Final Nun נ Nun ם Final Mem מ Mem ל Lamed ך Final Kaf כ Kaf
ת Tav ש Shin ר Resh ק Kuf ץ Final Tzadik צ Tzadik ף Final Feh פ Peh ע Ayin

ין תחע פרעסאנץ אף תחע געד אף יעקב,

In the Presence of the God of Jacob,

הו קאעשד א רוק תו געשה ינתו א ואתער פול,

Who caused a rock to gush into a water pool,

פלינטי רוק ינתו א ואתער פאונטאן.

Flinty rock into a water fountain.

ב

- 115 -

נעת פור עש, ו לורד,

Not for us, O Lord.

נעת פור עש,

Not for us,

בעת פור יור נאם [שם] בישתוו הונור,

But for Your Name bestow honor,

אככורדינג תו יור פאיתפול לובינג-קינדנעשס [חסד] אנד יור וערא‌סיתי!

According to Your faithful loving-kindness and Your veracity!

וי שוד עתחער פיפעלס [עמים] ינקויער:

Why should other peoples [AMEEM] inquire:

"נאו תחען, וער יש תחער געד"?

"Now then, where is their God?"

ביהולד ,אור געד יש ין תחע העאבענז [שמים],

Behold, our God is in the heavens,

ואטאבער הי דעשיערז הי פערפורמז!

Whatever He desires He performs!

אנד תחער אידולז אף שילבער אנד גולד,

And their idols on silver and gold,

אר מאד בי תחע האנדז אף מאן [אדם].

Are made by the hands of men.

תהאי האב בין פאשהאנד וית מאותס,

They have been fashioned with mouths,

בעת תהאי כאננוט שפיק;

But they cannot speak;

תהאי האב בין פאשהאנד וית עיז,

They have been fashioned with eyes,

בעת תהאי כאננוט שי;

But they cannot see;

תהאי האב בין פאשהאנד וית עארז,

They have been fashioned with ears,

בעת תהאי כאננוט העאר;

But they cannot hear;

תהאי האב בין פאשהאנד וית א נוז,

They have been fashioned with a nose,

בעת תהאי כאננוט שמעלל;

But they cannot smell;

תהאי האב בין פאשהאנד וית האנדז,

They have been fashioned with hands,

בעת תהאי כאננוט פיל;

But they cannot feel;

תהאי האב בין פאשהאנד וית פיט,

They have been fashioned with feet,

בעת תהאי כאננוט ואלך;

But they cannot walk;

ניתחער כאן תהאי עטטער א שאונד פרום תחער תחרוטץ.

Neither can they utter a sound from their throats.

י Yod ט Tet ח Chet ז Zayin ו Vav ה Hei ד Dalet ג Gimel ב Beit א Aleph
ס Samech ן Final Nun נ Nun ם Final Mem מ Mem ל Lamed ך Final Kaf כ Kaf
ת Tav ש Shin ר Resh ק Kuf ץ Final Tzadik צ Tzadik ף Final Feh פ Peh ע Ayin

לעט תהוז תחאט פאשהאנד תהעם,

Let those that fashioned and them,

ביכום געסט ליק תהעם,

Become just like them,

תהוז תחאט פלאס תחער תרעשט ין תהעם!

Those that place their trust in them!

ו ישראל!

O Israel!

תרעשט תחע לורד!

Trust in the Lord!

הי יש תחער העלפער אנד דיפענדער!

He is their helper and defender!

ו האוס אף אהרן!

O house of Aaron!

פלאס יור תרעשט ין געד!

Place your trust in God!

י Yod ט Tet ח Chet ז Zayin ו Vav ה Hei ד Dalet ג Gimel ב Beit א Aleph
ס Samech ן Final Nun נ Nun ם Final Mem מ Mem ל Lamed ך Final Kaf כ Kaf
ת Tav ש Shin ר Resh ק Kuf ץ Final Tzadik צ Tzadik ף Final Feh פ Peh ע Ayin

הי יש תחער העלפער אנד דיפענדר !

He is their helper and defender!

אלל אף יו,

All of you,

הו אר ין או אף תחע לורד!

Who are in awe of the Lord!

תרעשט תחע לורד!

Trust in the Lord!

הי יש תחער העלפער אנד דיפענדר!

He is their helper and defender!

תחע לורד הו האש בין מינדפול אף עש,

The Lord who has been mindful of us,

הי וילל בלעשש עס;

He will bless us;

היז בלעססינגז וילל בי ען תחע האוס אף ישראל;

His blessings will be on the House of Israel;

י Yod ט Tet ח Chet ז Zayin ו Vav ה Hei ד Dalet ג Gimel ב Beit א Aleph
ס Samech ן Final Nun נ Nun ם Final Mem מ Mem ל Lamed ך Final Kaf כ Kaf
ת Tav ש Shin ר Resh ק Kuf ץ Final Tzadik צ Tzadik ף Final Feh פ Peh ע Ayin

היש בלעססינגז וילל בי ען תחע האוס אף אהרן;

His blessings will be on the House of Aaron;

היש בלעססינגז וילל בי ען אלל הו אר ין או אף תחע לורד–

His blessings will be on all who are in awe of the Lord--

תחע יענג, טוגעתחער וית תחע ולד.

The young, together with the old.

תחע לורד,

The Lord

שחאלל ינקריס יור פאמילי,

Shall increase your family,

אנד תחאט אף יור עפפשפרינג!

And that your offspring!

יו אר בלאששד [ברוך],

You are blessed,

בי תחע וילל אף תחע לורד,

By the will of the Lord,

י Yod ט Tet ח Chet ז Zayin ן Vav ה Hei ד Dalet ג Gimel ב Beit א Aleph
ס Samech ן Final Nun נ Nun ם Final Mem מ Mem ל Lamed ך Final Kaf כ Kaf
ת Tav ש Shin ר Resh ק Kuf ץ Final Tzadik צ Tzadik ף Final Feh פ Peh ע Ayin

הו מאד תחע העאבען [שמים] אנד עארתח [ארץ].

Who made the heaven and earth.

אנד תחע העאבענז [שמים],

And the heavens,

תהאי אר תחע לורד'ס דומיניען,

They are the Lord's dominion,

אנד תחע עארתח [ארץ],

And the earth,

תחאט הי האש גיבען תו מאנקינד.

That He has given to mankind.

נון אף תהוז הו אר דעאד,

None of those who are dead,

כאן פראיז תחע לורד;

Can praise the Lord;

ניתחער כאן תהוז הו האב דישענדעד,

Neither can those who have descended,

י Yod ט Tet ח Chet ז Zayin ו Vav ה Hei ד Dalet ג Gimel ב Beit א Aleph
ס Samech ן Final Nun נ Nun ם Final Mem מ Mem ל Lamed ך Final Kaf כ Kaf
ת Tav ש Shin ר Resh ק Kuf ץ Final Tzadik צ Tzadik ף Final Feh פ Peh ע Ayin

ינתו קויעט.

Into quiet.

בעת אור בלעססינגז שחאלל בי עפון תחע לורד,

But our blessing shall be upon the Lord,

פרום תחיס תימ פורתח תו יתערנאטי,

From this time forth to eternity,

הללו יה!

Praise [Halleloo] God [[Yah]!

- 116 -

דעארלי ,אי לוב תחע לורד,

Dearly, I love the Lord,

פור הי העארז מי פליז ,אנד מי פראיערז.

For he hears my pleas, and my prayers.

פור הי בענדז היז עאר טוארד מי,

For He bends His ear toward me,

אנד אי וילל כאלל עפון הים,

And I will call upon Him,

אלל תחע דאיז אף מי ליף.

All the days of my life.

באונד בי תחע פאינז אף דעאתח,

Bound by the pains of death,

כונפאונדעד בי תחע טורמענטץ אף תחע גראב,

Confounded by the torments of the grave,

אי דישכובערד מיספורצען אנד גריף.

I discovered misfortune and grief.

אנד תחען, אי ינבוקד תחע נאם [שם] אף תחע לורד:

And then, I invoked the Name of the Lord:

"אי בישיץ יו, ו לורד ,רעשקיו מי שול [נפש]"!

"I beseech you, O Lord, rescue my soul!"

תחע לורד יש פיללד וית גראס,

The Lord is filled with grace,

אנד לובינג-קינדנעשס [חסד].

And loving-kindness.

אנד אור געד יש כומפאשענאת.

And our God is compassionate.

ו לורד ,פרוטעקתור אף תחע שימפאל!

O Lord, Protector of the simple!

אי ואס ברועט דאון,

I was brought down,

אנד הי רעשקיוד מי.

And He rescued me.

טערן באק אנד בי רעשתפול ,מי שול [נפש];

Turn back and be restful, my soul;

פור תחע לורד האש בין גענערוס,

For the Lord has been generous,

תו יו.

To you.

יו האב ברועט פורתח,

You have brought forth,

מי שול [נפש] פרום דעאתח,

My soul from death,

אנד קעפת טעארז,

And kept tears,

פרום מי עיז,

From my eyes,

אנד מי פיט,

And my feet,

פרום תריפפינג.

From tripping.

ביפור תחע לורד שחאלל אי ואלק,

Before the Lord shall I walk,

אנד דועלל ין תחע לאנד אף תחע ליבינג.

And dwell in the land of the living.

אס אי האב שפוקען אף מי גרעאט תורמענת,

As I have spoken of my great torment,

ין מי הוררי אי שטאטעד:

In my hurry I stated:

"אלל מאנקינד אר פיללד וית דישיט".

"All mankind are filled with deceit."

הוו קאן אי ופפער ריפאימענט,

How can I offer repayment,

תו תחע לורד פור אלל היש ריוארדז תו מי?

To the Lord for all His rewards to me?

י Yod ט Tet ח Chet ז Zayin ן Vav ה Hei ד Dalet ג Gimel ב Beit א Aleph
ס Samech ן Final Nun נ Nun ם Final Mem מ Mem ל Lamed ך Final Kaf כ Kaf
ת Tav ש Shin ר Resh ק Kuf ץ Final Tzadik צ Tzadik ף Final Feh פ Peh ע Ayin

אי וילל הולד הי א צאליס אף דיליבעראנץ,

I will hold high a chalice of deliverance,

אס אי ינבוך תחע נאם [שם] אף תחע לורד,

As I invoke the Name of the Lord,

אנד אי וילל ריפאי תו תחע לורד,

And I will repay to the Lord,

מי ואוז,

My vows,

תו בי ויתנעססד בי אלל אף היש פיפעל [עם].

To be witnessed by all of His people.

בילובעד ביפור תחע עיז אף תחע לורד,

Beloved before the eyes of the Lord,

יש תחע דעאתח אף היש פאיתפול וונז.

Is the death of his faithful ones.

אי ביסיץ יו, ו לורד,

I beseech you, O Lord,

י Yod ט Tet ח Chet ז Zayin ו Vav ה Hei ד Dalet ג Gimel ב Beit א Aleph
ס Samech ן Final Nun נ Nun ם Final Mem מ Mem ל Lamed ך Final Kaf כ Kaf
ת Tav ש Shin ר Resh ק Kuf ץ Final Tzadik צ Tzadik ף Final Feh פ Peh ע Ayin

אס אי אם יור סערבאנט,

As I am Your servant,

יור סערבאנט,

Your servant,

יור האנדמאידיס שון,

Your handmaid's son,

יו האב ענדון מי שהאקעלז.

You have undone my shackles.

תחאנקשגיבינג ופפערינגס,

Thanksgiving offerings,

שחאלל אי שאקריפיס תו יו,

Shall I sacrifice to You,

ינבוכינג תחע נאם [שם] אף תחע לורד.

Invoking the Name of the Lord,

אי וילל ריפאי תו תחע לורד,

I will repay to the Lord,

מי ואוז,

My vows,

אי וילל ופפער תהעם,

I will offer them,

ין תחע פרעסאנץ אף אלל היש פיפעל [עם].

In the presence of all His people.

ויתהין תחע קורתיארדז אף תחע האוס אף תחע לורד ,

Within the courtyards of the House of the Lord,

ויתהין יור מידצת,

Within your midst,

ו ירושלם.

O Jerusalem.

הללו יה!

Praise [HALL-EL-OO] God [YAH]!

י Yod ט Tet ח Chet ז Zayin ו Vav ה Hei ד Dalet ג Gimel ב Beit א Aleph
ס Samech ן Final Nun נ Nun ם Final Mem מ Mem ל Lamed ך Final Kaf כ Kaf
ת Tav ש Shin ר Resh ק Kuf ץ Final Tzadik צ Tzadik ף Final Feh פ Peh ע Ayin

- 117 -

הללו יה!

Praise [HALL-EL-OO] the Lord [YAH]!

אלל יו פיפעל [עם]!

All you people!

אקצטול הים ,אלל נאתענז!

Extol Him, all nations!

פור היש אבענדאנט לובינג-קינדנעשס [חסד] תו עש.

For His abundant loving-kindness to us.

תחע לורד'ס ועראסיתי ענדורז פוראבער!

The Lord's veracity endures forever!

הללויה!

Praise [Hallelloo] God [Yah]!

- 118 -

אקשפרעסס אפפרישיאשען תו תחע לורד,

Express appreciation to the Lord,

פור היז גוודנעסס!

For His goodness!

"היש לובינג-קינדנעשס [חסד] יש אנדורינג"!

"His loving-kindness is enduring!"

לעט ישראל מאיך א דעכלאראשען:

Let Israel make a declaration:

"היז לובינג-קינדנעשס [חסד] יש אנדורינג"!

"His loving-kindness is enduring!"

לעט תחע האוס אף אהרן מאיך א דעכלאראשען:

Let the house of Aron make a declaration:

"היש לובינג-קינדנעשס [חסד] יש אנדורינג"!

"His loving-kindness is enduring!"

לעט תהוז הו נוו תו פיר תחע לורד שאי:

Let those who know to fear the Lord say:

"היש לובינג-קינדנעשס [חסד] יש אנדורינג"!

"His loving-kindness is enduring!"

אפפליקתעד וית תרעבבעל ,אי כאללד עפון תחע לורד:

Afflicted with trouble, I called upon the Lord:

עכספאנשיבלי ,הי אנשערד מי!

Expansively, He answered me!

וית תחע לורד את מי סיד, אי פיר נותחינג;

With the Lord at my side, I fear nothing;

ואת כאן אני מאן [אדם] דו תו מי?

What can any man do to me?

תחע לורד שתאנדז וית מי,

The Lord stands with me,

אנד תהוז הו העלף מי.

And those who help me.

מי אנעמיז שחאלל בי פרעשתראטעד.

My enemies shall be frustrated.

יט יש מור דישיראבעל תו פלאס תרעשט ין תחע לורד,

It is more desirable to place trust in the Lord,

תהאן תרעשט ין מאנקינד.

Than trust in mankind.

יט יש מור דישיראבעל תו פלאס תרעשט ין תחע לורד,

It is more desirable to place trust in the Lord,

תהאן תרעשט ין נוביליטי.

Than trust in nobility.

אלל תחע מיריאד נאתענז שורראונד מי,

All the myriad nations surround me,

ין תחע נאם [שם] אף תחע לורד,

In the Name of the Lord,

אי שחאלל קעת תהעם דאון!

I shall cut them down!

תהאי תהרעטען מי פרום אלל סידז,

They threaten me from all sides,

תהאי אנסירכעל מי;

They encircle me;

ין תחע נאם [שם] אף תחע לורד,

In the Name of the Lord,

אי שחאלל קעת תהעם דאון!

I shall cut them down!

תהאי תהרעטען מי פרום אלל שידס,

They threatened me from all sides,

ליק ביז;

Like bees;

תהאי שחאלל בי עכצטינגוישד,

They shall be extinguished,

קונסומד ליק בערנינג תחורנז.

Consumed like burning thorns.

ין תחע נאם [שם] אף תחע לורד,

In the Name of the Lord,

אי שחאלל קעת תהעם דאון!

I shall cut them down!

תהאי אדבאנצד אגאינצט מי שו הארד,

They advanced against me so hard,

אי אלמושט פעלל,

I almost fell,

בעת תחע לורד סתוד בי מי.

But the Lord stood by me.

תחע לורד פרובידז מי וית סטרענת [כח],

The Lord provides me with strength,

אנד תחע שונג [שיר] תחאט אי שינג,

And the song that I sing,

פור הי יש מי סאלבאשען [ישועה].

For He is my salvation.

תחע וויסעז אף גוי [שמחה] אנד דיליבעראנץ,

The voices of joy and deliverance,

אר העארד ין תחע תענטץ אף תחע רעיצעס [צדיק]:

Are heard in the tents of the righteous:

"ין תריעמף תחע רעיט האנד אף תחע לורד פערפורמז!

In triumph the right hand of the Lord performs!

תחע רעיט האנד אף תחע לורד יש העלד הי!

The right hand of the Lord is held high!

ין תריעמף תחע לורד'ז רעיט האנד פערפורמז"!

In triumph the Lord's right hand performs!

דעאתח שחאלל נעת האב מי,

Death shall not have me,

פור אי ליב תו דיקלאר תחע לורד'ס וורקש.

For I live to declare the Lord's works.

אי האב בין דישאפלינד בי תחע לורד,

I have been disciplined by the Lord,

בעת, הי דיד נעת שוררענדער מי תו דעאתח.

But, He did not surrender me to death.

י Yod ט Tet ח Chet ז Zayin ן Vav ה Hei ד Dalet ג Gimel ב Beit א Aleph
ס Samech ן Final Nun נ Nun ם Final Mem מ Mem ל Lamed ך Final Kaf כ Kaf
ת Tav ש Shin ר Resh ק Kuf ץ Final Tzadik צ Tzadik ף Final Feh פ Peh ע Ayin

כאשט אופען תחע גאיתץ אף ריצאסנעשס [צדק] פור מי,

Cast open the gates of righteousness for me,

אנד אי שחאלל אנתער תהעם ,פראיזינג תחע לורד.

And I shall enter them, praising the Lord.

ביהולד תחע גאט תו תחע לורד,

Behold the gate to the Lord,

תחע פורתאל תחאט תחע רעיצעס [צדיק] שחאלל אנתער.

The portal that the righteous shall enter.

אי שינג יור פראיזעס,

I sing Your praises,

פור יו האב ריספונדעד תו מי,

For You have responded to me,

יו האב ביכום מי דעליבערער.

You have become my deliverer.

אנד תחע סתון,

And the stone,

תחאט ואס ריגעקתעד בי תחע בילדערז,

That was rejected by the builders,

האש ביכום תחע כורנערסטון!

Has become the cornerstone!

יט האש קעם אבאוט פרום תחע לורד,

It has come about from the Lord,

יט האש פיללד אור עיז וית וונדער.

It has filled our eyes with wonder.

תחע לורד האש מאד תחיס דאי,

The Lord has made this day,

אנד וי שחאלל סעלאבראט הים,

And we shall celebrate Him,

וית אקסאלטאשען אנד גוי [שמחה]!

With exultation and joy!

ו לורד ,קינדלי בי אור סאלבאשען [ישועה]!

O Lord, kindly Be our salvation!

י Yod ט Tet ח Chet ז Zayin ו Vav ה Hei ד Dalet ג Gimel ב Beit א Aleph
ס Samech ן Final Nun נ Nun ם Final Mem מ Mem ל Lamed ך Final Kaf כ Kaf
ת Tav ש Shin ר Resh ק Kuf ץ Final Tzadik צ Tzadik ף Final Feh פ Peh ע Ayin

ו לורד ,קינדלי גראנט עש גווד פורצען!

O Lord, kindly grant us good fortune!

בלאששעד [ברוך] יש הי הו ארריבז,

Blessed is he who arrives,

ין תחע נאם [שם] אף תחע לורד!

In the Name of the Lord!

וי בלעשש יו פרום תחע לורד׳ז האוס.

We bless you from the Lord's house.

תחע לורד יש געד הו האש שון עס תחע ליט;

The Lord is God Who has shown us the light;

בינד תחע שאקראפיס ופפעריינג,

Bind the sacrifice offering,

תו תחע קורנער הורנז אף תחע אלתער וית רופס.

To the corner horns of the altar with ropes.

יו אר מי געד אנד אי וילל אקנוולעדג יו,

You are my God and I will acknowledge You.

י Yod ט Tet ח Chet ז Zayin ו Vav ה Hei ד Dalet ג Gimel ב Beit א Aleph
ס Samech ן Final Nun נ Nun ם Final Mem מ Mem ל Lamed ך Final Kaf כ Kaf
ת Tav ש Shin ר Resh ק Kuf ץ Final Tzadik צ Tzadik ף Final Feh פ Peh ע Ayin

יו אר מי געד אנד יו אי וילל אכזאלט!

You are my God and You I will exalt!

ו גיב פראיז תו תחע לורד,

O give praise to the Lord,

אס הי יש כארינג,

As He is caring,

אנד היש לובינג-קינדנעשס [חסד],

And His loving-kindness,

יש נעבער- ענדינג!

Is never-ending!

- 119 -

א

האפפי אר תהוז הוז ואיז אר פיללד וית ינטעגראתי,

Happy are those whose ways are filled with integrity,

הוש פאתחואיז אר געידעד בי תחע פרישעפתץ [מצות] אף תחע לורד.

Whose pathways are guided by the precepts of the Lord.

האפפי אר תהוז הו גארד היז פרישעפתץ [מצות],

Happy are those who guard His precepts,

אנד הולהעארתעדלי שיק תו פאללוו תהעם.

And wholeheartedly seek to follow them.

תהאי יוען דו נעת אכט ענגעשתלי,

They even do not act unjustly,

תהאי פאללוו היז פאתחואיז.

They follow His pathways.

יו האב ורדערד יור פרישעפתץ [מצות],

You have ordered Your precepts,

תו בי דיליגענטלי עבשערבד.

To be diligently observed.

הופוללי תחע פאתחס תחאט אי האב פאללווד,

Hopefully the paths that I have followed,

וער ין קיפינג וית יור פרישעפתץ [מצות].

Were in keeping with Your precepts.

אככורדינגלי שהאם ויללנעת בי מין,

Accordingly shame will not be mine,

שינץ אי האב רישפעקתעד אלל יור קוממאנדמאנטץ [מצות].

Since I have respected all Your commandments.

אי גיב מי העארתפעלט פראיזעס תו יו ויתאוט פריטענץ,

I give my heartfelt praises to You without pretense,

אס אי לעארן אף יור געידינג געדגמענטץ.

As I learn of Your guiding judgments.

אי שחאלל קיף יור פרישעפתץ [מצות],

I shall keep your precepts,

י Yod ט Tet ח Chet ז Zayin ו Vav ה Hei ד Dalet ג Gimel ב Beit א Aleph
ס Samech ן Final Nun נ Nun ם Final Mem מ Mem ל Lamed ך Final Kaf כ Kaf
ת Tav ש Shin ר Resh ק Kuf ץ Final Tzadik צ Tzadik ף Final Feh פ Peh ע Ayin

דו נעת פוללי כאשט מי אשיד!

Do not fully cast me aside!

ב

ענדער ואת כונדישענז כאן א יענג מאן [אדם] פאללוו א פיור פאתח?

Under what conditions can a young man follow a pure path?

בי אדהירינג תו יור ינשטרעקשענז.

By adhering to Your instructions.

הולהעארתעדלי האב אי שועת יו,

Wholeheartedly have I sought You,

ו, תחאט אי נעת דיביאט פרום יור קומּמאנדמאנטץ [מצות].

O, that I not deviate from Your commandments.

אי האב כונסילד יור שאיינגס ויתהין מי העארט.

I have concealed Your sayings within my heart.

תו ריזיסת מי סין אגאינצט יו.

To resist my sin against You.

בלאששעד [ברוך] אר יו, ו לורד,

Blessed are You, O Lord,

י Yod ט Tet ח Chet ז Zayin ו Vav ה Hei ד Dalet ג Gimel ב Beit א Aleph
ס Samech ן Final Nun נ Nun ם Final Mem מ Mem ל Lamed ך Final Kaf כ Kaf
ת Tav ש Shin ר Resh ק Kuf ץ Final Tzadik צ Tzadik ף Final Feh פ Peh ע Ayin

ינצטרעקת מי ין יור סתאצוטץ.

Instruct me in Your statutes.

מי ליפס האב דיכלארד אלל תחע סתאצוטץ,

My lips have declared all the statutes,

אנד תחע פרוקלאמאשענז אף יור מאותח.

And the proclamations of Your mouth.

אי האב דיליטעד ין פוללווינג יור פרישעפתץ [מצות],

I have delighted in following Your precepts,

אס מעך אס יף תהאי ועך ענבאונדעד ועלתח .

As much as if they were unbounded wealth.

אף יור פרישעפתץ [מצות] ויללל אי שפיק,

Of Your precepts will I speak,

אנד אי וילל רישפעכטפוללי פאללוו יור פאתואיז.

And I will respectfully follow Your pathways.

יור סתאצוטץ שחאלל ברינג גוי [שמחה] ענתו מי ביינג,

Your statutes shall bring joy unto my being,

י Yod ט Tet ח Chet ז Zayin ו Vav ה Hei ד Dalet ג Gimel ב Beit א Aleph
ס Samech ן Final Nun נ Nun ם Final Mem מ Mem ל Lamed ך Final Kaf כ Kaf
ת Tav ש Shin ר Resh ק Kuf ץ Final Tzadik צ Tzadik ף Final Feh פ Peh ע Ayin

נעבער שחאלל אי נעגלעכט יור וורדז.

Never shall I neglect Your words.

ג

אללוקאט יור סערבאנט'ץ פורשען,

Allocate Your servant's portion,

אללוו מי תחע דאיס אף מי ליף,

Allow me the days of my life,

תחאט אי מאי פאללוו יור וורד.

That I may follow Your word.

ענכובער מי עיז אנד אי כאן עבשערב,

Uncover my eyes and I can observe,

תחע וונדערז אף יור תיצינגס,

The wonders of Your teachings,

אס אי אם אונלי א שוגורנער ין יור וורלד,

As I am only a sojourner in Your world,

דו נעת ויתהולד יור קוממאנדמאנטץ [מצות],

Do not withhold Your commandments,

פרום מי ינסטרעקשען.

From my instruction.

מי שול [נפש] יש בערשתינג וית דעשיער,

My soul is bursting with desire,

פור תחע גאסטיש [משפט] אף יור דיקריז ,אלואיס.

For the justice of Your decrees, always.

יו רעפרימאנדעד תחע דיסריספעקתפול סיננערז,

You reprimanded the disrespectful sinners,

הו ואנדערד אואי פרום יור קוממאנדמאנטץ [מצות].

Who wandered away from your commandments.

דישפלאס פרום מי דישגראס אנד דיסדאין,

Displace for me disgrace and disdain,

ביקאעס אי עבשערב יור תיצינגס.

Because I observe your teachings.

אלתחו נובעלמען כונבינד,

Although noblemen convened,

אנד אכספרעששד וורדז אגאינצט מי,

And expressed words against me,

אי ,יור העמבל סערבאנט ,רעבעל ין ריבילינג יור לאוז.

I, Your humble servant, revel in revealing your laws.

תרולי ,תחע פרוקלאמאשענז אף יור לאו מאיך מי גויעס;

Truly, the proclamations of Your law make me joyous;

תהאי אר תחע וורדז תחאט כאונסיל מי.

They are words that council me.

ד

מי שול [נפש] קלינגס תו דעשת,

My soul clings to dust,

ריביב מי ו לורד,

Revive me O Lord,

תחאט אי מאי בי,

That I may be,

יו אכּורד וית יור ריבילד וורד.

In accord with Your revealed word.

אי האב מאד נוון אלל אף מי אקצפיריענצעז תו יו,

I have made known all of my experiences to You,

אנד יו האב אקנוולעדגד מי וויס;

And you have acknowledged my voice;

ינצטרעקת מי ין יור לאוז.

Instruct me in Your laws.

אללוו מי תו ענדערשטאנד תחע מינינג,

Allow me to understand the meaning,

אף יור פרישעפתץ [מצות];

Of your precepts;

אנד אי וילל תאלק אבאוט יור מארבעלוס דידז.

And I will talk about Your marvelous deeds.

גריף האש קאעשד תחע דעשולאשען אף מי שול [נפש],

Grief has caused the desolation of my soul,

גראנט מי שאסטאנאנץ וית יור וורד.

Grant me sustenance with Your word.

י Yod ט Tet ח Chet ז Zayin ו Vav ה Hei ד Dalet ג Gimel ב Beit א Aleph
ס Samech ן Final Nun נ Nun ם Final Mem מ Mem ל Lamed ך Final Kaf כ Kaf
ת Tav ש Shin ר Resh ק Kuf ץ Final Tzadik צ Tzadik ף Final Feh פ Peh ע Ayin

רימוב דופליסיתי פרום מי פאתחואי,

Remove duplicity from my pathway,

אנד אללו מי שול [נפש] תו בי פערמיאתעד,

And allow my soul to be permeated,

וית יור תיצינגס.

With Your teachings.

מי צוזען פאתחואי יש פאיתח,

My chosen pathway is faith,

אנד יור געדגמענטץ אר מי געידאנץ,

And Your judgments on my guidance,

אי אם באונד בי יור לאוז.

I am bound by Your laws.

ו לורד ,דו נעת הומיליאט מי,

O Lord, do not humiliate me,

אי וילל פערשו תחע פאתחואיז,

I will pursue the pathways,

אף יור קוממאנדמאנטץ [מצות],

Of Your commandments,

אס יו עקצפאנד,

As You expand,

מי יננערמוסט ביינג .

My innermost being.

ה

ינצטרעקת מי ,ו לורד ,ין תחע תיצינגס אף יור לאו,

Instruct me, O Lord, in the teachings of Your law,

אנד אי שחאלל פאללו תהעם ענדלעסשלי.

And I shall follow them endlessly.

אללוו מי תו קומפריהענד,

Allow me to comprehend,

שו אי מאי פאללו יור סתאצוטץ,

So I may follow Your statutes,

אנד קיף תהעם וית מי העארתפעלט דיבושען.

And keep them with my heartfelt devotion.

י Yod ט Tet ח Chet ז Zayin ו Vav ה Hei ד Dalet ג Gimel ב Beit א Aleph
ס Samech ן Final Nun נ Nun ם Final Mem מ Mem ל Lamed ך Final Kaf כ Kaf
ת Tav ש Shin ר Resh ק Kuf ץ Final Tzadik צ Tzadik ף Final Feh פ Peh ע Ayin

געיד מי ען תחע פאתחואיז אף יור קוממאנדמאנטץ [מצות],

Guide me on the pathways of Your commandments,

תחאט יש מי העארתפעלט ויש.

That is my heartfelt wish.

פושישען מי העארט טוארד יור סתאצוטץ,

Position my heart toward Your statutes,

אנד נעת טוארד תחע גאתחערינג אף מאטיריאל תחינגז.

And not toward the gathering of material things.

טערן מי עיז אואי,

Turn my eyes away,

פרום תחע עמפתינעסס אף ואניטי,

From the emptiness of vanity,

אנד פרישערב מי תו פאללוו יור פאתחואיז.

And preserve me to follow Your pathways.

קיף יור פרומיס ויתּ יור סערבאנט,

Keep your promise with your servant,

הו הולדז יו ין או.

Who holds You in awe.

רימוב פרום מי מי דישגראס תחאט תעריפיז מי,

Remove from me my disgrace that terrifies me,

פור תחע גוודנעסס אף יור לאוז.

For the goodness of Your laws,

ביהולד מי דיבותעד וילל,

Behold my devoted will,

תו דעשיער יור פרישעפתץ [מצות],

To desire Your precepts,

יור ריצאסנעשס [צדק] וילל פרישערב מי.

Your righteousness [tzedek] will preserve me.

ו

דיליבער יור לובינג-קינדנעשס [חסד] תו מי ,ו לורד,

Deliver in Your loving kindness to me, O Lord,

תחע סאלבאשען [ישועה] תחאט יו פורטולד.

The salvation that You foretold.

י Yod ט Tet ח Chet ז Zayin ו Vav ה Hei ד Dalet ג Gimel ב Beit א Aleph
ס Samech ן Final Nun נ Nun ם Final Mem מ Mem ל Lamed ך Final Kaf כ Kaf
ת Tav ש Shin ר Resh ק Kuf ץ Final Tzadik צ Tzadik ף Final Feh פ Peh ע Ayin

תחען אי שחאלל ריספונד תו תהוז הו סקורן מי,

Then I shall respond to those who scorn me,

פור אי האב פלאסד מי פאיתח ין יור וורד.

For I have placed my faith in Your word.

דו נעת כומפליטלי דישלודג וורדז אף טרותה,

Do not completely dislodge words of truth,

פרום אוט אף מי מאותח,

From out of my mouth,

פור אי האו לווקד תו,

For I have looked to,

יור געדגמענטץ.

Your judgments.

אי ויילל בי תחע גארדיאן אף יור תיצינגס,

I will be the guardian of Your teachings,

פור אלל-תים ,פוראבער ; לדר ודר.

For all-time, for ever; from generation to generation.

אנד אי וילל גו,

And I will go,

אלונג ענבאונעד פאתחואיז,

Along unbounded pathways,

ביקאעס אי סועט יור קוממאנדמאנטץ [מצות] .

Because I sought Your commandments.

אנד אי וילל דיקלאר יור סתאצוטץ,

And I will declare your statutes,

ביפור תחע פרעסאנץ אף קינגז,

Before the presence of kings,

אנד נעבער פיל שהאם.

And never feel shame.

אי וילל בי גויעשלי גלאדענד,

I will be joyously gladdened,

בי תחע פלעזור,

By the pleasure,

י Yod ט Tet ח Chet ז Zayin ו Vav ה Hei ד Dalet ג Gimel ב Beit א Aleph
ס Samech ן Final Nun נ Nun ם Final Mem מ Mem ל Lamed ך Final Kaf כ Kaf
ת Tav ש Shin ר Resh ק Kuf ץ Final Tzadik צ Tzadik ף Final Feh פ Peh ע Ayin

אף יור קוממאנדמאנטץ [מצות],

Of your commandments,

שו לובד בי מי,

So loved by me,

אי שחאלל עמבראס תחע סתעדי,

I shall embrace the study,

אף יור סתאצוטץ.

Of Your statutes.

אנד אי וילל ראיז מי האנדז,

And I will raise my hands,

ריצינג פור יור קוממאנדמאנטץ [מצות];

Reaching for Your commandments;

אי צעריש תהעם--

I cherish them --

אנד אי וילל שתעדי יור סתאצוטץ.

And I will study Your statutes.

ז

ריכאלל תחע וורדז יו גאב תו יור סערבאנט,

Recall the words You gave to Your servant,

בי ויכח יו גאב כומפורט תו מי.

By which You gave comfort to me.

תחאט יש ואת שעשתאינד מי ין מי תורמענת,

That is what sustained me in my torment,

ביקאעס יור פרומאשינג וורדז האב מאינטאינד מי.

Because Your promising words have maintained me.

שינפול וונז גרעאתלי ועקס מי,

Sinful ones greatly vex me,

בעת אי האב נעת דיפארתעד פרום יור לאו.

But I have not departed from Your law.

אי ריכאלל יור איג-ולד פרישעפתץ [מצות] ו לורד,

I recall Your age-old precepts O Lord,

אנד תהאי כומפורט מי.

And they comfort me.

י Yod ט Tet ח Chet ז Zayin ו Vav ה Hei ד Dalet ג Gimel ב Beit א Aleph
ס Samech ן Final Nun נ Nun ם Final Mem מ Mem ל Lamed ך Final Kaf כ Kaf
ת Tav ש Shin ר Resh ק Kuf ץ Final Tzadik צ Tzadik ף Final Feh פ Peh ע Ayin

אי כואך וית פורי אובער תחע ויקעד
וונז,

I quake with fury over the wicked ones,

הו דישערט תחע סתאצוטץ אף יור לאו.

Who desert the statutes of Your law.

פור תהוז סתאצוטץ אף יור לאו,

For the statutes of Your law,

אר תחע סונגס אף מי סטרענת [כח],

Are the songs of my strength,

תחאט שפרעד תחרואוט,

That spread throughout,

וערעבער אי דועלל.

Whereever I dwell.

אי ריכאלל יור נאם [שם] את נעיט ו לורד,

I recall Your Name at night O Lord,

אנד אי עבשערב יור תיצינגז.

And I observe Your teachings.

י Yod ט Tet ח Chet ז Zayin ו Vav ה Hei ד Dalet ג Gimel ב Beit א Aleph
ס Samech ן Final Nun נ Nun ם Final Mem מ Mem ל Lamed ך Final Kaf כ Kaf
ת Tav ש Shin ר Resh ק Kuf ץ Final Tzadik צ Tzadik ף Final Feh פ Peh ע Ayin

אלל תחיס ואס מין,

All this was mine,

ביקאעס אי עבשערבד יור לאוז .

Because I observed Your laws.

ח

"ו לורד ,יו אר מי דעשתיני":

"0 Lord, You are my destiny:"

אי האב דיכלארד,

I have declared,

אי וןד עבשערב יור קוממאנדמאנטץ [מצות].

I would observe Your commandments.

אי האב בישיצד יו עארנעשתלי,

I have beseeched You earnestly,

וית הולהעארתעד שעפליכאשען,

With wholehearted supplication,

גראנט מי יור מערסי,

Grant me Your mercy,

אככורדינג תו יור פרומיס.

According to Your promise.

אי האב ריפלעכתעד ען תחע רודז,

I have reflected on the roads,

תחאט אי האו פאללווד,

That I have followed,

אנד אי וילל ברינג מי פיט באק תו יור דיקריז.

And I will bring my feet back to Your decrees.

אי מאד הוררי,

I made hurry,

אנד דיד נעת לינגער,

And did not linger,

ין תחע קיפינג אף יור קוממאנדמאנטץ [מצות].

In the keeping of your commandments.

ו תחע רופס אף ויכעד מען,

O the ropes of wicked men,

ענכומפאסס אנד פלענדער מי,

Encompass and plunder me,

אי האב נעת פורשאכען יור תיצינגז.

I have not forsaken your teachings.

אי וילל ריז עף את מידניט,

I will rise up at midnight,

תו ופפער יו מי פראיז,

To offer You my praise,

פור יור מערסיפול געדגמענטץ.

For Your merciful judgments.

אי אם א פרענד,

I am a friend,

תו אלל הו הולד יו ין או,

To all who hold You in awe,

אנד עפהולד יור פרישעפתץ [מצות].

And uphold Your precepts.

יור לובינג-קינדנעשס [חסד] ,ו לורד ,ענבעלופס תחע עארתח [ארץ],

Your loving-kindness, O Lord, envelops the earth,

ינצטרעקת מי ין תחע פאתחואיז אף יור סתאצוטץ.

Instruct me in the pathways of Your statutes.

ט

יור סערבאנט האש בין ועלל-תריטעד,

Your servant has been well-treated,

ו לורד ,יו האב קעפת פאיתפול,

O Lord, You have kept faithful,

ען אככורדאנץ וית יור וורד.

In accordance with Your word.

פור מי תרעשט יש ין יור קוממאנדמאנטץ [מצות].

For my trust is in Your commandments.

ביפור אי ואס תורמענטעד,

Before I was tormented,

אי ואס ין עררור,

I was in error,

בעת ,נוו אי עבשערב יור שאיינגז.

But, now I observe Your sayings.

יו אר וירציו אנד יו שפרעד גוודנעסס,

You are virtue and You spread goodness,

ינצטרעקת מי ין יור לאוז.

Instruct me in Your laws.

תחע פראודלי אררוגאנט האב כונשפיערד,

The proudly arrogant have conspired,

אנד בעאר פאלס ויתנעסס אגאינצט מי.

And bear false witness against me.

אי שחאלל הולד פאשט תו אלל אף יור פרישעפתץ [מצות],

I shall hold fast to all of Your precepts,

ויתמי הול העארט.

With my whole heart.

תחער מינדלעסס העארטץ האב גרון אס תחיך אס פאט;

Their mindless hearts have grown as thick as fat;

י Yod ט Tet ח Chet ז Zayin ו Vav ה Hei ד Dalet ג Gimel ב Beit א Aleph
ס Samech ן Final Nun נ Nun ם Final Mem מ Mem ל Lamed ך Final Kaf כ Kaf
ת Tav ש Shin ר Resh ק Kuf ץ Final Tzadik צ Tzadik ף Final Feh פ Peh ע Ayin

אס פור מי ,יור תיצינגס,

As for me, Your teachings,

אר מי פלעזור.

Are my pleasure.

מי אפפליקשען סערבד מי ועלל;

My affliction served me well;

יט געידעד מי טוארד לערנינג יור סתאצוטץ.

It guided me toward learning Your statutes.

אי פריפער תיצינגס פרום יור מאותח,

I prefer teachings from your mouth,

תו תחאושאנדז ין גולד אנד שילבער.

To thousands in gold and silver.

י

יור האנדז כריאטעד אנד עשטאבלישהד מי;

Your hands created and established me;

ענדוו מי ויתּ כומפריהענשען,

Endow me with comprehension,

י Yod ט Tet ח Chet ז Zayin ו Vav ה Hei ד Dalet ג Gimel ב Beit א Aleph
ס Samech ן Final Nun נ Nun ם Final Mem מ Mem ל Lamed ך Final Kaf כ Kaf
ת Tav ש Shin ר Resh ק Kuf ץ Final Tzadik צ Tzadik ף Final Feh פ Peh ע Ayin

שו אי מאי ועלל שתעדי,

So I may well study,

יור פרישעפתץ [מצות].

Your precepts.

תהוז הו שהו רעבעראנץ תו יו,

Those who show reverence to You,

שחאלל גויעשלי ויתנעסס מי פרעסאנץ,

Shall joyously witness my presence,

פור ,אי פות מי תרעשט,

For, I put my trust,

ין יור וורד.

In Your word

אי אקנוולעדג ,ו לורד,

I acknowledge, O Lord,

תחע גאסטיש [משפט] אף יור לאוז,

The justice of Your laws,

אנד ין יור פאיתפול געדגמענט [משפט],

And in Your faithful judgment,

יו קאעשד מי תו שעפפער.

You caused me to suffer.

אי ביסיך יו,

I beseech you,

תחאט באנעבולענץ בי גיבען תו מי פור מי שולאס,

That benevolence be given to me for my solace,

אס יו האב שעד תו יור פאיתפול סערבאנט.

As You have said to Your faithful servant.

סענד יור מערשי תו ענועלוף מי,

Send Your mercy to envelop me,

אללווינג מי תו ליב;

Allowing me to live;

ביקאעס אי תאק פלעזור ין יור תיצינגס.

Because I take pleasure in your teachings.

מאי תהוז הו שין,

May those who sin,

בי הומיליאתעד;

Be humiliated;

ביקאעס ויתאוט ריזון,

Because without reason,

תהאי בעאר פאלס ויתנעסס אגאינצט מי;

They bear false witness against me;

אי ויגל כונתיניו תו תאלק אף יור פרישעפתץ [מצות].

I will continue to talk of Your precepts.

לעט תהוז הו ריביר יו,

Let those who revere You,

ריטורן אגאין תו מי,

Return again to me,

אלונג וית תהוז,

Along with those,

הו נוו יור דעקלאראשענז.

Who know Your declarations.

י Yod ט Tet ח Chet ז Zayin ו Vav ה Hei ד Dalet ג Gimel ב Beit א Aleph
ס Samech ן Final Nun נ Nun ם Final Mem מ Mem ל Lamed ך Final Kaf כ Kaf
ת Tav ש Shin ר Resh ק Kuf ץ Final Tzadik צ Tzadik ף Final Feh פ Peh ע Ayin

מאי מי שינסיר העארט ריפלעכט יור סתאצוטץ,

May my sincere heart reflect Your statutes,

תחאט אי דו נעת נוע שחאם אור גריף.

That I do not know shame or grief.

כ

מי יננערמוסט ביינג יארנז פור יור שאבינג גראס,

My innermost being yearns for Your saving grace,

מי תרעשט יש פלאשד ין יור וורד.

My trust is placed in Your word.

מי עיז גרוו דים אואתינג,

My eyes grow dim awaiting,

תחע וורדז אף יור בונד,

The words of Your bond,

אנד אי שאי,

And I say,

"וען וילל יו ברינג שולאס תו מי"?

"When will you bring solace to me?"

ו ,אי האב בין ליק א שמוך דריד וין שקין,

O, I have been like a smoke dried wine skin,

בעת ,אי דיד נות אבאנדון יור סתאצוטץ.

But, I did not abandon Your statutes.

האו לונג אר יור סערבאנט׳ץ דאיס?

How long are Your servant's days?

וען וילל יו ראין געדגמענט [משפט] דאון,

When will You rain judgment down,

עפון מי פערשוערז?

Upon my pursuers?

עיבעלדוערז [רשעים] האב דעג פיטץ פור מי,

Evildoers have dug pits for me,

ויכח ויולאתץ יור סתאצוטץ.

Which violates Your statutes.

אלל יור פרישעפתץ [מצות] אר וורתהי אף תרעשט,

All Your precepts are worthy of trust,

מי פערשוערז בעאר פאלס ויתנעסס אגאינצט מי,

My pursuers bear false witness against me,

גראנט מי יור העלף!

Grant me Your help!

תהאי האב נעארלי שטופפד מי עארתחלי גערני,

They have nearly stopped my earthly journey,

בעת ,אי האב נעבער דעשערתעד יור קוממאנדמאנטץ [מצות].

But, I have never deserted Your commandments.

ין קיפינג וית יור באנעבולענץ,

In keeping with Your benevolence,

שאב מי!

Save me!

אנד אי שחאלל קיף תחע סתאצוטץ תחאט יו האב דיכלארד.

And I shall keep the statutes that You have declared.

ל

יתערנאללי ,ו לורד ,יור פירם וורד,

Eternally, O Lord, your firm word,

יש העאבען סענט.

Is heaven sent.

אנד יור כונשטאנת תרעסט קונטיניוז,

And Your constant trust continues,

לדר ודר.

From generation to generation.

יו כריאטעד תחע עארתח [ארץ],

You created the earth,

אנד יט שתאנדז פירם,

And it stands firm,

תו כאררי אוט יור געדגמענטץ עברי דאי,

To carry out Your judgments every day,

שינץ אלל אר יור סערבאנטץ.

Since all are Your servants.

האד אי נות תאקען פלעזור ין תחע סטעדי,

Had I not taking pleasure in the study,

אף יור תיצינגס,

Of Your teachings,

שורלי ,אי ווד האב פעּרישחד,

Surely, I would have perished,

דורינג מי שעפפערינג.

During my suffering.

נעבער וילל אי נעגלעכט,

Never will I neglect,

יור קוממאנדמאנטץ [מצות],

Your commandments,

פור בי תחער דירעכשען,

For by their direction,

יו האב פרישערבד מי ליף.

You have preserved my life.

י Yod ט Tet ח Chet ז Zayin ו Vav ה Hei ד Dalet ג Gimel ב Beit א Aleph
ס Samech ן Final Nun נ Nun ם Final Mem מ Mem ל Lamed ך Final Kaf כ Kaf
ת Tav ש Shin ר Resh ק Kuf ץ Final Tzadik צ Tzadik ף Final Feh פ Peh ע Ayin

אי בילונג תו יו;

I belong to you;

בי מי סאלבאשען [ישועה]!

Be my salvation!

ביקאעס אי האב שועת תו אביד,

Because I have sought to abide,

בי יור קוממאנדמאנטץ [מצות].

By Your commandments.

ויכעד וונז הוף פור מי דעשטרעכשען ;

Wicked ones hope for my destruction;

אי שתעדי יור דעקלאראשענז.

I study Your declarations.

אי האב ויתנעששד תחאט עבערי תאשק האש אן ענדינג;

I have witnessed that every task has an ending;

תחע ברעאדתח אף יור תיצינגס יש מעשורלעס.

The breadth of Your teachings is measureless.

י Yod ט Tet ח Chet ז Zayin ו Vav ה Hei ד Dalet ג Gimel ב Beit א Aleph
ס Samech ן Final Nun נ Nun ם Final Mem מ Mem ל Lamed ך Final Kaf כ Kaf
ת Tav ש Shin ר Resh ק Kuf ץ Final Tzadik צ Tzadik ף Final Feh פ Peh ע Ayin

מ

ו האו מעץ דו אי צעריש יור תיצינגז!

O how much do I cherish Your teachings!

אלל תחע דאי לונג,

All the day long,

יט יש מי מעדיטאטיב שתעדי.

It is my meditative study.

יור קוממאנדמאנטץ [מצות],

Your commandments,

גיב מי מור ויזדעם,

Give me more wisdom,

תהאן מי אנעמיז,

Than my enemies,

ביקאעס תהאי אר אלואיס ויתּ מי.

Because they are always with me

אי אם מור ענליתענד תחאן מי תיצערז,

I am more enlightened than my teachers,

פור אי האב שטעדיד אנד דיסקעשד,

For I have studied and discussed,

יור טעשתימוניז.

Your testimonies.

אי האב כונתימפלאתעד מור תהאן מי אלדערז,

I have contemplated more than my elders,

פור אי האו עבשערבד,

For I have observed,

יור פרישעפתץ [מצות].

Your precepts.

אנד פרום אלל תחע פאתחואיז אף יבעל,

And from all the pathways of evil,

אי האב דיתאינד מי פיט,

I have detained my feet,

תו מאינתאין יור וורד.

To maintain Your word.

אי האו נעת טערנד אואי פרום יור לאוז,

I have not turned away from Your laws,

פור יו האב שון מי יור ינשטרעקשענז;

For You have shown me Your instructions;

תחע שויטנעסס אף יור וורדז ין מי מאותח,

The sweetness of Your words in my mouth,

מור תהאן הוני תו מי טאשט.

More than honey to my taste.

יט יש תחרו יור קוממאנדמאנטץ [מצות],

It is through Your commandments,

תחאט אי כונתעמפלאט,

That I contemplate,

אנד פינד האתפול,

And find hateful,

פאלס פאתחואיז.

False pathways.

נ

יור וורד יש א כאנדעל את מי פיט,

Your word is a candle at my feet,

אס תחע ליט תו געיד מי פאתח.

As the light to guide my path.

אי האב מאד א שולעם ואו,

I have made a solemn vow,

אנד אי אם כוממיטעד,

And I am committed,

תו הולד פאשט תו יור,

To hold fast to Your,

רעיצעס געסט לאוז.

Righteous just laws.

אי אם תערריבלי דישטרעששד,

I am terribly distressed,

ו לורד ,שאב מי,

O Lord, save me,

י Yod ט Tet ח Chet ז Zayin ן Vav ה Hei ד Dalet ג Gimel ב Beit א Aleph
ס Samech ן Final Nun נ Nun ם Final Mem מ Mem ל Lamed ך Final Kaf כ Kaf
ת Tav ש Shin ר Resh ק Kuf ץ Final Tzadik צ Tzadik ף Final Feh פ Peh ע Ayin

אככורדינג תו יור טעשטימוניז.

According to Your testimonies.

פליז פאבור מי וית יור אקקסעפטאנץ,

Please favor me with Your acceptance,

ו לורד,

O Lord,

אף מי מאותח׳ש ופפערינגז ין יור לאוז.

Of my mouth's offerings in Your laws.

אלתחו מי ליף יש כונשטאנתלי ין דאנגער,

Although my life is constantly in danger,

אי האב נעת דישריגארדעד יור תיצינגס.

I have not disregarded Your teachings.

תחע ויכעד האב שעט תראפס פור מי,

The wicked have set traps for me,

בעת אי האב נעת ואנדערד פרום יור קוממאנדמאנטץ [מצות].

But I have not wandered from Your commandments.

י Yod ט Tet ח Chet ז Zayin ו Vav ה Hei ד Dalet ג Gimel ב Beit א Aleph
ס Samech ן Final Nun נ Nun ם Final Mem מ Mem ל Lamed ך Final Kaf כ Kaf
ת Tav ש Shin ר Resh ק Kuf ץ Final Tzadik צ Tzadik ף Final Feh פ Peh ע Ayin

יור דעקלאראשענז אר יתערנאללי מי העריטאג,

Your declarations are eternally my heritage,

אי האו תערנד מי העארט,

I have turned my heart,

טוארד עבשערווינג,

Toward observing,

יור לאוז;

Your laws;

פוראבער אנד עבער.

Forever and ever.

ס

אי דעשפייז דיביעס דאבעל-תאלקערז,

I despise devious double-talkers,

בעת ,אי לוב תחע תיצינג אף יור סתאצוטץ.

But, I love the teaching of Your statutes.

יו אר מי פרוטעקטיב כובער,

You are my protective cover,

אנד מי דיפענץ;

And my defense;

מי תרעשט,

My trust,

דועללז ין יור וורד.

Dwells in Your word.

גו אואי פרום מי פרעסאנץ,

Go away from my presence,

יו הו אר יבעל,

You who are evil,

תחאט אי פאיתפוללי,

That I faithfully,

היד תחע קוממאנדמאנטץ [מצות],

Heed the commandments,

אף מי געד.

Of my God.

מאינתאין מי אככורדינג תו יור פרומיס,

Maintain me according to Your promise,

תחאט אי מאי שערויב,

That I may survive,

אנד דו נעת דישאפפוינט מי דעשיערז.

And do not disappoint my desires.

שעפפורת מי אנד אללוו מי סאפטי,

Support me and allow me safety,

שו תחאט אי וילל היד,

So that I will heed,

יור תיצינגס את אלל תימז.

Your teachings at all times.

יו האב כרעשד אלל הו ואנדערד,

You have crushed all who wandered,

אואי פרום יור לאו,

Away from Your law,

פור תחער געיל יש דישיטפול.

For their guile is deceitful.

ליק דרוס ,תחע ואשט אף מעלתינג מעטאל,

Like dross, the waste of melting metal,

יו כלינד אוט תחע ויכעד וונז,

You cleaned out the wicked ones,

ען עארתח [ארץ].

On earth.

אנד שו ,אי צעריש יור פרישעפתץ [מצות].

And so, I cherish Your precepts.

מי בודי בריסעלז ין דרעאד,

My body bristles in dread,

אנד אי אם ין או אף יור לאוז.

And I am in awe of Your laws.

ע

מי אקשענז וער דען,

My actions were done,

י Yod ט Tet ח Chet ז Zayin ו Vav ה Hei ד Dalet ג Gimel ב Beit א Aleph
ס Samech ן Final Nun נ Nun ם Final Mem מ Mem ל Lamed ך Final Kaf כ Kaf
ת Tav ש Shin ר Resh ק Kuf ץ Final Tzadik צ Tzadik ף Final Feh פ Peh ע Ayin

ין גאסטיש [משפט] אנד ין ריצאסנעשס [צדק],

In justice and in righteousness,

דו נעת דישכארד מי תו תהוז הו ווד,

Do not discard me to those who would,

שעלפישהלי תאק אדבאנטאג אף מי.

Selfishly take advantage of me.

בי תחע גאראנטור פור גוודנעסס פור יור סערבאנט ,אלואיס,

Be the guarantor for goodness for Your servant, always,

דו נעת לעט האעטי סיננערז,

Do not let haughty sinners,

תאק אדבאנטאג אף מי.

Take advantage of me,

מי עיז גרוו דים,

My eyes grow dim,

אס אי ואית פור יור סאלבאשען [ישועה],

As I wait for Your salvation,

י Yod ט Tet ח Chet ז Zayin ו Vav ה Hei ד Dalet ג Gimel ב Beit א Aleph
ס Samech ן Final Nun נ Nun ם Final Mem מ Mem ל Lamed ך Final Kaf כ Kaf
ת Tav ש Shin ר Resh ק Kuf ץ Final Tzadik צ Tzadik ף Final Feh פ Peh ע Ayin

אנד פור יור געסט פרומעשיז.

And for Your just promises.

רילאט תו יור סערבאנט,

Relate to Your servant,

אס ביכומז יור לובינג-קינדנעשס [חסד],

As becomes Your loving-kindness,

אנד ינצטרעקת מי אככורדינג תו יור לאו.

And instruct me according to Your law.

אס אי אם יור סערבאנט ,אללוו מי כומפריהענשען,

As I am your servant, allow me comprehension.

תחאט אי מאי לעארן יור סתאצוטץ.

That I may learn of Your statutes.

תחער יש א תים תחע לורד קיפס תו אכט,

There is a time the Lord keeps to act,

אס תהאי האב ויולאטעד תחע לאו.

As they have violated the law.

בעת אי צעריש יור קוממאנדמאנטץ [מצות],

But I cherish your commandments,

יוען אבוב גולד ,מור תהאן פיור גולד.

Even above gold, more than pure gold.

אנד אי דיקלאר תחע גאסטיש אף אלל יור פרישעפתץ [מצות],

And I declare the justice of all Your precepts.

אנד עבערי פאלס פאתחואי האתפול.

And every false pathway hateful.

פ

וונדרעס אר יור פרישעפתץ [מצות],

Wondrous are Your precepts,

פיתינגלי מי שול [נפש] עבשערוז תהעם.

Fittingly my soul observes them.

יור ינתרודעכתורי וורדז יללומינאט,

Your introductory words illuminate,

אללווינג עיוען תחע שימפאל תו גראשף תחער מינינג.

Allowing even the simple to grasp their meaning.

מי מאותח גאפש אנד אי קאטך מי ברעאתה,

My mouth gapes and I catch my breath,

יט יש ביקאעס אי יעארן פור יור פרישעפתץ [מצות].

It is because I yearn for Your precepts.

טערן טוארד מי אנד אללוו מי יור גראס,

Turn toward me and allow me Your grace,

אס יש תחע כאס פור תהוז הו צעריש יור נאם [שם].

As is the case for those who cherish Your Name.

רישולב מי פאתחואי טוארד יור תיצינגס,

Resolve my pathway toward Your teachings,

אנד אללו נו ויקעדנעשס תו רול מי פאתח.

And allow no wickedness to rule my path.

קאעז מי סאלבאשען [ישועה] פרום עפפרעששיב מאן [אדם],

Cause me salvation from oppressive men,

תחאט אי מאי עבשערב יור קוממאנדמאנטץ [מצות].

That I may observe Your commandments.

פערמיט תחע ראדיאנץ אף יור פאש,

Permit the radiance of Your face,

תו יללומינאט יור סערבאנט,

To illuminate Your servant,

תיצינג מי יור לאוז.

Teaching me Your laws.

שטרימז אף ואתער [מים] פאלל פרום מי עיז,

Streams of water fall from my eyes,

תחאט מען דו נעת עבשערב יור תיצינגס.

That men do not observe Your teachings.

צ

ו לורד ,יו אר געסט אנד הונעשט ין יור לאוז.

O Lord, You are just an honest in your laws.

יור פרישעפתץ [מצות] תחאט יו האב אורדאינד,

Your precepts that You have ordained,

אר כומפוזד אף גאסטיש [משפט] אנד אבערלאשתינג פאיתח.

Are composed of justice and everlasting faith.

אי אם ינשענסד בי מי פיוריעש ראג.

I am incensed by my furious rage.

י Yod ט Tet ח Chet ז Zayin ו Vav ה Hei ד Dalet ג Gimel ב Beit א Aleph
ס Samech ן Final Nun נ Nun ם Final Mem מ Mem ל Lamed ך Final Kaf כ Kaf
ת Tav ש Shin ר Resh ק Kuf ץ Final Tzadik צ Tzadik ף Final Feh פ Peh ע Ayin

פור מי אנעמיז האב נעגלעקתעד יור וורדז.

For my enemies have neglected Your words.

יור וורד עקוז וית גרעאט פיוריתי,

Your word echoes with great purity,

אנד יט יש צערישד בי יור סערבאנט.

And it is cherished by Your servant

אלתהו אי אם יותחפול,

Although I am youthful,

אנד תריטעד וית כונתעמפט,

And treated with contempt,

אי האו נעת נעגלעקתעד יור פרישעפתץ [מצות].

I have not neglected Your precepts.

יור וערצועס ריצאסנעשס [צדק] יש אבערלאשתינג,

Your virtuous righteousness is everlasting,

אנד תחע סתאצוטץ אף יור לאו,

And the statutes of Your law,

י Yod ט Tet ח Chet ז Zayin ו Vav ה Hei ד Dalet ג Gimel ב Beit א Aleph
ס Samech ן Final Nun נ Nun ם Final Mem מ Mem ל Lamed ך Final Kaf כ Kaf
ת Tav ש Shin ר Resh ק Kuf ץ Final Tzadik צ Tzadik ף Final Feh פ Peh ע Ayin

אר תרעשטוורתחי.

Are trustworthy.

מיספורצען אנד דישטרעסס האב פאונד מי;

Misfortune and distress have found me;

תחע שתעדי אף יור קוממאנדמאנטץ [מצות],

The study of Your commandments.

גלאדענז מי שול [נפש].

Gladdens my soul.

תחע גאסטיש [משפט] אף יור פרישעפתץ [מצות],

The justice of Your precepts,

שחאלל שתאנד יתערנאללי,

Shall stand eternally,

אללוו מי תו קומפריהענד,

Allow me to comprehend,

ין ורדער תחאט אי מאי כונתיניו תו ליב.

In order that I may continue to live.

ק

וית אלל מי הערט אי קרי אוט תו יו ,ו לורד,

With all my heart I cry out to You, O Lord,

ריספונד תו מי.

Respond to me.

אי וילל געארד יור לאוז,

I will guard Your laws,

אי קרי אוט תו יו תו גראנט מי סאלבאשען [ישועה],

I cry out to You to grant me salvation,

פור אי וילל עבשערב יור טעשטימוניז.

For I will observe Your testimonies.

רישינג ביפור תחע דאון אף תחע מורנינג,

Rising before the dawn of the morning,

אי קריד פור יור סאלבאשען [ישועה] ;תרעשטינג ין יור שאיינגז.

I cried for your salvation; trusting in your sayings.

מי עיז ופען ביפור עיך אף תחע נעית ואטצעז,

My eyes open before each of the night watches,

סו תחאט אי מאי תחעוטפוללי ריביו יור וורד.

So that I may thoughtfully review Your word.

הארקען תו מי אפפעאל,

Hearken to my appeal,

אס ביפיתץ יור פאבור.

As befits Your favor.

ו לורד ,גראנט מי יור סאלבאשען [ישועה],

O Lord, grant me Your salvation,

ין קיפינג וית יור לאוז.

In keeping with Your laws.

כונשפיעריגג פערשוערז אר אפפרוצינג מי,

Conspiring pursuers are approaching me,

תהאי אר רימות פרום יור לאו.

They are remote from Your law.

בעת יו אר נירבי ,ו לורד,

But You are nearby, O Lord

אנד יור טרותס אר ין אלל יור פרישעפתץ [מצות].

And Your truths are in all Your precepts.

פרום מי כוממענצמענת אף ענדערשתאנדינג,

From my commencement of understanding,

אי נו תחאט יור טעשטימוניז אף ולד,

I knew that Your testimonies of old,

וער עסטאבלישד בי יו יתערנאללי.

Were established by You eternally.

ר

עבשערב מי שעפפערינג אנד שעט מי פרי,

Observe my suffering and set me free,

פור אי האב נעת פאילד תו היד יור לאו.

For I have not failed to heed Your law.

סעפפורת מי אפפעאל אנד רעשקיו מי,

Support my appeal and rescue me,

בי מי סאלבאשען [ישועה] אככורדינג תו יור וורד.

Be my salvation according to Your word.

תחע ויכעד אר רימות פרום סאלבאשען [ישועה],

The wicked are remote from salvation,

פור יור לאוז אר נעת סועט אפתער בי תהעם.

For Your laws are not sought after by them.

ו לורד ,אס יור מערסי יז באונתיפול,

O Lord, as Your mercy is bountiful,

דעליבער מי ין קיפינג וית יור לאוז.

Deliver me in keeping with Your laws.

מי פערשוערז אנד אנעמיז אר מאני,

My pursuers and enemies are many,

אי האב נעבער סתראיד,

I have never strayed,

פרום תחע תיצינג אף יור פרישעפתץ [מצות].

From the teaching of Your precepts.

וען אי בור ויתנעסס תו טראיטורס,

When I bore witness to traitors,

י Yod ט Tet ח Chet ז Zayin ו Vav ה Hei ד Dalet ג Gimel ב Beit א Aleph
ס Samech ן Final Nun נ Nun ם Final Mem מ Mem ל Lamed ך Final Kaf כ Kaf
ת Tav ש Shin ר Resh ק Kuf ץ Final Tzadik צ Tzadik ף Final Feh פ Peh ע Ayin

אי האו ארגיוד וית תהעם,

I have argued with them,

ביקאעס תהאי דיד נעת געארד,

Because they did not guard,

יור וורד.

Your word

ביהולד, אי צעריש יור קוממאנדמאנטץ [מצות],

Behold, I cherish Your commandments,

ו לורד ,בי מי סאלבאשען [ישועה],

O Lord, be my salvation,

אככורדינג תו יור פאבור.

According to Your favor.

פרום תחע ביגינינג ,

From the beginning,

יור וערי עששענץ יש טרותה,

Your very essence is truth,

יור געדגמענטץ אר יתערנאללי רעיצעס.

Your judgments are eternally righteous.

ש

מי פערשוערז אר פרינצעס,

My pursuers are princes,

הו פערשעקיוט מי ויתאוט ריזון,

Who persecute me without reason,

בעת מי העארט יש ין פיר אף יור וורד.

But my heart is in fear of Your word.

יור וורד ברינגז גוי [שמחה] תו מי,

Your word brings joy to me,

אס וון הו פינדז א גרעאט תרעזור.

As one who finds a great treasure.

אי לותח אנד דעתעשט פאלס וורדז,

I loathe and detest false words,

בעת ,אי צעריש יור תיצינגס.

But, I cherish Your teachings.

אי פראיז יו שעבען תימז דאילי,

I praise You seven times daily,

פור תחע גאסטיש [משפט] אף יור סתאצוטץ.

For the justice of Your statutes.

פור תהוז הו לוב יור תיצינג,

For those who love Your teaching,

ועלל-ביינג יש באונטיפוללי פיספול.

Well-being is bountifully peaceful.

אנד תחער יש נו שטעמבלינג בלוך ין תחער ואי.

And there is no stumbling block in their way.

ו לורד ,אי אנטיסיפאט יור סאבינג גראס,

O Lord, I anticipate Your saving grace,

אי האב בין פאיתפול תו יור פרישעפתץ [מצות] .

I have been faithful to Your precepts.

וית אלל מי שול [נפש] אי האו קעפת יור סתאצוטץ [מצוות],

With all my soul I have kept Your statutes,

י Yod ט Tet ח Chet ז Zayin ו Vav ה Hei ד Dalet ג Gimel ב Beit א Aleph
ס Samech ן Final Nun נ Nun ם Final Mem מ Mem ל Lamed ך Final Kaf כ Kaf
ת Tav ש Shin ר Resh ק Kuf ץ Final Tzadik צ Tzadik ף Final Feh פ Peh ע Ayin

אנד אי צעריש תהעם גרעאתלי.

And I cherish them greatly,

אי האב עבשערבד,

I have observed,

יור קוממאנדמאנטץ [מצות],

Your commandments,

אנד יור דעקריז,

And Your decrees,

ביקאעס ביפור יו אר אלל מי ואיז.

Because before You are all my ways.

ת

אי פראי תחאט מי שונג [שיר] כומז,

I pray that my song comes,

ביפור יור פרעסאנץ ,ו לורד,

Before Your presence, O Lord

אנד אללוו מי אנליטענמענת ,ין קיפינג ויתּ יור וורד.

And allow me enlightenment, in keeping with Your word.

פערמיט מי ענטריטי תו פריסענט יתשעלף ביפור יו,

Permit my entreaty to present itself before You,

בי מי סאלבאשען [ישועה] ין אככורדאנץ וית יור וורד.

Be my salvation in accordance with Your word.

מי פראיז שחאלל אובערפלוו מי ליפס,

My praise shall overflow my lips,

פור יו ינשתרעקטעד מי ין יור לאו.

For you instructed me in Your law.

מי תונג שחאלל פורם תחע וורדז,

My tongue shall form the words,

תחאט פרוכלאימז תחע גאסטיש [משפט] אף יור טעשטימוניז,

That proclaims the justice of Your testimonies,

אנד תחע ריצאסנעשס [צדק] אף אלל יור קוממאנדמאנטץ [מצות].

The righteousness of all Your commandments.

לענד מי יור העלפינג האנד,

Lend me Your helping hand,

פור אי האב בין פאיתפול תו יור קוממאנדמאנטץ [מצות].

For I have been faithful to Your commandments.

אי יעארן פור יור דיליבעראנץ ,ו לורד,

I yearn for Your deliverance, O Lord,

פור יור תיצינגס אר מי כונשטאנת פלעזור.

For Your teachings are my constant pleasure.

פערמיט מי שול [נפש] תו כונתיניו יטץ ליף,

Permit my soul to continue its life,

תחאט יט שחאלל אלואיס פראיז יו,

That it shall always praise You,

אנד יור לאוז געיד מי.

And Your laws guide me.

אי האו ואנדערד ען מי פאתח,

I have wandered on my path,

אס א לושט שיף.

As a lost sheep.

שערך אוט יור סערבאנט,

Search out Your servant,

פור אי האב נעת פורשאכאן,

For I have not forsaken,

יור פרישעפתץ [מצות].

Your precepts.

- 120 -

א שונג [שיר] אף אשענץ.

A song of Ascents.

ין מי אנגויש אי כאללד אוט תו תחע לורד,

In my I anguish I called out to the Lord,

אנד הי ריספונדעד תו מי.

And He responded to me.

ו לורד ,דעליבער מי,

O Lord, deliver me,

פרום דישיטפול ליפס,

From deceitful lips,

אנד א ליינג תונג.

And a lying tongue.

ואת כאן הי פרוביד יו?

What can he provide You?

אנד ואת פרושידס വילל בי ריטורנד,

And what proceeds will be returned,

י Yod ט Tet ח Chet ז Zayin ו Vav ה Hei ד Dalet ג Gimel ב Beit א Aleph
ס Samech ן Final Nun נ Nun ם Final Mem מ Mem ל Lamed ך Final Kaf כ Kaf
ת Tav ש Shin ר Resh ק Kuf ץ Final Tzadik צ Tzadik ף Final Feh פ Peh ע Ayin

פרום א ליינג תונג?

From a lying tongue?

תחע מיתי וארריורז׳ ארררוז האב בין שארפענד,

The mighty warriors' arrows have been sharpened,

וית העת קולז אף גוניפר וודֿ.

With hot coals of juniper wood.

אי אם ווֿפול פור מי עקצתענדעד ויזיט תו משך,

I am woeful for my extended visit to Meshech,

אנד תחאט אי דועלט אמונג תחע טריב אף קדר.

And that I dwelt among the tribe of Kedar.

מי שול [נפש] האס שוגערנד תו לונג,

My soul has sojourned too long,

וית תהוז הו דעשפיז שלום.

With those who despise peace.

אי אם אלל פור שלום,

I am all for peace,

אי שפיק פור שלום,

I speak for peace,

תהאי שפיק פור ואר.

They speak for war.

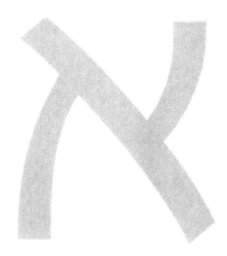

- 121 -

א שונג [שיר] תו תחע אשענץ.

A song to the Ascents.

אי כאשט מי עיז עף תו תחע מאונתאנז [הרים];

I cast my eyes up to the mountains;

פרום ווער וילל מי איד קעם?

From where will my aid come?

מי איד אררױבז פרום תחע לורד,

My aid arrives from the Lord,

תחע קריאטור אף העאבען אנד עארתח [ארץ].

The Creator of heaven and earth.

הי וילל נעת אללוו,

He will not allow,

יור פותסתעפס תו שטעמבעל,

Your footsteps to stumble,

יור געארדיאן דעז נעת עבער רעשת;

Your Guardian does not ever rest;

ביהולד ,תחע געארדיאן אף ישראל,

Behold, the Guardian of Israel,

נעבער רעשתס ור שליפס.

Never rests or sleeps.

תחע לורד יש יור געארדיאן,

The Lord is your Guardian,

תחע לורד יש יור שהעלטער,

The Lord is your shelter,

את יור ריט האנד.

At your right hand.

תחע שען וילל נעת הארם יו דורינג תחע דאי,

The sun will not harm you during the day,

נור תחע מון את ניט.

Nor the moon at night.

געד שחאלל פרותעקט יו פרום אלל עיבעל;

God shall protect you from all evil;

י Yod ט Tet ח Chet ז Zayin ו Vav ה Hei ד Dalet ג Gimel ב Beit א Aleph
ס Samech ן Final Nun נ Nun ם Final Mem מ Mem ל Lamed ך Final Kaf כ Kaf
ת Tav ש Shin ר Resh ק Kuf ץ Final Tzadik צ Tzadik ף Final Feh פ Peh ע Ayin

הי וילל געארד יור שול [נפש].

He will guard your soul.

הי וילל געארד יור כומינגז אנד יור גוינגז,

He will guard your comings and your goings,

פרום תחיס תים, נאו אנד פורעבערמור.

From this time now, and for evermore.

נ

- 122 -

א שונג [שיר] אף אשענץ ,בי דוד.

A song of Ascents, by David.

אי ואס פיללד וית גוי [שמחה],

I was filled with joy,

וען תהאי סאעד תו מי,

When they said to me,

"לעט עש אלל גו עף תו תחע האוש אף תחע לורד ".

"Let us all go up to the House of the Lord."

אור פיט סתוד אפיקצת,

Our feet stood affixed,

ויתהין יור גאתץ ,ו ירושלם.

Within your gates, O Jerusalem.

א בילט-עף ירושלם,

A built-up Jerusalem,

א יוניתעד סיטי, וובען תוגעתחער,

A united city, woven together,

י Yod ט Tet ח Chet ז Zayin ו Vav ה Hei ד Dalet ג Gimel ב Beit א Aleph
ס Samech ן Final Nun נ Nun ם Final Mem מ Mem ל Lamed ך Final Kaf כ Kaf
ת Tav ש Shin ר Resh ק Kuf ץ Final Tzadik צ Tzadik ף Final Feh פ Peh ע Ayin

ינתו א כוננעקטעד הול.

Into a connected whole.

א פלאס אף פילגראמאג,

A place of pilgrimage,

פור תחע תריבז תו אשענד;

For the tribes to ascend;

תחע לורד'ס תריבז,

The Lord's tribes,

הו אר תחע ויתנעששעס אף ישראל,

Who are the witnesses of Israel,

תו תהאנקפוללי פראיז תחע לורד'ז נאם [שם].

To thankfully praise the Lord's Name.

ביקאעס תחעאר שאט תחע תחרונז אף געדגמענט [משפט],

Because there sat the thrones of judgment,

תחע תחרונז פור תחע האוס אף דוד.

The thrones for the House of David.

י Yod ט Tet ח Chet ז Zayin ו Vav ה Hei ד Dalet ג Gimel ב Beit א Aleph
ס Samech ן Final Nun נ Nun ם Final Mem מ Mem ל Lamed ך Final Kaf כ Kaf
ת Tav ש Shin ר Resh ק Kuf ץ Final Tzadik צ Tzadik ף Final Feh פ Peh ע Ayin

פראי פור תחע שלום אף ירושלם;

Pray for the peace of Jerusalem;

אלל תהוז הו צעריש יו שחאלל האב שלום.

All those who cherish You shall have peace.

"מאי תחער בי פיספול ועלל-ביינג,

"May there be peaceful well-being,

ויתהין יור וואללז,

Within your walls.

אנד מאי סערעניתי פרושפער,

And may serenity prosper,

ויתהין יור סטרונג האוסעז".

Within your strong houses."

ען ביהאלף אף מי פאמילי אנד פרענדז,

On behalf of my family and friends,

אי פראי פור שלום ויתהין יור מידצת.

I pray for peace within your midst.

י Yod ט Tet ח Chet ז Zayin ו Vav ה Hei ד Dalet ג Gimel ב Beit א Aleph
ס Samech ן Final Nun נ Nun ם Final Mem מ Mem ל Lamed ך Final Kaf כ Kaf
ת Tav ש Shin ר Resh ק Kuf ץ Final Tzadik צ Tzadik ף Final Feh פ Peh ע Ayin

ען ביהאלף אף תחע האוס אף תחע לורד ,אור געד,

On behalf of the House of the Lord, our God,

יט יז פור יור גווד,

It is for your good,

תחאט אי פראי.

That I pray.

ו

- 123 -

א שונג [שיר] אף אשענץ.

A Song of Ascents.

תו יו ,אי כאשט עף מי עיז;

To You, I cast up my eyes;

ו יו הו אר ענתרונד,

O You Who are enthroned,

ין תחע העאבענז [שמים].

In the heavens.

ביהולד!

Behold!

מין אר ליק תחע עיז אף א סערבאנט,

Mine are like the eyes of a servant,

לוכינג טוארד היז מאסתעריס האנד;

Looking toward his master's hand;

ליק תחע עיז אף א מאידען,

Like the eyes of a maiden,

י Yod ט Tet ח Chet ז Zayin ו Vav ה Hei ד Dalet ג Gimel ב Beit א Aleph
ס Samech ן Final Nun נ Nun ם Final Mem מ Mem ל Lamed ך Final Kaf כ Kaf
ת Tav ש Shin ר Resh ק Kuf ץ Final Tzadik צ Tzadik ף Final Feh פ Peh ע Ayin

לוקינג טוארד הער מישתרעש'ס האנד;

Looking toward her mistress's hand;

שו אור עיז סעט עפון תחע לורד ,אור געד,

So our eyes set upon the Lord, our God,

אס וי ואית עפון הים תו פאבור עש וית מערסי,

As we wait upon Him to favor us with mercy,

גראנט עש מערסי ,ו לורד ,גראנט עש מערסי,

Grant us mercy, O Lord, grant us mercy,

פור וי אר גרעאתלי פיללד וית סכורן,

For we are greatly filled with scorn,

אנד אור שול [נפש] אובערפלווז,

And our soul overflows,

וית תחע דיסדאין,

With the disdain,

אף תחע כומפלאסענט,

Of the complacent,

אנד שהאם,

And shame,

אף תחע אררוגאנט.

Of the arrogant.

מ

- 124 -

א שונג [שיר] אף אשענץ – בי דוד.

A Song of Ascents - by David

יף יט וער נעת פור תחע לורד ,הו ואס וית עש--

If it were not for the Lord, Who was with us --

נאו ,אלל ישראל מאיך א דעכלאראשען--

Now, all Israel make a declaration --

יף נעת פור תחע לורד, הו ואס וית עש,

If not for the Lord, Who was with us,

וען מען פערשוד עש,

When men pursued us,

תהאי וود האב,

They would have,

קונשומד עש,

Consumed us,

אליב,

Alive,

וען תחער פורי,

When their fury,

ואס יגניטעד אגאינצט עש.

Was ignited against us.

תחע ואתערז [מים] ווד האב שועפט אובער עש,

The waters would have swept over us,

א ריבער ווד האו פאששד אובער אור סול [נפש].

A river would have passed over our soul.

ויללפול ואתערז [מים] ווד האב פאששד אובער אור שול [נפש],

Willful waters with passed over our soul,

בלאששעד [ברוך] בי תחע לורד ,הו דיד נעת אללוו עס אס תחער פראי,

Blessed be the Lord, Who did not allow us as their prey,

גריפפד ביטוין תחער טייתה.

Gripped between their teeth.

אור שול [נפש] פלעד ליק א בירד,

Our soul fled like a bird,

יבאדינג תחע הענטער׳ז תראף,

Evading the hunter's trap,

תחע תראף ברוך,

The trap broke,

אנד וי פלעד.

And we fled.

אור העלפער,

Our helper,

יש תחע נאם [שם] אף תחע לורד,

Is the Name of the Lord,

קריאטור אף העאבען אנד עארתח [ארץ].

Creator of heaven and earth.

- 125 -

א שונג [שיר] אף אשענץ.

A Song of Ascents.

תהוז הו פלאס תחער תרעשט ין תחע לורד,

Those who place their trust in the Lord,

מאי בי כומפארד תו מאונת ציון,

May be comparted to Mount Zion,

ויך קאננוט בי מובד,

Which cannot be moved,

אנד עקזיסטץ פורעבער.

And exists forever.

אס תחע מאונתאנז [הרים] וראף אראונד ירושלם,

As the mountains wrap around Jerusalem,

תחע לורד וראפס אראונד היז פיפעל [עם],

The Lord wraps around His people,

נאו אנד פורעבערמור.

Now and forevermore.

י Yod ט Tet ח Chet ז Zayin ו Vav ה Hei ד Dalet ג Gimel ב Beit א Aleph
ס Samech ן Final Nun נ Nun ם Final Mem מ Mem ל Lamed ך Final Kaf כ Kaf
ת Tav ש Shin ר Resh ק Kuf ץ Final Tzadik צ Tzadik ף Final Feh פ Peh ע Ayin

ביקאעז תחע שעפתער בורן בי תחע ויכעד שחאלל נעת בי פלאשד,

Because the scepter borne by their wicked shall not be placed,

ען תחע דעשתיני בילונגינג תו תחע רעיצעס [צדיק],

On the destiny belonging to the righteous,

שו תחאט תחע רעיצעס [צדיק] וילל קיף תחער האנדז,

So that the righteous will keep their hands,

פרי פרום ויכעד דוינגז.

Free from wicked doings.

גראנט גוודנעסס ,ו לורד ,תו גווד פיפעל,

Grant goodness, O Lord, to good people,

אס ועלל אס תהאי הו אר הונישט ין תחער העארטץ,

As well as they who are honest in their hearts,

בעת תהוז הו תערנד,

But those who turned,

טו תויסטעד ואיז,

To twisted ways,

י Yod ט Tet ח Chet ז Zayin ו Vav ה Hei ד Dalet ג Gimel ב Beit א Aleph
ס Samech ן Final Nun נ Nun ם Final Mem מ Mem ל Lamed ך Final Kaf כ Kaf
ת Tav ש Shin ר Resh ק Kuf ץ Final Tzadik צ Tzadik ף Final Feh פ Peh ע Ayin

תחע לורד וילל שענד תהעם,

The Lord will send them,

אלונג תחע ואי אף עיבעלדוערז [רשעים].

Along the way of evildoers.

בעת תו ישראל ,תחער שחאלל בי שלום.

But to Israel, there shall be peace.

י Yod ט Tet ח Chet ז Zayin ו Vav ה Hei ד Dalet ג Gimel ב Beit א Aleph
ס Samech ן Final Nun נ Nun ם Final Mem מ Mem ל Lamed ך Final Kaf כ Kaf
ת Tav ש Shin ר Resh ק Kuf ץ Final Tzadik צ Tzadik ף Final Feh פ Peh ע Ayin

- 126 -

א שונג [שיר] אף אשענץ.

A Song of Ascents.

וען תחע לורד ריטערנז עש פרום ציון'ז כאפתיביטי,

When the Lord returns us from Zion's captivity,

ווי וילל אכט אס דרימערז.

We will act as dreamers.

יט וילל בי תחען תחאט אור מאותס,

It will be then that our mouths,

אר שו פיללד וית לאפינג,

Are so filled with laughing,

אנד אור תונגז גויפולי,

And our tongues joyfully,

רעזונאט וית שונג [שיר].

Resonate with song.

אנד תחען תהוז אמונג תחע נאתענז ,תהאי שחאלל שאי,

And then those among the nations, they shall say,

י Yod ט Tet ח Chet ז Zayin ן Vav ה Hei ד Dalet ג Gimel ב Beit א Aleph
ס Samech ן Final Nun נ Nun ם Final Mem מ Mem ל Lamed ך Final Kaf כ Kaf
ת Tav ש Shin ר Resh ק Kuf ץ Final Tzadik צ Tzadik ף Final Feh פ Peh ע Ayin

"תחע לורד האש דון גרעאט תחינגז פור תהעם"!

"The Lord has done great things for them!"

תחע לורד האז פרובידעד גרעאתלי פור עש,

The Lord has provided greatly for us,

גלאדלי דו וי ריגויס!

Gladly do we rejoice!

ו לורד ,רישתור עס פרום כאפתיביטי,

O Lord, restore us from captivity,

אס ריבערבעדז ין תחע נגב דעזערט,

As riverbeds in the Negev desert,

אללוו תהוז הו פלאנט ין טעארז ,תו הארועשת ין גוי [שמחה],

Allow those who plant in tears, to harvest in joy,

אנד תהוז הו גו ויפינג, הו קאררי א וורתהי סיד,

And those who go weeping, who carry a worthy seed,

שחאלל ריטורן וית גויעס שונג [שיר] בארינג היז שהיבז אף ויט.

Shall return with joyous song bearing his sheaves of wheat.

י Yod ט Tet ח Chet ז Zayin ו Vav ה Hei ד Dalet ג Gimel ב Beit א Aleph
ס Samech ן Final Nun נ Nun ם Final Mem מ Mem ל Lamed ך Final Kaf כ Kaf
ת Tav ש Shin ר Resh ק Kuf ץ Final Tzadik צ Tzadik ף Final Feh פ Peh ע Ayin

- 127 -

א שונג [שיר] אף אשענץ פור שולומון [שלמה].

A Song of Ascents for Solomon.

יף תחע לורד דעז נעת בילד תחע האוס,

If the Lord does not build the House,

תחע תויל אף תחע בילדערז אף יט יש פור נאעט.

The toil of the builders of it is for naught.

יף תחע לורד דעז נעת ואתץ אובער תחע סיתי,

If the Lord does not watch over the city,

תחע ואתצמאן'ז ויגיל יש פור נאעט.

The watchman's vigil is for naught.

אנד יט יש פור נאעט פור יו תו ריז עף את דאון,

And it is for naught for you to rise up at dawn,

שתאי עף לאט ,אנד וורק ין גריף פור תחע ברעד יו עיט,

Stay up late, and work in grief for the bread you eat,

פור הי פרובידז פור היז בילובעד דורינג תחער סלעמבער .

For He provides for His beloved during their slumber.

י Yod ט Tet ח Chet ז Zayin ו Vav ה Hei ד Dalet ג Gimel ב Beit א Aleph
ס Samech ן Final Nun נ Nun ם Final Mem מ Mem ל Lamed ך Final Kaf כ Kaf
ת Tav ש Shin ר Resh ק Kuf ץ Final Tzadik צ Tzadik ף Final Feh פ Peh ע Ayin

ביהולד !צילדרען אר תחע ביקועשט גיבען בי תחע לורד,

Behold! Children are the bequest given by the Lord,

הי גיבז תחע פרוט אף תחע וומב אס היז ריוארד.

He gives the fruit of the womb as His reward.

אס אררווז ין תחע האנדז אף א וארליק מאן [אדם],

As arrows in the hands of a warlike man,

שו אר צילדרען בורן תו תחע יענג.

So are children born to the young.

וורתהי אף פראיז יש תחע מאן [אדם],

Worthy of praise is the man,

הו פיללס היש קויבער,

Who fills his quiver,

וית תהעם.

With them.

שהאם שחאלל נעת פאלל עפון תהעם,

Shame shall not fall upon them,

וען תהאי מעסט כונבערס את תחע גאט וית תהער פוז.

When they must converse at the gate with their foes.

י Yod ט Tet ח Chet ז Zayin ו Vav ה Hei ד Dalet ג Gimel ב Beit א Aleph
ס Samech ן Final Nun נ Nun ם Final Mem מ Mem ל Lamed ך Final Kaf כ Kaf
ת Tav ש Shin ר Resh ק Kuf ץ Final Tzadik צ Tzadik ף Final Feh פ Peh ע Ayin

- 128 -

א שונג [שיר] אף אשענץ.

A Song of Ascents.

בלעססינגז עפון עבעריוון הו פירז תחע לורד,

Blessings upon everyone who fears the Lord,

אנד הו פוללווז היז פאתחואיז,

And who follows His pathways,

יו שחאלל פארתאק אף,

You shall partake of,

תחע וורק אף יור וון האנדז,

The work of your own hands,

אנד יו שחאלל בי פיללד,

And you shall be filled,

וית האפפינעסס,

With happiness,

אנד יו שחאלל, פרושפער.

And you shall prosper.

יור ויף ויילל בי פרוטפול ליק א גראפבין,

Your wife will be fruitful like a grapevine,

ויתהין תחע כונפינז אף יור הום;

Within the confines of your home;

אנד יור צילדרען שחאלל בי,

And your children shall be,

ליק יענג עליב תריז,

Like young olive trees,

אראונד יור תאבעל.

Around your table.

ביהולד!

Behold!

פור תחיס יש תחע ואי תחע מאן [אדם],

For this is the way the man,

הו פירז תחע לורד,

Who fears the Lord,

י Yod ט Tet ח Chet ז Zayin ו Vav ה Hei ד Dalet ג Gimel ב Beit א Aleph
ס Samech ן Final Nun נ Nun ם Final Mem מ Mem ל Lamed ך Final Kaf כ Kaf
ת Tav ש Shin ר Resh ק Kuf ץ Final Tzadik צ Tzadik ף Final Feh פ Peh ע Ayin

יש בלאששד [ברוך].

Is blessed.

מאי תחע לורד גראנט יו בלעססינגז,

May the Lord grant you blessings,

פרום אוט אף ציון,

From out of Zion,

אנד מאי יו ויתנעסס תחע גוודנעסס,

And may you witness the goodness,

אף ירושלם ,אלל תחע דאיס אף יור ליף;

Of Jerusalem, all the days of your life;

אנד מאי יו ליב תו שי,

And may you live to see,

יור צילדרען האב צילדרען,

Your children have children,

אנד מאי אלל ישראל בי פיספול.

And may all Israel be peaceful.

י Yod ט Tet ח Chet ז Zayin ו Vav ה Hei ד Dalet ג Gimel ב Beit א Aleph
ס Samech ן Final Nun נ Nun ם Final Mem מ Mem ל Lamed ך Final Kaf כ Kaf
ת Tav ש Shin ר Resh ק Kuf ץ Final Tzadik צ Tzadik ף Final Feh פ Peh ע Ayin

- 129 -

א שונג [שיר] אף אשענץ.

A Song of Ascents.

עפט-תימז ,עבער שינץ מי יות,

Oft-times, ever since my youth,

תהאי האו ופתען קאעשד מי אפפליקשען,

They have often caused my affliction,

אנד נאו לעט תחע דעכלאראשען קעם פרום ישראל;

And now let the declaration come from Israel;

שינץ מי יות תהאי האב ופתען קאעשד מי אפפליקשען,

Since my youth they have caused me affliction,

בעת נעבער דיד תהאי ואנקוישח מי!

But never did they vanquish me!

אלונג מי באק תחע פלוומען פלווד,

Along my back the plowmen plowed,

אנד תהאי קאעשד לונג פוררווז.

And they caused long furrows.

געד יש געסט!

God is just!

הי שעבערד תחע רופס,

He severed the ropes,

אף תחע ויכעד.

Of the wicked.

דישגראשד אנד תערנד אואי,

Disgraced and turned away,

וילל בי אלל תהוז הו אר האתערז אף ציון.

Will be all those who are haters of Zion.

תהאי אר ליכענד תו תחע האי ען תחע רופטעפס,

They are likened to the hay on the rooftops,

תחאט ויתחערז ביפור יט כאן בי ענשהאיתד ,

That withers before it can be unsheathed,

אנד תחע ריפער כאננוט עיואן גאתחער א האנדפול,

And the reaper cannot even gather a handful,

נור תחע בינדער אף האי פילל היז ארם.

Nor the binder of hay fill his arm.

אנד תהוז הו אר פאשערזבי ,האב נעת שאעד,

And those who are passersby, have not said,

"מאי געד'ז בלעססינג,

"May God's blessing,

בי עפון יו."

Be upon you."

"וי בלעשש יו,

"We bless you,

ין תחע נאם [שם] אף תחע לורד."

In the Name of the Lord."

ווי גיב יו אור בלעססינג ין תחע [חי] נאם [שם] אף תחע לורד [אדוני].

We give you our blessing in the [Ha] Name [Shem] of the Lord [Adonai].

- 130 -

א שונג [שיר] אף אשענץ.

A Song of Ascents.

פרום אוט אף תחע דעפץ אי קרי אוט תו יו ,ו לורד.

From out of the depths I cry out to you, O Lord.

ו לורד ,לישתען תו מי כאלל,

O Lord, listen to my call,

אללוו יור עארז תו בי רעסעפתיב,

Allow Your ears to be receptive,

תו תחע סאונדז אף מי פלידינגז פור העלף.

To the sounds of my pleadings for help.

יף יו ,ו לורד ,פרישערבד א רעכורדינג אף שינז,

If you, O Lord, preserved a recording of sins,

ו מי לורד ,הו קוד כונתיניו תו ליב?

O my Lord, who could continue to live?

פור יו פארדון,

For You pardon,

אנד פור תחאט יו מאי בי העלד ין או.

And for that You may be held in awe.

אי פות מי טרעשט ין תחע לורד,

I put my trust in the Lord

מי שול [נפש] הופץ פור הים,

My soul hopes for Him,

אנד ין היש וורד ,אי תרעשט.

And in His word, I trust.

מי יננערמוסט ביינג לונגז פור מי לורד,

My innermost being longs for my Lord,

מור תהאן תחע ואצמען,

More than the watchmen,

הו אואית תחע מורנינג,

Who await the morning,

עיואן תחע ואצמען,

Even the watchmen,

פור תחע מורנינג.

For the morning.

לעט ישראל טרעשט ין תחע לורד,

Let Israel trust in the Lord,

פור וית תחע לורד תחער יש לובינג-קינדנעשס [חסד],

For with the Lord there is loving-kindness,

אנד הי ברינגז וית הים באונטיפול דיליבעראנץ,

And he brings with Him bountiful deliverance,

פור יט יש הי הו שחאלל דעליבער ישראל פרום אלל יטץ ויקעדנעשס.

For it is He Who shall deliver Israel from all its wickedness.

- 131 -

א שונג [שיר] אף אשענץ ,בי דוד.

A Song of Ascents, by David.

ו לורד ,מי הערט יש נעת פיללד וית אררוגאנץ,

O Lord, my heart is not filled with arrogance,

אנד תחע לווק אף מי עיז יז נעת האעטי;

And the look of my eyes is not haughty;

אנד אי דיד נות אתתעמפט תו אתטאין גרעאתנעסס ור וונדערז,

And I did not attempt to attain greatness or wonders,

תחאט וער בייונד מי ריך.

That were beyond my reach.

אי אפפירם תחאט מי שול [נפש] דועללז,

I affirm that my soul dwells,

קויעט אנד כונטענטעד,

Quiet and contented,

נו לונגער א נערסינג צילד,

No longer a nursing child,

בי היז מותחער'ז שיד,

By his mother's side

מי יננערמוסט ביינג,

My innermost being,

יש נו לונגער ליק א נערשינג צילד.

Is no longer like a nursing child.

ו לעט ישראל ,תרעשט ין תחע לורד,

O let Israel, trust in the Lord,

פרום תחיס תים אנד פוראבערמור.

From this time and for evermore.

ש

- 132 -

א שונג [שיר] אף אשענץ.

A Song of Ascents.

ו לורד ,ריכאלל דוד;

O Lord, recall David;

אלל אף היז שעפפערינגז,

All of his sufferings,

אנד היז ואוז תו תחע לורד,

And his vows to the Lord,

אנד פרומישעז תו תחע סטרונג וון אף יעקב .

And promises to the Strong One of Jacob.

"אי שחאלל נעת אנתער תחע תענט אף מי הום ,נור וילל אי אנתער מי בעד,

I shall not enter the tent of my home, nor will I enter my bed,

אנד אללוו שליף תו אנתער מי עיז ,תחאט כאעזעז מי עילידז תו כלוז,

And allow sleep to enter my eyes, that causes my eyelids to close,

ביפור אי פינד א תאבערנאקאל פור תחע לורד ;א דועללינג פלאס
פור תחע סטרונג וון אף יעקב."

Before I find a tabernacle for the Lord; a dwelling place for the Strong One of Jacob."

ביהולד !וען וי העארד תחאט יט ואס ין אפרת, וי פאונד יט,

Behold! When we heard that it was in Ephrath, we found it,

ין תחע מעדווז אף תחע פורעסט.

In the meadows of the forest.

היר וי וילל גו תו היז אבוד ,היז תאבערנאקאל,

Here we will go to His abode, His tabernacle,

תחער וי וילל פרושתראט עורשעלבז את היז פותסתול.

There we will prostrate ourselves at His footstool.

ריז עף ו לורד את יור רעשתינג פלאס,

Rise up O Lord at Your resting place,

יו אנד יור סטרונג ארק.

You and Your strong ark.

ו ,לעט יור פרישטס בי קלותד ין געסטיש [משפט],

O, let Your priests be clothed in justice,

י Yod ט Tet ח Chet ז Zayin ו Vav ה Hei ד Dalet ג Gimel ב Beit א Aleph
ס Samech ן Final Nun נ Nun ם Final Mem מ Mem ל Lamed ך Final Kaf כ Kaf
ת Tav ש Shin ר Resh ק Kuf ץ Final Tzadik צ Tzadik ף Final Feh פ Peh ע Ayin

אנד יור פאיתהפוללי דעבאות גויעשלי שינג.

And Your faithfully devout joyously sing.

דו תחיס פור יור סערבאנט דוד'ז שאך,

Do this for Your servant David's sake,

דו נעת ריגעקט דוד'ז פאש,

Do not reject David's face,

יור אנוינתעד וון.

Your anointed one.

תחע לורד,

The Lord,

האש אפירמד תו דוד,

Has affirmed to David,

א טרו אותח הי וילל נעבער רינאונץ,

A true oath He will never renounce,

"פרום תחע פרוט אף יור בודי,

"From the fruit of your body,

אי וילל פלאס עף ען יור תחרון,

I will place up on your throne,

יף יור צילדרען עבשערב מי קובענאנט,

If your children observe My covenant,

אנד מי פרישעפתץ [מצות] ין ויך אי שחאלל ינצטרעקת תהעם,

And My precepts in which I shall instruct them,

אנד תחער צילדרען אס ועלל.

And their children as well.

לדר ודר ,פוראבער,

From generation to generation, forever,

שחאלל שיט עפון יור תחרון.

Shall sit upon your throne.

ביקאעס תחע לורד צוס אנד דעשיערד ציון אס היז דועללינג פלאס,

Because the Lord chose and desired Zion as His dwelling place,

יט יש היר תחאט אי וילל בי פיספול פוראבער אנד שעתתעל,

It is here that I will be peaceful forever and settle,

י Yod ט Tet ח Chet ז Zayin ו Vav ה Hei ד Dalet ג Gimel ב Beit א Aleph
ס Samech ן Final Nun נ Nun ם Final Mem מ Mem ל Lamed ך Final Kaf כ Kaf
ת Tav ש Shin ר Resh ק Kuf ץ Final Tzadik צ Tzadik ף Final Feh פ Peh ע Ayin

פור תחאט יז מי דעשיער.

For that is My desire.

אי וילל בלעסש הער נידי אנד פולפיל תהעם וית שאשטאנאנץ,

I will bless her needy and fulfill them with sustenance,

הער פרישטס ,תו ,כובערד וית סאלבאשען [ישועה],

Her priests, too, covered with salvation,

אנד הער דעבאות וית שונגז אף גוי [שמחה],

And her devout with songs of joy,

אי שחאלל קאוז פריד תו ספראות,

I shall cause pride to sprout,

פור דוד;

For David;

א כאנדעל האב אי כריאטעד,

A candle have I created,

פור מי אנוינתעד.

For my anointed.

היז אנעמיז שחאלל בי,

His enemies shall be,

כובערד וית ינפאמי.

Covered with infamy.

אנד עפון הים,

And upon him,

שחאלל שפרינג עף א כרוון.

Shall spring up a crown.

- 133 -

א שונג [שיר] אף אשענץ, בי דוד:

A Song of Ascents, by David:

ביהולד, האו ניס אנד פליזינג יט יז,

Behold, how nice and pleasing it is,

פור תחע דוללינג תוגעתער אף ברותערס ין יוניתי.

For the dwelling together of brothers in unity.

אס תחע פינעשת אויל עפון תחע העאד רענז דאון עפון תחע בירד,

As the finest oil upon the head runs down upon the beard,

אס תחע בירד אף אהרן ראן דאון אובער תחע כוללאר אף היז רוב.

As the beard of Aaron ran down over the collar of his robe.

יט יש ליק תחע דו אף מאונת חרמון ,פאללינג עפון תחע מאונתאנז [הרים] אף ציון,

It is like the dew of Mount Herman, falling upon the mountains of Zion,

פור יט ואס תחער תחאט תחע לורד אורדאינד א בלעססינג : עבערלאשתינג ליף -- פוראבער!

For it was there that the Lord ordained a blessing: Everlasting life -- forever!

- 134 -

א שונג [שיר] אף אשענץ.

A Song of Ascents.

ביהולד ,בלעשש תחע לורד,

Behold, bless the Lord,

אלל יו הו אר תחע לורד'ז סערבאנטץ,

All you who are the Lord's servants,

הו שתאנד ין תחע האוס אף תחע לורד עברי ניט,

Who stand in the House of the Lord every night,

ראיז יור האנדז תחרואוט תחע שאנכצוארי אנד בלעששש תחע לורד,

Raise your hands throughout the sanctuary and bless the Lord,

מאי תחע לורד ,הו כריאטעד העאבען [שמים] אנד עארתח [ארץ] , בלעשש יו פרום אוט אף ציון.

May the Lord, Who created heaven and earth, bless you from out of Zion.

- 135 -

הללויה !פראיז תחע נאם [שם] אף תחע לורד;

Praise [Hall-el-oo] God [Yah]! Praise the Name of the Lord;

רענדער פראיז ,יו פאיתפול סערבאנטץ אף תחע לורד,

Render praise, you faithful servants of the Lord,

אלל תהוז הו שתאנד ין תחע האוס אף תחע לורד,

All those who stand in the House of the Lord,

ין תחע קורתיארדז אף תחע האוס אף אור לורד.

In the courtyards of the House of our Lord.

פראיזעס תו געד !ביקאעס תחע לורד יש גווד,

Praises to God! Because the Lord is good,

שינג פראיזעס תו היש נאם [שם],

Sing praises to His Name,

ביקאעס יט יש פליזינג.

Because it is pleasing.

ביקאעס געד צוס יעקב,

Because God chose Jacob,

י Yod ט Tet ח Chet ז Zayin ו Vav ה Hei ד Dalet ג Gimel ב Beit א Aleph
ס Samech ן Final Nun נ Nun ם Final Mem מ Mem ל Lamed ך Final Kaf כ Kaf
ת Tav ש Shin ר Resh ק Kuf ץ Final Tzadik צ Tzadik ף Final Feh פ Peh ע Ayin

אנד צוז אז היז תרעזור,

And chose as His treasure,

ישראל.

Israel.

ין טרותה ,אי נוע ,תחאט תחע לורד יש טרולי גרעאט,

In truth, I know, that the Lord is truly great,

תחאט אור לורד יש גרעאתעשט אבוו אלל גודס.

That our Lord is greatest above all gods.

אלל תחע לורד דעשיערז ;יט יז דון,

All the Lord desires; it is done,

ין תחע העאבענז [שמים] אנד ען תחע עארתח [ארץ],

In the heavens and on the earth,

ין תחע שיז אנד את אלל דעפתץ.

In the seas and at all depths.

הי ראיזעז היש כלאודס,

He raises His clouds,

י Yod ט Tet ח Chet ז Zayin ו Vav ה Hei ד Dalet ג Gimel ב Beit א Aleph
ס Samech ן Final Nun נ Nun ם Final Mem מ Mem ל Lamed ך Final Kaf כ Kaf
ת Tav ש Shin ר Resh ק Kuf ץ Final Tzadik צ Tzadik ף Final Feh פ Peh ע Ayin

פרום תחע ועריִ ענדז אף תחע עארתח [ארץ],

From the very ends of the earth,

הי כאעזעז ליתנינג בולתץ פור תחע ראין,

He causes lightning bolts for the rain,

פרום היש תרעזור ואעלתץ ,הי כאזעז תחע וינד תו בלוו.

From His treasure vaults, He causes the wind to blow.

הי קעת דאון תחע פירשת בורן אף יגיפט ,בותח מאן [אדם] אנד בישט.

He cut down the first born of Egypt, both man and beast.

הי סענט שינז אנד מיראכאלז ינתו תחע מידצת אף יגיפט,

He sent signs and miracles into the midst of Egypt,

הי סענט תהעם אגאינצט פרעה אנד אלל אף היז סערבאנטץ;

He set them against Pharaoh and all of his servants;

יט ואס הי הו שתרעק דאון מאני נאתענז,

It was He Who struck down many nations,

אנד קעת דאון גרעאט קינגז:

And cut down great kings:

י Yod ט Tet ח Chet ז Zayin ו Vav ה Hei ד Dalet ג Gimel ב Beit א Aleph
ס Samech ן Final Nun נ Nun ם Final Mem מ Mem ל Lamed ך Final Kaf כ Kaf
ת Tav ש Shin ר Resh ק Kuf ץ Final Tzadik צ Tzadik ף Final Feh פ Peh ע Ayin

סיחון ,כינג אף תחע אמוריטץ,

Sihon, king of the Amorites,

אנד עוג ,כינג אף בשן,

And Og, king of Bashan,

אנד אלל כנען'ז רויאלטי.

And all Canaan's royalty.

אנד הי פרעשענתעד אלל,

And He presented all,

אף תחער לאנדז,

Of their lands,

אז א ביקואסט תו ישראל,

As a bequest to Israel,

אס א העריטאג תו היש פיפעל [עם] -- ישראל.

As a heritage to His people -- Israel.

ו לורד ,פוראבער דעז יור נאם [שם] אקזישט,

O Lord, forever does Your Name exist,

אנד יור נאם [שם] יש מעמוריאליזד לדר ודר,

And Your Name is memorialized from generation to generation,

ביקאעס יט יש תחע לורד הו וילל געדג היז נאשען ,אנד פארדון היש פאיתפול סערבאנטץ.

Because it is the Lord Who will judge His nation, and pardon and His faithful servants.

תחע היתהאן נאתשענז' אידולס אר אונלי אף שילבער אנד גולד, מאד בי תחע האנד אף מאן [אדם].

The heathen nations' idols are only of silver and gold, made by the hand of man.

מאותס תהאי האב; בעת תהאי כאננוט שפיק .עיז תהאי האו ;בעת תהאי קאננוט סי.

Mouths they have; but they cannot speak. Eyes they have; but they cannot see.

עארז תהאי האב; בעת תהאי כאננוט העאר .אנד תחער יז נו ברעאתה תחאט כומז אוט אף תחער מאותס.

Ears they have; but they cannot hear. And there is no breath that comes out of their mouths.

אס תהאי אר, שחאלל תחער מאקערז הו פאשחאנד תהעם ביכום,

As they are, shall their makers who fashioned them become,

אנד עבעריוון הו פלאשעס תרעסט ין תהעם.

And everyone who places trust in them.

י Yod ט Tet ח Chet ז Zayin ו Vav ה Hei ד Dalet ג Gimel ב Beit א Aleph
ס Samech ן Final Nun נ Nun ם Final Mem מ Mem ל Lamed ך Final Kaf כ Kaf
ת Tav ש Shin ר Resh ק Kuf ץ Final Tzadik צ Tzadik ף Final Feh פ Peh ע Ayin

ו האוס אף ישראל ,בלעססינגז עפון תחע לורד,

O House of Israel, blessings upon the Lord,

ו האוס אף אהרן ,בלעססינגז עפון תחע לורד.

O House of Aaron, blessings upon the Lord.

ו האוש אף לוי, בלעססינגז עפון תחע לורד,

O House of Levi, blessings upon the Lord,

ו יו געד פירינג וונז ,בלעססינגז עפון תחע לורד.

O you God-fearing ones, blessings upon the Lord.

בלעססינגז עפון תחע לורד פרום ציון,

Blessings upon the Lord from Zion,

הי ,הו אבידז ין ירושלם : הללויה!

He, who abides in Jerusalem: Praise [HALL-EL-OO] God [YAH]!

- 136 -

ו ,ופפער תחאנקשגיבינג תו תחע לורד ;פור היז גוודנעסס,

O, offer thanksgiving to the Lord; for His goodness,

היש לובינג-קינדנעשס [חסד] עקזיסטץ פור יתערנאטי.

His loving-kindness exists for eternity.

ו ,ופפער תחאנקשגיבינג תו תחע געד אף אלל גודז,

O, offer thanksgiving to the God of all gods,

היז לובינג-קינדנעשס [חסד] עקזיסטץ פור יתערנאטי.

His loving-kindness exists for eternity.

ו ,ופפער תחאנקשגיבינג תו תחע לורד אף אלל לורדז,

O, offer Thanksgiving to the Lord of all lords,

היש לובינג-קינדנעשס [חסד] עקזיסטץ פור יתערנאטי.

His loving-kindness exists for eternity.

יט יז הי אלון הו פערפורמז וונדרעס וורקש,

It is He alone Who performs wondrous works,

היש לובינג-קינדנעשס [חסד] עקזיסטץ פור יתערנאטי.

His loving-kindness exists for eternity.

י Yod ט Tet ח Chet ז Zayin ו Vav ה Hei ד Dalet ג Gimel ב Beit א Aleph
ס Samech ן Final Nun נ Nun ם Final Mem מ Mem ל Lamed ך Final Kaf כ Kaf
ת Tav ש Shin ר Resh ק Kuf ץ Final Tzadik צ Tzadik ף Final Feh פ Peh ע Ayin

יט יז הי הו תחאעטפוללי כריאטעד תחע העאבענז [שמים],

It is He Who thoughtfully created the heavens,

היש לובינג-קינדנעשס [חסד] עקזיסטץ פור יתערנאטי.

His loving-kindness exists for eternity.

יט יש הי הו שפרעד אוט תחע עארתח [ארץ] אובער תחע ואתערז [מים],

It is He Who spread out the earth over the waters,

היז לובינג-קינדנעשס [חסד] עקזיסטץ פור יתערנאטי.

His loving-kindness exists for eternity.

יט יש הי הו כריאטעד תחע גרעאט עשענשאל ליטץ,

It is He Who created the great essential lights,

היז לובינג-קינדנעשס [חסד] עקזיסטץ פור יתערנאטי.

His loving-kindness exists for eternity.

יט יז הי הו סענט תחע שען תו רול תחע דאי,

It is He Who sent the sun to rule the day,

היש לובינג-קינדנעשס [חסד] עקזיסטץ פור יתערנאטי.

His loving-kindness exists for eternity.

יט יש הי הו סענט תחע מון אנד שתארז תו רול תחע ניט,

It is He Who sent the moon and stars to rule the night,

היז לובינג-קינדנעשס [חסד] עקזיסטץ פור יתערנאטי.

His loving-kindness exists for eternity.

יט יז הי הו שתרעך דאון יגיפת בי תחער פירסת בורן,

It is He Who struck down Egypt by their firstborn,

היש לובינג-קינדנעשס [חסד] עקזיסטץ פור יתערנאטי.

His loving-kindness exists for eternity.

יט יש הי הו דיליבערד ישראל פרום תחער מידצת,

It is He Who delivered Israel from their midst,

היז לובינג-קינדנעשס [חסד] עקזיסטץ פור יתערנאטי.

His loving-kindness exists for eternity.

יט יש הי הו וית א סטרונג האנד אנד אותשטרעצד ארם,

It is He Who with a strong hand and outstretched arm,

היש לובינג-קינדנעשס [חסד] עקזיסטץ פור יתערנאטי.

His loving-kindness exists for eternity.

א Aleph ב Beit ג Gimel ד Dalet ה Hei ו Vav ז Zayin ח Chet ט Tet י Yod
כ Kaf ך Final Kaf ל Lamed מ Mem ם Final Mem נ Nun ן Final Nun ס Samech
ע Ayin פ Peh ף Final Feh צ Tzadik ץ Final Tzadik ק Kuf ר Resh ש Shin ת Tav

הו שפליט תחע שי אף רידז ינתו סעכשענז,

Who split the Sea of Reeds into sections,

היש לובינג-קינדנעשס [חסד] עקזיסטץ פור יתערנאטי.

His loving-kindness exists for eternity.

אנד געידעד ישראל תו פאסש תחרו יט,

And guided Israel to pass through it,

היז לובינג-קינדנעשס [חסד] עקזיסטץ פור יתערנאטי.

His loving-kindness exists for eternity.

יט ואס הי הו כאשט פרעה אנד היש ארמי ינתו תחע שי אף רידס,

It was He Who cast Pharaoh and his army into the Sea of Reeds,

היז לובינג-קינדנעשס [חסד] עקזיסטץ פור יתערנאטי.

His loving-kindness exists for eternity.

יט ואס הי הו לעד היש פיפעל [עם] תחרו תחע דעזערט,

It was He Who led his people through the desert,

היש לובינג-קינדנעשס [חסד] עקזיסטץ פור יתערנאטי.

His loving-kindness exists for eternity.

יט ואס הי הו שתרעך דאון מיתי קינגז,

It was He Who struck down mighty kings,

היש לובינג-קינדנעשס [חסד] עקזיסטץ פור יתערנאטי.

His loving-kindness exists for eternity.

יט ואס הי הו שתרעך דאון פווערפול קינגז,

It was He Who struck down powerful kings,

היז לובינג-קינדנעשס [חסד] עקזיסטץ פור יתערנאטי.

His loving-kindness exists for eternity.

יט ואס הי הו שלו סיחון ,כינג אף תחע אמוריטץ,

It was He Who slew Sichon, king of the Amorites,

היש לובינג-קינדנעשס [חסד] עקזיסטץ פור יתערנאטי.

His loving-kindness exists for eternity.

יט ואס הי הו שלו עוג ,קינג אף בשן,

It was He Who slew Og, king of Bashan,

היש לובינג-קינדנעשס [חסד] עקזיסטץ פור יתערנאטי.

His loving-kindness exists for eternity.

יט ואס הי הו גאב תחער לאנד אז א ביקואשט,

It was He Who gave their land as a bequest,

היז לובינג-קינדנעשס [חסד] עקזיסטץ פור יתערנאטי.

His loving-kindness exists for eternity.

יט ואס הי הו גאב תחער לאנד תו היז סערבאנט ישראל,

It was He Who gave their land to His servant Israel,

היש לובינג-קינדנעשס [חסד] עקזיסטץ פור יתערנאטי.

His loving-kindness exists for eternity.

יט ואס הי הו שתוד בי עש ין אור דיגראדעד כונדישען,

It was He Who stood by us in our degraded condition,

היש לובינג-קינדנעשס [חסד] עקזיסטץ פור יתערנאטי.

His loving-kindness exists for eternity.

יט ואס הי הו שאבד עש פרום אור אנעמיז,

It was He Who saved us from our enemies,

היז לובינג-קינדנעשס [חסד] עקזיסטץ פור יתערנאטי.

His loving-kindness exists for eternity.

י Yod ט Tet ח Chet ז Zayin ו Vav ה Hei ד Dalet ג Gimel ב Beit א Aleph
ס Samech ן Final Nun נ Nun ם Final Mem מ Mem ל Lamed ך Final Kaf כ Kaf
ת Tav ש Shin ר Resh ק Kuf ץ Final Tzadik צ Tzadik ף Final Feh פ Peh ע Ayin

יט יש הי הו שעשתאינז אלל פלעש וית פוד,

It is He Who sustains all flesh with food,

היש לובינג-קינדנעשס [חסד] עקזיסטץ פור יתערנאטי.

His loving-kindness exists for eternity.

ו ,גיב תחאנקשגיבינג תו תחע געד אף העאבען,

O, give thanksgiving to the God of heaven,

היז לובינג-קינדנעשס [חסד] עקזיסטץ פור יתערנאטי.

His loving-kindness exists for eternity.

ת

י Yod ט Tet ח Chet ז Zayin ו Vav ה Hei ד Dalet ג Gimel ב Beit א Aleph
ס Samech ן Final Nun נ Nun ם Final Mem מ Mem ל Lamed ך Final Kaf כ Kaf
ת Tav ש Shin ר Resh ק Kuf ץ Final Tzadik צ Tzadik ף Final Feh פ Peh ע Ayin

- 137 -

בי תחע ריוערז אף באבאלון,

By the rivers of Babylon,

תחער וי שאט אנד עיואן קריד,

There we sat and even cried,

וען אור תחאעתץ רימעמבערד ציון.

When our thoughts remembered Zion.

תחער עפון תחע ויללווס וי העגג אור כנור הארפס,

There upon the Willows we hung our lyre harps,

אס אור כאפתורס ואנתעד עש תו סינג גויפוללי.

As our captors wanted us to sing joyfully.

"סינג פור עש וון אף תחע שונגס פרום ציון"!

"Sing for us one of the songs from Zion!"

"הוו כאן וי גיב פורתח וית געד'ס שונג [שיר],

"How can we give forth with God's song,

ען פורען שויעל"?

On foreign soil?"

י Yod ט Tet ח Chet ז Zayin ו Vav ה Hei ד Dalet ג Gimel ב Beit א Aleph
ס Samech ן Final Nun נ Nun ם Final Mem מ Mem ל Lamed ך Final Kaf כ Kaf
ת Tav ש Shin ר Resh ק Kuf ץ Final Tzadik צ Tzadik ף Final Feh פ Peh ע Ayin

יף אי פורגעט יו ,ו ירושלם,

If I forget you, O Jerusalem,

לעט מי ריט האנד פורגעט יטץ שקילפול כענינג.

Let my right hand forget its skillful cunning.

לעט מי תונג אדהיר תו מי פאלאט.

Let my tongue adhere to my palate.

יף אי שיז תו רימעמבער יו,

If I cease to remember you,

אנד ראיז עף ירושלם,

And raise up Jerusalem,

אבעו מי גרעאתעשט,

Above my greatest,

גוי [שמחה].

Joy.

רימעמבער ,ו לורד,

Remember, O Lord,

י Yod ט Tet ח Chet ז Zayin ו Vav ה Hei ד Dalet ג Gimel ב Beit א Aleph
ס Samech ן Final Nun נ Nun ם Final Mem מ Mem ל Lamed ך Final Kaf כ Kaf
ת Tav ש Shin ר Resh ק Kuf ץ Final Tzadik צ Tzadik ף Final Feh פ Peh ע Ayin

יט ואס תחע עפפשפרינג אף תחע עדומיטץ,

It was the offspring of the Edomites,

ען תחע וערי דאי תחאט ירושלם פעלל,

On the very day that Jerusalem fell,

תהאי שעד:

They said:

"דעשטרוי הער !דעשטרוי הער!

"Destroy her! Destroy her!

תו הער וערי פאונדאשענז".

To her very foundations."

ו יו ראבעגד דאעתער אף באבאלון,

O you ravaged daughter of Babylon,

בלעססינגז תו הים הו ברינגז פאימענת טו יו,

Blessing to him who brings payment to you,

יור דו יו האב ריוארדעד עש,

Your due as you have rewarded us,

א בלעססינג עפון הים,

A blessing upon him,

כאתצינג אנד שמאשהינג יור באביז,

Catching and smashing your babies,

אגאינצט תחע רוקס!

Against the rocks!

ט

י Yod ט Tet ח Chet ז Zayin ו Vav ה Hei ד Dalet ג Gimel ב Beit א Aleph
ס Samech ן Final Nun נ Nun ם Final Mem מ Mem ל Lamed ך Final Kaf כ Kaf
ת Tav ש Shin ר Resh ק Kuf ץ Final Tzadik צ Tzadik ף Final Feh פ Peh ע Ayin

- 138 -

אף דוד.

Of David.

אי וילל פראיז יו וית העארתפעלט תחאנקשגיבינג,

I will praise You with heartfelt thanksgiving,

ביפור תהוז הו מאך געדגמענטץ.

Before those who make judgments.

אי וילל ופפער פראיזעס תו יו.

I will offer praises to You.

אי וילל פרושתראט מישעלף,

I will prostrate myself,

פאסינג יור הולי שאנכצואָרי,

Facing Your Holy Sanctuary,

אנד ופפער פראיזעס אף תחאנקשגיבינג תו יור נאם [שם],

And offer praises of Thanksgiving in Your Name,

פור יור באנעבולענץ אנד יור יטערנאל טרותה.

For Your benevolence and Your eternal truth.

יט יז ביקאעז יו האו ינקרישד יור פרומיס,

It is because You have increased Your promise.

בייונד יור הול נאם [שם].

Beyond Your whole Name.

ען תחע וערי דאי תחאט אי קריד אוט תו יו ,יו הארקענד תו מי,

On the very day that I cried out to You, You hearkened to me,

אנד שתרענתחענד מי ;יו פורטיפיד מי שול [נפש] וית כוראג.

And strengthened me; You fortified my soul with courage.

אלל תחע עארתח'ס קינגז שחאלל ופפער תחאנקשגיבינג תו יו,

All the earth's kings shall offer thanksgiving to You,

עפון העארינג תחע וורדז פרום יור מאותח,

Upon hearing the words from Your mouth,

אנד תהאי שחאלל שינג אף תחע לורד'ז פאתח.

And they shall sing of the Lord's path.

אס אקזאלטעד יז תחע הונור אף תחע לורד,

י Yod ט Tet ח Chet ז Zayin ו Vav ה Hei ד Dalet ג Gimel ב Beit א Aleph
ס Samech ן Final Nun נ Nun ם Final Mem מ Mem ל Lamed ך Final Kaf כ Kaf
ת Tav ש Shin ר Resh ק Kuf ץ Final Tzadik צ Tzadik ף Final Feh פ Peh ע Ayin

הי לוקס עף תו תחע העמבעל,

He looks up to the humble,

בעת תחע ארּרוגאנט וונז,

But the arrogant ones,

הי טאקש נוט אף פרום א דישתאנץ.

He takes note of from a distance.

אלתחו תחע פאתחואיז תחאט אי ואלק אר אמונג אנעמיז,

Although the pathways that I walk are among enemies,

יו ויּלל שאב מי דעשפיט מי פוז' פיורי.

You will save me despite my foes' fury.

יו ויּלל ברינג פורתח יור האנד ,אנד יור ריט האנד ויּלל שאב מי.

You will bring forth Your hand, and Your right hand will save me.

ו לורד אי פראי תחאט יו ויּלל שעתתאל מי כונסערנז פור מי!

O Lord I pray that you will settle my concerns for me!

ו מי לורד ,יור לובינג-קינדנעשס [חסד] עקזיסטץ פוראבער;

O my Lord, Your loving-kindness exists forever;

דו נעת ליב עפף תחע וורק אף יור האנדז.

Do not leave off the work of Your hands.

י Yod ט Tet ח Chet ז Zayin ו Vav ה Hei ד Dalet ג Gimel ב Beit א Aleph
ס Samech ן Final Nun נ Nun ם Final Mem מ Mem ל Lamed ך Final Kaf כ Kaf
ת Tav ש Shin ר Resh ק Kuf ץ Final Tzadik צ Tzadik ף Final Feh פ Peh ע Ayin

- 139 -

פור תחע לידער ,בי דוד ,א שונג [שיר].

For the leader, by David, a song.

ו לורד ,יו האב ינספעכטעד מי כלושלי,

O Lord, You have inspected me closely,

אנד יו נוו עבעריתחינג אבאוט מי,

And You know everything about me,

יו נוע וען אי שיט אנד יו נוע וען אי ריז,

You know when I sit and You know what I rise,

אנד פרום אפאר יו נוו מי תחאעתץ--

And from afar You know my thoughts --

מי פאתחואיז וען אי ואלק אנד וען אי ריקלין;

My pathways when I walk and when I recline;

יו נוע אלל מי ואיז.

You know all my ways.

ביקאעס תחער יז נעת א וורד תחאט פורמז ען מי תונג,

Because there is not a word that forms on my tongue,

אנד ביהולד ,ו לורד ,יו אר אואר אף יט.

And behold, O Lord, You are aware of it.

פרום מי באק אנד פרונט,

From my back and front,

יו קאעזד מי שעפפערינג,

You caused me suffering,

אנד פלאשד יור האנד ען מי.

And placed Your hand on me.

תחיס ענדערסתאנדינג יש א מארבעל תו מי:

This understanding is a marvel to me:

אקזאלטעד בייונד מי תחאעתץ,

Exalted beyond my thoughts,

וער כאן אי גו אואי פרום יור שפיריט?

Where can I go away from Your spirit?

אנד וער כאן אי פלי פרום יור פרעזאנץ?

And where can I flee from Your presence?

יף אי שוד ריז עף תו העאבען:

If I should rise up to heaven:

יו אר תחער!

You are there!

יף אי בעד דאון ין תחע לוער וורלד:

If I bed down in the lower world:

ביהולד !יו אר תחער!

Behold! You are there!

עיוען יף אי ווער תו תאק עף תחע וינגז אף תחע דאון,

Even if I were to take up the wings of the dawn,

אנד רישיד את תחע ענד אף תחע שי,

And reside at the end of the sea,

תחער ,עיוען תחער,

There, even there,

יור האנד וד געיד מי,

Your hand would guide me,

י Yod ט Tet ח Chet ז Zayin ו Vav ה Hei ד Dalet ג Gimel ב Beit א Aleph
ס Samech ן Final Nun נ Nun ם Final Mem מ Mem ל Lamed ך Final Kaf כ Kaf
ת Tav ש Shin ר Resh ק Kuf ץ Final Tzadik צ Tzadik ף Final Feh פ Peh ע Ayin

אנד יור ריט האנד ווד הולד פאשט תו מי.

And Your right hand would hold fast to me.

אנד שוד אי שאי, "יט יש שור תחאט דארקנעסס וילל כונסיל מי",

And should I say, "It is sure that darkness will conceal me,"

אי נוע ניט וילל ילומינאת מי,

I know night will illuminate me,

פור עיוען תחע דארקנעסס כונסילס נעתחינג פרום יו,

For even darkness conceals nothing from You,

אנד תחע ניט יז אז בריט אז תחע דאי,

And the night is as bright as the day,

פור תו יו תחע דארקנעסס אף ניט אנד תחע ליט אף תחע דאי אר אס וון.

For to You the darkness of night and the light of the day are as one.

יט יש יו הו האב שעלתערד מי ין מי מותחער'ז וומב.

It is You Who have sheltered me in my mother's womb.

וית תחאנקשגיבינג אי פראיז יו,

With Thanksgiving I praise You,

י Yod ט Tet ח Chet ז Zayin ו Vav ה Hei ד Dalet ג Gimel ב Beit א Aleph
ס Samech ן Final Nun נ Nun ם Final Mem מ Mem ל Lamed ך Final Kaf כ Kaf
ת Tav ש Shin ר Resh ק Kuf ץ Final Tzadik צ Tzadik ף Final Feh פ Peh ע Ayin

פור תחע אוסעמנעשס אנד מיראקעל אף מי ביינג,

For the awesomeness and miracle of my being,

יור וורקש אר פיללד וית וונדר,

Your works are filled with wonder,

אנד מי שול [נפש] מעך אקנוולעדגעז תחיס.

And my soul much acknowledges this.

מי ביינג ואס נעת כונסילד פרום יו,

My being was not concealed from You,

עיוען וען אי ואז סיכרעתלי כומפוזד;

Even when I was secretly composed;

עיוען אס אי ואס כומפוזד ין תחע יננערמוסט עארתח [ארץ].

Even when I was composed in the innermost earth.

תחער יור עיז שאו מי ענשהאפד לימבז,

There Your eyes saw my unshaped limbs,

אנד אלל אר ריכורדעד ין יור בוק פור אס מאני דאיז תחאט אי
ואס פורמד;

And all are recorded in Your book for as many days that I was formed;

י Yod ט Tet ח Chet ז Zayin ו Vav ה Hei ד Dalet ג Gimel ב Beit א Aleph
ס Samech ן Final Nun נ Nun ם Final Mem מ Mem ל Lamed ך Final Kaf כ Kaf
ת Tav ש Shin ר Resh ק Kuf ץ Final Tzadik צ Tzadik ף Final Feh פ Peh ע Ayin

אף גרעאט וורתח אר יור נותענז תו מי ,ו געד! תחער לישט יש פורמידאבעל.

Of great worth are Your notions to me, O God! Their list is formidable.

יף אי קוד נעמבער תהעם ,תהאי אקשיד תחע גראינז אף שאנד,

If I could number them, they exceed the grains of sand,

אס אי קעם תו תחע ענד ,אי וילל אביד וית יו.

As I come to the end, I will abide with You.

ו לורד ,גראנט תחאט יו קיל תחע ויכעד!

O Lord, grant that You kill the wicked!

שו דיפארט, גו פרום מי יו ויכעד ויולנט וונז!

So depart, go from me you wicked violent ones!

תהאי קונשפיער אגאינצט יו וית תחער וורדז,

They conspire against You with their words,

יור אנעמיז,

Your enemies,

תאק יור נאם [שם] ין ואין.

Take Your Name in vain.

י Yod ט Tet ח Chet ז Zayin ו Vav ה Hei ד Dalet ג Gimel ב Beit א Aleph
ס Samech ן Final Nun נ Nun ם Final Mem מ Mem ל Lamed ך Final Kaf כ Kaf
ת Tav ש Shin ר Resh ק Kuf ץ Final Tzadik צ Tzadik ף Final Feh פ Peh ע Ayin

ו לורד ,תהוז הו האת יו :דו אי נעת האת תהעם?

O Lord, those who hate You: Do I not hate them?

אנד תאק ישׁשיו וית תהוז הו ריז עף אגאינצט יו.

And take issue with those who rise up against You.

אי האב תחע עטמושׁת דיסדאין אנד האתרעד טוארד אלל אף תהעם,

I have the utmost disdain and hatred toward all of them,

אי שׁי תהעם אס מי פערשׁונאל אנעמיז .אקזאמין מי ,ו לורד,

I see them as my personal enemies. Examine me, O Lord,

אנד לווק ינתו מי העארט ,אקזאמין אנד לעארן מי יננערמוסט תחאעתץ,

And look into my heart, examine and learn my innermost thoughts,

אנד שׁי עף אי האו אני תרעבעלינג ואיז,

And see if I have any troubling ways,

אנד געיד מי טוארד תחע פאתחואיז אף יתערנאטי.

And guide me toward the pathways of eternity.

- 140 -

פור תחע לידער :א שונג [שיר] אף דוד.

For the Leader: A song of David.

גראנט מי סאלבאשען [ישועה] ,ו מי לורד ,פרום ויכעד מאן [אדם] ;
גיב מי דיליבעראנץ פרום ויולנט מאן [אדם],

Grant me salvation, O my Lord, from wicked man; give me deliverance from violent man,

הוז הערטץ כונתעמפלאט עיבעל סקימז :תהאי הו גאתחער עברי
דאי תו פלאן ואר.

Whose hearts contemplate evil schemes: They who gather every day to plan war.

תהאי שהארפין תחער תונגז ליק א שנאך ;ענדער תחער ליפס תחער
יש א שפידער׳ז וענום .אמן.

They sharpen their tongues like a snake; under their lips there is a spider's venom. Amen.

ו לורד ,קיף מי פרום תחע ויכעד׳ש כלעצינג האנדז .שאב מי פרום
תחע ויולענט וונז.

O Lord, keep me from the wicked's clutching hands Save me from the violent ones.

תהאי שיך תו תריף מי פיט ;תחיז אררוגאנט מען האב שעט תראפס
פור מי.

They seek to trip my feet; these arrogant men have set traps for me.

י Yod ט Tet ח Chet ז Zayin ו Vav ה Hei ד Dalet ג Gimel ב Beit א Aleph
ס Samech ן Final Nun נ Nun ם Final Mem מ Mem ל Lamed ך Final Kaf כ Kaf
ת Tav ש Shin ר Resh ק Kuf ץ Final Tzadik צ Tzadik ף Final Feh פ Peh ע Ayin

תהאי שפרעד אוט נעתץ אנד רופס אלונג מי פאתחואיז,

They spread out nets and ropes along my pathways,

תהאי האב שעט אוט תראפס פור מי .אמן.

They have set out traps for me. Amen.

אי כאללד תו תחע לורד" ,יו אר מי געד!

I called to the Lord, "You are my God!

ו לורד ,גיב עאר תו מי פליז."

O Lord, give ear to my pleas."

ו לורד ,מי געד,

O Lord, my God,

יו אר תחע מיט אף מי דיליבעראנץ ;יו שעלתערד מי העאד ין תחע דאי אף ואר.

You are the might of my deliverance; You sheltered my head in the day of war.

דו נעת אללוו תחע וישעז ,ו לורד ,אף תחע ויכעד וונז ,אנד פרעשטראט תחער עיבעל פלאנז,

Do not allow the wishes, O Lord, of the wicked ones, and frustrate their evil plans,

ור תהאי וילל בי עפליפטעד .אמן.

Or they will be uplifted. Amen

י Yod ט Tet ח Chet ז Zayin ו Vav ה Hei ד Dalet ג Gimel ב Beit א Aleph
ס Samech ן Final Nun נ Nun ם Final Mem מ Mem ל Lamed ך Final Kaf כ Kaf
ת Tav ש Shin ר Resh ק Kuf ץ Final Tzadik צ Tzadik ף Final Feh פ Peh ע Ayin

מאי תחע לידערס אף תהוז הו קענשפיער אגאינצט מי בי קונדעימנוד,

May the leaders of those who conspire against me be condemned,

לעט תהעם האב תחע עיבעל כונשפראשי תחאט כומז פרום תחער ון ליפס שפרעד אובער תהעם,

Let them have the evil conspiracy that comes from their own lips spread over them,

בי דישענדעד עפון תהעם ליק פיערי קולז,

Be descended upon them like fiery coals,

אנד לעט תהעם בי תהרון דאון ינתו תחע פיער,

And let them be thrown down into the fire,

אנד ינתו תחע דיפעשט פיטץ,

And into the deepest pits

נעבער אגאין תו ריז.

Never again to rise.

לעט תהוז הו שפיק שלאנדער נעת בי שעט א פלאס ען עארתח [ארץ];

Let those who speak slander not be set a place on earth;

לעט ויקעדנעשס שטאלק אנד דריב אוט תחע ויולנט מאן [אדם].

Let wickedness stalk and drive out the violent man.

י Yod ט Tet ח Chet ז Zayin ו Vav ה Hei ד Dalet ג Gimel ב Beit א Aleph
ס Samech ן Final Nun נ Nun ם Final Mem מ Mem ל Lamed ך Final Kaf כ Kaf
ת Tav ש Shin ר Resh ק Kuf ץ Final Tzadik צ Tzadik ף Final Feh פ Peh ע Ayin

אי נוע תחאט תחע לורד יש תחע דיפענדער אף תחע נידי אנד
פרובידז גאסטיש [משפט] תו תחע דעשטיתוט;

I know that the Lord is the defender of the needy and provides justice to the destitute;

תחע ריצעס שחאלל שערלי פראיז יור נאם [שם],

The righteous shall surely praise Your Name,

אנד תחע הונוראבעל שחאלל רישיד ויתהין יור פרעזאנץ.

And the honorable shall reside within Your Presence.

ג

י Yod ט Tet ח Chet ז Zayin ו Vav ה Hei ד Dalet ג Gimel ב Beit א Aleph
ס Samech ן Final Nun נ Nun ם Final Mem מ Mem ל Lamed ך Final Kaf כ Kaf
ת Tav ש Shin ר Resh ק Kuf ץ Final Tzadik צ Tzadik ף Final Feh פ Peh ע Ayin

- 141 -

א שונג [שיר] אף דוד.

A Song of David

ו מי לורד ,אי קרי אוט תו יו;

O my Lord, I cry out to you;

הוררי תו מי אנד לישתען תו מי וויס וען אי כאלל יו.

Hurry to me and listen to my voice when I call you.

לעט מי פראיער בי עישטאבלישהד אס אן ינשענץ ופפערינג ין יור פרעסאנץ;

Let my prayer be established as an incense offering in your presence;

מי האנדז אר ליפטעד ין אן אפתערנון אפפערינג.

My hands are lifted in an afternoon offering.

שתאשען א געארדיאן אובער מי מאותח ו לורד ,אנד א ואצמאן את תחע דוורואי אף מי ליפץ.

Station a guardian over my mouth O Lord, and a watchman at the doorway of my lips.

לעט מי תחאעתץ נעת קונשידער אני עיבעל, ור ויכעד דידז וית ויכעד מען,

Let my thoughts not consider any evil, or wicked deeds with wicked men,

אנד געיד מי פרום בראקינג ברעד וית תחע ויכעד וונז,

י Yod ט Tet ח Chet ז Zayin ו Vav ה Hei ד Dalet ג Gimel ב Beit א Aleph
ס Samech ן Final Nun נ Nun ם Final Mem מ Mem ל Lamed ך Final Kaf כ Kaf
ת Tav ש Shin ר Resh ק Kuf ץ Final Tzadik צ Tzadik ף Final Feh פ Peh ע Ayin

אנד געיד מי פרום בראקינג ברעד וית תחע ויכעד וונז,

And guide me from breaking bread with the wicked ones,

וען תהאי שיט דאון תו באנקועתץ אף דעליקאסיז.

When they sit down to banquets of delicacies.

עף א רעיצעס [צדיק] מאן [אדם] שטרקס מי ין לובינג קינדנעשס [חסד] יט וועד בי מערשיפול,

If a righteous man strikes me in loving kindness, it would be merciful,

אנד עף הי רעבוקס מי ,יט יש ליק תחע פינעשת אויל.

And if he rebukes me it is like the finest oil.

מי העאד שחאלל נעת ריפיוס יטץ באלם אגאינצט עיבעל.

My head shall not refuse its balm against evil.

שתרעך דאון עפון תחע רוקס וער תחער געדגעז,

Struck down upon the rocks were their judges,

אנד תהאי שחאלל העאר מי וורדז ויך אר פלעזאנת.

And they shall hear my words which are pleasant.

אס א פערשון שלעיסעז אנד שפליטץ תחע עארתח [ארץ],

As a person slices and splits the earth,

י Yod ט Tet ח Chet ז Zayin ו Vav ה Hei ד Dalet ג Gimel ב Beit א Aleph
ס Samech ן Final Nun נ Nun ם Final Mem מ Mem ל Lamed ך Final Kaf כ Kaf
ת Tav ש Shin ר Resh ק Kuf ץ Final Tzadik צ Tzadik ף Final Feh פ Peh ע Ayin

אור בונז אר שכאטתערד את תחע מאותח אף תחע גראב.

Our bones are scattered at the mouth of the grave.

בעת מי עיז אר פוכעסד עפון יו ו לורד ,מי געד:

But my eyes are focused upon You O Lord, my God:

אי שיך מי סאלבאשען [ישועה] ין יו ,דו נעת אללוו מי שול [נפש] תו בי דעשערתעד.

I seek my salvation in You, do not allow my soul to be deserted.

פרותעכט מי פרום תחע תראפס אנד שנארז שיט פור מי,

Protect me from the traps and snares set for me,

אנד תחע תראפס אף תחע עיבעל-דוערז.

And the traps of the evildoers.

מאי אלל תחע ויכעד וונז תוגעתחער בי תראפד ין תחער וון נעתץ,

May all the wicked ones together be trapped in their own nets,

ענטיל אי פאסש.

Until I pass.

- 142 -

א משכיל בי דוד.

A Maskil by David.

א פראיער וען הי וענת ינתו תחע כאב.

A prayer when he went into the cave.

וית מי וויס אי שהותעד אוט תו תחע לורד,

With my voice I shouted out to the Lord,

אנד וית מי וויס אי פלידעד וית תחע לורד,

And with my voice I pleaded with the Lord,

מי קרי פלווד ביפור הים ,אס אי שעט מי תרובעלז ביפור הים;

My cry flowed before Him, as I set my troubles before Him;

את תחע תים מי שפיריט, ויקענד יש אובערכום,

At the time my spirit, weakened is overcome,

יו נוע תחע דירעכשענז ין ויך אי גו;

You know the directions in which I go;

תהאי האב שעט א תראף פור מי ען תחע פאתחואיז אף תחע רוד תחאט אי תראבעל.

They have set a trap for me on the pathways of the road that I travel.

י Yod ט Tet ח Chet ז Zayin ו Vav ה Hei ד Dalet ג Gimel ב Beit א Aleph
ס Samech ן Final Nun נ Nun ם Final Mem מ Mem ל Lamed ך Final Kaf כ Kaf
ת Tav ש Shin ר Resh ק Kuf ץ Final Tzadik צ Tzadik ף Final Feh פ Peh ע Ayin

ען מי ריט ,לווק אנד שי– תחער יש נון הו נוס מי ;תחער יז נו עשכאף.

On my right, look and see -- there is none who knows me; there is no escape.

תחער יש נון תו שאב מי ליף ;אי האב קריד אוט תו יו ,ו לורד,

There is none to save my life; I have cried out to You O Lord,

אי שעד" ,יו אר מי שהעלטער ,מי לוט ין תחע לאנד אף תחע ליבינג."

I said, "You are my shelter, my lot in the land of the living."

ו ,העאר מי קרי ;פור אי האו ביכום וערי לוולי.

O, hear my cry; for I have become very lowly.

דעליבער מי פרום מי פערשוערז,

Deliver me from my pursuers,

הו אר מיתיער תהאן אי אם.

Who are mightier than I am.

ריליס מי שול [נפש] פרום תחיס ענכלוזער .

Release my soul from this enclosure.

תו שינג פראיזעס ,תו יור נאם [שם].

To sing praises, to Your Name.

י Yod ט Tet ח Chet ז Zayin ו Vav ה Hei ד Dalet ג Gimel ב Beit א Aleph
ס Samech ן Final Nun נ Nun ם Final Mem מ Mem ל Lamed ך Final Kaf כ Kaf
ת Tav ש Shin ר Resh ק Kuf ץ Final Tzadik צ Tzadik ף Final Feh פ Peh ע Ayin

אנד תחע ריצעס שחאלל גאתחער אראונד מי,

And the righteous shall gather around me,

פור יו האב ריוארדעד מי.

For You have rewarded me.

ר

י Yod ט Tet ח Chet ז Zayin ו Vav ה Hei ד Dalet ג Gimel ב Beit א Aleph
ס Samech ן Final Nun נ Nun ם Final Mem מ Mem ל Lamed ך Final Kaf כ Kaf
ת Tav ש Shin ר Resh ק Kuf ץ Final Tzadik צ Tzadik ף Final Feh פ Peh ע Ayin

- 143 -

א שונג [שיר] אף דוד.

A Song of David.

ו לורד ,העאר מי פראיער ,אנד הארקען תו מי פלידינגז,

O Lord, hear my prayer, and hearken to my pleadings,

אנד ריביל יור פאיתפולנעסס אנד גאסטיש [משפט].

And reveal Your faithfulness and justice.

אנד דו נעת רענדער יור געדגמענט [משפט] טוארד יור סערבאנט;

And do not render Your judgment toward your servant;

ביקאעז ין יור פרעזאנץ נו וון יש יננושענת.

Because in Your presence no one is innocent.

ביקאעס מי פוז פערשוד מי שול [נפש] ,גראונד מי ביינג ין תחע דירט,

Because my foes pursued my soul, ground my being in the dirt,

אנד ריטערנד מי תו תותאל דארקנעסס ,ליק תהוז לונג דעאד.

And returned me to total darkness, like those long dead.

אנד מי יננער שפיריט ואס אובערכום, אנד מי יננער העארט ואס כונפיוזד.

And my inner spirit was overcome, and my inner spirit was confused.

אנד תחען אי רימעמבערד תחע ולדען דאיס ,אנד אי ריפלעכתעד אבאוט יור דידז,

And I remembered the olden days, and I reflected about Your deeds,

אי תחאעט אבאוט תחע קריאתענז אף יור האנדז.

I thought about the creations of your hands.

אי ריץ מי האנדז אוט תו יו,

I reached my hands out to you,

ו לורד ,מי שול [נפש] ליק א ועארי לאנד לונגז פור יו .אמן.

O Lord, my soul like a weary land longs for You. Amen

ריספונד תו מי שפידילי ,ו לורד ,פור מי שפיריט יש עכזאעשטעד,

Respond to me speedily, O Lord, for my spirit is exhausted,

דו נעת כונסיל יור פרעזאנץ פרום מי,

Do not conceal your presence from me,

לעשט אי בי כומפארד תו תהוז,

Lest I be compared to those,

הו דישענד ינתו תחע פיט.

Who descend into the pit.

אננאונץ תו מי,

Announce to me,

יור באנעבולענץ,

Your benevolence,

עפון תחע דאונינג אף תחע מורנינג,

Upon the dawning of the morning,

פור אי פלאס מי תרעשט ין יו תו ינצטרעקת מי ין מי פאתח,

For I place my trust in You to instruct me in my path,

יט יש תחע פאתח אי וילל תאק ,פור אי האב ראיזד מי שול [נפש] עף תו יו.

It is the path I will take, for I have raised my soul up to You.

גראנט מי סאלבאשען [ישועה] פרום מי פוז ,ו לורד ,אי שיק רעפיוג וית יו.

Grant me salvation from my foes, O Lord, I seek refuge with You.

ינצטרעקת מי ין יור ואי ,אס יו אר מי געד ;לעט יור גווד שפיריט
געיד מי,

Instruct me in Your way, as You are my God; let Your good spirit guide me,

תו ואלק עפריט ען לעבאל גראונד :פור תחע שאך אף יור נאם [שם] ,
ו לורד,

To walk upright on level ground: For the sake of Your Name, O Lord,

אללוו מי סאלבאשען [ישועה] אנד וית יור ריצעס לובינג-קינדנעשס
[חסד],

Allow me salvation and with Your righteous loving-kindness,

קאעז מי שול [נפש] תו בי דיליבערד פרום יטץ דישטרעסס.

Cause my soul to be delivered from its distress.

אנד ין יור באנעבולענץ, דיסתרוי מי אנעמיז,

And in Your benevolence, destroy my enemies,

אנד קאעז רוין תו תחע פערשוערז תחאט תורמענת מי שול [נפש],

And cause ruin to the pursuers that torment my soul,

אס אי אם יור סערבאנט.

As I am Your servant.

י Yod ט Tet ח Chet ז Zayin ן Vav ה Hei ד Dalet ג Gimel ב Beit א Aleph
ס Samech ן Final Nun נ Nun ם Final Mem מ Mem ל Lamed ך Final Kaf כ Kaf
ת Tav ש Shin ר Resh ק Kuf ץ Final Tzadik צ Tzadik ף Final Feh פ Peh ע Ayin

- 144 -

בי דוד.

By David.

ו ,בלאששעד [ברוך], יש תחע לורד מי רוך,

O, blessed is the Lord my Rock,

הו האש תאעט באתתעל תו מי האנדז אנד ואר תו מי פינגערז.

Who has taught battle to my hands and war to my fingers.

מי פאבור ,מי פורתיפיכאשען ,מי תוועד אף סטרענת [כח] ,מי רידימער ,מי געארדיאן,

My Favor, my Fortification, my Tower of Strength, my Redeemer, my Guardian,

ין הוז שהעלטער אי תרעשט ,אנד הו האז אללווד מי תו ברינג מי פיפעל [עם] ענדער מי כונטרול.

In Whose shelter I trust, and Who has allowed me to bring my people under control.

ו לורד ,ואת יז מאן [אדם] תחאט יו שוד אקנוולעדג הים ?תחע עפפשפרינג אף א מורתאל,

O Lord, what is man that You should acknowledge him? The offspring of a mortal,

תחאט יו שוד גיב ימפורט תו הים ?א מאן [אדם] יש ליק א פאששינג ברעאתח ;

That You should give import to him? A man is like a passing breath;

א פותיל פריטענשען;

A futile pretension;

היש דאיז אר ליקענד תו א שחאדוו תחאט מובז אואי.

His days are likened to a shadow that moves away.

ו לורד ,קאעז יור העאבענז [שמים] תו בוו שו יו מאי דישענד;

O Lord, cause Your heavens to bow so you may descend;

יף יו תעץ תחע מאונתאנז [הרים] תהאי וילל שמוך;

If You touch the mountains they will smoke;

קאעז ליתנינג בולטץ תו פלאשה ,אנד דישפערס תהעם;

Cause lightening bolts to flash, and disperse them;

שענד יור אררווז ,תו ואנקוישח תהעם.

Send Your arrows, to vanquish them.

כאשט יור האנדז פרום אבוב תחע העאבענז [שמים];

Cast Your hands from above the heavens;

רידים אנד שאב מי פרום מיתי ואתערז [מים];

Redeem and save me from mighty waters;

י Yod ט Tet ח Chet ז Zayin ו Vav ה Hei ד Dalet ג Gimel ב Beit א Aleph
ס Samech ן Final Nun נ Nun ם Final Mem מ Mem ל Lamed ך Final Kaf כ Kaf
ת Tav ש Shin ר Resh ק Kuf ץ Final Tzadik צ Tzadik ף Final Feh פ Peh ע Ayin

אוט אף תחע גראשפס אף שטראנגערז.

Out of the grasps of strangers.

תהוז הוז מאותס שפיק פאלס וורדז;

Those whose mouths speak false words;

תחער שולעם ותחס אר תחע ריט האנד אף ליז.

Their solemn oaths are the right hand of lies.

ו געד ,תו יו וילל אי שינג א נו שונג [שיר],

O God, to You I will sing a new song,

ען א תען שטרינג נבל;

On a ten string harp [NEV-EL];

מי שונג [שיר] וילל בי א הימ תו יו.

My song will be at hymn to You.

הי הו גראנתץ רידעמפשען תו קינגז,

He Who grants redemption to Kings,

אנד הו שאבד דוד ,היז סערבאנט ,פרום תחע עיבעל שורד.

And Who saved David, His servant, from the evil sword.

י Yod ט Tet ח Chet ז Zayin ו Vav ה Hei ד Dalet ג Gimel ב Beit א Aleph
ס Samech ן Final Nun נ Nun ם Final Mem מ Mem ל Lamed ך Final Kaf כ Kaf
ת Tav ש Shin ר Resh ק Kuf ץ Final Tzadik צ Tzadik ף Final Feh פ Peh ע Ayin

רידים אנד שאב מי פרום שטראנגערס' האנדז;

Redeem and save me from strangers' hands;

תהוז הוז מאותס שפיק פאלס וורדז;

Those whose mouths speak false words;

אנד תחער שולעם אותהס אר תחע ריט האנד אף ליז.

And their solemn oaths are the right hand of lies.

פור אור שונז אר גרוון ליק מאצור פלאנתץ ,ין תחער יענג דאיס,

For our sons are grown like mature plants, in their young days,

אור דאעטערז אר כראפטעד ליק כורנערשתונז,

Our daughters are crafted like cornerstones,

קארבד אס א פאונדאשען אף א תעמפעל.

Carved as a foundation of a temple.

אור סטורהאוסעז אר ועלל-שטוכד ,פרובידינג אלל קינדז אף פוד,

Our storehouses are well-stocked, providing all kinds of food,

אללווינג אור שיף תו ינקריס מאני תימז אובער,

Allowing our sheep to increase many times over,

י Yod ט Tet ח Chet ז Zayin ו Vav ה Hei ד Dalet ג Gimel ב Beit א Aleph
ס Samech ן Final Nun נ Nun ם Final Mem מ Mem ל Lamed ך Final Kaf כ Kaf
ת Tav ש Shin ר Resh ק Kuf ץ Final Tzadik צ Tzadik ף Final Feh פ Peh ע Ayin

תחרואוט תחע אופען שפאשעס;

Throughout the open spaces;

אנד אור עקצען אר העארתי.

And our oxen are hearty.

תחער אר נו בריץ-ינז ור גוינגס-אוט,

There are no breach-ins or goings-out,

תחער יש נו ואילינג פרום אור סטריטץ.

There is no wailing from our streets.

האפפינעסס יש שפרעד אובער שעך א פיפעל [עם],

Happiness is spread over such a people,

האפפינעשש יש שפרעד אובער תחיס נאישען,

Happiness is spread over this nation,

הוז געד יש תחע לורד.

Whose God is the Lord.

- 145 -

א פראיז ,בי דוד:

A praise, by David:

א

אי ויּלל עלאואת יו ;יו אר מי געד ,תחע כינג ;אי ויּלל בלעשש יור נאם [שם] פור אבער אנד עבער.

I will elevate You; You are my God, the King; I will bless Your Name for ever and ever.

ב

אי ויּלל בלעשש יו עברי דאי אנד אי ויּלל גלוריפי יור נאם [שם] וית פראיז פור עבער אנד עבער.

I will bless You every day and I will glorify Your Name with praise for ever and ever.

ג

תחע לורד יש אקזאלטעד אנד עקצידינגלי אככלאימד ;היז מאגניתוד יש ביינד ענדערשתאנדינג.

The Lord is exalted and exceedingly acclaimed; His magnitude is beyond understanding.

ד

לדר ודר ,עיך ויּלל אקשכלאים יור וונדרעס דידז אנד תאלק אבאוט יור מיטי גודלינעסס .

From generation to generation, each will exclaim Your wondrous deeds and talk about Your mighty godliness.

י Yod ט Tet ח Chet ז Zayin ו Vav ה Hei ד Dalet ג Gimel ב Beit א Aleph
ס Samech ן Final Nun נ Nun ם Final Mem מ Mem ל Lamed ך Final Kaf כ Kaf
ת Tav ש Shin ר Resh ק Kuf ץ Final Tzadik צ Tzadik ף Final Feh פ Peh ע Ayin

ה

אי וילל שינג וורדז תו הונור יור מאגעשטייש גלוריעש שפלענדור אנד יור מאגניפעסענת דידז.

I will sing words to honor Your Majesty's glorious splendor and Your magnificent deeds.

ו

אנד וען תהאי תאלק אף יור אושעם פוואער אי וילל שפיק אף יור גרעאתנעסס.

And when they talk of Your awesome power I will speak of Your greatness.

ז

תהאי וילל רעכולעקט אנד תאלק אף יור ואשט לובינג-קינדנעשס [חסד], אנד שחאלל גויפולי פראיז יור ריצאסנעשס [צדק].

They will recollect and talk of Your vast loving-kindness, and shall joyfully praise Your righteousness.

ח

תחע לורד'ש נאתער יש גראשעס, אנד מערשיפול; פאתענט, אנד פולל אף לובינג-קינדנעשס [חסד].

The Lord's nature is gracious, and merciful; patient, and full of loving-kindness.

ט

תחע לורד'ז גוודנעסס יש אקשטענדעד תו אלל אנד היש כעמפאששען יש עפון אלל היז קריצערז.

The Lord's goodness is extended to all and his compassion is upon all his creatures.

י Yod ט Tet ח Chet ז Zayin ו Vav ה Hei ד Dalet ג Gimel ב Beit א Aleph
ס Samech ן Final Nun נ Nun ם Final Mem מ Mem ל Lamed ך Final Kaf כ Kaf
ת Tav ש Shin ר Resh ק Kuf ץ Final Tzadik צ Tzadik ף Final Feh פ Peh ע Ayin

י

אלל אף יור וורקש פראיז יו, ו לורד ,אנד יור פאיתפול וונז בלעשש יו.

All of Your works praise you, O Lord, and Your faithful ones bless You.

כ

תהאי שחאלל שפיק אף יור גלוריעש קינגדום אנד תהאי וילל ריכאונט יור גרעאט דידז.

They shall speak of Your glorious kingdom and they will recount Your great deeds.

ל

תהאי וילל אננאונץ תו אלל היש גרעאט דידז אנד תחע גלוריעש שפלענדור אף היש כינגדום.

They will announce to all His great deeds and the glorious splendor of His kingdom.

מ

פור יור כינגדום יש אן יטערנאל קינגדום ,אנד יור רול יש לדר ודר.

For your kingdom is an eternal kingdom, and Your rule is generation to generation.

ס

יט יש תחע לורד תחאט שעשתאינז אלל תהוז הו האב פאללען, אנד ראיזעז עף אלל תהוז הו אר בווד.

It is the Lord that sustains all those who have fallen, and raises up all those who are bowed.

ע

אלל מאנקינד'ש עיז לווק תו יו ין עקצפעכטעד תרעשט אנד את תחע ריט תים יו פרוביד תהעם וית פוד.

All mankind's eyes look to You in expected trust and at the right time You provide them with food.

פ

ויתּ אן ופּען האנד יו לווק תו פולפילל תחע ואנתץ אף עבערי ליבינג קריצער.

With an open hand You look to fulfill the wants of every living creature.

צ

תחע לורד'ז ריצאסנעשס [צדק] עקזיסטץ ין אלל היש ואיז , אקשפרעששינג לובינג-קינדנעשס [חסד] ין אלל היש דידז.

The Lord's righteousness exists in all His ways, expressing loving-kindness in all His deeds.

ק

תחע לורד יז כלוס תו אלל הו כאלל ען הים ,אנד הו כאלל עפון הים ויתּ סינסעריטי.

The Lord is close to all who call on Him, and who call upon Him with sincerity.

י Yod **ט** Tet **ח** Chet **ז** Zayin **ו** Vav **ה** Hei **ד** Dalet **ג** Gimel **ב** Beit **א** Aleph
ס Samech **ן** Final Nun **נ** Nun **ם** Final Mem **מ** Mem **ל** Lamed **ך** Final Kaf **כ** Kaf
ת Tav **ש** Shin **ר** Resh **ק** Kuf **ץ** Final Tzadik **צ** Tzadik **ף** Final Feh **פ** Peh **ע** Ayin

ר

הי וילל אכט ען ביהאלף אף תהוז הו רעשפעכת הים; הי העארז תחער וויסעז קרי אנד תהאי וילל בי שאבד.

He will act on behalf of those who respect Him; He hears their voices cry and they will be saved.

ש

יט יש תחע לורד הו פרוטעכתץ אלל הו לוב הים, בעת הי שחאלל דעשטרוי אלל הו אר ויכעד.

It is the Lord Who protects all who love Him, but He shall destroy all who are wicked.

ת

לעט מי מאותח שפיק תחע פראיזעס אף תחע לורד; אנד אלל תחע ליבינג בלעשש היז הולי נאם [שם] פוראבער אנד אבערמור.

Let my mouth speak the praises of the Lord; and all the living bless
His Holy Name forever and evermore.

- 146 -

מי שול [נפש] !הללויה!

My soul! Praise [Hall-el-oo] the Lord [Yah]!

אלל תחע דאיז אף מי ליף אי וילל פראיז תחע לורד,

All the days of my life I will praise the Lord,

אי וילל פראיז תחע לורד ויל אי האב ליף ין מי,

I will praise the Lord while I have life in me,

דו נעת פלאס יור תרעשט ען תחע הי אנד תחע מיטי ור ין אני מורתאל ביינג,

Do not place your trust on the high and the mighty or in any mortal being,

פור נו מורתאל ביינג כאן אששור סאלבאשען [ישועה] ;וען היש שפיריט דיז ,הי וילל גו באק תו תחע עארתח [ארץ] פרום ויך הי כאם,

For no mortal being can assure salvation; when his spirit dies, he will go back to the earth from which he came.

ען תחאט סאם דאי ,אלל היש כונתעמפלאשענז אר לוסט.

On that same day, all his contemplations are lost.

גויעס יש תחע מורתאל הו יש אידעד בי תחע געד אף יעקב;

Joyous is the mortal who is aided by the God of Jacob;

י Yod ט Tet ח Chet ז Zayin ו Vav ה Hei ד Dalet ג Gimel ב Beit א Aleph
ס Samech ן Final Nun נ Nun ם Final Mem מ Mem ל Lamed ך Final Kaf כ Kaf
ת Tav ש Shin ר Resh ק Kuf ץ Final Tzadik צ Tzadik ף Final Feh פ Peh ע Ayin

הו פלאשעז היש תרעשט ין תחע לורד היש געד.

Who places his trust in the Lord his God.

פור יט יז תחע לורד ,קריאטור אף העאבען [שמים] אנד עארתח [ארץ],

For it is the Lord, Creator of heaven and earth,

אנד תחע שיז אנד אלל תחאט דועלל ויתהין תהעם,

And the seas and all that dwell within them,

הו פריזערבס פאיתח פוראבער,

Who preserves faith forever,

קיפינג גאסטיש [משפט] פור תהוז עקשפלויטעד,

Keeping justice for those exploited,

אנד פוד פור תחע הענגרי.

And food for the hungry.

תחע לורד ליבעראתץ כאפטיבז,

The Lord liberates captives,

תחע לורד רעסטורז שיט תו תחע בלינד,

The Lord restores sight to the blind,

י Yod ט Tet ח Chet ז Zayin ו Vav ה Hei ד Dalet ג Gimel ב Beit א Aleph
ס Samech ן Final Nun נ Nun ם Final Mem מ Mem ל Lamed ך Final Kaf כ Kaf
ת Tav ש Shin ר Resh ק Kuf ץ Final Tzadik צ Tzadik ף Final Feh פ Peh ע Ayin

תחע לורד שטראיתענס תהוז הו אר בענת,

The Lord straightens those who are bent,

תחע לורד צערישעז תחע געסט,

Lloyd cherishes the just,

תחע לורד פרוטעכתץ שטראנגערז,

The Lord protects strangers,

תחע לורד ענקוראגעס תחע וידוו אנד תחע פאתחערלעסס,

The Lord encourages the widow and the fatherless

אנד תחע פאתחואיז אף עיבעלדוערז [רשעים] הי תוישטס .

And the pathways of evildoers He twists.

געד וילל רול פוראבער;

God will rule forever;

יור געד ,ו ציון, לדר ודר.

Your God, O Zion, from generation to generation.

הללויה!

Praise God!

י Yod ט Tet ח Chet ז Zayin ו Vav ה Hei ד Dalet ג Gimel ב Beit א Aleph
ס Samech ן Final Nun נ Nun ם Final Mem מ Mem ל Lamed ך Final Kaf כ Kaf
ת Tav ש Shin ר Resh ק Kuf ץ Final Tzadik צ Tzadik ף Final Feh פ Peh ע Ayin

- 147 -

הללויה,

Praise O Lord,

ביקאעז יט יש וונדערפול תו שינג הימז תו אור געד;

Because it is wonderful to sing hymns to our God;

אס יט יש פליזינג אנד ביוטיפול תו גיב אקלאים.

As it is pleasing and beautiful to give acclaim.

יט יש תחע לורד הו בילדז ירושלם,

It is the Lord who builds Jerusalem,

אנד ברינגז פורתח תחע רעגעקתעד אף ישראל.

And brings forth the rejected of Israel.

הי יש א העאלער אף תחע ברוקענהעארטעד אנד מענדז תחער פאין.

He is a Healer of the brokenhearted and mends their pain.

הי קיפס אקאונט אף תחע נעמבער אף תחע שתארז,

He keeps account of the numbers of the stars,

אנד אשינז עיך וון בי יטץ און נאם [שם].

And assigns each one by its own Name.

י Yod ט Tet ח Chet ז Zayin ו Vav ה Hei ד Dalet ג Gimel ב Beit א Aleph
ס Samech ן Final Nun נ Nun ם Final Mem מ Mem ל Lamed ך Final Kaf כ Kaf
ת Tav ש Shin ר Resh ק Kuf ץ Final Tzadik צ Tzadik ף Final Feh פ Peh ע Ayin

אור לורד יש גרעאט אנד מושט פאוורפול אנד היש ויזדום יש ענדלעסס.

Our Lord is great and most powerful and his wisdom is endless.

תחע לורד העארתענז תהוז הו אר העמבאל,

The Lord heartens those who are humble,

בעת עיבעלדוערז [רשעים] הי ברינגז דאון תו תחע גראונד.

But evildoers He brings down to the ground.

שינג אוט תו תחע לורד וית תחאנקשגיבינג פראיזעס,

Sing out to the Lord with thanksgiving praises,

שינג הימז טו אור געד ען תחע כנור.

Sing hymns to our God on the lyre.

הי הו בלאנקעתץ העאבען [שמים] וית כלאודז,

He Who blankets heaven with the clouds,

הו מאקס רעאדי ראין תו פאלל עפון תחע עארתח [ארץ],

Who makes ready rain to fall on the earth,

הו כאעשעז פודדער תו גרוו עפון תחע מאונתאנשיד.

Who causes fodder to grow upon the mountain side.

הו פרובידז פוד תו אנימאלז אנד תו תחע ראבעןץס יענג וען תהאי כאלל אוט;

Who provides food to animals and to the raven's young when they call out;

הי דעז נעת קראב תחע הורשעיס סטרענגת [כח] נור יש הי ימפראששד בי תחע לעגז אף א מאן [אדם].

He does not crave the horse's strength nor is He impressed by the legs of a man.

תחע לורד יש ינכלינד טוארד תהוז הו הולד הים ין או אנד אשפיער תו היז לובינג-קינדנעשס [חסד].

The Lord is inclined toward those who hold Him in awe and aspire to his loving-kindness.

אקלאים תחע לורד ,ו ירושלם ,לאעד יור געד ,ו ציון.

Acclaim the Lord, O Jerusalem, laud your God, O Zion.

אס הי האז פורטיפיד תחע בארז לאצינג יור גאתץ אנד בלאששד יור צילדרען ין יור מידצת;

As He has fortified the bars latching your gates and blessed your children in your midst;

הי ,הו האז מאד תחע בורדערס אף יור רעלם פיספול,

He, Who has made the borders of your realm peaceful,

אנד שעשתאינז יו וית תחע פינעשת ויט;

And sustains you with the finest wheat;

הי ,הו האז סענט היש טעשטימוניז תו אלל תחע עארתח [ארץ],

He, Who has sent His testimonies to all the earth,

היש קוממאנדמאנטץ [מצות] שפרעד קויכלי;

His commandments spread quickly;

הי כאשטס סנוו אבאוט ליק פליס ,אנד דישבורשעז פרושט ליק אשעס;

He casts snow about like fleece, and disburses frost like ashes;

הי תחרווס דאון היש האילשתונז ליק כרעמבז,

He throws down His hailstones like crumbs,

ואת מורתאל כאן ויתהשתאנד היש ציל?

What mortal can withstand His chill?

הי דיליבערס היז כומאנד אנד תהאי מעלט,

He delivers His command and they melt,

הי בלווז היש וינד אנד תחע ואתערז [מים] שתרים,

He blows His wind and the waters stream,

הי דעכלארז היז וורד תו יעקב,

He declares His word to Jacob,

י Yod ט Tet ח Chet ז Zayin ו Vav ה Hei ד Dalet ג Gimel ב Beit א Aleph
ס Samech ן Final Nun נ Nun ם Final Mem מ Mem ל Lamed ך Final Kaf כ Kaf
ת Tav ש Shin ר Resh ק Kuf ץ Final Tzadik צ Tzadik ף Final Feh פ Peh ע Ayin

הי גאב ישראל היש טעשטימוניז אנד לאוז.

He gave Israel His testimonies and laws.

הי דיד נעת דו תחיס פור אני עתחער נאשען,

He did not do this for any other nation,

אנד תהאי נוו נעת אף תחע לורד'ש לאוז.

And they know not of the Lord's laws.

הללויה!

Praise God!

ו

י Yod ט Tet ח Chet ז Zayin ו Vav ה Hei ד Dalet ג Gimel ב Beit א Aleph
ס Samech ן Final Nun נ Nun ם Final Mem מ Mem ל Lamed ך Final Kaf כ Kaf
ת Tav ש Shin ר Resh ק Kuf ץ Final Tzadik צ Tzadik ף Final Feh פ Peh ע Ayin

- 148 -

הללויה!

Praise God!

הללויה פרום תחע העאבענז [שמים],

Praise God from the heavens,

פראיז הים פרום תחע העיטץ,

Praise Him from the heights,

פראיז הים אנד אלל היז אנגעלז,

Praise Him and all His angels,

פראיז הים אלל היז העלפערס,

Praise Him all His helpers,

פראיז הים ,תחע שען אנד מון,

Praise Him, the sun and the moon,

פראיז הים ,עבערי בריט סתאר,

Praise Him, every bright star,

פראיז הים תו תחע הי העאבענז [שמים],

Praise Him, to the high heavens,

אנד תחע ואתערז [מים] תחאט דועלל אבוב העאבעןיש כלועדז;

And the waters that dwell above heaven's clouds;

תהאי וילל אלל אקלאים תחע נאם [שם] אף געד,

They will all acclaim the Name of God,

פור וען הי גאב היש כוממאנד,

For when He gave His command,

תהאי כאם ינתו קריאשען,

They came into creation,

אנד שעט תהעם פור יתערנאטי;

And set them for eternity;

אנד היז דיכלארד דעקרי,

And His declared decree,

יז ענצאנגינג!

Is unchanging!

הללויה!

Praise the Lord!

י Yod ט Tet ח Chet ז Zayin ן Vav ה Hei ד Dalet ג Gimel ב Beit א Aleph
ס Samech ן Final Nun נ Nun ם Final Mem מ Mem ל Lamed ך Final Kaf כ Kaf
ת Tav ש Shin ר Resh ק Kuf ץ Final Tzadik צ Tzadik ף Final Feh פ Peh ע Ayin

פרום אלל תחע עארתח [ארץ]: תחע קריצערס תחאט דועלל ויתהין
תחע שי אנד ין אלל יטץ דיפעשט ואתערז [מים],

From all the earth: The creatures that dwell within the sea
and in all its deepest waters,

פיער, האיל, שנוו, מיסתי ואפור, אנד תחע תעמפעשט וינדס תחאט
דו אז הי כומּמאנדז;

Fire, hail, snow, misty vapor, and the tempest winds that do as He commands;

אלל תחע מאונתאנז [הרים] אנד תחע הי פלאשעז, תחע תריז
תחאט בעאר פרוט אנד אלל סידארס,

All the mountains and the high places, the trees that bear fruit and all cedars,

אלל תחע וילד בישתס אנד אלל אנימאלז, אנד אלל כראולינג
תחינגס, אנד וינגד בירדז.

All the wild beasts and all animals, and all crawling things, and winged birds.

אלל תחע קינגז הו דועלל ען עארתח [ארץ] אנד אלל נאתענז;

All the kings who dwell on earth and all nations;

העאדס אף סטאת אנד עבערי גאסטיש תחאט יש ען תחע עארתח
[ארץ],

Heads of state and every justice that is on the earth,

אלל תחע יותחס, וית מאדענז, תחע ולד וית תחע יענג,

All the youths, with maidens, the old with the young,

י Yod ט Tet ח Chet ז Zayin ו Vav ה Hei ד Dalet ג Gimel ב Beit א Aleph
ס Samech ן Final Nun נ Nun ם Final Mem מ Mem ל Lamed ך Final Kaf כ Kaf
ת Tav ש Shin ר Resh ק Kuf ץ Final Tzadik צ Tzadik ף Final Feh פ Peh ע Ayin

אלל ויילל אקלאים תחע נאם [שם] אף געד ,אס היש נאם [שם] אלון יש אקזאלטעד.

All will acclaim the Name of God, as His Name alone is exalted.

אנד היז גלוריעש מאגעשטי תווערז אובער העאבען [שמים] אנד עארתח [ארץ].

And His glorious majesty towers over heaven and earth.

אנד הי האז בראעט גלורי [כבוד] תו תחע רעפותאשען אף היש פיפעל [עם],

And He has brought glory to the reputation of His people

אנד גרעאט הונור תו אלל היש דעבותעד פאיתפול וונז,

And great honor to all His devoted faithful ones,

אנד תו היש פיפעל [עם] ,ישראל,

And to His people, Israel,

א נאשען כלוס תו הים.

A nation close to Him.

הללויה!

Praise God!

י Yod ט Tet ח Chet ז Zayin ו Vav ה Hei ד Dalet ג Gimel ב Beit א Aleph
ס Samech ן Final Nun נ Nun ם Final Mem מ Mem ל Lamed ך Final Kaf כ Kaf
ת Tav ש Shin ר Resh ק Kuf ץ Final Tzadik צ Tzadik ף Final Feh פ Peh ע Ayin

- 149 -

הללויה!

Praise God!

שינג אוט תו תחע לורד וית א נו שונג [שיר] ,אנד אקלאים הים,

Sing out to the Lord with the new song, and acclaim Him,

ין תחע כונגרעגאשען אמונג תחע פאיתפול.

In the congregation among the faithful.

ישראל וילל ריגויס ין יטץ קריאטור,

Israel will rejoice in its Creator,

אלל ציון'ש עפפשפרינג וילל ריגויס ין תחער כינג.

All Zion's offspring will rejoice in their King.

תהאי וילל דאנץ אס תהאי אקלאים היז נאם [שם],

They will dance as they acclaim His Name,

תהאי וילל שינג הימז תו הים וית תחע דרעם אנד כנור.

They will sing hymns to Him with the drum and lyre [kinor].

ביקאעז תחע לורד יש פליזד וית היז פיפעל [עם],

Because the Lord is pleased with His people,

אנד ברינגז פורתח תחע העמבאל תו שפלענדור וית סאלבאשען [ישועה].

And brings forth the humble to splendor with salvation.

תחע פאיתפול וילל שעלאבראט ין גלורי [כבוד],

The faithful will celebrate in glory,

תהאי וילל שינג גויעשלי וען עפון תחער בעדז.

They will sing joyously when upon their beds.

תחער תחרוט'ץ פראיז וילל אקזאלט געד .

Their throat's praise will exalt God.

ין תחער האנדז וילל בי א דעבאל עדגד שורד;

In their hands will be a double edged sword;

תו אזאקיות וענגפול רעתרעבושען אמונג נאתענז,

To execute vengeful retribution among nations,

אנד כונדעמנאשען אמונג פיפעלס [עמים].

And condemnation among peoples.

תו ימפריזון תחער קינגז ין בינדז,

To imprison their kings in binds,

אנד רעשתראין תחער דיגניטאריז ין צאינז אף עירון.

And restrain their dignitaries in chains of iron.

תו שעאל ין ריטינג א דעכלאראשען פור א געדגמענט [משפט]
אגאינצט תהעם.

To seal in writing a declaration for a judgment against them.

הי ראינז ין גלוריעש מאגעשטי אובער אלל היש פאיתפול.

He reigns in glorious majesty of all His faithful.

הללויה!

Praise God!

- 150 -

הללויה!

Praise God!

פראיז הים ין היש הולי פלאס,

Praise Him in His holy place,

פראיז הים ין תחע ואעלתעד העאבענז [שמים] אף היש מיט.

Praise Him in the vaulted heavens of his might.

פראיז הים פור היש אלל-פוורפול דידז.

Praise Him for His all-powerful deeds.

פראיז הים ביפיתתינג היז אותשטאנדינג עמינאנץ.

Praise Him befitting His outstanding Eminence.

פראיז הים וית תחע פוורפול בלאשט אף תחע הורן.

Praise Him with the powerful blast of the horn.

פראיז הים וית תחע נבל אנד תחע כנור.

Praise Him with the harp and the lyre.

פראיז הים וית תחע דרעמז אנד דאנצינג.

Praise Him with the drums and dancing.

י Yod ט Tet ח Chet ז Zayin ו Vav ה Hei ד Dalet ג Gimel ב Beit א Aleph
ס Samech ן Final Nun נ Nun ם Final Mem מ Mem ל Lamed ך Final Kaf כ Kaf
ת Tav ש Shin ר Resh ק Kuf ץ Final Tzadik צ Tzadik ף Final Feh פ Peh ע Ayin

פראיז הים וית תחע טאמבורין אנד תחע פיף.

Praise Him with the tambourine and the pipe.

פראיז הים וית תחע זילעפון אנד רעקורדער.

Praise Him with the xylophone and recorder.

פראיז הים וית לארג שימבולז אנד קאסתאנעטץ.

Praise Him with large symbols and castanets.

עוערי בריתחינג קריציור וילל פראיז תחע לורד.

Every breathing creature will praise the Lord.

הללויה!

Praise God!

י Yod ט Tet ח Chet ז Zayin ו Vav ה Hei ד Dalet ג Gimel ב Beit א Aleph
ס Samech ן Final Nun נ Nun ם Final Mem מ Mem ל Lamed ך Final Kaf כ Kaf
ת Tav ש Shin ר Resh ק Kuf ץ Final Tzadik צ Tzadik ף Final Feh פ Peh ע Ayin

lossary Me-lone מלון

on	Aharon	אהרן
aham	Avraham	אברהם
n	amen	אמן
jamin	Benyamin	בנימין
sed	baruch	ברוך
mand- nts	meetzvot	מצות
vid	David	דוד
h	aretz	ארץ
raim	Ephraim	אפרים
doers	reshaeem	רשעים
eration	dor	דור
eration to eration	le dor ve dor	לדר ודר
ry	kavod	כבוד
ven(s)	shamayim	שמים
el	Yisrael	ישראל
ac	Yitzchak	יצחק
ob	Yakov	יעקב
usalem	Yerushalayim	ירושלם
eph	Yosef	יוסף
hua	Yeshua	ישועה
	seemcha	שמחה
tice	meeshpat	משפט
rd	Yah, Adonai	יה, אדוני
ving-kind- ss	chesed	חסד

Glossary Me-lone מלון

lyre, violin	kinor	כנור
man	adam	אדם
Menasseh	Menashe	מנשה
Moses	Moshe	משה
mountains	hareem	הרים
name	shem	שם
people	om	עם
peoples	ameem	עמים
praise	hallelu	הללו
praise the Lord	hallelujah	הללויה
precepts	meetzvot	מצות
righteousness	tzedek	צדק
righteous (person)	Tzadeek	צדיק
salvation	yeshua	ישועה
Shiloh	Shiloh	שלו
Solomon	Shlomo	שלמה
song	shir	שיר
soul	nefesh	נפש
strength	koach	כח
ten string harp	nevel	נבל
the	ha	ה
water(s)	mayeem	מים
Zion	Zion	ציון

י Yod ט Tet ח Chet ז Zayin ו Vav ה Hei ד Dalet ג Gimel ב Beit א Aleph

ס Samech ן Final Nun נ Nun ם Final Mem מ Mem ל Lamed ך Final Kaf כ Kaf

ת Tav ש Shin ר Resh ק Kuf ץ Final Tzadik צ Tzadik ף Final Feh פ Peh ע Ayin

The Jewish Dentist and the Eskimo = The Breidner Linguistic Method (BLM)

Background

A Jewish dentist and an Eskimo started it all. Sometime during the late 1980s while serving as headmaster of the American Jewish Academy, our school's secretary notified me that there was a couple with a high school age young man requesting interview for admission to our school. The young man was approximately 16 years old as I recall, and his mother and father were from distinctly different backgrounds. His father came from a Jewish family with a limited income that lived in Brooklyn. The man had a dream of becoming a dentist, but the funds were not available to pay for tuition. He discovered a Federal program that granted tuition for medical education on condition that payback would be made by providing dental services in a depressed area after graduation for a specific period. The father chose Alaska in an Inuit community above the Arctic Circle. Considering his physical needs of the time as a young man, he was attracted to an Inuit young lady who was now his wife. After the couple moved to the New York area, and registered their son at Midwood High School in Brooklyn, they became aware of social problems he was having that reflected his formative years in an Inuit village. He just did not seem to fit in with its large Jewish student population, when describing the glories of the whale hunt in his Inuit village.

His mother was not Jewish and his father's only exposure to Judaism was memorizing his bar mitzvah part and enjoying the party that followed. The family relocated to Long Island, and now sought to register the 16 year old at the American Jewish Academy where he could become acclimatized to American social attitudes and get a firm foundation in his religious heritage. I made it very clear that this young man would have to have a bar mitzvah and be able to pass the New York State Regents examination in Hebrew. They could not agree and the young man was not enrolled at the American Jewish Academy.

Following that interview, I sat down at my desk to ponder the problem; I noted a newspaper which our school secretary had placed on my desk with the morning mail. I do not have any knowledge of Yiddish, except for a few common expressions. In fact, I remember going to an evening class at Taft High School in the Bronx where I lived at the time to learn Yiddish in an adult education program, in 1948 or 49 after World War II when we became aware of the true dimensions of the Holocaust. I left the classroom rapidly, thoroughly aghast at my neighbors attempting to learn what sounded to me like a German language. Little did I know as a young man that Yiddish was the cultural language of the Ashkenazi Jews, of which I am a part, and that so many of us had died with that language on our lips. As I looked across the desk at the newspaper, I felt a new understanding was about to come my way. The newspaper was written with Hebrew letters. I read the masthead from right to left as any Hebrew text. It said "Forward." I knew that I was holding a piece of a puzzle that would unlock language acquisition through a linguistic keyhole. However, the key to the puzzle was yet to be defined.

Here was a problem. A significant number of American Jews had prepared for their bar and bat mitzvah ceremony by attending synagogue classes that were devoted to religious and cultural education, but did not adequately address Hebrew literacy. The Hebrew that was used by the bar or bat mitzvah youngster during the service was rote memorized for presentation. America's Jewish community's most pressing problem, as I saw it, was Hebrew literacy in order to maintain and grow synagogue membership.

A few days after that interview, when I returned from the school's parking lot where all of the students had boarded buses for the journey home, a teacher motioned me into her classroom and pointed to the chalkboard. It said: סוב אהת תא ימ תיימ [Meet me at the bus]. One of our students provided the piece that solved the language acquisition puzzle and created a form for the key that opened the door to the BLM.

The BLM opens with hinges that turn within a cultural structure that is distinctly American energized by our attitudes toward free will. As a people we resent rote learning. Preparation for school examinations have rarely produced retained knowledge. The same may be said for memorizing a Bar/Bat Mitzvah presentation. Large numbers of American Jews have rejected membership or active inclusion in synagogue life resulting from an inability to understand the Hebrew that they memorized for their Bar/Bat Mitzvah performance. The gates of return are opening! After awhile a structure for the key to unlocking Hebrew literacy began to take shape as the BLM. If Yiddish based upon German could be read with Hebrew letters, why not English? Perhaps this would be a pathway to Hebrew literacy. A Social Studies high school assignment for a Southern Jewish cook book, targeting primary Hebrew literacy might look like this:

"The Southern Jewish Cookbook"

Pאssoveר section:

Sארi Sephארdi's Heרoic Hארoset

½ cup pitted dאtes-two אpples, peeled אnd finely chopped
100 pרoof רum אnd honey to moisten
½ cup dארk ראisins
¼ cup chopped nuts

Gרind אll fרuit togetheר, moisten libeראlly with 100 pרoof רum אnd א little honey.
אdd nuts.
אvoid open flאmes

Elviרא MאcאBee-SאlאzאR's Sho-Fly Mאtzo-Bרi

4 eggs
½ teאspoons sאlt
2 tאblespoons chopped onion
6 mאtzos
2 ounces bouרbon אnd peאnut oil
oר
2 tאblespoons butteר oר mארgארine
Beאt the eggs, mix well with sאlt אnd onion.
Cרumble the mאtzos into the eggs אnd mix well
Foרm into hush puppies
Heאt the peאnut oil (oר butteר אnd mארgארine) in א fרying pאn
Dip into good quאlity Southeרn bouרbon אnd fרy until lightly bרowned

Judy Hאlevi's Jolly Fרuitcאke

2 tאblespoons melted unsאlted butteר oר nondאiry mארgארine
2 cups pitted dאtes, thinly sliced
2 cups dרied אpרicots, quארteרed
1 cup golden ראisins
1 - ½ cups posted whole אlmonds
1 - ½ cups toאsted wאlnut pieces
1 ounce mix of sweet Pאssoveר wine/100 pרoof רum
¾ cup mאtzo cאke meאl
1 tאblespoon potאto stארch
¾ cup sugאר
3 eggs
1 teאspoon vאnillא

Heאt oven to 300°bרush א (5x9 inch) loאf pאn with melted butteר oר nondאiry mארgארine אnd line with foil

In א lארge mixing bowl, combine the dאtes, אpרicots, ראisins, אlmonds, wאlnuts, אnd wine/100 pרoof רum.

Combine the mאtzo cאke meאl, the potאto stארch, אnd sugאר - mix well.

Blend foר the mixtuרe אnd mix evenly. Beאt eggs אnd vאnillא to blend.

Stiר into fרuit mixtuרe. Spoon bאtteר into pרepארed loאf pאn אnd spרeאd evenly, pרess into coרneרs of pאn.

Bאke until golden bרown, אbout 1 - ½ to 1-¾ houרs. Cool in pאn on ראck foר 10 minutes, then tuרn out of pאn. Peel off foil אnd let cool on ראck.

Wראp in plאstic wראp אnd foil. Chill foר אt leאst 24 houרs. To seרve, plאce cאke on wooden boארd, אnd using א shארp knife, cut into thin slices.

אvoid אn open flאme

No culture on planet earth has ever survived a loss of its cultural language! Fortunately, the establishment of the State of Israel has created a rebirth of Hebrew as a language which has been our catalyst for over 3,500 years binding the Jewish people together. Those ties that bind had been lost for the most part to American Jewry. Assimilation and lack of Jewish identification have been accelerated by a lack of literacy in Hebrew when attending synagogue services. While Hebrew is the native language of Israelis, in the United States and the English-speaking world it is not a "foreign language" it is our heritage. Our cultural language records our culture: Talmud/Torah! The use of transliterations in Hebrew further acknowledges the problem. Universally, synagogues use music that triggers a sequence of transliterated words that are not understood by the congregants but sung in cadence with the music mimicking the sounds of words in another language. That illustrates the problem. Many Jews are estranged from synagogue membership because they lack Hebrew literacy which denies their feeling of "belonging." Synagogue membership is vital to the survival of Judaism in the United States and everywhere else in the world. Hebrew and synagogues provide the emotional energy that unifies a Jewish community. The Hebrew language is vital to Jewish survival.

Throughout the history of the world there are many examples of cultures that have vanished from the world stage because only their holy men and an esoteric few were literate in their holy language. By an accident of history, the religious Jewish community in Europe provided a conduit to reading Hebrew letters for the average Ashkenazi Jew.

A key has been forged upon the crucible of cultural assimilation in the English-speaking world to unlock Hebrew literacy for American Jewry and revitalize the catalyst language of the Jewish people: Hebrew. The BLM key's calibration to open the door for English language fluency to achieve Hebrew literacy was proven by millions of Yiddish speakers. After all, humans have learned how to write what they speak. The reverse is also true. If the sound of spoken word is recorded in letters, the letters that they know will be recorded. For the Ashkenazi Jew those letters were Hebrew; the language was Yiddish.

Once again, the rich heritage of the Jewish people shall provide a proven solution to the problem. The solutions may be found in the Ashkenazi culture for those in Eastern Europe who did not experience liberation from the ghettos during the French revolution, when Jews were recognized for the first time as citizens of countries in which they lived. Yiddish, [ahsht] = Jewish, is a German language that established itself as early as the 10th century as Ashkenaz [Genesis 10:3] following an early Aramaic vernacular, reflecting the trading population of the Roman provinces, which soon became replete with an influx of words from Eastern European culture. Mame-loshn was the mother tongue of Eastern European and non-assimilated Jews and Loshn-Koydesh was the holy tongue or Hebrew. A Hebrew prayer book produced in approximately 1272 contains the following:

גוט טֵק אִים בְטָגָא שְׁוֵיר דִיש מַחֲזוֹר אִין בֵית הַכְּנֶסֶת טְרַגְ In Yiddish.

Gut tak im betage se vaer dis makhazor in beis hakneses trage: In transliteration.

In English: May a good day come to him who carries this prayer book into the synagogue.

The BLM opens the door for English language fluency to achieve Hebrew literacy. This approach to language was proven by millions of Yiddish speakers, but it seemed farfetched to Jewish educators who earn their living processing bar and bat mitzvah students. The BLM was introduced in The Psalms in 2009 as a hardcover edition through advertisements in Biblical Archaeology Review; the response quickly justified full page advertisements and books were shipped all over the world; not one was ever returned for refund. The Evangelical Christian community responded enthusiastically to the ability to read in its original their "Old Testament" using the BLM.

Highly recommended: All members of the Jewish community [Orthodox, Conservative, Reconstructionist, and Reform] please read the following!

Hebrew is not a foreign language in any synagogue. It is the holy tongue of the Jewish people. It is the official language of the State of Israel. It is our heritage!

English speaking Christians throughout the world have used the BLM to read the first book in their Bible, "The Old Testament" in its interlinear English/Hebrew edition in order to understand the text in the language that it was written. Since the English word is printed immediately under the Hebrew word, comprehension is immediate and the use of a dictionary is not necessary. Hebrew language acquisition is rapid.

Jews do not refer to the Hebrew Bible as the Old Testament; it is "Tanakh" - The Torah, The Prophets, [Nevi'im] and The Writings [Kethuvim] = [Ta-Na-Kh].

Once you have completed reading The Psalms using BLM you'll be able to read the entire Tanakh in Hebrew.

The publishers would like to highly recommend that if you are using an Interlinear NIV Hebrew-English Old Testament from a non- Jewish publishing house in order to quickly attain Hebrew literacy for Bar/Bat Mitzvah preparation, you should review the portion you will be reading with your Rabbi. Remember - If you can read it you can speak it!

Knowledge Is Your Great Strength – Know How You Think

You can Use the Breidner Linguistic Method [BLM]: English = Hebrew

Here are some Educational Terms You Might Wish to Know

METHODOLOGY:

Any program of *learning* by its very nature requires *teaching*, either by one's experience or by formal instruction. The process of *teaching* follows an interaction with anything that exists, and learning a relationship to it. The method depends completely upon the *elements* of *education*. It is helpful to consider this as if you were an experienced master teacher transmitting education to a class of individuals with widely varied backgrounds. Marketing this to a large population requires both methodology and apperception [see below].

Learning: To know or to *discover* and to *identify* anything that exists. This creates cognition — which is the act of *knowing* or *identifying* — it may be called perception — according to each individual's mode of *learning* — their *modality*. The task oriented result: *Education*.

Education: A modification of individual behavior is "*education*." It does not matter whether an individual is *learning* to tie shoelaces, to housebreak a dog, resolve complex mathematical equations, or to develop a marketing campaign for canned chicken soup, education occurs when prior *learning* enables the modification to be achieved. However, achievement is based upon the elements of education functioning within two concepts -- "*intelligence*" and/or "*intellect*."

Intelligence: All humans exhibit intelligence, which may be defined as *memory* or *recall*. It is through experience that individuals proceed from conscious memory or recall to an *imprinted action* that requires no conscious effort. The experience of learning how to tie shoelaces or open or close a water faucet at first requires conscious memory/recall, but after repetitive actions a modification of behavior takes place and a *stimulus* to an individual will create a *rote response* - this is called *imprinting*. This basic element of education makes it possible for an individual to touch-type, play the piano, drive a car, — or to read, write, and speak words that *transmit thoughts*.

Intellect: All humans exhibit intellect in varying degrees, which is the ability *to understand relationships*. *Intellect* is the ability to take elements of intelligence and understand their relationship to each other in order to produce *reason*, as an outcome of *learning*. This element of education is evidenced by a modification of behavior that may be called *understanding* or *comprehension*, and permits the individual to solve highly complex problems.

Convergent Thinking: Everyone uses *convergent thinking* in order to do daily tasks, whether making breakfast, dressing, or going to the supermarket; *intelligence* permits routines to easily be accomplished. Repetitive tasks are more easily accomplished through convergent thinking operations. The degree to which individuals are convergent in their thinking is generally environmentally generated. Convergent thinkers tend to be very literal in their understandings of concepts, and especially new concepts. They tend to associate themselves with rigid and unyielding attitudes and policies regarding nation, political party, culture, organization, or a belief system in which they have been imprinted. The degree to which this behavioral mode is a function of an individual's behavior modification impacts greatly on their education. For convergent thinkers, literal understandings can be a major driving force motivating a method for learning subject matter through the use of high-interest level material for immediate gratification. Convergent thinkers derive satisfaction assembling learnings transmitted through *imprinting*. Convergent thinkers rely heavily upon their intelligence — memory/recall. To the convergent thinker a brick may be used to build a house, build a fireplace, construct a brick walkway, or to build a wall — after all, a brick is a brick!

Divergent Thinking: Environment plays a major role in creating *divergent thinking* skills. The ability to consider divergent understandings of *learning* anything is called *intellect. Knowing* or *identifying* anything is *cognition* — once it is registered in the individual's memory it may be re - *cognated,* or recognized. Combinations of previously learned material are brought together by the divergent thinker in order to provide reasoned understandings of new concepts. These new concepts come together in a confluent amalgam to produce *education* — a new understanding that has modified the individual's behavior. Divergent thinkers rely heavily upon their intellect — the ability to see relationships. To the divergent thinker a brick may be ground in to red powder and mixed with plaster in order to make a relief map of the Rocky Mountains; place two bricks in a lavatory's reservoir to reduce water consumption; hollow out the inside of a brick, fill it with jewelry and place it in a brick wall to hinder burglars.

Imprinting: The result of repetitive action is called — "Imprinting." Turning off a water faucet after opening it, is an act of imprinting. Cognition and reaction — stimulus and response — are the result of repetitive actions that have been imprinted upon the individual within the parameters of their specific modalities. The touch typist may listen to a radio while typing a script, or watch television typing from audio input through earphones — the typist's response to the cognition of a specific letter or word is to type it. Your ability to read this results from imprinting.

Modality: Learning is completely dependent upon the individual's modalities during the act of cognition. A brief examination of some of the *modalities* of *learning,* and its impact upon the modification of the learner's behavior is imperative if education is to take place. Convergent and divergent thinking operations are performed by individuals using their favorite combination of methods solving problems, because their experience has shown them that the mindset of methods that they are using to think has been the most productive way to learn anything they consider. Those methods of solving problems are called *modalities.*

A FEW OF THE MAJOR MODALITIES:

Auditory Discrimination — Auditory discrimination is vital if the individual is to pursue language in a meaningful way. Primary to their effective use is an understanding of the sounds of printed letters as they are blended together into a word which is identifiable as a component of an idea. English language learners following a phonetic approach, which is based on convergent thinking, quickly move from decoding letters into sound to whole word recognition, in order to form word clusters that can be said together with lucidity. In our Anglo- Saxon language the sounds *of* the word are often different than the sounds *in* the word. Sugar is not "soogar." The visual discrimination of gum/gun, when expressed in the context of a sentence, is often difficult if auditory discrimination, which proceeds visual discrimination in human development, has not been properly dealt with. For example: "He took the gum/gun in his hand," requires the use of divergent thinking abilities as the reader adjusts the literal decoding of the word as perceived and discriminates its meaning as evidenced by the words proper pronunciation because the reader is aware of the "sense" of the sentence. Example: You *can* open the can. This visual discrimination follows perceptions/cognition and is completely dependent upon auditory discrimination.

Cadent Thinking – The cadence of a spoken language - its modulation and intonation - as the speaker's words rise and fall permits the listener of that language to anticipate future words along a line of thought. Cadent thinking is a function of auditory discrimination. After being imprinted by sounds of words in a line of print - the reader can often associate those sounds with words that are going to be immediately presented in a word cluster [i.e. "Can you catch a cat" as a word cluster, becomes "kenyaketchjaket" when spoken]. Cadent thinking permits opera singers to render an entire opera in a foreign-language although they have no literal knowledge of the words they are singing. Throughout the world large numbers of people use cadent memory. In this manner, Latin was read and spoken in church liturgy by congregants and many Jewish boys and girls read and spoke Hebrew in the course of their Bar/Bat Mitzvah without literal comprehension. For some non-Indo-European language systems which are basically tonal in nature [Chinese for example] cadent comprehension is essential to obtain meaning from language.

Schematic Thinking — The ability to read a map, follow a blueprint, understand a design, navigate a course, and conceive geometric concepts is the result of a schematic modality which has very important implications for learning. Generally, schematic thinking is two-dimensional. Many people have learned to read using "flash cards," which enable individuals to see and be imprinted with "whole" words that they might have difficulty spelling: Lieutenant, cafeteria, Mississippi, boulevard. However, these words are readily understood in the context of a sentence thanks to schematic ability imprinting whole words upon the reader. Schematic thinking occurs when the imprinting of the word's design is established in a convergent inventory of knowledge and it is this cognition that permits recognition of a word that represents identifiable thought. A common example is the logo for Coca-Cola.

Figural Thinking — Language learning for individuals with a strong *figural modality* can be strengthened using *imprinting* as an outcome of *convergent thinking*. The symbiotic relationship of mathematics to musical ability, which is often used in the playing of an instrument with both hands, requires the functional understanding of an equation. The popularity of Dr. Seuss's basic use of poetical music in a series of children's books to young children creates a right/left brain equation which stimulates, through a cadent understanding, the schematic memory of specific words. Each "whole" word is imprinted upon the child's mindset as an individual schematic image as if it were presented in a "flash card." After puberty, when a better understanding of relationships provokes intellectual thinking, the subliminal use of cadent operations in our language gathers imprinted whole words into word clusters as phrases that have meaning within an individual's inventory of knowledge, resulting from convergent thinking operations. Coupled with cadent thinking childish jingles, advertising slogans, popular tunes, are understood and retained through the modality of *figural thinking* operations.

Apperception - Any individual's *apperceptive* base is completely dependent upon their cognitive inventory which allows the absorption of new information added to their inventory of knowledge. The assimilation of a new perception creates cognition as a result of the learner's inventory of knowledge already in the individual's mind, and produces a modification of behavior which we identify as *education*. The apperceptive base is entirely environmental and has no relationship to a genetic predisposition. It is most often thought that there is a symbiotic relationship between age and maturity, and that is the reason children and adolescents tend to have a short attention span. That concept is false. Children and adolescents can absorb themselves in a video game or an age appropriate television show for hours at a time. Adults, at any age, evidence a very short attention span except for one intervening variable - their *apperceptive base. Apperception* is the ability to perceive clearly, to observe, and to recognize and have full understanding of the assimilation of new information as a result of *convergent thinking* (memory/recall) operations provoking the individual's inventory of knowledge, which may produce - in the case of a divergent thinker — intellectual outcomes. An expanded attention span fuels the desire not to leave in the middle of a movie, television show, interesting book, or other sedentary intellectual involvement and is often identified as motivation. Attention span relies heavily upon an *apperceptive base* which motivates the individual's desire for an outcome focused on the task oriented activity at hand. That outcome has been projected by the individual's prior *inventory of knowledge*. The motivating result is *satisfaction*, because the individual projected the end of the movie, the television show, the interesting book, or other activity.

Spatial Thinking – Spatial thinking differs from schematic thinking because it is more global in its approach. Schematic thinking may be very useful in understanding a blueprint or similar design on paper or other medium. Spatial thinking immediately changes that design - geometric forms - letters - musical notes - into a picture. Generally, spatial thinking is three dimensional. Readers with high levels of spatial thinking skills tend to be able to picture what they read. That picture may be three-dimensional or two-dimensional. It may be in color or black-and-white. But in any event it is a picture in space - "spatial." Composers have done this for many years by creating music that evokes an image in the listener's mind drawn from that individual's apperceptive base. The confluence of cadent, spatial and schematic thinking implemented during imprinting when learning an ideographic language code — such as Chinese — is extremely useful. It is also used in a church or synagogue when praying or singing in a language other than English and speaking words without literal comprehension, such as Hebrew.

Phoneme Inventory – The phoneme inventory is commonly referred to as accent or dialect. The variant sounds of an individual's speech are the speakers' *phoneme inventory*, which permits the consonants to transmit meaning as the vowels communicate sound. The phoneme inventory reflects the individuals' environment during early childhood, when they were creating the sounds of a primary language during its acquisition. The phoneme inventory does not inhibit the acquisition or fluency of reading skills in a native language. Speakers of a specific language may have a wide variation in their phoneme inventory but all have the same decoding skills when reading.

Ideographic Language – Ideographic representations are ideograms used in a language as a picture or symbol; they are a spatial object/icon to represent a thing or an idea but not a particular word or phrase for it; they represent the word as a whole without any indication of its sounds/phonemes. Its identification is purely spatial/schematic. When transmitted in speech, the individual's phoneme inventory for an ideographic language must rely on environmental imprinting, resulting in an understanding of tonal inflections to communicate meaning into ideographic expressions. Just as in Indo-European languages, tonal inflections, expressed from the phoneme inventory inflect meaning, but do not impede reading comprehension. The BLM approach to language acquisition uses the native language of the learner to modify the sounds of a target language, regardless of the phoneme inventory, even as it morphs from Indo-European to ideographic and vice versa. It permits formidable language acquisition in as little as one day. [See: SamuelGordonLLC.com.]

CPSIA information can be obtained at www.ICGtesting.com
Printed in the USA
LVOW111302120712

289782LV00003B/11/P

9 780615 491226